GOD'S WISDOM
FOR MARRIAGE & *the* HOME

FOR *the* GLORY
OF *the* LORD

PASTOR SCOTT MARKLE

Shepherding the Flock Ministries
7971 Washington St. ❖ Melvin, MI 48454
(810) 378-5323
www.shepherdingtheflock.com

God's Wisdom for Marriage & The Home
(Second Edition)
by Pastor Scott Markle

Printed in the United States of America

ISBN 978-0692408759

Shepherding the Flock Ministries
7971 Washington St.
Melvin, MI 48454
(810) 378-5323
www.shepherdingtheflock.com

DEDICATION

First and foremost,
To my Lord and Savior Jesus Christ,
Who as my Savior loved me and gave Himself for me
That I might have newness of spiritual life,
And who as my Head directs me each day
In the way everlasting
That I might walk in abundance of spiritual life.

Furthermore,
To my beloved wife, Kerry,
Who is a precious treasure from the hand of the Lord,
Who is truly a helper that is meet for me
And a crown upon my head,
In whom my heart doth safely trust and ever rejoice.

TABLE OF CONTENTS

PREFACE

Through wisdom is an house builded;
and by understanding it is established.
Proverbs 24:3

B rethren, how important is it for us to know, understand, and follow God's wisdom concerning the home? Certainly all of us in one manner or another, either as a child, as a spouse, as a parent, or as a sibling, have had, and may yet have, a relationship with the home. In fact, most of us expect to have some relationship with the home for the entire extent of our lives. Thus the home is a significant element of our lives from beginning to end.

Furthermore, the marriage relationship itself is of primary significance in most of our lives. Yes, our Lord does indeed call some to be single. Yet the majority of us will enter into the marriage relationship, and for most of us that relationship will extend over the majority of our lives. Yea, even before we enter into the marriage relationship, we generally spend some period of time thinking about, planning for, and developing relationships that might lead to marriage. Thus the marriage relationship is indeed a significant element in our lives.

Finally, the marriage and home relationships are the foundational building blocks of society. As goes the marriage, so goes the home. As goes the home; so goes the church, and so goes the country. Since marriage and the home are so significant to our existence in this present life, certainly it is of great importance that we find trustworthy guidance concerning their success. How much more trustworthy guidance may we find than that of the wisdom of the Lord our God!

Yet the home, as the Lord our God would have it, is under severe attack. This attack does not find its primary source in "flesh and blood." *"For we wrestle not against flesh and blood, but against principalities, against powers, against the rulers of the darkness of this world, against spiritual wickedness in high places."* (Ephesians 6:12) The primary source of attack against the home is not to be found in societal corruption, in governmental agenda, in educational error, etc. Rather, the primary source of attack is to be found in our adversary the devil and in his forces of spiritual darkness and wickedness.

It is our adversary the devil who is out seeking to stir up division between husband and wife, and thus to destroy the marriage bond. It is our adversary the devil who is out seeking to turn parents away from the training up of their children in the right way. It is our adversary the devil who is out seeking to turn children away from following the authority and training of their parents. It is our adversary the devil who is out seeking to stir up contention among the relationships of the home.

Where then shall we find the means of victory over the severe and unrelenting attacks of our adversary the devil? We shall find the place of victory only in the wisdom and power of the Lord our God. So then, it is of great importance that we come to know, understand, and follow God's wisdom concerning the home. It is my desire through this book to search the Scriptures for that very wisdom.

Now, most of the material of this book centers upon the marriage relationship. If our Lord will permit, I also desire to write on the Biblical doctrine of parenting and the home. However, the material of this book has been written by our Lord's grace with a desire to present an extensive Biblical study on marriage and the home. Yet this material is certainly not exhaustive. There is always more wondrous truth in the living Word of God than this author could possibly glean in a lifetime.

Furthermore, I do not write this material as one who has perfected its application in my own life. I fully recognize that much growth is needed on my part. In fact, this study began with my own need and desire to learn what the Lord our God expected of me as the husband of my wife and as the man of my home. Oh, how very convicting this study has been to my heart! Thus I have written this material simply to share the Biblical truths to which the Lord our God has opened my eyes concerning marriage and the home.

This material has not been written in the popular style of our time. I do not believe that I am well equipped to write in such a style, and I do not believe that our Lord has called me to such a task for this book. The reader will not find many anecdotal stories or psychological philosophies herein. Rather, I have simply sought to present the truths and teachings of God's Holy Word on the matter of marriage and the home. I have written, not for those who desire to be thrilled or entertained, nor for those who are committed to the world's philosophies and ideas, but for those who desire to walk in our Lord's truth.

It is my prayer that our Lord might graciously use the following study to direct the attention of the reader unto the wisdom and counsel of His Holy Word. It is my prayer that it might be "***good to the use of edifying, that it may minister grace unto the hearers.***" (Ephesians 4:29) Yea, it is my prayer that in all things it might be found unto the glory of our Lord.

For the Excellency of the Knowledge of Christ Jesus our Lord,
Abiding in Christ, and Christ in us,
Pastor Scott Markle

1

In the Beginning

Where then do we begin on this matter of marriage and the home? It would seem best to begin at the beginning. Thus we turn to the Book of Beginnings. In Genesis 1:1-5 we read, "*In the beginning God created the heaven and the earth. And the earth was without form, and void; and darkness was upon the face of the deep. And the Spirit of God moved upon the face of the waters. And God said, Let there be light: and there was light. And God saw the light, that it was good: and God divided the light from the darkness. And God called the light Day, and the darkness he called Night. And the evening and the morning were the first day.*" Then verses 6-8 reveal the creation of the firmament on the second day. Verses 9-13 reveal the creation of the dry land and the plant life on the third day. Verses 14-19 reveal the creation of the sun, moon, and stars on the fourth day. Verses 20-23 reveal the creation of the water animals and the fowl on the fifth day. And verses 24-25 reveal the creation of the land animals and "creeping things" on the sixth day.

The Creation of Mankind

Yet the Lord our God performed a second work of creation on the sixth day. On that day He also created mankind, both the man and the woman. In Genesis 1:26-27 we read, "*And God said, Let us make man* [that is – mankind] *in our image, after our likeness: and let them have dominion over the fish of the sea, and over the fowl of the air, and over the cattle, and over all the earth, and over every creeping thing that creepeth upon the earth. So God created man* [that is – mankind] *in his own image, in the image of God created he him; male and female created he them.*" Here we must take notice that the Lord our God created *both* the man *and* the woman "in His own image," after His own likeness. Thus we must recognize that there is no superiority or inferiority between the man and the woman in their spiritual relationship toward the Lord their God. In the divine work of creation, *both* the man *and* the woman were created with the spiritual capacity to walk in fellowship with the Lord their God. Neither men nor women are naturally more spiritual or less spiritual than the other. In the matter of spiritual things, both men and women stand on the same ground before the Lord our God.

Furthermore, we must recognize that there is no superiority or inferiority between the man and the woman in their natural relationship to the human race. Such is revealed, not only in that the Lord our God created *both* the man *and* the woman "in His own image," but also in that the Lord our God gave to *both* the man *and* the woman dominion over the creation. In Genesis 1:28 we read, "*And God blessed them* [*both* the man *and* the woman]*, and God said unto them* [*both* the man *and* the woman]*, Be fruitful, and multiply, and replenish the earth, and subdue it: and have dominion over the fish of the sea, and over the fowl of the air, and over every living thing that moveth upon the earth.*" Although (as we shall learn later in this study through the wisdom of God's Word) there may be different levels of authority and submission between the roles of the husband and wife within the marriage and home, there is no superiority or inferiority between them spiritually or naturally in the sight of the Lord their God.

Genesis 2 then gives us further details concerning this creation of the man and the woman. In Genesis 1:26-28 the creation of the first man and woman is reported in summary. In Genesis 2:4-25 the creation of the first man and woman is reported in greater detail. There we learn that this creation occurred in a process. First, the Lord our God created the man. Then the Lord planted the garden of Eden and placed the man therein. Finally, the Lord created the woman to be the man's wife.

14

The Creation of the First Man

In Genesis 2:4-7 we read, *"These are the generations of the heavens and of the earth when they were created, in the day that the LORD God made the earth and the heavens, and every plant of the field before it was in the earth, and every herb of the field before it grew: for the LORD God had not caused it to rain upon the earth, and there was not a man to till the ground. But there went up a mist from the earth, and watered the whole face of the ground. And the LORD God formed man of the dust of the ground, and breathed into his nostrils the breath of life; and man became a living soul."* Then in verses 8-15 we learn that *"the LORD God planted a garden eastward in Eden,"* and that He *"took the man, and put him into the garden of Eden to dress it and to keep it."* Such reveals the first responsibility that was assigned to the man – to take care of the Garden of Eden. It is also worthy of notice that this responsibility was first assigned to the man *only,* since the woman had not yet been created.

Verses 16-17 then reveal the provision and the precept that the LORD God delivered unto the man. There we read, *"And the LORD God commanded the man, saying, Of every tree of the garden thou mayest freely eat: but of the tree of the knowledge of good and evil, thou shalt not eat of it: for in the day that thou eatest thereof thou shalt surely die."* Again it is worthy of notice that this charge was first given to the man *before* the woman had been created. Through all of this we begin to see the role and responsibility of *leadership* that the Lord our God intended for the man within the structure of the marriage and home.

In fact, in 1 Timothy 2:12-13 the apostle Paul employed this very matter concerning the order of the creation as evidence for the man's role of leadership and for the woman's role of submission. There we read, *"But I suffer not a woman to teach, nor to usurp authority over the man, but to be in silence. For Adam was first formed, then Eve."* Some in our time have spoken against this principle, claiming that such was simply a cultural matter intended only for the time and place of the apostle. Yet the order of creation precedes any system of culture that developed thereafter. Thus we may conclude that the roles of leadership for the man and of submission for the woman were intended by the Lord our God *from the beginning.*

The Creation of the Man's Wife

Having learned of the creation of the man in Genesis 2:4-17, we come in the second place to the creation of the woman in Genesis 2:18-25. Such begins with verse 18 where the LORD God Himself made the assessment concerning the man, saying, "*It is not good that the man should be alone; I will make him an help meet for him.*" This assessment is of great interest when we consider that it is the only occasion where the Lord our God concluded that something was *not* good in His work of creation. All throughout Genesis 1 we find Him considering that which He had made "that it was good." Yet here He concluded, "It is *not* good that the man should be alone." The man was in need of "an help meet for him," and in loving kindness the Lord our God determined to create a wife for him. Even so, the principle of Proverbs 18:22 continues unto this day – "*Whoso findeth a wife findeth a good thing, and obtaineth favour of the LORD.*"

In Genesis 2:18 we also find God's greatest calling for the wife within the marriage relationship. The first purpose that the Lord our God designated for the wife was to serve as "an help meet" for her husband. Even to this day this is the primary purpose that the Lord our God Himself has set before the wife – that she should serve as "an help meet" for her husband. What then does it mean to be "an help meet for him"? First, it means that the wife is to be her husband's *help*er. The first man had been assigned the responsibility to care for the Garden of Eden. His wife, as "an help meet for him," was to be his helper in fulfilling this God-given responsibility. Second, it means that the wife is to be a helper who is *meet* for her husband. She is to be a helper that is suitable and fitting for her husband. She is to be a helper that perfectly compliments her husband in fulfilling the responsibilities and calling that the Lord has set before him. She is not to go her own separate way from him, doing her own thing. Rather, she is to come together with her husband that they may serve together as a perfectly unified whole.

16

Yet in His infinite wisdom the Lord our God did not immediately create the woman as "an help meet" for the man. Rather, He brought the man to the realization that he *was* in need of such "an help meet for him," and that none of the animals could adequately meet this need. Thus in Genesis 2:19-20 we read, *"And out of the ground the LORD God formed every beast of the field, and every fowl of the air; and brought them unto Adam to see what he would call them: and whatsoever Adam called every living creature, that was the name thereof. And Adam gave names to all cattle, and to the fowl of the air, and to every beast of the field; but for Adam there was not found an help meet for him."*

Therefore, verses 21-22 continue, *"And the LORD God caused a deep sleep to fall upon Adam, and he slept: and he took one of his ribs, and closed up the flesh instead thereof; and the rib, which the LORD God had taken from man, made he a woman, and brought her unto the man."* The LORD God formed the man Adam out of "the dust of the ground." The LORD God made the woman out of the rib of the man. Yea, He took one of the man's ribs and transformed that very rib into the woman. The first woman very literally was a part of the man. Even so, Adam himself declared in verse 23, *"This is now bone of my bones, and flesh of my flesh: she shall be called Woman, because she was taken out of Man."*

The Creation of the Marriage Relationship

Herein we find that the Lord our God Himself established the first marriage and home. At the end of verse 22, the LORD God Himself brought the woman unto the man to be his wife. Then in verse 24 the LORD God Himself confirmed that marriage with these words – *"Therefore shall a man leave his father and his mother, and shall cleave unto his wife: and they shall be one flesh."* (Note: Although it may be uncertain in the context of Genesis 2 as to who actually spoke these words, in Matthew 19:4-5 our Lord Jesus Christ specifically attributed these words to the Creator God.) We might even view this as the first marriage ceremony. The Creator God gave away the bride in verse 22; the man received his bride in verse 23; and the LORD God Himself pronounced them man and wife in verse 24. The marriage relationship was not invented by mankind, but was ordained and established by the Lord our God. Thus it is not to be defined, directed, or discarded by the will of mankind. Rather, the marriage relationship is to be defined, directed, and developed according to the will of the Creator God.

Furthermore, in verse 24 we find the three foundational principles that the Lord our God, the Creator of marriage, proscribed for a good marriage. Now, the first two of these principles are directed *only* to the husband, and the last of these principles is directed to *both* the husband and the wife. First, the husband must "leave his father and his mother." Second, the husband must "cleave unto his wife." Third, the husband and the wife are to "be one flesh." Thus we learn that the Lord our God intends for the husband *to take the leadership* in developing a one-flesh unity within the marriage, and thus we learn that the Lord our God intends for the husband and the wife *to work together* in developing and maintaining this one-flesh unity.

Finally, in the closing verse of the chapter, we encounter a beautiful example of this one-flesh unity. In Genesis 2:25 we read, *"And they were both naked, the man and his wife, and were not ashamed."* How could they, "the man and his wife," be so open with one another and yet be "not ashamed"? They could do so because, before the entrance of sin, they walked in perfect, one-flesh unity with one another.

Yet before we conclude this chapter we should consider one further charge that the Lord our God gave unto "the man and his wife." For this charge we must return to the account of Genesis 1. In verse 28 we read, *"And God blessed them, and God said unto them, Be fruitful, and multiply, and replenish the earth, and subdue it: and have dominion over the fish of the sea, and over the fowl of the air, and over every living thing that moveth upon the earth."* The Lord our God charged "the man and his wife" to "be fruitful, and multiply, and replenish the earth," that is – to raise up a family and to develop a home. This He delivered unto them as His *blessing* upon them. He poured out His blessing upon them, and they were to develop a home for Him.

Then the sixth day of creation ends with the words of Genesis 1:31 – *"And God saw every thing that he had made, and, behold, it was very good. And the evening and the morning were the sixth day."* Before the creation of the woman as "an help meet" for the man and before the completion of the marriage relationship, something was *"not* good." Now, however, everything is *"very* good." Everything, including the one-flesh marriage relationship between the man and his wife, was "very good."

Truth for Meditation

"In the beginning" we find the following principles concerning marriage and the home –

1. There is no superiority or inferiority between men and women in their spiritual relationship with the Lord. (Gen. 1:26-27)

2. There is no superiority or inferiority between men and women in their natural relationship to the human race. (Gen. 1:26-28)

3. The husband is to serve in the role of leadership within the marriage and home. (Gen. 2:7, 15-17; 1 Tim. 2:12-13)

4. The wife is to serve as "an help meet" for her husband within the marriage and home. (Gen. 2:18)

5. The husband needs his wife as "an help meet for him." (Gen. 2:18-20)

6. The wife is a good gift from the Lord to her husband. (Gen. 2:18-22; Prov. 18:22)

7. The Lord our God established the first marriage and the basic principles of a good marriage. (Gen. 2:22-24)

8. The husband is to take the leadership in developing the one-flesh unity within the marriage. (Gen. 2:24)

9. The husband and his wife are to work together to develop and maintain the one-flesh unity of the marriage. (Gen. 2:24)

10. The husband and his wife are to develop a home for the Lord. (Gen. 1:28)

Verses for Memorization

Proverbs 24:3: Through wisdom is an house builded: and by understanding it is established.

Genesis 1:27: So God created man in his own image, in the image of God created he him; male and female created he them.

2

The Unity Destroyed

At the end of Genesis 2, the man and his wife were walking in perfect unity with one another, even as they were walking in perfect obedience to and perfect fellowship with the Lord their God and Creator. However, in Genesis 3 we encounter an attack upon that obedience to the Lord, that fellowship with the Lord, and that unity within the marriage relationship.

The Devil's Temptation to Sin

In Genesis 3:1-5 we read, *"Now the serpent was more subtil than any beast of the field which the LORD God had made. And he said unto the woman, Yea, hath God said, Ye shall not eat of every tree of the garden? And the woman said unto the serpent, We may eat of the fruit of the trees of the garden: but of the fruit of the tree which is in the midst of the garden, God hath said, Ye shall not eat of it, neither shall ye touch it, lest ye die. And the serpent said unto the woman, Ye shall not surely die: for God doth know that in the day ye eat thereof, then your eyes shall be opened, and ye shall be as gods, knowing good and evil."*

That old serpent, the devil, came to attack and to destroy that which the LORD God had made. He came to destroy the fellowship between the LORD God and mankind, and he came to destroy the unity between the man and his wife. This destruction he sought to accomplish through the attack of temptation, tempting the man and his wife unto disobedience against the Lord their God. That old serpent, the devil, began his temptation by *questioning* the Word of God and thereby *questioning* the goodness of God. In fact, God had *not* said that they could not eat of every tree of the garden. Yea, God *had* said that they *could* eat of every tree of the garden except one.

Having questioned the Word of God, that old serpent, the devil, then *directly denied* the Word of God and thereby *denied* the goodness of God. God had said that in the day that they ate of the forbidden tree, they would surely die. The devil said that they would *not* surely die. In addition, that old serpent, the devil, indicated that God was withholding something profitable from them. He indicated that eating the fruit of the forbidden tree would open their eyes to greater, godlike knowledge and that God knew this and was just keeping this knowledge from them.

How then did the man and his wife respond to this attack and this temptation? Verse 6 gives answer, saying, *"And when the woman saw that the tree was good for food, and that it was pleasant to the eyes, and a tree to be desired to make one wise, she took of the fruit thereof, and did eat, and gave also unto her husband with her; and he did eat."* Both the man and his wife yielded to the temptation. That old serpent, the devil, first approached the woman, tempting her to eat of the forbidden tree; and she yielded to that temptation, "and did eat" thereof. Then she gave the fruit unto her husband that he might join with her, "and he did eat" also.

The Broken Fellowship by Sin

What affect did this act of disobedience have upon the man and his wife? Immediately their fellowship with the LORD God and their unity with one another were broken. In verses 7-8 we read, *"And the eyes of them both were opened, and they knew that they were naked; and they sewed fig leaves together, and made themselves aprons. And they heard the voice of the LORD God walking in the garden in the cool of the day: and Adam and his wife hid themselves from the presence of the LORD God amongst the trees of the garden."*

That old serpent, the devil, had said that eating the forbidden fruit would open their eyes unto greater, godlike knowledge. Even so, their eyes were indeed opened. Yet they only knew sin and shame. In Genesis 2:25 we observed the man and his wife walking in perfect unity and openness with one another. *"And they were both naked, the man and his wife, and were not ashamed."* However, with the entrance of sin "they knew that they were naked" and *were* ashamed. Therefore, they sought to cover themselves with fig-leaf aprons.

Before the entrance of sin, they were willing to be completely open with one another, and that without any shame. Yet that unashamed openness had been lost with the entrance of sin. Sin had created a division between them. Furthermore, when "they heard the voice of the LORD God walking in the garden," they "hid themselves" from His presence. Sin had also created a division between them and the Lord their God.

Then verses 9-11 reveal the LORD God's confrontation of the man, saying, *"And the LORD God called unto Adam, and said unto him, Where art thou? And he said, I heard thy voice in the garden, and I was afraid, because I was naked; and I hid myself. And he said, Who told thee that thou wast naked? Hast thou eaten of the tree, whereof I commanded thee that thou shouldest not eat?"* It is worthy of our notice that the LORD God began His confrontation of this matter with the man. The LORD God had placed the man in the leadership role within the home, and He first held the man responsible for the direction of that home.

Although that old serpent, the devil, began his temptation with the woman, and although the woman first yielded to that temptation, the LORD God first confronted the man and leader of the home for the disobedience. Even so, the LORD God challenged Adam with the question, "Where art thou?" Certainly the Lord knew where Adam was hiding. His desire with this question was to convict Adam and bring him to face and acknowledge his sin and shame.

How then did the man respond to the LORD God's confrontation? He immediately pointed his finger at his wife. In verse 12 we read, *"And the man said, The woman whom thou gavest to be with me, she gave me of the tree, and I did eat."* Oh, how greatly had sin destroyed the unity between the man and his wife! Now the man was no longer walking in perfect unity with his wife. Now the man was trying to shift the blame of his own sin onto his wife.

In addition, the man in sin also attempted to draw the LORD God into the blame and guilt of that sin, saying, "The woman *whom thou gavest* to be with me." Basically the man was complaining against the LORD God for giving to him such a faulty wife. Before the entrance of sin, the man was wonderfully pleased with the "help meet" that the LORD God had given to him; but with the entrance of sin, he was now complaining against the LORD God for the gift of his wife. Without a doubt sin had broken the unity and fellowship of the man with his wife and with his God.

The Continuing Conflict through Sin

Then verse 13 reveals the LORD God's confrontation of the woman for her disobedience, saying, *"And the LORD God said unto the woman, What is this that thou hast done? And the woman said, The serpent beguiled me, and I did eat."* In addition, verses 14-15 reveal the LORD God's curse on that old serpent, the devil, for his temptation of the man and his wife – *"And the LORD God said unto the serpent, Because thou hast done this, thou art cursed above all cattle, and above every beast of the field; upon thy belly shalt thou go, and dust shalt thou eat all the days of thy life: and I will put enmity between thee and the woman, and between thy seed and her seed; it shall bruise thy head, and thou shalt bruise his heel."* From that point forward that old serpent, the devil, would be the great spiritual adversary of mankind. Continually he would attack and tempt us in order to direct us toward sin and its destruction.

In verses 16-19 the LORD God then pronounced His curse on the man and his wife. First, verse 16 reveals the curse upon the woman, saying, *"Unto the woman He said, I will greatly multiply thy sorrow*

24

and thy conception; in sorrow thou shalt bring forth children; and thy desire shall be to thy husband, and he shall rule over thee." Here we take notice of the closing portion of this curse. From this point forward the wife would struggle in her relationship with her husband. Now within her sinful nature, there would be a resistance to her role as the helper and to his role as the leader. As a part of sins curse upon her, the wife would now have within her sinful nature a *negative* desire directed *toward and against* her husband's *authority and rule* over her. Thus sin would continually be a force of *disunity* within the marriage relationship.

Second, verses 17-19 reveal the curse upon the man, saying, "*And unto Adam He said, Because thou hast hearkened unto the voice of thy wife, and hast eaten of the tree, of which I commanded thee, saying, Thou shalt not eat of it: cursed is the ground for thy sake; in sorrow shalt thou eat of it all the days of thy life; thorns also and thistles shall it bring forth to thee; and thou shalt eat the herb of the field; in the sweat of thy face shalt thou eat bread, till thou return unto the ground; for out of it wast thou taken: for dust thou art, and unto dust shalt thou return.*" Here we take notice of the opening portion of this curse. Instead of taking up the responsibility to lead in obedience unto the voice of the Lord, the man had hearkened unto the voice of his wife and thereby had yielded himself to disobedience. Even so, within the sinful nature of the husband there would now be *a lethargy* to take up *the responsibility* of *spiritual leadership* for his marriage and home. Thus sin would continually be a force of *corruption* within the home.

Finally, Genesis 3 ends with a powerful picture of the broken fellowship between mankind and the LORD God and of the LORD God's gracious provision to deal with that sin. In verses 20-24 we read, "*And Adam called his wife's name Eve; because she was the mother of all living. Unto Adam also and to his wife did the LORD God make coats of skins, and clothed them. And the LORD God said, Behold, the man is become as one of us, to know good and evil: and now, lest he put forth his hand, and take also of the tree of life, and eat, and live for ever: therefore the LORD God sent him forth from the garden of Eden, to till the ground from whence he was taken. So He drove out the man; and He placed at the east of the garden of Eden Cherubims, and a flaming sword which turned every way, to keep the way of the tree of life.*"

The Destructive Force of Sin

Yet before we conclude this chapter, there is another account that we must consider concerning the destructive force of sin within the home. In Genesis 4:1-8 we learn how sin destroyed the relationship between Adam and Eve's first two sons, Cain and Abel. In verse 1 we read, *"And Adam knew Eve his wife; and she conceived, and bare Cain, and said, I have gotten a man from the LORD."* Here we find that Eve viewed her first-born son Cain as a precious blessing from the Lord. Yet as the account continues, we find that sin destroyed this also.

Even so, in verses 2-5 we read, *"And she again bare his brother Abel. And Abel was a keeper of sheep, but Cain was a tiller of the ground. And in process of time it came to pass, that Cain brought of the fruit of the ground an offering unto the LORD. And Abel, he also brought of the firstlings of his flock and of the fat thereof. And the LORD had respect unto Abel and to his offering: but unto Cain and to his offering he had not respect. And Cain was very wroth, and his countenance fell.*" Thus we observe that the force of sin in Cain's sinful attitude created division in his relationship with his brother.

Then in verses 6-7 the Lord confronted Cain for his sinful attitude and warned him of its destructive nature. There we read, *"And the LORD said unto Cain, Why art thou wroth? And why is thy countenance fallen? If thou doest well, shalt thou not be accepted? And if thou doest not well, sin lieth at the door. And unto thee shall be his desire, and thou shalt rule over him."* Herein the Lord declared to Cain that if he did not do well, then sin was lying in wait at the door. With such words our Lord was describing the force of sin as a wild animal just waiting at the door to attack and devour those who were not on their guard against it. Cain, however, did not heed the Lord's warning. In verse 8 we read, *"And Cain talked with Abel his*

brother: and it came to pass, when they were in the field, that Cain rose up against Abel his brother, and slew him." Yet again sin won the day and brought disunity, destruction, and death into the home.

To this day our adversary the devil continues his attacks of temptation against the marriage and home relationships, ever seeking to devour our lives, marriages, and homes. In 1 Peter 5:8 the instruction and warning is given, ***"Be sober, be vigilant; because your adversary the devil, as a roaring lion, walketh about, seeking whom he may devour."*** Such is the battle before us if we desire to have a home that is as the Lord our God would have it to be.

Furthermore, the force of sin in our nature, attitudes, words, and actions ever continues its work of destruction within our marriages and homes. As long as the home is made of sinners who yield unto temptation, the problems and battles of disunity, contention, and strife shall continue within the home. James 4:1 declares, ***"From whence come wars and fightings among you? Come they not hence, even of your lusts*** [that is – of your sinful and selfish desires] ***that war in your members?"***

Yea, the first half of Proverbs 13:10 proclaims, ***"Only by pride cometh contention;"*** and the first half of Proverbs 28:25 adds, ***"He that is of a proud heart stirreth up strife."*** Proverbs 6:14 speaks of the ungodly in heart, saying, ***"Frowardness is in his heart, he deviseth mischief continually; he soweth discord."*** Proverbs 14:1 speaks of the contrast between the spiritually wise woman and the spiritually foolish woman, saying, ***"Every wise woman buildeth her house: but the foolish plucketh it down with her hands."*** Finally, Proverbs 15:1 speaks of the contrast between gentle and grievous words, saying, ***"A soft answer turneth away wrath: but grievous words stir up anger."*** Yes, the sinfulness of our *own* hearts, our *own* attitudes, our *own* words, and our *own* actions is the destroyer of our marriages and homes.

Truth for Meditation

In the first disobedience of the man and his wife against the LORD God, we learn these truths concerning the great adversary and the great destroyer of our marriages and homes –

1. Our adversary the devil is ever attacking our Lord God's design for the marriage and home, seeking to devour our lives, marriages, and homes. (Gen. 3:1-5; 1 Pet. 5:8)

2. Our adversary the devil's weapons of choice in these attacks are deception and temptation to sin. (Gen. 3:1-5)

3. Our sinfulness and selfishness of nature, attitude, word, and action is the great destroyer of our marriages and homes. (Gen. 3:7, 12; Gen. 4:5-8; Jam. 4:1)

4. The force of sin destroys marriages and homes by creating disunity, contention, and strife. (Gen. 3:7, 12; Gen 4:5-8; Jam. 4:1; Prov. 13:10, 14:1; 15:1; 28:25)

5. The temptation of the devil and the force of sin will ever direct the husband and the wife to walk contrary to the roles of the marriage relationship that the Lord our God intended. (Gen. 3:16-17)

Verses for Memorization

James 4:1: From whence come wars and fightings among you? Come they not hence, even of your lusts that war in your members?

1 Peter 5:8: Be sober, be vigilant; because your adversary the devil, as a roaring lion, walketh about, seeking whom he may devour.

3

Hope for the Home

A t the end of the previous chapter, we learned that the home is now on a battlefield, fighting a fierce spiritual battle to survive and flourish as the Lord our God intended. Our adversary the devil is the great spiritual opponent against our marriages and homes, ever seeking to deceive us and tempt us unto sin. In addition, the force of our own selfishness and sinfulness is the great destroyer of our marriages and homes. The battle now rages; and the cry is raised – "Is there any hope for the home?" To this question the answer rings back from heaven through the Word of God – "Yes, there is *abundant hope* for the home!" Where then is this abundant hope to be found? It is wholly and wondrously to be found *in our Lord and Savior Jesus the Christ.*

God's Promise of a Great Savior

Even before He proclaimed the curse upon the woman and the man, the LORD God had revealed this hope in Genesis 3:15. There He declared unto that old serpent, the devil, *"And I will put enmity between thee and the woman, and between thy seed and her seed; it shall bruise thy head, and thou shalt bruise his heel."* Normally God's Word speaks concerning the seed of the man, but here the Lord our God spoke concerning the seed of the woman. This was the first promise concerning the One who would be born of a virgin woman. This was the first promise the coming of God the Son into this world as God in the flesh.

Here also we learn that this promised One would bruise the head of that old serpent, the devil. Although that old serpent would bruise His heel with the poison of death, yet the promised One would crush the serpent's head with that same bruised heel (that is – through His own death). In Hebrews 2:14-15 we read, "***Forasmuch then as the children are partakers of flesh and blood, he also himself likewise took part of the same; that through death he might destroy him that had the power of death, that is, the devil; and deliver them who through fear of death were all their lifetime subject to bondage.***" Through His death upon the cross, God the Son, the Lord Jesus Christ, destroyed that old serpent, the devil, and brought deliverance to us from the devil's power. Oh, what a Savior is our Lord and Savior Jesus Christ! Oh, what wondrous hope we have in Him!

Another point of hope is found immediately after the LORD God pronounced the curse upon the woman and the man. In Genesis 3:21 we read, "***Unto Adam also and to his wife did the LORD God make coats of skins, and clothed them.***" From Genesis 3:7 we learn that after Adam and Eve had sinned, "***the eyes of them both were opened, and they knew that they were naked.***" We also learn that "***they sewed fig leaves together, and made themselves aprons.***" This was their own human attempt to cover their shame and their sinfulness, but the attempts of sinners to cover their own sinfulness are not acceptable with the Lord our God. Thus in Genesis 3:21 we find that the LORD God Himself made coats of animal skins and that He Himself clothed them.

This was no longer their own human attempt to cover their sinfulness. This was the gracious work of the LORD God Himself on their behalf to deal with their sin through the shed blood and sacrificial death of an animal. Even so, the Lord our God proclaimed unto the children of Israel in Leviticus 17:11, "***For the life of the flesh is in the blood: and I have given it to you upon the altar to make an atonement for your souls: for it is the blood that maketh an atonement for the soul.***" Furthermore, this sacrifice was a figure and type of the shed blood and sacrificial death of God the Son, our Lord and Savior Jesus Christ, the eternal Lamb of God, to pay for our sin. Even so, Colossians 1:14 declares concerning Him, "***In whom we have*** *redemption through his blood, even the forgiveness of sins.*" Oh, how precious is the blood of our Savior Jesus Christ by which He "*obtained eternal redemption for us*" (Hebrews 9:12) and "*washed us from our sins*" (Revelation 1:5)!

Our Eternal Salvation through Faith

However, the delivering power of our Lord Jesus Christ's shed blood and sacrificial death is only effective and available to those who receive Him through faith as their personal Savior. The apostle Paul declared in Romans 1:16, "*For I am not ashamed of the gospel of Christ: for it is the power of God unto salvation to every one that believeth; to the Jew first, and also to the Greek.*" The gospel of Christ is the good news of His shed blood and sacrificial death for us sinners; and this gospel message is the very power of God Himself unto eternal salvation to every single individual that believes on God the Son, the Lord Jesus Christ, as Savior.

Yet again the apostle Paul declared in 1 Corinthians 1:18, "*For the preaching of the cross is to them that perish foolishness; but unto us which are saved it is the power of God.*" Who then are those that are saved, to whom the preaching of the cross is the very power of God? Verse 21 gives the answer, saying, "*For after that in the wisdom of God the world by wisdom knew not God, it pleased God by the foolishness of preaching to save them that believe.*" The truth of Christ's shed blood and sacrificial death upon the cross is the delivering power of God unto "them that *believe.*" As Ephesians 1:19 gives the description, it is "*the exceeding greatness of his power to usward who believe.*"

Furthermore, John 1:12-13 reveals that those who believe on the Lord Jesus Christ as Savior, not only receive the power of God unto salvation, but also receive the power to become God's own dear children. There we read, "*But as many as received him, to them gave he power to become the sons of God, even to them that believe on his name: which were born, not of blood, nor of the will of the flesh, nor of the will of man, but of God.*" Now, the power to become a child of God is the power of new spiritual birth. By His

31

exceeding great power, God the Father delivers all believers from the power of spiritual darkness (that is – from the power of sin and of the devil) and translates them into the spiritual kingdom of His dear Son as the children of God and the citizens of heaven. This is our wondrous hope in our Lord and Savior Jesus Christ through faith in Him as our eternal Savior.

Yet how is this delivering power over the forces of sin and the devil to be applied unto our daily Christian living in the home? The answer is completely rooted in our spiritual union with our Lord and Savior Jesus Christ.

Our Spiritual Union with Christ

In the first place, *we must recognize the absolute truth of our spiritual union with Christ.* In Romans 6:4 we read, "***Therefore we are buried with him by baptism into death: that like as Christ was raised up from the dead by the glory of the Father, even so we also should walk in newness of life.***" Also in verses 6 we read, "***Knowing this, that our old man is crucified with him, that the body of sin might be destroyed, that henceforth we should not serve sin.***" Finally, in Ephesians 2:4-5 we read, "***But God, who is rich in mercy, for his great love wherewith he loved us, even when we were dead in sins, hath quickened us*** [or, made us alive] ***together with Christ, (by grace ye are saved).***"

In all three of these verses, we find the phrase "with Him." From Romans 6:4 we learn that we have been spiritually "buried *with Him* . . . into death." Furthermore, from Romans 6:6 we learn that we have had our old, unsaved man spiritually "crucified *with Him*." Finally, from Ephesians 2:4-5 we learn that we have been made alive "together *with Christ*." At the moment of our salvation through Christ, we were placed into spiritual union with Christ; and being placed into such a spiritual union, we were spiritually unified with Him in His death and in His resurrection.

Therefore, Romans 6:10-11 describes the character of Christ's death and resurrection life and then applies such to us believers, saying, "***For in that he died, he died unto sin once: but in that he liveth, he*** *liveth unto God. Likewise reckon ye also yourselves to be dead indeed unto sin, but alive unto God through Jesus Christ our Lord.*" Our Lord Jesus Christ's death was a death "unto sin," and His resurrection life is a life "unto God." Even so, in our spiritual union with His death and resurrection, we must recognize that we ourselves also are "dead indeed unto sin, but alive unto God." What does this mean for our daily living? As the closing phrase of verse 6 reveals, it means that "henceforth we should not serve sin;" and as the closing phrase of verse 4 reveals, it means that "we also should walk in newness of life." Yea, it means that through our spiritual union with our Lord and Savior Jesus Christ, we are now able to have *daily victory* over sin and to live in *daily obedience* unto God.

The Lord's Power for Daily Living

In the second place, to have our Lord's delivering power applied to our daily Christian living in our homes, *we must stand firm by faith in our Lord's almighty power for our daily living.* We do not possess the power in ourselves to stand victorious over the temptation of sin and to bring forth spiritual fruit unto God's glory. Yet those things that are impossible in our own strength are abundantly possible in our Lord's almighty strength; and through our spiritual union with Christ, we have access to that almighty strength.

Thus we are instructed in Ephesians 6:10-11, "*Finally, my brethren, be strong in the Lord, and in the power of his might. Put on the whole armour of God, that ye may be able to stand against the wiles of the devil.*" To this verse 13 adds, "*Wherefore take unto you the whole armour of God, that ye may be able to withstand in the evil day, and having done all, to stand.*" By firmly standing and faithfully trusting in our Lord's strength for the battle, we are able to overcome the deceptions and temptations of our adversary the devil and to stand victorious in the evil day of temptation and tribulation.

Yea, concerning that part of the armor which is called the shield of faith, verse 16 declares, "*Above all, taking the shield of faith, wherewith ye shall be able to quench all of the fiery darts of the wicked.*" Our daily, moment-by-moment faith in our Lord *is* our

33

shield against the attacks of our wicked adversary. By this shield of faith (that is – by our faithful trusting in our Lord's strength), we are able to defeat *all* of the fiery darts that our wicked adversary might shoot against us. Even so, James 4:7 gives us the two-fold instruction, ***"Submit yourselves therefore to God. Resist the devil, and he will flee from you."*** If we will first submit ourselves unto the Lord our God, firmly standing and faithfully trusting in His almighty power for the battle, we will be able to resist the devil in such a victorious manner that the devil will actually *flee* from us.

Yet there is more. In our Lord's strength we not only find the power to stand victorious over our adversary the devil and over the temptation of sin, but in our Lord's strength we also find the power to bring forth much spiritual fruit unto the glory of God. In John 15:4-5 our Lord Jesus Christ gave the instruction, ***"Abide in me, and I in you. As the branch cannot bear fruit of itself, except it abide in the vine; no more can ye, except ye abide in me. I am the vine, ye are the branches. He that abideth in me, and I in him, the same bringeth forth much fruit: for without me ye can do nothing."*** Our Lord gives us the solemn warning that we cannot bring forth any spiritual fruit at all unless we abide in Him. Without Him we stand in our own strength, and in our own strength we can do nothing.

Yet here our Lord also gives us the glorious promise that those who are abiding in Him and allowing Him to be abiding in them will be bringing forth *much* spiritual fruit. Even so, the apostle Paul gave personal testimony in Philippians 4:13, saying, ***"I can do all things through Christ which strengtheneth me."*** This then is the solemn warning – *No thing without Christ.* Yet this is the glorious promise – *All things through Christ.* Yea, the truth is given in Philippians 1:11, ***"Being filled with the fruits of righteousness, which are by Jesus Christ, unto the glory and praise of God."*** Again we read in Hebrews 13:20-21, ***"Now the God of peace, that brought again from the dead our Lord Jesus, that great shepherd of the sheep, through the blood of the everlasting covenant, make you perfect in every good work to do his will, working in you that which is wellpleasing in his sight, through Jesus Christ; to whom be glory for ever and ever. Amen."*** We are "filled with the fruits of

34

righteousness" *by Jesus Christ*, and we are made "perfect in every good work" to do God's will and to live well pleasing in God's sight *"through Jesus Christ."*

The Lord's Sufficiency for Our Lives

In the third place, to have our Lord's delivering power applied to our daily Christian living in our homes, *we must be assured of our Lord's complete sufficiency for our daily lives.* In Colossians 1:19 we read concerning our Lord and Savior Jesus Christ, *"For it pleased the Father that in him should all fulness dwell."* Again in Colossians 2:3 we read concerning Him, *"In whom are hid all the treasures of wisdom and knowledge."* Then we are warned in verse 4, *"And this I say, lest any man beguile you with enticing words;"* and again we a warned in verse 8, *"Beware lest any man spoil you through philosophy and vain deceit, after the tradition of men, after the rudiments of the world, and not after Christ."*

The warning is that we might not be turned aside from our Lord and Savior Jesus Christ through the philosophies and deceptions of this world. Rather, we are ever to follow hard after Christ. Why? Verses 9-10 give answer, saying, *"For in him dwelleth all the fulness of the Godhead bodily. And ye are complete in him, which is the head of all principalities and power."* We believers are complete in our Lord Jesus Christ. *All* that we need for life and godliness is to be found in Him. *He* is our all in all, and *He* is sufficient for *all.* In Him dwells *"all* the fulness of the Godhead," and in Him "are hid *all* the treasures of wisdom and knowledge." Thus our Lord proclaimed in the second half of John 10:10, *"I am come that they might have life, and that they might have it more abundantly."* He alone is our *all-sufficient* Source for abundant Christian living. Yea, in Him *alone* is to be found *all* spiritual help and hope for our lives, our marriages, and our homes.

The Filling Influence of the Holy Spirit

In the fourth place, to have our Lord's delivering power applied to our daily Christian living in our homes, *we must walk step-by-step under the filling influence of the Holy Spirit of Christ.* In Ephesians 5:18

we are instructed, *"And be not drunk with wine, wherein is excess; but be filled with the Spirit."* Then in verses 19-21 the instruction continues, *"Speaking to yourselves in psalms and hymns and spiritual songs, singing and making melody in your heart to the Lord; giving thanks always for all things unto God and the Father in the name of our Lord Jesus Christ; submitting yourselves one to another in the fear of God."* Following this we find a lengthy passage of Scripture concerning Christian living in the home. In Ephesians 5:22-33 we find a passage concerning the husband-wife relationship, and in Ephesians 6:1-4 we find a passage concerning the parent-child relationship. In the structure of this context, all of these things flow out of the instruction of Ephesians 5:18 to *"be filled with the Spirit."*

All that our Lord would have to be true of our home relationships is built upon the foundation of our being filled with the Spirit. Thus we are instructed in Galatians 5:16, *"This I say then, Walk in the Spirit, and ye shall not fulfill the lust of the flesh."* As we have already learned, the force of our selfish, sinful flesh is the great destroyer of our marriages and homes. Yet as we walk in and after the direction of the Holy Spirit, we shall find victory over these sinful ways and over their destructive force in our lives and in our homes. In addition, as we walk in and after the direction of the Holy Spirit, we shall bring forth the fruit of the Spirit as revealed in verses 22-23 – *"But the fruit of the Spirit is love, joy, peace, longsuffering, gentleness, goodness, faith, meekness, temperance: against such there is no law."* Such is the spiritual fruit that shall cause our marriages and homes to survive and flourish as the Lord our God intends. *"This I say then, Walk in the Spirit."*

The Rich Indwelling of Our Lord's Word

In the fifth place, to have our Lord's delivering power applied to our daily Christian living in our homes, *we must allow the Word of Christ to dwell in us richly in all wisdom.* In Colossians 3:16 we are instructed, *"Let the word of Christ dwell in you richly in all wisdom; teaching and admonishing one another in psalms and hymns and spiritual songs, singing with grace in your hearts to the Lord."*

Also in verse 17 we are instructed, "*And whatsoever ye do in word or deed, do all in the name of the Lord Jesus, giving thanks to God and the Father by him.*" Then in verses 18-21 each member of the home is given instruction.

Here we learn that whatever we do in word or deed in the relationships of our homes, we are to do all in the name of our Lord and Savior Jesus Christ. How then shall we accomplish this? We do so by allowing the Word of our Lord to dwell richly in our hearts as the governing principle of our lives. Just as all that our Lord would have to be true of our home relationships is built upon the foundation of our being filled with the Spirit, even so all that He would have to be true of our home relationships is also built upon our allowing His Word to dwell in us richly. Thus the instruction and promise is given in Joshua 1:8, "*This book of the law shall not depart out of thy mouth; but thou shalt meditate therein day and night, that thou mayest observe to do according to all that is written therein: for then thou shalt make thy way prosperous, and then thou shalt have good success.*" Yes, *then* our marriages and homes shall *survive and flourish* as the Lord our God intends.

A Faithful Walk with Our Lord

Finally then, to have our Lord's delivering power applied to our daily Christian living in our homes, *we must daily and faithfully walk with our Lord in righteousness.* In Genesis 6:5-7 we read, "*And God saw that the wickedness of man was great in the earth, and that every imagination of the thoughts of his heart was only evil continually. And it repented the LORD that he had made man on the earth, and it grieved him at his heart. And the LORD said, I will destroy man whom I have created from the face of the earth; both man, and beast, and the creeping thing, and the fowls of the air; for it repenteth me that I have made them.*" Because of the wickedness of mankind upon the earth, the Lord our God determined to destroy mankind. "*But,*" verse 8 adds, "*Noah found grace in the eyes of the LORD.*" Why did Noah find such grace in the LORD's sight? Verse 9 reveals the answer, saying, "*These are the generations of Noah: Noah was a just man and perfect in his generation, and Noah walked with God.*"

Thus in verses 13-21 God instructed Noah to build an ark unto the saving of his household. Yea, in verses 17-18 God declared unto him, *"And, behold, I, even I, do bring a flood of waters upon the earth, to destroy all flesh, wherein is the breath of life, from under heaven; and every thing that is in the earth shall die. But with thee will I establish my covenant; and thou shalt come into the ark, thou, and thy sons, and thy wife, and thy sons' wives with thee."* Then verse 22 reveals that Noah obeyed God in this matter. Yea, in Genesis 7:1 we read, *"And the LORD said unto Noah, Come thou and all thy house into the ark; for thee have I seen righteous before me in this generation."* Then Genesis 7:23 gives report concerning the judgment of the flood, *"Every living substance was destroyed which was upon the face of the ground, both man, and cattle, and the creeping thing, and the fowl of the heaven; and they were destroyed from the earth: and Noah only remained alive, and they that were with him in the ark."*

At that time of God's judgment upon that wicked generation, Noah and his household were the only individuals that were delivered. Why were they delivered? Noah and his household were delivered because "Noah *walked with God*" and because Noah was seen to be *righteous before God.* Even so, if we desire that our own marriages and homes might survive and flourish as the Lord our God intends, we ourselves must daily and faithfully walk with the Lord our God in our generation, no matter how wicked that generation may be.

How then shall we walk with our Lord? Colossians 2:6-7 gives answer, saying, *"As ye have therefore received Christ Jesus the Lord, so walk ye in him: rooted and built up in him, and stablished in the faith, as ye have been taught, abounding therein with thanksgiving."* We walk and abide in our Lord Jesus Christ in the same manner that we received Him as our eternal Savior. We received Him as Savior through faith. Therefore, we must also walk and abide in Him through steadfastness of faith. Thereby we are "rooted and built up in Him," and thereby we come to know and experience the spiritual victory that we have in Him. Even so, the apostle Paul gave testimony in 2 Corinthians 2:14, saying, *"Now thanks be unto God, which always causeth us to triumph in Christ, and maketh manifest the savour of his knowledge by us in every place.*" In Christ Jesus our Lord and Savior there is abundant hope for us, for our marriages, and for our homes. Amen, and AMEN.

Truth for Meditation

The hope for our homes is wholly and wondrously to be found in our Lord and Savior Jesus Christ, that is –

1. In the sacrificial death of Christ. (Gen. 3:15; Heb. 2:14-15)

2. In the cleansing blood of Christ. (Gen. 3:21; Col. 1:14)

3. In our eternal salvation through Christ. (Rom. 1:16; 1 Cor. 1:18, 21; John 1:12-13)

4. In our spiritual union with Christ. (Rom. 6:4, 6, 10-11; Eph. 2:4-5)

5. In the almighty power of Christ. (Eph. 6:10-11, 13, 16; Jam. 4:7; John 15:4-5; Phil. 4:13; Phil. 1:11; Heb. 13:20-21)

6. In the complete sufficiency of Christ. (Col. 1:19; 2:3, 9-10; John 10:10)

7. In the Holy Spirit of Christ. (Eph. 5:18 – 6: 4; Gal. 5:16, 22-23)

8. In the true Word of Christ. (Col. 3:16-21; Josh. 1:8)

9. In our faithful walk with Christ. (Gen. 6:8-9; 7:1; Col. 2:6-7)

10. In our sure victory through Christ. (2 Cor. 2:14)

Verses for Memorization

Romans 6:11: Likewise reckon ye also yourselves to be dead indeed unto sin, but alive unto God through Jesus Christ our Lord.

Ephesians 6:10-11: Finally, my brethren, be strong in the Lord, and in the power of his might. Put on the whole armour of God, that ye may be able to stand against the wiles of the devil.

James 4:7: Submit yourselves therefore to God. Resist the devil, and he will flee from you.

John 15:4-5: Abide in me, and I in you. As the branch cannot bear fruit of itself except it abide in the vine; no more can ye, except ye abide in me. I am the vine, ye are the branches. He that abideth in me, and I in him, the same bringeth forth much fruit: for without me ye can do nothing.

Philippians 4:13: I can do all things through Christ which strengtheneth me.

Galatians 5:16: This I say then, Walk in the Spirit, and ye shall not fulfil the lust of the flesh.

Joshua 1:8: This book of the law shall not depart out of thy mouth; but thou shalt meditate therein day and night, that thou mayest observe to do according to all that is written therein: for then thou shalt make thy way prosperous, and then thou shalt have good success.

Colossians 2:6: As ye have therefore received Christ Jesus the Lord, so walk ye in him.

4

Leadership in the Home

Previously, in considering Genesis 2 concerning the creation of the man and his wife, we took notice that the Lord our God created the man for the role of leadership within the structure of the marriage and home. Is this conclusion Biblically valid? Does God's Word truly reveal that the Lord our God has ordained for the man of the home to serve in the role of leadership for his marriage and home? If so, what are the Biblical evidences for this truth?

The Order of the Creation

The man Adam was created first, and then his wife Eve was created as "an help meet for him." Even before his wife had been created, the man Adam was placed into the Garden of Eden and assigned the responsibility "to dress it and to keep it." Even before his wife had been created, the man Adam was given the provision of every tree of the garden for food to eat and the precept that he should not eat of the tree of the knowledge of good and evil. Even before his wife had been created, the man Adam was responsible to name all of the land animals. Even so, in 1 Timothy 2:12-13 the apostle Paul, under the inspiration of God the Holy Spirit, argued from *the order of the creation* for the role of leadership for the man and the role of submission for the woman. There we read, ***"But I suffer not a woman to teach, nor to usurp authority over the man, but to be in silence. For Adam was first formed, then Eve."***

The Nature of the First Temptation

In addition, the apostle, under the inspiration of God the Holy Spirit, gave a second argument for the roles of leadership for the man and of submission for the woman. In 1 Timothy 2:14 we read, *"And Adam was not deceived, but the woman being deceived was in the transgression."* When that old serpent, the devil, came into the garden in temptation, he approached the woman, not the man. In this temptation he sought to deceive her into believing that eating the fruit of the forbidden tree would be of spiritual benefit to her and her husband. Yea, he sought to deceive her concerning the consequences of eating the forbidden fruit. In Genesis 3:4-5 we read, *"And the serpent said unto the woman, Ye shall not surely die: for God doth know that in the day ye eat thereof, then your eyes shall be opened, and ye shall be as gods, knowing good and evil."*

Then verse 6 reveals the woman's response, saying, *"And when the woman saw that the tree was good for food, and that it was pleasant to the eyes, and a tree to be desired to make one wise, she took of the fruit thereof, and did eat, and gave also unto her husband with her; and he did eat."* That old serpent, the devil, did indeed deceive the woman into believing that the forbidden fruit was spiritually desirable to make one spiritually wise.

Yet what about her husband? There is no record in God's Word that the devil ever directly tempted the man. Rather, God's Word indicates that the woman gave of the fruit also unto her husband and that he did eat at *her* hand. He was not deceived by the devil. He was not deceived concerning the consequences of his disobedience. He was not deceived into believing that the forbidden fruit would be of spiritual benefit to him and his wife. Therefore, in 1 Timothy 2:14 the apostle Paul, under the inspiration of God the Holy Spirit, argued from *the nature of the first temptation* for the roles of leadership for the man and of submission for the woman. This he did on the grounds that the man is less easily deceived by the deceptions of the devil.

The Declaration of God's Word

Furthermore, in 1 Corinthians 11 the apostle Paul, under the inspiration of God the Holy Spirit, delivered another argument from the original creation for the roles of leadership for the man and of submission for the woman. In verse 3 the apostle declared, "***But I would have you know, that the head of every man is Christ; and the head of the woman is the man; and the head of Christ is God.***" Here we learn who holds the role of leadership in three relationships. We learn that God the Father is the Head of God the Son. Furthermore, we learn that God the Son is the Head of the man of the home. Finally, we learn that the man of the home is the head of his wife. This is *the declaration of God's Word.*

Now, headship is the position of leadership. Thus we learn that God the Father is in the role of leadership over God the Son, that God the Son is in the role of leadership over the man, and that the man is in the role of leadership over his wife. Yet this matter of headship is not to be viewed as a matter of natural superiority or inferiority. God the Son is not inferior to God the Father. Yea, God the Father and God the Son are eternally equal in the essence of the triune Godhead. Yet in the plan of redemption for us sinners, God the Father entered into the role of leadership; and God the Son willingly submitted Himself to the Father's headship by taking upon Himself the form of a servant and by becoming obedient unto the Father's will even unto the death of the cross. (Philippians 2:5-8) In like manner, the wife is *not humanly or spiritually inferior* to the husband. Yet in the marriage relationship, the husband has been assigned by the Lord our God to the role of leadership over his wife and his home.

The Nature of the Creation

Now, in 1 Corinthians 11:4-5 the headship of the man is applied to the matter of praying or prophesying in the public gathering of the church. There we read, "***Every man praying or prophesying, having his head covered, dishonoureth his head. But every woman that prayeth or prophesieth with her head uncovered dishonoureth her head: for that is even all one as if she were shaven.***" For our purposes we shall not enter into the question of what constitutes a head covering. Yet we shall consider the application of headship in this matter.

Here we learn that every man who prays or prophesies in the public gathering of the church while having his physical head covered with some form of head covering brings dishonor upon his head. Who then is the head of every man? According to verse 3, *"the head of every man is Christ."* By praying or prophesying with his physical head covered, a man brings dishonor upon his Lord and Savior Jesus Christ. We also learn that every woman who prays or prophesies in the public gathering of the church while not having her physical head covered with some form of head covering brings dishonor upon her head. Who then is the head of the woman? According to verse 3, *"the head of the woman is the man."* By praying or prophesying without her physical head covered, a wife brings dishonor upon her husband.

To this 1 Corinthians 11:7 adds, *"For a man indeed ought not to cover his head, forasmuch as he is the image and glory of God: but the woman is the glory of the man."* On the one hand, the reason that a man ought not to cover his physical head in such a case is because "he is the image and glory of God." On the other hand, the reason that the wife ought to cover her physical head in such a case is because she is the glory of her husband.

Thus the wife ought to wear some form of head covering in such a case as a *symbol* of her *willing submission* to her *husband's* role of *headship and leadership* over her. The argument that the apostle gives for this, under the inspiration of God the Holy Spirit, is again rooted in the creation account. In verses 8-9 we read, *"For the man is not of the woman; but the woman of the man. Neither was the man created for the woman; but the woman for the man."* Here the argument is rooted, not in the order of the creation, but in the nature of the creation. The Lord our God did not create the first man Adam out of the first woman Eve. Rather, He created the first woman Eve out of the first man Adam's rib. Furthermore, the Lord our God did not create the first man Adam for the sake of the first woman Eve. Rather, He created the first woman Eve for the sake of her husband Adam – to be "an help meet *for him.*" Thus *the nature of the original creation* also reveals the roles of leadership for the husband and of submission for the wife.

Yet again we must understand that this is not a matter of superiority or inferiority; for the man and the woman are *not independent* of one another, but are *interdependent upon* one another. Even so, 1 Corinthians 11:11-12 declares, *"Nevertheless neither is the man without the woman, neither the woman without the man, in the Lord. For as the woman is of the man, even so is the man also by the woman; but all things of God."* Just as it is true that the first woman Eve was created out of the rib of the first man Adam, even so it is also true that every other man except Adam has been born into this world by a woman. Yea, even our Lord Jesus Christ, who was not physically begotten by a human father, was born into this world by a woman.

The Command of God's Word

However, the Lord our God Himself has established the headship of the husband over his wife. In giving instruction to the wives, Ephesians 5:22-24 declares, *"Wives, submit yourselves unto your own husbands, as unto the Lord. For the husband is the head of the wife, even as Christ is the head of the church: and he is the saviour of the body. Therefore as the church is subject unto Christ, so let the wives be to their own husbands in every thing."* Here we learn that the husband is the head of his wife in the same manner that our Lord Jesus Christ is the Head of the church. Just as our Lord Jesus Christ possesses the role of authority and leadership over His church, even so the husband possesses the God-given role of authority and leadership over his wife. In addition, just as Christ's church is to subject itself unto His authority and leadership, even so the wife is to subject herself unto her husband's authority and leadership. This is *the command of God's Word.*

Yea, in verse 22 God's Word commands the wife to submit herself unto her own husband as if she was submitting unto the Lord Himself, for in some sense a wife's own husband stands before her as a representative of the Lord Himself. Furthermore, in Colossians 3:18 God's Word gives instruction to the wives, saying, ***"Wives, submit yourselves unto your own husbands, as it is fit in the Lord."*** In our Lord's sight and according to our Lord's will, it is fitting and proper for a wife to submit herself unto the leadership of her husband.

The Responsibility of Leadership

Yet here is where many a man makes a great and grave mistake in his home. When many a man learns of his God-given role of leadership in the marriage and home, he tends to concentrate his attention upon the privilege of that leadership role. Yea, he tends to take up the privilege of authority in a selfish manner and to lord it selfishly over his wife and household. Such is indeed the way of this sinful world and its view of leadership. However, in the Biblical view, the role of leadership in the home is first and foremost a role of responsibility *for the sake of* one's wife and household. Thus to be a true man and leader in his home, a man must be a man of *responsibility*.

Now, it must be understood that the man of the home is the head and leader of his home no matter how poorly he might lead. In Scripture the Lord our God never instructs the man of the home to *become* the head of his wife and household. Rather, the Lord our God declares in His Word that the man of the home *is* the head of his wife and household. The question is not whether or not the man of the home is able to be the head and leader of his home. Rather, the question is what kind of head and leader the man of the home will be. The question is whether the man of the home will be a good, godly, and faithful leader of his home or a poor, ungodly, and irresponsible leader of his home.

Yet what if the man of the home decides to cast aside his role of leadership in the home, or what if the man of the home is irresponsible and unfaithful in his role of leadership in the home? Even in this the man of the home still serves as the leader of his home. However, in such a case he leads his home down a path of spiritual darkness and destruction. Just as such a man lives his own life as if God's will and ways for the matters of life are unnecessary, unwanted, and unacceptable, even so he leads his wife and household into the same view that God's will and ways for the matters of their lives are unnecessary, unwanted, and unacceptable. Just as he lives after his own way, rather than after God's way, even so he leads his wife and household to live after their own way, rather than after God's way. Just as he lives selfishly in his daily walk, even so he leads his wife and household to be selfish and self-serving in their daily walk. Just as he lives irresponsibly and unfaithfully in his own life and responsibilities as the man of the home, even so he leads his wife and household to be irresponsible and unfaithful in their own responsibilities in life. Oh, how many a man needs to humble himself before the Lord in repentance with a broken and contrite heart for his selfish, self-serving, irresponsible, unfaithful, unspiritual leadership within his marriage and home!

What then are the responsibilities that the role of leadership requires of the man of the home?

Accountable before the Lord for His Leadership

In the first place, the man of the home is responsible and accountable *before the Lord for the manner in which he leads his wife and household.* We must remember the *first* truth of 1 Corinthians 11:3 – *"But I would have you know, that the head of every man is Christ."* The man of the home is divinely appointed as head over his own home, but he himself also has a Head over him. His role of leadership is not an ultimate headship, but is a *delegated* headship from his own Head and Lord, Jesus Christ. Thus the man of the home will be held accountable before the Lord for every bit of his faithfulness or failure in the leadership of his home.

Responsible to Serve and Minister in Humility

In the second place, the man of the home is responsible *to serve and minister in humility unto his wife and household.* In Mark 10:42-45 our Lord Jesus Christ instructed His disciples concerning those who would possess roles of leadership among His people. There we read, *"But Jesus called them to him, and saith unto them, Ye know that*

47

they which are accounted to rule over the Gentiles exercise lordship over them; and their great ones exercise authority upon them. But so shall it not be among you: but whosoever will be great among you, shall be your minister: and whosoever of you will be the chiefest, shall be servant of all. For even the Son of man came not to be ministered unto, but to minister, and to give his life a ransom for many."

In the view of this sinful, selfish world, a position of leadership is a position of *power* over others and of *privilege* for self. In the ways of this world, those in leadership roles selfishly concentrate their focus upon their privilege of lordship, dominion, and authority. Yet our Lord would not have such a view and such ways among His own people. It is His will that those in leadership roles should humbly concentrate their focus upon serving and ministering to those under their leadership. Thus the man of the home is not to view his leadership role selfishly as a benefit for himself, but to view his leadership role *humbly* as an opportunity and responsibility *to serve* his wife and household.

Responsible to Lead in Developing One-Flesh Unity

In the third place, the husband is responsible *to take the lead in developing the one-flesh unity of his marriage relationship.* In Genesis 2:24 the Lord our God gave three foundational principles for a good marriage relationship. There He declared, *"Therefore shall a man leave his father and his mother, and shall cleave unto his wife: and they shall be one flesh."* Now, the third of these foundational principles is delivered to *both* the husband and the wife. Together they are *both* to pursue and develop a one-flesh unity in their marriage relationship. Yet the first two of these foundational principles are delivered *only* to the husband. He is to leave his parents and to cleave unto his wife. These two principles that were delivered to the husband alone are placed in order *before* the principle that was delivered to both the husband and the wife. Thus the husband is responsible to take the lead in developing the one-flesh unity between him and his wife.

Furthermore, if the one-flesh unity of the marriage so fails that the husband divorces his wife, even still he is responsible and accountable for her. In Matthew 5:31-32 our Lord Jesus Christ proclaimed, "*It hath been said, Whosoever shall put away his wife, let him give her a writing of divorcement: but I say unto you, That whosoever shall put away his wife, saving for the cause of fornication, causeth her to commit adultery: and whosoever shall marry her that is divorced committeth adultery.*" If the divorced wife remarries in such a case, *three* individuals are accountable for the sin of adultery. The man who marries her is committing adultery; she herself is committing adultery; and the husband who originally divorced her is accountable for her sin of adultery. Yea, our Lord Himself proclaimed that the original husband, by divorcing his wife, is *causing* her to commit adultery. The divorce did not cancel his responsibility before the Lord for the one-flesh unity of their marriage relationship. He is still responsible and accountable.

Responsible for His Wife's Growth in Maturity

In the fourth place, the husband is responsible *for his wife's growth in spiritual, emotional, and mental maturity*. In giving instruction to the husbands, Ephesians 5:25-27 declares, "*Husbands, love your wives, even as Christ also loved the church, and gave himself for it; that he might sanctify and cleanse it with the washing of water by the word, that he might present it to himself a glorious church, not having spot, or wrinkle, or any such thing; but that it should be holy and without blemish.*" Here we find that the husband is to love his wife in the same manner that our Lord Jesus Christ loved the church. How then did Christ love the church? He loved the church by giving Himself for it. Why then did He give Himself for the church? He did so in order that He might sanctify and cleanse the church and that thereby He might present the church unto Himself as a glorious church, not having any spot or wrinkle, but being holy and without blemish. He did so in order that He might nourish and cherish the church unto growth and glory.

In like manner and for the same reason, the husband is responsible to love his wife. Thus verses 28-29 continue the instruction to husbands,

49

saying, "*So ought men to love their wives as their own bodies. He that loveth his wife loveth himself. For no man ever yet hated his own flesh; but nourisheth and cherisheth it, even as the Lord the church.*" Just as our Lord nourishes and cherishes the church in love for its growth and glory, even so the husband is responsible to nourish and cherish his wife in love for the purpose of her growth and glory in maturity.

Responsible for His Wife's and Daughter's Commitments

In the fifth place, the man of the home is responsible *for the commitments that his wife or daughter(s) might make.* This principle is found in the Law of our Lord to the children of Israel. In Numbers 30:2 we read, "*If a man vow a vow unto the LORD, or swear an oath to bind his soul with a bond; he shall not break his word, he shall do according to all that proceedeth out of his mouth.*" However, in verses 3-8 we read, "*If a woman also vow a vow unto the LORD, and bind herself by a bond, being in her father's house in her youth; and her father hear her vow, and her bond wherewith she hath bound her soul, and her father shall hold his peace at her: then all her vows shall stand, and every bond wherewith she hath bound her soul shall stand. But if her father disallow her in the day that he heareth; not any of her vows, or of her bonds wherewith she hath bound her soul, shall stand: and the LORD shall forgive her, because her father disallowed her. And if she had at all an husband, when she vowed, or uttered ought out of her lips, wherewith she bound her soul; and her husband heard it, and held his peace at her in the day that he heard it: then her vows shall stand, and her bonds wherewith she bound her soul shall stand. But if her husband disallowed her on the day that he heard it; then he shall make her vow which she vowed, and that which she uttered with her lips, wherewith she bound her soul, of none effect: and the LORD shall forgive her.*" Yea, verses 13-16 declare, "*Every vow, and every binding oath to afflict the soul, her husband may establish it, or her husband may make it void. But if her husband altogether hold his peace at her from day to day; then he establisheth all her vows, or all her bonds, which are upon her: he confirmeth them, because he held his peace at her in the day that he heard them. But if he shall any ways make them void after that he hath heard them; then he shall bear her iniquity. These are the statutes, which the LORD commanded Moses, between a man and his wife, between the father and his daughter, being yet in her youth in her father's house."*

It is the man's responsibility to condone, confirm, counteract, or cancel the commitments that his wife or daughter(s) might make, even when those commitments are made unto the Lord our God Himself. Furthermore, if some form of iniquity is produced by his cancellation of such a commitment, then according to verse 15 *he* must bear that iniquity before the Lord. The man himself is responsible and accountable for the matter.

Responsible for the Spiritual Direction of His Household

In the sixth place, the man of the home is responsible *for the spiritual direction and service of his household.* In Joshua 24:14-15 we observe the godly example of Joshua; for there he proclaimed unto the children of Israel, *"Now therefore fear the LORD, and serve him in sincerity and in truth: and put away the gods which your fathers served on the other side of the flood, and in Egypt; and serve ye the LORD. And if it seem evil unto you to serve the LORD, choose you this day whom ye will serve; whether the gods which your fathers served that were on the other side of the flood, or the gods of the Amorites, in whose land ye dwell: but as for me and my house, we will serve the LORD."*

The man of God Joshua set the spiritual direction for his household. He did not take a vote from his wife and children. Rather, he took the lead in the matter. Even so, every man of God today is responsible to set the spiritual direction for his household, firmly and faithfully leading them to follow and serve the Lord. Oh, how great is the need for men who will step forward and stand fast as men of God in *leading* their households to follow and serve the Lord! Oh, how great is the need in our homes for the men to make the *first* commitment in following and serving the Lord and to maintain the *foremost* commitment in the face of every temptation and trial!

51

Responsible to Provide Materially for His Household

In the seventh place, the man of the home is responsible *to provide materially for the needs of his household.* In 1 Timothy 5:8 the judgment is pronounced, *"But if any provide not for his own, and specially for those of his own house, he hath denied the faith, and is worse than an infidel."* In its immediate context this judgment was made concerning a man's provision for his widowed mother. Yet if such judgment holds true when a man does not strive to provide for his widowed mother, then certainly it would also hold true if a man did not strive to provide for his own wife and children. Now, it is understood that we all may suffer times of financial struggle. Yet it is the responsibility of the man of the home, as much as he is able, to work for the provision of his household with diligence and to manage the financial affairs of the home with integrity.

Responsible for the Upbringing of His Children

In the eighth place, the father is responsible *to bring up his children in the wisdom and ways of the Lord.* In Ephesians 6:4 God's Word commands, *"And, ye fathers, provoke not your children to wrath: but bring them up in the nurture and admonition of the Lord."* Certainly both the father and the mother are to have a part in the upbringing of their children. Yet God's Word reveals that the primary responsibility for this upbringing is set squarely upon the shoulders of the father. In like manner, Colossians 3:21 focuses upon the fathers when it warns them, saying, *"Fathers, provoke not your children to anger, lest they be discouraged."* Furthermore, Deuteronomy 8:5 employs the father's responsibility to chasten his son as an example for our Lord's chastening of his own people, saying, *"Thou shalt also consider in thine heart, that, as a man chasteneth his son, so the LORD thy God chasteneth thee."* Thus we find that, although others may be involved, the father is the one who is first and foremost responsible before God for the upbringing and discipline of his children.

Responsible for the Sexual Purity of His Daughter

In the ninth place, the father is responsible *for the sexual purity of his daughter(s)*. Again this principle is found in the Law of our Lord unto the children of Israel. In Deuteronomy 22:13-17 we encounter a case in which a man marries a woman and afterward makes an accusation against her that she was not a virgin when he married her. There we read, *"If any man take a wife, and go in unto her, and hate her, and give occasions of speech against her, and bring up an evil name upon her, and say, I took this woman, and when I came to her, I found her not a maid* [that is – not a virgin]*: then shall the father of the damsel, and her mother, take and bring forth the tokens of the damsel's virginity unto the elders of the city in the gate: and the damsel's father shall say unto the elders, I gave my daughter unto this man to wife, and he hateth her; and, lo, he hath given occasions of speech against her, saying, I found not thy daughter a maid; and yet these are the tokens of my daughter's virginity. And they shall spread the cloth before the elders of the city."* Here we find that it is the *father* who was to speak in the defense of his daughter's virginity and sexual purity.

If the accusation was found to be false, then verses 18-19 pronounced the judgment, *"And the elders of that city shall take that man and chastise him; and they shall amerce him in an hundred shekels of silver, and give them unto the father of the damsel, because he hath brought up an evil name upon a virgin of Israel: and she shall be his wife; he may not put her away all his days."* Here we find that a monetary fine was charged against the husband who had falsely accused this sexually pure damsel of God's people, and that the amount of the fine was to be paid to the *father* of that sexually pure damsel. However, if the accusation was found to be true, then verses 20-21 pronounced the judgment, *"But if this thing be true, and the tokens of virginity be not found for the damsel: then they shall bring out the damsel to the door of her father's house, and the men of her city shall stone her with stones that she die: because she hath wrought folly in Israel, to play the whore in her father's house: so shalt thou put evil away from among you."* Here we find that the sexually impure damsel was to be stoned unto death at the very door of her *father's* house. Through all of these things, we learn that her father stands personally responsible for his daughter's sexual purity until her marriage.

Responsible for the Future Blessing of His Household

In the tenth and final place, the man of the home is responsible *for the future blessing of his household.* In Psalm 112:1-2 God's Word declares, *"Praise ye the LORD. Blessed is the man that feareth the LORD, that delighteth greatly in his commandments. His seed shall be mighty upon earth: the generation of the upright shall be blessed."* In like manner, Psalm 102:28 speaks concerning the children of our Lord's faithful servants, saying, *"The children of thy servants shall continue, and their seed shall be established before thee."* Thus Noah's entire household was delivered from the judgment of the flood for the sake of Noah's righteousness.

Again Proverbs 20:7 declares, *"The just man walketh in his integrity: his children are blessed after him."* Thus the children of Israel were blessed for the sake of their fathers, Abraham, Isaac, and Jacob. Yet again Proverbs 12:7 gives the warning and promise, saying, *"The wicked are overthrown, and are not: but the house of the righteous shall stand."* Thus even the unfaithful descendants of David were graciously blessed for their father David's sake. Finally, Psalm 128:1-4 declares, *"Blessed is every one that feareth the LORD; that walketh in his ways. For thou shalt eat the labour of thine hands: happy shalt thou be, and it shall be well with thee. Thy wife shall be as a fruitful vine by the sides of thine house: thy children like olive plants round about thy table. Behold, that thus shall the man be blessed that feareth the LORD."* When a man of God faithfully follows and serves the Lord, not only is he blessed at the hand of the Lord, but also his wife and children are so blessed.

Yet faithful men are quite rare. Indeed, Proverbs 20:6 proclaims, *"Most men will proclaim every one his own goodness: but a faithful man who can find?"* Most men only talk a good talk, proclaiming their own goodness unto all who will hear. Yet such talk is cheap and empty. As the divinely appointed leaders of our homes, we men have been given a stewardship from the hand of the Lord our God Himself. We are the divinely appointed stewards of our marriages and homes; and God's Holy Word declares in 1 Corinthians 4:2, "***Moreover it is required in stewards, that a man be found faithful.***" Such is the need of our times – faithful, responsible, godly men. Such is the need of our homes – faithful, responsible, godly men. Such is that for which our Lord is searching – faithful, responsible, godly men. To such men a great promise is given in the opening half of Proverbs 28:20 – "***A faithful man shall abound with blessings.***" My dear brothers in Christ, considering these things, let us ever seek and strive to be faithful, responsible, godly leaders in our homes!

Truth for Meditation

The truth of the husband's role of leadership over his wife is rooted in –

1. The order of the creation, that the man Adam was created first, and then his wife Eve. (Gen. 2:7-23; 1 Tim. 2:12-13)

2. The nature of the first temptation, that the woman Eve was deceived, but the man Adam was not deceived. (Gen. 3:1-6; 1 Tim. 2:12-14)

3. The declaration of God's Word that the husband is the head of his wife. (1 Cor. 11:3; Eph. 5:23-24)

4. The nature of the creation, that the woman Eve was formed out of the man Adam as a help meet for the man Adam. (Gen. 2:18-23; 1 Cor. 11:7-9)

5. The command of God's Word that the wife is to submit herself unto her husband's leadership. (Eph. 5:22-24; Col. 3:18)

The responsibility of the man's leadership role includes –

1. His accountability before the Lord for the manner in which he leads his wife and household. (1 Cor. 11:3)

2. His responsibility to serve and minister in humility unto his wife and household. (Mark 10:42-45)

3. His responsibility to take the lead in developing the one-flesh unity of his marriage relationship. (Gen. 2:24; Matt. 5:31-32)

4. His responsibility for his wife's growth in spiritual, emotional, and mental maturity. (Eph. 5:25-29)

5. His responsibility for the commitments that his wife or daughter(s) might make. (Num. 30)

6. His responsibility for the spiritual direction and service of his household. (Josh. 24:14-15)

7. His responsibility to provide materially for the needs of his household. (1 Tim. 5:8)

8. His responsibility to bring up his children in the wisdom and ways of the Lord. (Eph. 6:4; Col. 3:21; Deut. 8:5)

9. His responsibility for the sexual purity of his daughter(s). (Deut. 22:13-21)

10. His responsibility for the future blessing of his household. (Psa. 102:28; 112:1-2; 128:1-4; Prov. 12:7; 20:7)

Verses for Memorization

1 Corinthians 11:3: But I would have you know, that the head of every man is Christ; and the head of the woman is the man; and the head of Christ is God.

Psalm 128:3-4: Thy wife shall be as a fruitful vine by the sides of thine house: thy children like olive plants round about thy table. Behold, that thus shall the man be blessed that feareth the LORD.

5

The Priority of Marriage

Certainly we should understand that it is not our Lord's will
for every man and every woman to enter into the marriage
relationship.

The Will of God to Remain Unmarried

In Matthew 19:11-12 we read, ***"But he said unto them, All men
cannot receive this saying, save they to whom it is given. For there
are some eunuchs, which were so born from their mother's womb:
and there are some eunuchs, which were made eunuchs of men:
and there be eunuchs, which have made themselves eunuchs for
the kingdom of heaven's sake. He that is able to receive it, let
him receive it."*** In verses 3-9 our Lord had been dealing with the
Pharisees on the matters of marriage, divorce, and remarriage.
Then in verse 10 Jesus' disciples said unto Him, ***"If the case of the
man be so with his wife, it is not good to marry."*** Apparently the
extent of the husband's responsibilities in the marriage relationship
had brought the disciples to conclude that marriage itself was not a
good thing. To this our Lord responded in verses 11-12, and in this
response our Lord revealed that there are three groups of men for
whom it is not God's will that they should enter into the marriage
relationship.

❖ First, our Lord made reference to those who are born eunuchs from their mother's womb. In this our Lord was referring to all those who are born with such a physical problem that it is either not possible or not practical for them to enter into the marriage relationship. Now, since the Lord our God Himself is the One who determines the traits with which we are born, it would certainly be God's own will that such individuals not enter into the marriage relationship.

❖ Second, our Lord made reference to those who are made eunuchs by the hands of men. In this our Lord was referring to all those who are literally castrated at the hands of men. Some Biblical examples of such a case would include the men of God, Daniel, Hananiah, Mishael, and Azariah. (Daniel 1:3-7) Again, since the Lord our God Himself is the One who governs such circumstances of life, it would certainly be God's own will that such individuals not enter into the marriage relationship.

❖ Third, our Lord made reference to those who make themselves eunuchs "for the kingdom of heaven's sake." In this our Lord was not necessarily referring to those who literally castrate themselves for spiritual purposes, but to those who purposefully choose not to enter into the marriage relationship in order that they might concentrate their time and energy toward the work and ministry of the Lord in some fashion. Some Biblical examples of such a case would include John the Baptist, the apostle Paul, and our Lord Jesus Christ Himself. Certainly we may conclude that God's will was followed in these cases.

The truth of 1 Corinthians 7:25-26 also reveals that it is not necessarily our Lord's will for every man and every woman to enter into the marriage relationship. In these verses the apostle Paul expressed his personal, Spirit-filled discernment on the matter, saying, *"Now concerning virgins I have no commandment of the Lord: yet I give my judgment, as one that hath obtained mercy of the Lord to be faithful. I suppose therefore that this is good for the present distress, I say, that it is good for a man so to be."* The apostle counseled that "for the present distress" of persecution and affliction in his time, it would be profitable for individuals not to enter into the marriage relationship. This counsel the apostle gave under the inspiration of God the Holy Spirit. Thus we may conclude that this counsel was in accord with God's own will.

Yet earlier in the chapter the apostle had already indicated that each one must follow God's specific will and calling for his or her own life in this matter. Yea, in verse 7 the apostle had declared, *"For I would that all men were even as I myself. But every man hath his proper gift of God, one after this manner, and another after that."* Some have received the gift and calling of God not to enter into the marriage relationship, whereas others have received the gift and calling of God to enter into the marriage relationship. Each one must walk in accord with the particular gift and calling of God for his or her own life.

On the other hand, we must take warning against those false teachers and that false teaching that would forbid marriage altogether. In 1 Timothy 4:1-3 the warning is given, *"Now the Spirit speaketh expressly, that in the latter times some shall depart from the faith, giving heed to seducing spirits, and doctrines of devils; speaking lies in hypocrisy; having their conscience seared with a hot iron; forbidding to marry, and commanding to abstain from meats, which God hath created to be received with thanksgiving of them which believe and know the truth."* In this passage those who would forbid marriage altogether are also described as departing from the faith, giving heed to seducing spirits and doctrines of devils, speaking lies in hypocrisy, and having their conscience seared with a hot iron. Certainly we should beware of such and should withdraw ourselves from them. (1 Timothy 6:3-5)

The Purpose of God for the Unmarried

Finally, we should understand that when an individual receives the gift and calling of our Lord to remain unmarried, it is specifically so that individual might concentrate his or her time and effort unto the work and ministry of the Lord. Thus we read in 1 Corinthians 7:32-35, *"But I would have you without carefulness. He that is unmarried careth for the things that belong to the Lord, how he may please the Lord: but he that is married careth for the things that are of the world, how he may please his wife. There is difference also between a wife and a virgin. The unmarried woman careth for the things of the Lord, that she may be holy both in body and in spirit: but she that is married careth for the things of the world, how she may please her husband. And this I speak for your own profit; not that I may cast a snare upon you, but for that which is comely, and that ye may attend upon the Lord without distraction."*

Those who have been called by our Lord into the marriage relationship have certain God-given responsibilities that those who remain unmarried do not have. In his God-given responsibility toward his wife, the married man must give some care for the things of the world "how he may please his wife" in the unity of their marriage relationship. In her God-given responsibility toward her husband, the married woman must give some care for the things of the world "how she may please her husband" in the unity of their marriage relationship.

Yet the unmarried individual does not have such a call upon his or her time and effort. Rather, the unmarried individual is to concentrate his or her time and effort "for the things that belong to the Lord." The time and effort that such would have concentrated on their relationship with their spouse is rather to be concentrated toward the work and ministry of the Lord. Now, this is not intended as a snare for those who are unmarried, but as that which is spiritually profitable and proper. It is intended as a means of demonstrating devotion toward the Lord. The unmarried individual is ever to attend upon the Lord without distraction just as a servant is ever to attend upon his master or as a handmaid is ever to attend upon her mistress.

The Will of God to Pursue Marriage

However, although it is not our Lord's will that every man and every woman should enter into the marriage relationship, it is our Lord's will that the *majority* of men and women should. In Genesis 2:18 we read, *"And the LORD God said, It is not good that the man should be alone; I will make him an help meet for him.*" The Lord our God Himself declared that it was not good for the first man Adam to be alone. The first man Adam was a perfectly created man without sin. Yet the Lord our God Himself determined that he needed a wife. This was not Adam's determination. This was God's determination, and the same holds true unto this day. The majority of the men in the world today need a wife, a helper who is meet for them.

Furthermore, just as Genesis 2:18 reveals, even so 1 Corinthians 11:9 proclaims, *"Neither was the man created for the woman; but the woman for the man."* The first woman Eve was created specifically to be Adam's wife. The Lord our God specifically created her to be a helper meet for Adam, and the same also holds true unto this day. The majority of women in the world today have been called of God to enter into the marriage relationship as the wife and helper of God's chosen husband for her.

Since it is our Lord's will that the majority of us should enter into the marriage relationship, what place should this relationship be given in our married lives? From the truth and teaching of God's Word, we learn that the marriage relationship should be given a place of priority above every other human relationship in our lives. In fact, according to the truth and teaching of God's Word, the only relationship that should be in a place of priority above our marriage relationship is our personal relationship and walk with the Lord our God and Savior Himself. All other human relationships should find their place below the marriage relationship.

The Principle of Leaving One's Parents

As we have noted previously, in Genesis 2:24 the Lord our God delivered three foundational principles for a good marriage relationship. There He declared, *"Therefore shall a man leave his father and his mother, and shall cleave unto his wife: and they shall be one flesh."* The first of these foundational principles is that a man must leave his father and his mother in order that he may enter aright into the marriage relationship with his wife. Before a young man is married and has established his own home, his primary human relationship is to be his relationship with his parents. He is to obey them and honor them. He is to hear the instruction of his father and not to forsake the law of his mother. Yet when that young man enters into the marriage relationship, he is commanded by the Lord his God *to leave* the priority of his relationship with his parents in order that he may *cleave unto* his wife aright.

This does not mean that he must cease all contact with his parents, or that he must cease to show honor unto his parents. Yet it does mean that his marriage relationship with his wife must take the place of priority in his life over his relationship with his parents. His wife and his relationship with her must come *first*. Such is the very precept and principle of the Lord our God concerning the marriage relationship. It also stands to reason that if the marriage relationship is to be in the place of priority even over the parent-child relationship, then it must certainly take the place of priority over the other relationships of this life. It must take the place of priority over one's children, one's family, one's friends, one's job, one's hobbies, and even one's ministry.

The Principle of Cleaving unto One's Wife

The second foundational principle for a good marriage relationship that the Lord our God delivered in Genesis 2:24 was that a man must cleave unto his wife in his marriage relationship with her. Now, this word "cleave" carries the idea of being glued together. As such, it means that a husband is to be *unified together* with his wife in an *intimate* and *inseparable* fashion. In addition, this word "cleave" can carry the idea of pursuing hard after an individual in order to draw as close to them as possible. As such, it means that a husband is *actively* and *fervently* to *pursue after* his wife with the intent of developing a *one-flesh unity* with her. Such is the very precept and principle of the Lord our God, and the *only* other personal relationship in which the Lord our God commands us to cleave in this manner is in our personal relationship with Him.

In Deuteronomy 13:4 the man of God Moses gave instruction to the people of God, saying, "*Ye shall walk after the LORD your God, and fear him, and keep his commandments, and obey his voice, and ye shall serve him, and cleave unto him."* Again in Joshua 22:5 the man of God Joshua instructed the people of God, saying, *"But take diligent heed to do the commandment and the law, which Moses the servant of the LORD charged you, to love the LORD your God, and to walk in all his ways, and to keep his commandments, and to cleave unto him, and to serve him with all your heart and with all your soul."* Yet again in Acts 11:23 we read concerning the exhortation that the man of God Barnabas delivered unto the believers at Antioch – *"That with purpose of heart they would cleave unto the Lord."* Certainly in Romans 12:9 we are given the general precept and principle that we are to *"abhor that which is evil"* and to *"cleave to that which is good."* Yet in all of God's Word the *only two* personal relationships in which we are commanded to cleave is *in our personal relationship with our Lord* and *in a husband's marriage relationship with his wife*. Thereby our Lord raises the priority of the marriage relationship to the highest level, placing it just below our personal relationship with Him.

The Principle of Pursuing One-Flesh Unity

The third foundational principle for a good marriage relationship that the Lord our God delivered in Genesis 2:24 is that both the husband and the wife are ever to work together to develop and maintain one-flesh unity in their marriage relationship. The *only* other personal relationship in which we are to grow in such a one-flesh unity is in our spiritual relationship with our Lord and Savior Jesus Christ. In Ephesians 5:30 the truth is given, *"For we are members of his body, of his flesh, and of his bones."* In accord with this truth, Ephesians 4:15 teaches us that by *"speaking the truth in love,"* we are to *"grow up into him in all things, which is the head, even Christ."*

Now, in Ephesians 5:28-30 this truth is employed under the inspiration of God the Holy Spirit in the context of the marriage relationship between a husband and his wife. There we read, *"So ought men to love their wives as their own bodies. He that loveth his wife loveth himself. For no man ever yet hated his own flesh; but nourisheth and cherisheth it, even as the Lord the church: for we are members of his body, of his flesh, and of his bones."* Just as we believers are in a one-flesh relationship with our Lord Jesus Christ as the spiritual members of His body, even so in the one-flesh relationship of marriage a husband is to view his wife as his own body and his own flesh. Furthermore, in Ephesians 5:30-32 the one-flesh relationship of marriage is presented as a physical illustration of the spiritual unity between our Lord Jesus Christ and His church. There we read, "*For we are members of his body, of his flesh, and of his bones. For this cause shall a man leave his father and mother, and shall be joined unto his wife, and they two shall be one flesh. This is a great mystery: but I speak concerning Christ and the church.*"

In *no other* human relationship are we instructed to have a one-flesh relationship. Parents and children are not instructed to have such a one-flesh relationship together. Extended family is not instructed to have such a one-flesh relationship together. Employers and employees are not instructed to have such a one-flesh relationship together. Friends are not instructed to have such a one-flesh relationship together. Yet a husband and his wife are instructed to develop a one-flesh relationship together as a divinely chosen illustration of our Lord's one-flesh relationship with His church. Thereby we learn that the marriage relationship is to be the most intimate of human relationships, and as such that it is to be in a place of priority above all other human relationships.

The Principle of Governing Ministry Involvement

In fact, according to the truth and teaching of God's Word, the responsibility of a husband and wife toward one another in the marriage relationship is even to govern their involvement in the work and ministry of the Lord. One's personal walk and fellowship with the Lord is to take a place of priority above the marriage relationship, but the marriage relationship is to take a place of priority above one's public service in the work and ministry of the Lord. As we have already seen, 1 Corinthians 7:32-35 sets the concentration and involvement of the unmarried individual in the work and ministry of the Lord in contrast to that of the married individual. There again we read, "*But I would have you without carefulness. He that is unmarried careth for the things that belong to the Lord, how he may please the Lord: but he that is married careth for the things that are of the world, how he may please his wife. There is difference also between a wife and a virgin. The unmarried woman careth for the things of the Lord, that she may be holy both in body and in spirit: but she that is married careth for the things of the world, how she may please her husband. And this I speak for your own profit; not that I may cast a snare upon you, but for that which is comely, and that ye may attend upon the Lord without distraction."*

Here we find that an unmarried individual is able to focus his or her attention wholly upon the extended work and ministry of the Lord. The unmarried individual is able to care "for the things that belong to the Lord," how he or she "may please the Lord," because the unmarried individual does not have to give any attention toward pleasing a spouse. However, the married individual is not able to focus his or her attention wholly upon the extended work and ministry of the Lord. The married individual has the *God-given* responsibility to give attention toward pleasing his or her spouse. Yea, the married individual should view his or her God-given responsibility in the marriage relationship as his or her *first* ministry from the Lord. Thus the married man must care "for the things of the world, how he may please his wife;" and the married woman must care "for the things of the world, how she may please her husband." So then, we find that the God-given responsibility of the marriage relationship *governs* and *sets a boundary* upon one's involvement in the extended work and ministry of the Lord.

The Principle of Qualification for Pastoral Ministry

Furthermore, concerning the pastoral ministry God's Word teaches that a man's relationship with his wife is a very matter of qualification for that particular ministry role. In 1 Timothy 3:1-7 and Titus 1:5-9 we find the Biblical list of qualifications for pastoral ministry. In both of these passages of Scripture, we find that a man who would serve in pastoral ministry must be "the husband of one wife." His relationship to his wife is a matter of qualification. In addition, we read in 1 Timothy 3:4-5 that a man who would serve in pastoral ministry must be *"one that ruleth well his own house, having his children in subjection with all gravity: (For if a man know not how to rule his own house, how shall he take care of the house of God?)."* In verse 4 we find a direct mention of how this man handles his children. However, we also find that he must rule his entire household well, which would include his relationship both to his wife and to his children.

Now, if a man is not relating well toward his wife in the marriage relationship according to the precepts and principles of God's Holy Word, then he is not ruling his own house well. Thus he is not qualified for pastoral ministry. Yea, verse 5 teaches us that such a man actually lacks understanding for pastoral ministry. The very fact that he does not know how to relate aright unto his wife directly indicates that he does not know how to relate aright unto the church. The very fact that he is not spiritually mature enough to fulfill his God-given responsibilities in the marriage relationship directly indicates that he is not spiritually mature enough to fulfill the responsibilities of the pastoral ministry. Even in this then, we find that the marriage relationship takes the place of priority.

Yet a note of caution must be sounded forth at this point lest we seek to over-compartmentalize an individual's life. The first and central priority of our lives should always be our personal walk before God our heavenly Father as obedient children and with our Lord Jesus Christ as faithful disciples. Now, to married individuals God's Word gives precepts and principles concerning that which the Lord our God Himself requires of the husband and the wife in their marriage relationship toward one another. In order to walk aright in the will of our Lord, the married individual *must* walk in faithful obedience to these precepts and principles. In addition, to all believers God's Word gives precepts and principles concerning that which the Lord our God Himself requires of us for our involvement in the work and ministry of the Lord. Again, in order to walk aright in the will of our Lord, all believers *must* walk in faithful obedience to these precepts and principles.

However, we must not view these precepts and principles concerning the marriage relationship and concerning ministry responsibilities as standing in competition and contradiction to one another. The will of our Lord on the one hand does not stand in competition with and contradiction to the will of our Lord on the other hand. That which is actually our Lord's will for our lives does not contradict and compete with itself. At any given time in our lives, that which is *actually* our Lord's will for us in our marriage relationship will not contradict and compete with that which is *actually* our Lord's will for us in our ministry responsibilities. Therefore, if some competition and contradiction does appear to arise between our God-given responsibilities in our marriage and our God-given responsibilities in our ministry, then some matter in our marriage, in our ministry, or in both is not actually in accord with our Lord's will for our lives.

The Principle of a Hindered Prayer Life

In conclusion then, two other Biblical admonitions also reveal the importance and priority of the marriage relationship. In 1 Peter 3:7 we learn that if a husband does not relate aright unto his wife in the marriage relationship, then his very prayers before the Lord will be hindered. There we read, *"Likewise, ye husbands, dwell with them* [that is – with the wife] *according to knowledge, giving honour unto the wife, as unto the weaker vessel, and as being heirs together of the grace of life; that your prayers be not hindered."* Husbands, the effectiveness of our prayer lives is at stake; and considering how important our prayer lives are to our daily, personal walk with our Lord, such a warning places the marriage relationship at a high level of priority.

The Principle of Blasphemy to God's Word

Furthermore, in Titus 2:4-5 we learn that if a wife does not relate aright unto her husband, then such wrong behavior will cause God's Holy Word to be blasphemed by the world. There we find that the older women in the Lord are to walk and behave in a holy manner *"that they may teach the young women to be sober, to love their husbands, to love their children, to be discreet, chaste, keepers at home, good, obedient to their own husbands, that the word of God be not blasphemed.*" Wives, the testimony of God's Holy Word is at stake; and considering how important the testimony of His Word is to our Lord, such a warning places the marriage relationship at a high level of priority.

How important then is it for husbands and wives to learn all that our Lord teaches in His Word concerning the marriage relationship, and how to relate aright unto one another in their marriage relationship?

Truth for Meditation

The truth that it is not our Lord's will that everyone should marry is taught through –

1. Our Lord's statement that some are born eunuchs from their mother's womb. (Matt. 19:12)

2. Our Lord's statement that some are made eunuchs at the hands of men. (Matt. 19:12)

3. Our Lord's statement that some purposefully choose not to marry for the kingdom of heaven's sake. (Matt. 19:12)

4. The truth that some should not marry during times of severe persecution and distress. (1 Cor. 7:25-26)

5. The truth that some are given the gift and calling of God not to marry (specifically that they may concentrate their time and effort unto the work and ministry of the Lord). (1 Cor. 7:7, 32-35)

The priority of the marriage relationship over all other human relationships is taught through –

1. The call for the husband to leave the priority of his relationship with his parents for the sake of his relationship with his wife. (Gen. 2:24)

2. The call for the husband to actively cleave unto his wife (considering that the only other relationship in which we are called to cleave is in our personal relationship with our Lord). (Gen. 2:24)

3. The call for both the husband and the wife to actively develop a one-flesh unity within their marriage relationship (considering that no other human relationship receives such a call). (Gen. 2:24)

4. The fact that the husband and the wife have a God-given responsibility to give attention toward pleasing their spouse and thus to govern the attention that they give toward the work and ministry of the Lord. (1 Cor. 7:32-35)

5. The fact that a man's relationship toward his wife is a direct matter of qualification and maturity for pastoral ministry. (1 Tim. 3:4-5)

6. The admonition to the husband that his prayers will be hindered if he does not relate aright unto his wife. (1 Pet. 3:7)

7. The admonition to the wife that God's Word will be blasphemed if she does not relate aright unto her husband. (Tit. 2:4-5)

Verse for Memorization

Genesis 2:24: Therefore shall a man leave his father and his mother, and shall cleave unto his wife: and they shall be one flesh.

6

The Permanency of Marriage

Already we have learned that the Lord our God Himself instituted the marriage relationship as a very part of His work of creation, even before sin had entered into the world. Furthermore, we have noted that at that very time the Lord our God Himself gave three foundational principles for a good marriage relationship. In Genesis 2:24 He proclaimed, "*Therefore shall a man leave his father and his mother, and shall cleave unto his wife; and they shall be one flesh.*" Now, the third of these foundational principles teaches us that both the husband and the wife are actively to pursue a one-flesh unity in their marriage relationship. In this principle we find our Lord God's intent concerning the marriage relationship – not that the husband and the wife should be moving away from one another in their relationship, until the marriage completely breaks apart; but that the husband and the wife should ever be growing *together* in their relationship of unity, fellowship, and companionship. Herein we find our Lord God's intent for the permanency of the marriage relationship.

Our Lord's Definition of Marriage

Even so, in Matthew 19:4-6 our Lord Jesus Christ spoke concerning God's intended permanency for the marriage relationship. From verse 3 we learn that the Pharisees had come to the Lord Jesus with a question concerning the matter of divorce and the justifiable reasons for divorce. This they asked, seeking to ensnare Him in His answer.

Thus we read, "***The Pharisees also came unto him, tempting him, and saying unto him, Is it lawful for a man to put away his wife for every cause?***" To this question our Lord gave answer in verses 4-6 – "***And he answered and said unto them, Have ye not read, that he which made them at the beginning made them male and female, and said, For this cause shall a man leave father and mother, and shall cleave to his wife: and they twain shall be one flesh? Wherefore they are no more twain, but one flesh. What therefore God hath joined together, let not man put asunder.***"

In response to the question of the Pharisees, our Lord immediately turned their attention to the account of creation – to *God's institution* of the marriage relationship at the creation and to *God's original purpose and principles* for that marriage relationship. Yea, in response to the Pharisees' question concerning the justification of divorce, our Lord focused their attention upon the foundational principles for a good marriage that the Lord our God delivered in Genesis 2:24. In particular our Lord gave emphasis to the third of these foundational principles – "***And they twain shall be one flesh?***" Upon the ground of this foundational principle our Lord gave the explanation – "***Wherefore they are no more twain, but one flesh.***" According to our Lord's own Word, at the moment that a man and a woman are married, they are no longer two independent individuals, but have now entered into a one-flesh relationship with one another. They are no longer to live as two separate persons, but are now to live as one single unit. Such is the very definition of the Lord our God for marriage – "***Wherefore they are no more twain, but one flesh.***"

Our Lord's Prohibition against the Division of a Marriage

Furthermore, our Lord Jesus Christ gave instruction, saying, "***What therefore God hath joined together, let not man put asunder.***" From the two parts of this instruction we learn two truths. First, in every marriage the Lord our God Himself is the One who joins together the husband and his wife into a one-flesh relationship. The two are joined into one flesh by the divine hand of God Himself. This is not simply a convention of society or government. This is a specific work of the Lord God of heaven and earth. Second, we are

72

specifically commanded not to allow the hand of man to "put asunder" the one-flesh marriage relationship that the Lord our God Himself has put together. Now, that phrase "put asunder" means "to separate, to divide." Through its use in this command, we understand that the Lord our God does not intend for any marriage to end in a divorce. Rather, the foundational intent of the Lord our God is that every marriage should continue in one-flesh unity "until death do us part." Yea, the foundational intent of the Lord our God is for the permanency of the marriage relationship.

Yet the principle of this instruction runs somewhat deeper. It is not simply that the Lord our God is against the putting asunder of the one-flesh marriage relationship through divorce. It is also that the Lord our God is against *any* selfishness and sinfulness of man that would work contrary to the one-flesh unity between a husband and a wife. Therefore, we must not allow *anything* of this world into our marriage relationships that would create division and separation in that one-flesh relationship. Rather, as we have previously learned, the husband and the wife must *actively pursue* the development and maintenance of their one-flesh relationship. Such must be done in order that the marriage might *continually grow* in strength and stability that in turn it might *stand permanent* even as the Lord our God intends.

Our Lord's Assessment of the Foundational Reason for Divorce

However, the Pharisees were not satisfied with our Lord's response; and they pressed the matter with a second question. In Matthew 19:7 we read, *"They say unto Him, Why did Moses then command to give a writing of divorcement, and to put her away?"* To this our Lord Jesus Christ first gave response concerning the nature of Moses' Law on this matter. We read in verse 8, *"He saith unto them, Moses because of the hardness of your hearts suffered you to put away your wives: but from the beginning it was not so."* In contrast to the Pharisees' word choice that Moses had *commanded* the putting away of one's wife, our Lord revealed that Moses had only granted a legal *permission* for such. In addition, our Lord revealed that this legal permission was rooted, not in the original intent of the Lord our God, but in the sinful hardness of men's hearts.

Our Lord's Judgment against Divorce and Remarriage

Since the beginning of creation, the foundational intent of the Lord our God has always been for the permanency of the marriage relationship. Therefore, in verse 9 our Lord added the judgment, *"And I say unto you, Whosoever shall put away his wife, except it be for fornication, and shall marry another, committeth adultery: and whoso marrieth her which is put away doth commit adultery."* The Lord our God neither holds nor supports a casual view of divorce and remarriage. His foundational intent for the marriage relationship is that of permanency, and a casual view of divorce and remarriage stands against this foundational intent. Even so, if an individual passes through a divorce and enters into marriage with another, the Lord our God holds that individual accountable for committing the sin of adultery.

Our Lord's Foundational Instruction to the Husband

In addition, the second foundational principle of a good marriage, that a husband is to cleave unto his wife, also reveals the foundational intent of the Lord our God for the permanency of marriage. As we have noted in a previous chapter, this word "cleave" carries the two-fold idea of following hard after an individual in order to be close to that individual and of holding an individual close to one's heart in a relationship of intimacy. The husband is required by the Lord our God and responsible before the Lord our God ever to pursue after his wife and to hold her close to his heart in order to develop and maintain the one-flesh intimacy of their marriage relationship.

Our Lord's Holding the Husband Accountable for a Divorce

Thus, if the marriage relationship is broken in a divorce, the Lord our God holds the husband accountable. In Matthew 5:32 our Lord Jesus Christ declared, *"But I say unto you, That whosoever shall put away his wife, saving for the cause of fornication, causeth her to commit adultery: and whosoever shall marry her that is divorced committeth adultery."* If a divorced wife marries another man, both she and the man who marries her commit the sin of adultery in God's sight. Yet the first husband is *also* responsible and accountable for this sin of adultery. Yea, our Lord proclaimed that the first husband himself, by divorcing his wife, *caused* her to commit the sin of adultery. How did he do this? He did this by failing in the God-given requirement and responsibility to cleave unto his wife – to pursue after her and hold her close to himself. Even so, the foundational intent of the Lord our God is that a husband must *cleave unto* his wife in a one-flesh relationship, not *put away* his wife in divorcement.

Our Lord's Foundational Attitude against Divorce

In Malachi 2:13-16 the prophet of the Lord delivered the Lord's rebuke against the men of Israel, saying, ***"And this have ye done again, covering the altar of the LORD with tears, with weeping, and with crying out, insomuch that he regardeth not the offering any more, or receiveth it with good will at your hand. Yet ye say, Wherefore? Because the LORD hath been witness between thee and the wife of thy youth, against whom thou hast dealt treacherously: yet is she thy companion, and the wife of thy covenant. And did not he make one? Yet had he the residue of the spirit. And wherefore one? That he might seek a godly seed. Therefore take heed to your spirit, and let none deal treacherously against the wife of his youth. For the LORD, the God of Israel, saith that he hateth putting away: for one covereth violence with his garment, saith the LORD of hosts: therefore take heed to your spirit, that ye deal not treacherously."***

The focus of this rebuke is upon a husband's treacherous dealing against his wife. At that time, because of the treacherous dealings of the men of Israel against their wives, there were many tears, much weeping, and many groaning cries by the woman of Israel; and the Lord Himself took notice of the grief of these women. Yea, He took notice and viewed their tears, weeping, and groaning as covering over His holy altar, so much so that He would no longer look with favor upon the sacrifices that the men of Israel brought before His altar. He would no longer receive with pleasure the sacrifices and offerings of worship from the hands of these men. *Because of* the tears of the wives, the Lord our God *completely rejected* the sacrifices and worship of the husbands.

75

Thus, in turn, the men of Israel cried out unto the Lord, asking the question – Why? Why would the Lord no longer look with favor upon their sacrifices? Why would He no longer receive their offerings of worship? The answer rang back in verse 14, "***Because the LORD hath been witness between thee and the wife of thy youth, against whom thou hast dealt treacherously: yet is she thy companion, and the wife of thy covenant.***" The Lord our God completely rejected their sacrifices and offerings of worship specifically because they had dealt *treacherously* against their wives. The Lord Himself had seen the treacherous dealing that each of these husbands had committed against his own wife, and the Lord was greatly offended.

Why then was He so offended? The Lord our God was so offended because He Himself had been witness between each husband and his wife. At the time of the marriage, the husband had made *a life-long covenant* unto his wife before the Lord; and the Lord Himself had *confirmed the covenant* of their marriage relationship. Furthermore, at the time of the marriage, the husband had entered into *a one-flesh companionship* with his wife; and the Lord Himself had *joined them together* in the one-flesh companionship of their marriage. Yet the treacherous dealing of these husbands against their wives stood contrary to that one-flesh companionship and that divinely confirmed covenant.

What the Lord God Himself had joined together, these men were putting asunder through their treacherous dealings against their wives. Yea, through their treacherous dealings these men were standing contrary to the foundational intent of the Lord their God for the permanency of their marriages. The covenant of marriage that the Lord our God Himself confirms is *a covenant of permanency*. Yet the treacherous dealings of these men against their wives was striking against that covenant. The one-flesh companionship in which the Lord our God Himself joins a husband and his wife is *a relationship of permanency*. Yet the treacherous dealings of these men against their wives was damaging and destroying that one-flesh companionship.

Furthermore, verse 15 reveals one of the great purposes of the Lord our God for the one-flesh companionship of marriage – "***That he might seek a godly seed.***" The development of godly children is founded upon the permanency of the one-flesh companionship between the husband and his wife. Yet the treacherous dealings of these men against their wives was damaging and destroying that foundation.

Therefore, God's Holy Word reveals the foundational attitude of the Lord our God toward divorce in the opening portion of verse 16, saying, "***For the LORD, the God of Israel, saith that he hateth divorce.***" This is no light matter. The foundational attitude of the Lord our God toward the breakup of a marriage in divorce is that of *hatred*. He literally *hates* the very idea that a marriage might end in a divorce. So then, why is the foundational attitude of the Lord our God so strong toward the matter of divorce? It is because the foundational intent of the Lord our God for the one-flesh relationship and companionship of marriage is that of *permanency*.

In addition, the Lord our God stands against the idea that a legal divorce can somehow cover over the treachery and cruelty of abandoning one's own wife. Such is the point of the middle phrase in verse 16 – "***For one covereth violence with his garment, saith the LORD of hosts.***" In this context the word "violence" refers to the treachery and cruelty that a husband commits against his wife when he ceases to cleave unto her and abandons his one-flesh relationship with her. In the eyes of the world, a legal divorce might cover over this treachery and cruelty in order that it might be viewed with respectability. However, such treachery and cruelty cannot so easily be covered over in the sight of the Lord our God. He still stands against this treachery and cruelty. He still stands against the breakup of the marriage in divorce.

Our Lord's Admonition concerning the Husband's Attitude

Thus the admonition of God's Holy Word is given to every husband at the end of verse 15 – "***Therefore take heed to your spirit, and let none deal treacherously against the wife of his youth.***" Yet again the admonition is given at the end of verse 16 – "***Therefore take***

77

heed to your spirit, that ye deal not treacherously." The whole matter begins with a husband's *spirit* (that is – with his *heart attitude*) toward his wife. Attitude leads to and governs action. A husband must *ever take heed* concerning his heart attitude toward his wife in order that he might *never* deal treacherously in action against her. He must *ever guard* his heart attitude that it might *never* turn away from cleaving unto his wife. Yea, he must ever be on his guard that he might *never* turn away from holding his wife dear in his heart and from pursuing a one-flesh relationship with her with all of his heart.

Our Lord's Instruction to the Divorced Wife

Yet there is one further passage that must be considered concerning the foundational intent of the Lord our God for the permanency of marriage. In 1 Corinthians 7:10-11 the apostle Paul, under the inspiration of God the Holy Spirit, reiterated the principle and precept of our Lord Jesus Christ from Matthew 19:6. In the opening portion of 1 Corinthians 7:10 the apostle stated, "*And unto the married, I command, yet not I, but the Lord.*" Then at the end of verse 10 the apostle delivered our Lord's precept in relation to the wife, saying, "*Let not the wife depart from her husband.*" Also at the end of verse 11 the apostle delivered our Lord's precept in relation to the husband, saying, "*And let not the husband put away his wife.*" Thus the foundational intent of the Lord our God for the permanency of marriage is again lifted up and given emphasis.

However, the apostle also envisioned a case where the wife might be separated from her husband, possibly due to her husband's abandonment or abusiveness, or even due to her own disobedience unto the Lord. Even so, in the opening portion of verse 11 the instruction is delivered under the inspiration of God the Holy Spirit, "*But and if she depart, let her remain unmarried, or be reconciled to her husband.*" The instruction of God's Holy Word for such a case is either that this wife remain unmarried so as to avoid the sin of adultery that would be committed if she married another (Matthew 5:32), or that she be reconciled to her husband in reestablishing the unity of their marriage relationship if that opportunity might present itself. Even in this the foundational intent of the Lord our God for the permanency of marriage is given emphasis. On the one hand, this wife is instructed not to strike further against the permanency of the marriage by marrying another. On the other hand, she is instructed to pursue reconciliation with her husband and the restoration of their marriage.

Our Lord's Instruction to a Believer with an Unbelieving Spouse

Then in 1 Corinthians 7:12-16 the apostle moved to a case about which our Lord Jesus Christ Himself did not specifically speak during His walk upon this earth. In the opening line of verse 12 the apostle stated, "***But to the rest speak I, not the Lord.***" However, although our Lord Jesus Christ did not specifically speak concerning this case, nevertheless the apostle's teaching on this matter does not stand contrary to our Lord's teaching. Rather, the apostle's teaching was delivered under the inspiration of God the Holy Spirit as the very truth of God's Holy Word, not in contrast to our Lord's teaching, but in perfect correspondence to it.

What then is this special case about which the apostle is inspired of God the Holy Spirit to speak? It is the case of a marriage in which one spouse receives the Lord Jesus Christ through faith as Savior, but the other spouse remains an unbeliever. In verses 12-13 we read, "***But to the rest speak I, not the Lord: If any brother hath a wife that believeth not, and she be pleased to dwell with him, let him not put her away. And the woman which hath an husband that believeth not, and if he be pleased to dwell with her, let her not leave him.***"

Upon the ground of such instruction as is found in 2 Corinthians 6:14-18, that we believers are not to be unequally yoked together with unbelievers, but that we are to come out from among them and be separate from them, some question arose concerning the case at hand. In the case of an individual who became a believer, but whose spouse remained an unbeliever, should that believer separate himself or herself from that marriage relationship? The answer of the Holy Spirit inspired Word of God is this – If the unbelieving spouse is pleased to dwell with the believing spouse, then the believing spouse should *not* seek separation or divorce. Even in a spiritually mixed marriage such as this, the foundational intent of the Lord our God for the permanency of the marriage relationship is lifted up and given emphasis.

Even so, the supporting truth is given in verse 14 – *"For the unbelieving husband is sanctified by the wife, and the unbelieving wife is sanctified by the husband: else were your children unclean; but now are they holy."* To this verse 16 adds, *"For what knowest thou, O wife, whether thou shalt save thy husband? Or how knowest thou, O man, whether thou shalt save thy wife?"*

❖ First, we find that the believing spouse should remain in the marriage because that marriage is *sanctified* through the presence of the believing spouse. Rather than viewing the marriage as being spiritually corrupted by the unbelieving spouse, the Lord our God views the marriage as being spiritually sanctified by the believing spouse. Through the presence of the believing spouse, such a marriage is able to receive special outpourings of God's enabling grace upon it.

❖ Second, we find that the believing spouse should remain in the marriage because it will maintain the foundation of the marriage relationship upon which to train up the children unto godliness. Rather than giving up the children to the spiritual uncleanness of this world, the believing spouse will have greater opportunity to light the way spiritually in the upbringing of the children.

❖ Third, we find that the believing spouse should remain in the marriage because such will allow a greater opportunity for the light of the gospel of Jesus Christ to shine into the heart of the unbelieving spouse. Although there is no certain promise that such will result in the salvation of the unbelieving spouse, it certainly provides a greater possibility for it.

Yet what if the unbelieving spouse is not pleased to dwell with the believing spouse? To this verse 15 gives answer, *"But if the unbelieving depart, let him depart. A brother or a sister is not under bondage in such cases: but God hath called us to peace.*" If the unbelieving spouse seeks after a divorce, the believing spouse is not to be contentious, but is to accept such peaceably. In such a case the Lord our God does not hold the believing spouse accountable for the breakup of the marriage. Nor should their fellow believers hold them accountable.

Nevertheless, throughout God's Holy Word the foundational intent of the Lord our God for the permanency of the marriage relationship is clearly revealed:

"Therefore shall a man leave his father and his mother, and shall cleave unto his wife; and they shall be one flesh."

"Wherefore they are no more twain, but one flesh. What therefore God hath joined together, let not man put asunder."

"He saith unto them, Moses because of the hardness of your hearts suffered you to put away your wives: but from the beginning it was not so. And I say unto you, Whosoever shall put away his wife, except it be for fornication, and shall marry another, committeth adultery: and whoso marrieth her which is put away doth commit adultery."

"Therefore take heed to your spirit, and let none deal treacherously against the wife of his youth. For the LORD, the God of Israel, saith that he hateth putting away."

"And unto the married, I command, yet not I, but the Lord, Let not the wife depart from her husband; but and if she depart, let her remain unmarried, or be reconciled to her husband: and let not the husband put away his wife. But to the rest speak I, not the Lord: If any brother hath a wife that believeth not, and she be pleased to dwell with him, let him not put her away. And the woman which hath an husband that believeth not, and if he be pleased to dwell with her, let her not leave him."

81

Truth for Meditation

The foundational intent of the Lord our God for the permanence of the marriage relationship is found –

1. In our Lord God's definition of marriage – "Wherefore they are no more twain, but one flesh." (Matt. 19:6)

2. In our Lord God's prohibition against the division of a marriage – "What therefore God hath joined together, let not man put asunder." (Matt. 19:6)

3. In our Lord God's assessment concerning the foundational reason for divorce – "He saith unto them, Moses because of the hardness of your hearts suffered you to put away your wives: but from the beginning it was not so." (Matt. 19:8)

4. In our Lord God's judgment against divorce and remarriage – "And I say unto you, Whosoever shall put away his wife, except it be for fornication, and shall marry another, committeth adultery: and whoso marrieth her which is put away doth commit adultery." (Matt. 19:9)

5. In our Lord God's foundational instruction to the husband – "And shall cleave unto his wife." (Gen. 2:24)

6. In our Lord God's holding the husband accountable for the breakup of his marriage – "But I say unto you, That whosoever shall put away his wife, saving for the cause of fornication, causeth her to commit adultery." (Matt. 5:32)

7. In our Lord God's foundational attitude against divorce – "For the LORD, the God of Israel, saith that He hateth divorce." (Mal. 2:16)

8. In our Lord God's admonition concerning the attitude of the husband – "Therefore take heed to your spirit, and let none deal treacherously against the wife of his youth." (Mal. 2:15-16)

9. In our Lord God's instruction to the divorced wife – "But and if she depart, let her remain unmarried, or be reconciled to her husband." (1 Cor. 7:10-11)

10. In our Lord God's instruction to a believer with an unbelieving spouse – "But to the rest speak I, not the Lord: If any brother hath a wife that believeth not, and she be pleased to dwell with him, let him not put her away. And the woman which hath an husband that believeth not, and if he be pleased to dwell with her, let her not leave him." (1 Cor. 7:12-16)

Verse for Memorization

Matthew 19:6: Wherefore they are no more twain, but one flesh. What therefore God hath joined together, let not man put asunder.

7

The Purpose of Marriage

The marriage relationship was the first institution established for mankind, and it was instituted by the Lord our God Himself during the week of creation at the creation of mankind. In fact, in the creation of mankind the Lord our God did not simply create the male and the female and then allow them to develop the marriage relationship on their own. Rather, from the account of Genesis 2 we learn that the Lord our God specifically created them, the male and the female, as the man and his wife. Yea, the Lord our God was the very One who gave the woman unto the man to be his wife and the very One who confirmed their marriage bond. Thus the marriage relationship was instituted by the Lord our God as a very part of His work of creation.

So then, why did the Lord our God institute and establish the marriage relationship? Certainly in the infinite abundance and perfection of His wisdom, He had the most perfect reasons for doing so. Has He revealed any of those reasons to us through His Word? The answer is affirmative, for in His Word our Lord has revealed at least five reasons for the marriage relationship.

To Provide Human Companionship

In the first place, the Lord our God instituted and established the marriage relationship *to provide human companionship*. The Lord our God has created us as social beings who possess a natural need for companionship and fellowship with others. In the spiritual realm we possess a need for fellowship with the Lord our God Himself, and in the natural realm we possess a need for the companionship of other human beings. Even so, at the very creation the Lord our God declared in Genesis 2:18, *"It is not good that the man should be alone."*

Now, the first man Adam was not *completely* alone; for he was able to walk in daily fellowship with the Lord God Himself. Yet although this daily, spiritual fellowship with God was available to Adam, the Lord our God Himself referred to Adam as being *alone*. Even before sin had entered in to separate the spiritual fellowship between God and Adam, the first man Adam was in need of human companionship and fellowship. Yet in answer to this need the Lord our God did not simply provide a friend for Adam. Rather, in the infinite perfection of His wisdom, the Lord our God deemed it best to meet Adam's need for companionship by providing a *wife* for him. Even so, at the close of Malachi 2:14 the Lord referred to a man's wife as his companion, saying, *"Yet is she thy companion, and the wife of thy covenant."* Even so also, in the second half of the Song of Solomon 5:16, the wife declared concerning her beloved husband, *"This is my beloved, and this is my friend, O daughters of Jerusalem."*

In truth, there is no human relationship that can provide as deep a companionship and fellowship as a good, godly, growing marriage relationship. Yea, it is the one human relationship in which the Lord our God instructs us to develop and maintain a *one-flesh* companionship, fellowship, and unity. In Genesis 2:24 our Lord gave the three-fold command, saying, *"Therefore shall a man leave his father and his mother, and shall cleave unto his wife; and they shall be one flesh."* Yet from this we also learn that this one-flesh companionship, fellowship, and unity must be actively pursued. It will not simply happen. It will not be developed and maintained without an active, determined, faithful pursuit therein. The husband must actively and faithfully pursue such a companionship with his wife, and the wife must actively and faithfully pursue such with her husband. Both the husband and the wife must actively and faithfully pursue those elements that make for such an intimate, one-flesh companionship.

86

❖ Both the husband and the wife must pursue *open communication* with one another. In the opening portion of Exodus 33:11, God's Holy Word speaks of friendship in this manner, saying, "***And the LORD spake unto Moses face to face, as a man speaketh unto his friend.***" Furthermore, the opening half of Proverbs 27:6 declares, "***Faithful are the wounds of a friend;***" and verse 9 adds, "***Ointment and perfume rejoice the heart: so doth the sweetness of a man's friend by hearty counsel.***" Open, face-to-face communication, including hearty counsel and loving reproof, is essential to develop and maintain an intimate companionship.

❖ Both the husband and the wife must pursue *emotional camaraderie* with one another. In the opening half of Psalm 55:14, David described a time of friendship with another, saying, "***We took sweet counsel together.***" Furthermore, in describing the close friendship between David and Jonathan, 1 Samuel 18:1 reveals "***that the soul of Jonathan was knit with the soul of David, and Jonathan loved him as his own soul.***" The sweetness of fellowship and the knitting of hearts are necessary ingredients in any intimate companionship, and especially in the companionship of the one-flesh, marriage relationship.

❖ Both the husband and the wife must pursue a *firm and faithful commitment* to one another. The opening half of Proverbs 17:17 proclaims, "***A friend loveth at all times;***" and the closing half of Proverbs 18:24 adds, "***There is a friend that sticketh closer than a brother.***" Yea, this loving commitment must stand firm and faithful through smooth times and stormy times, through easy times and emotional times, through times of unity and times of offense.

❖ Both the husband and the wife must pursue a *caring compassion* for one another. In Psalm 35:13-14 David described the behavior of a true friend, saying, "***But as for me, when they were sick, my clothing was sackcloth: I humbled my soul with fasting; and my prayer returned into mine own bosom. I behaved myself as though he had been my friend or brother: I bowed down heavily, as one that mourneth for his mother.***" A true friend and companion cares more for the other's needs, concerns, and interests than for his

87

or her own. In addition, a true friend and companion shows such care and compassion, not for the selfish motive of manipulation, but out of a true heart of love.

❖ Finally, both the husband and the wife must pursue *intimate communion* with one another. With this we return to the three-fold command of Genesis 2:24 – "***Therefore shall a man leave his father and his mother, and shall cleave unto his wife; and they shall be one flesh.***" The second part of this three-fold command is that the husband "shall cleave unto his wife." He is to cling unto her and to hold her close. The husband is actively to pursue an intimate closeness and communion with his wife. Furthermore, the third part of this three-fold command is that both the husband and the wife "shall be one flesh." They both are actively to pursue one-flesh unity and communion with each other. Yea, in the companionship of their marriage they are to develop and maintain such a relationship of unity and fellowship that they are ever building up one another. Even so, Proverbs 27:17 declares, "***Iron sharpeneth iron; so a man sharpeneth the countenance of his friend.***" Thus in communion with his wife, the husband is ever to sharpen her countenance; and in communion with her husband, the wife is ever to sharpen his countenance.

To Form a Working Partnership

In the second place, the Lord our God instituted and established the marriage relationship *to form a working partnership.* As we have already noted, at the creation the Lord our God declared in the opening half of Genesis 2:18, "***It is not good that the man should be alone.***" Then in the closing half of that verse the Lord our God proscribed His answer out of his infinite wisdom, saying, "***I will make him an help meet for him.***" Now, in His all-wise response our Lord did not employ the single, compound word "help-meet" as we so often do. Rather, our Lord employed the phrase "an help meet." In this phrase there are two parts that must be understood. First, there is the noun phrase "an help." This phrase refers to one who is a *helper.* It refers to one who is *a partner in helping* to fulfill a task.

Second, there is the adjective "meet." This adjective is descriptive of the noun phrase "an help." It refers to a helper who is meet. It refers to one who *perfectly corresponds* unto the one being helped. It refers to a helper who is suitable, fitting, and complementary as a partner in helping to fulfill the task. In creating Eve the Lord our God did not simply create a human companion for the first man Adam to relieve his loneliness. In creating Eve He also created a complementary partner for the first man Adam to help him in fulfilling his responsibilities. Thus we learn the nature of the working partnership of the marriage relationship – The husband's *need* is for his wife's help, and the wife's *purpose* is to give her husband that help.

It is our Lord's purpose that the husband and wife should work together as *unified partners* to build, establish, and maintain a strong, godly home. It is our Lord's purpose that the husband and wife should work together as *unified partners* in raising up their children in the nurture and admonition of the Lord to serve Him unto His glory. It is our Lord's purpose that the husband and wife should work together as *unified partners* in the service and ministry of the Lord. Yea, it is our Lord's purpose that the marriage relationship should beautifully illustrate the Biblical principle of Ecclesiastes 4:9-10 – "***Two are better than one; because they have a good reward for their labour. For if they fall, the one will lift up his fellow: but woe to him that is alone when he falleth; for he hath not another to help him up.***"

Yet this does not mean that the husband and wife must at all times be involved in exactly the same activities and ministries. Rather, it is our Lord's purpose that the husband and wife should *complement* one another. It is His purpose that they two should form such a working partnership in which the two separate parts fit together into a single, unified whole. Yea, it is our Lord's purpose that the individual labors and ministries of the husband and of the wife should correspond with, support, and enhance the labors and ministries of the other. Furthermore, it is His purpose that the individual labors and ministries of the husband and of the wife should never contradict, undercut, or tear down the labors and

89

ministries of the other. It is His purpose that the husband and the wife should ever work, not to *compete* with one another, but to *complete* one another.

Thus the precepts and principles of unity that the Lord our God has delivered to us in His Word might especially apply to the working partnership of the marriage relationship. The prayer of Romans 15:5-6 might apply – "***Now the God of patience and consolation grant you to be likeminded one toward another according to Christ Jesus: that ye may with one mind and one mouth glorify God, even the Father of our Lord Jesus Christ.***" The principles of Philippians 2:2-4 might apply – "***Fulfil ye my joy, that ye be likeminded, having the same love, being of one accord, of one mind. Let nothing be done through strife or vainglory; but in lowliness of mind let each esteem other better than themselves. Look not every man on his own things, but every man also on the things of others.***" The precepts of 1 Peter 3:8-9 might apply – "***Finally, be ye all of one mind, having compassion one of another, love as brethren, be pitiful, be courteous: not rendering evil for evil, or railing for railing: but contrariwise blessing; knowing that ye are thereunto called, that ye should inherit a blessing.***"

To Raise Up a Godly Generation

In the third place, the Lord our God instituted and established the marriage relationship *to raise up a godly generation.* In Genesis 1:28 the Lord our God blessed the first man Adam and his wife and instructed them both, saying, "***Be fruitful, and multiply, and replenish the earth, and subdue it.***" Although our Lord does not grant that every married couple might have children, it is His purpose in the majority of cases that a married couple should bring forth children into this world. Yet there is more. A married couple is not only responsible to bring forth children, but is also responsible to train up those children; and our Lord would have those children brought up in godliness for the glory of His name. In Ephesians 6:4 the instruction of God's Word is given to every father, "***And, ye fathers, provoke not your children to wrath: but bring them up in the nurture and admonition of the Lord.***"

Even so, in the midst of a rebuke unto the men of Israel for their mistreatment of their wives, the Lord our God proclaimed in Malachi 2:15, "*And did not he make one? Yet had he the residue of the spirit. And wherefore one? That he might seek a godly seed. Therefore take heed to your spirit, and let none deal treacherously against the wife of his youth.*" The question is asked – Why did the Lord our God establish the one-flesh relationship of marriage. Then the answer is given – "That He might seek a godly seed." From the opening portion of this verse we learn that the Lord our God instituted and established the marriage relationship so that the married couple might raise up a godly generation. Thus the husband is challenged and warned in the closing portion of the verse to take heed unto his spirit toward his wife and not to deal treacherously against her. Why is he so warned in this context? The husband is so warned because the manner in which he treats his wife will have a direct impact upon the training of their children. A husband *must* give godly honor unto his wife in order to bring up his children aright "in the nurture and admonition of the Lord." Bringing up children in godliness is not simply founded upon the principles of godly parenting. It is even more deeply rooted in the relationship of a godly *marriage*.

To Protect against Sexual Immorality

In the fourth place, the Lord our God instituted and established the marriage relationship *to protect against sexual immorality*. In this life we believers still possess within us the old man of our sinful flesh. The lusts of our sinful flesh continue to war within us, and we continue to face the temptation to be drawn away of our sinful lusts and to be enticed unto sin. Among these lusts of our sinful flesh is the temptation to sexual immorality – sexual lust, fornication, adultery, etc. However, in 1 Corinthians 7:2 we learn that through the marriage relationship the Lord our God has granted us a very practical form of protection against the temptation to sexual immorality. There we read, "*Nevertheless, to avoid fornication, let every man have his own wife, and let every woman have her own husband.*" Although sexual immorality is a sinful abomination in our Lord's sight, He views the sexual relationship between a husband and wife as precious and worthy of honor. In Hebrews 13:4 God's Holy Word declares, *"Marriage is honourable in all, and the bed undefiled: but whoremongers and adulterers God will judge."* Thus a healthy sexual relationship between a husband and wife will help to protect them from the temptation of sexual immorality outside the marriage relationship.

In fact, in 1 Corinthians 7:3-5 the Lord our God through His Holy Word *commands* a husband and wife to maintain a healthy sexual relationship with one another. There we read, *"Let the husband render unto the wife due benevolence: and likewise also the wife unto the husband. The wife hath not power of her own body, but the husband: and likewise also the husband hath not power of his own body, but the wife. Defraud ye not one the other, except it be with consent for a time, that ye may give yourselves to fasting and prayer; and come together again, that Satan tempt you not for your incontinency."* Here we learn the definition of the Lord our God Himself for the sexual relationship between a husband and wife. He defines this sexual relationship as a *"due benevolence"* from the husband unto his wife and from the wife unto her husband.

First, we take notice that the sexual relationship between a husband and wife is a matter of *benevolence*. In the view of the Lord our God Himself, for a husband and wife to provide sexual pleasure one to another is an act of *good will* and *kindness* to one another. Furthermore, we take notice that the sexual relationship between a husband and wife is a *due* benevolence. To provide sexual pleasure one to another is an act of good will and kindness that a husband *owes* to his wife and that a wife *owes* to her husband. Finally, we take notice from verse 5 that in the view of the Lord our God, for a husband or wife to withhold such sexual pleasure from the other is an act of *defrauding* the other. It is an act of robbing from the other the benevolence that is owed to the other. Therefore, in verse 5 the Lord our God *commands* a husband and wife *not* to defraud one another of this due benevolence. In fact, our Lord grants only one exception to this command – that one might give himself or herself to fasting and prayer. Yet even in this exception the Lord our God requires mutual consent and a limited period of time. Why are these restrictions necessary? The answer is "that Satan tempt you not." The answer is that a husband and wife might be protected against the devil's temptation to sexual immorality.

To Testify of the Union between Christ and His Church

In the fifth and final place, the Lord our God instituted and established the marriage relationship *to illustrate and testify of the union between our Lord and Savior Jesus Christ and His church.* Now, this reason is given last in order because it is presented last in the progressive revelation of God's Holy Word. However, this reason is certainly not the least in importance. Rather, it serves as the cap stone for the other reasons. In Ephesians 5:23 God's Word declares, *"For the husband is the head of the wife, even as Christ is the head of the church: and he is the saviour of the body."* In verses 25-27 God's Word commands, *"Husbands, love your wives, even as Christ also loved the church, and gave himself for it; that he might sanctify and cleanse it with the washing of the word, that he might present it to himself a glorious church, not having spot, or wrinkle, or any such thing; but that it should be holy and without blemish."* In verses 29-30 God's Word proclaims, *"For no man ever yet hated his own flesh; but nourisheth and cherisheth it, even as the Lord the church; for we are members of his body, of his flesh, and of his bones."* Finally, in verse 32 God's Word reveals, *"This is a great mystery: but I speak concerning Christ and the church."*

Again and again in these passages, we are taught that a husband's relationship to his wife is *even as* Christ's relationship to His church. First, just as the husband is the head of his wife, even so Christ is the Head of His church. Second, just as a husband is required to love his wife, even so our Lord and Savior Jesus Christ has loved His church and has given Himself for it. This our Lord did in order that, first, He might sanctify and cleanse His church so that, in turn, He might present His church unto Himself as His own pure and glorious wife. Even so, Revelation 19:7-8 speaks of this coming day, saying, *"Let us be glad and rejoice, and give honour to him: for the marriage of the Lamb is come, and his wife hath made herself ready. And to her was granted that she should be arrayed in fine linen, clean and*

white: for the fine linen is the righteousness of saints." Third, just as a husband is required to nourish and cherish his wife as his very own flesh, even so our Lord Jesus Christ continues to nourish and cherish us who are the members of His church. This our Lord does because we are the very members of His body, "of His flesh and of His bone." This certainly is a great spiritual mystery – concerning the spiritual union between Christ and His church; and the one-flesh relationship between a husband and wife illustrates and testifies of this great and glorious spiritual mystery.

Truth for Meditation

The purpose of the Lord our God for the marriage relationship is –

1. To provide human companionship. (Gen. 2:18; Mal. 2:14; Song 5:16; Gen. 2:24)

2. To form a working partnership. (Gen. 2:18; Eccl. 4:9-10)

3. To raise up a godly generation. (Gen. 1:28; Eph. 6:4; Mal. 2:15)

4. To protect against sexual immorality. (1 Cor. 7:2-5; Heb. 13:4)

5. To testify of the union between Christ and His church. (Eph. 5:23, 25-27, 29-30, 32)

In order to develop and maintain an intimate, one-flesh companionship together, the husband and wife must –

1. Actively pursue open communication with one another. (Ex. 33:11; Prov. 27: 6, 9)

2. Actively pursue emotional camaraderie with one another. (Psa. 55:14; 1 Sam. 18:1)

3. Actively pursue a firm and faithful commitment to one another. (Prov. 17:17; 18:24)

4. Actively pursue a caring compassion for one another. (Psa. 35:13-14)

5. Actively pursue intimate communion with one another. (Gen. 2:24; Prov. 27:17)

Verses for Memorization

Genesis 2:18: And the LORD God said, It is not good that the man should be alone; I will make him an help meet for him.

1 Corinthians 7:2: Nevertheless, to avoid fornication, let every man have his own wife, and let every woman have her own husband.

8

Cleaving unto Thy Wife
(Part 1)

As we have previously noted, when the Lord our God instituted and established the marriage relationship at creation, He delivered three foundational principles for a good marriage. These we find in Genesis 2:24 – *"**Therefore shall a man leave his father and his mother, and shall cleave unto his wife; and they shall be one flesh.**"* From the last of these principles we learn that both the husband and the wife are actively to pursue an intimate, one-flesh relationship together. However, the first two of these foundational principles are delivered only to the husband in the marriage relationship. These two principles are that the husband must leave the priority of his relationship with his parents and that he must cleave unto his wife.

Already from the order of these three principles, we have learned that the Lord our God intends for the husband to take up the responsibility of leadership in developing and maintaining the one-flesh relationship of the marriage. Yet there is more depth for the husband to fathom in this matter of cleaving unto his wife. What does the Lord our God mean when He instructs the husband to cleave unto his wife? What all are the specific elements involved in a husband's cleaving unto his wife?

The Place of Priority

Some of these elements we have touched upon already. Yet we shall take them up in review as we begin. In the first place then, the husband is *to give his relationship with his wife the place of priority over all other human relationships.* Or, considered from the opposite perspective, the husband is not to allow any other human relationship to hinder his one-flesh relationship with his wife. In the order of the three foundational principles for a good marriage relationship found in Genesis 2:24, we may see three progressive layers. Yea, we may see each principle laying the foundation for the next. The instruction of the third principle is that both the husband and the wife are to pursue a one-flesh relationship with one another. That which lays the foundation for this third principle is the instruction of the second principle – that the husband is to take up the responsibility of leadership in first cleaving unto his wife. That which lays the foundation for this second principle is the instruction of the first principle – that the husband is first to leave the priority of his relationship with his parents.

Obedience to the first principle is necessary for obedience to the second. Before a young man is married, his priority human relationship is to be that with his father and his mother. Yet when he enters into the marriage relationship with his wife, the Lord our God Himself commands that he leave the priority of his relationship with his parents and that he replace it with the priority of his one-flesh relationship with his wife. Now, since the husband's marriage relationship with his wife must be set even above his relationship with his parents, then certainly his marriage relationship with his wife should be set above all other human relationships of lesser priority.

Furthermore, in the latter half of Matthew 19:6, our Lord Jesus Christ presented the precept and principle, saying, "***What therefore God hath joined together, let not man put asunder.***" On this particular occasion the Pharisees had come to the Lord, seeking to "entangle Him in His talk." The question that they presented unto

Him concerned the matter of divorce. In verse 3 we read, *"The Pharisees also came unto him, tempting him, and saying unto him, Is it lawful for a man to put away his wife for every cause?"*

In response the Lord immediately turned their attention toward the creation account and toward God's original purpose in His own institution of the marriage relationship. In verses 4-5 we read, *"And he answered and said unto them, Have ye not read, that he which made them at the beginning made them male and female, and said, For this cause shall a man leave his father and mother, and shall cleave to his wife: and they twain shall be one flesh?"* Then, having referred them to the account of creation, our Lord Jesus Christ presented His conclusion and His command in verse 6, saying, *"Wherefore they are no more twain, but one flesh. What therefore God hath joined together, let not man put asunder."*

Now, some may see this command in this context as having an application only to the matter of divorce. However, the principle of our Lord's precept reaches more deeply into the nature of the marriage relationship. First, we take note that our Lord builds His precept upon the foundational truth that a husband and wife are no longer two independent parts, but are now a one-flesh unit. Second, we take note that it is the Lord our God and heavenly Father Himself who joins together a husband and his wife into this one-flesh unit. Third, we take note that the words "put asunder" mean "to divide or to separate." Finally, we take note that our Lord's precept forbids "man" (that is – any relationship of mankind or element of this life) to become a matter of division and separation within the one-flesh relationship of a marriage.

Thus in the principle of our Lord's precept, He not only speaks against the practice of divorce, but also for the *priority* of the marriage relationship. In cleaving unto his wife, the husband must give his marriage relationship the place of priority over all other human relationships and must not allow any other human relationship to hinder his one-flesh relationship with his wife. They are one-flesh. The Lord God Himself has made them one-flesh. Therefore, the husband must not allow any force of man or of this world even to begin the process of pulling them asunder.

The husband must not allow his relationship with his parents to stir up strife and division in his relationship with his wife. Certainly he is required by the Lord his God to honor his father and his mother and to have affection of heart toward them. Yet he is to honor his wife and to have affection of heart toward her all the more. Yes, conflicts might arise between his wife and his parents; and certainly at such times the husband should seek the Lord's face in prayer for the spiritual discernment to honor both his wife and his parents, as he ought. Yet at such times he must ever remember that his relationship with his wife is to stand in the place of priority above his relationship with his parents. Thus at times of intense conflict, when he might be required to choose either his wife or his parents, he must choose the side of his wife.

Yet in standing with his wife, he must also stand as a spiritual guard for her heart, seeking to prevent or even to confront a sinful attitude on her part toward his parents. In addition, the husband must never use his relationship with his parents as an emotional weapon against his wife. Yea, he especially should not compare his wife with his mother in a derogatory and damaging manner. Rather, the husband should ever seek, as much as he is able, to draw his wife and his parents into a growing relationship of love, peace, and unity one with another.

The husband must not allow his relationship with his brother(s), or sister(s), or other extended family to rise higher than his relationship with his wife. Certainly he ought to seek, as much as he is able, to dwell in peace, unity, and brotherly love with his brother(s), sister(s), and other extended family. Yet his unity and intimate communion with his wife should ever rise higher, extend further, and go deeper.

The husband must not allow his affection for his children or his grandchildren to eclipse his affection and love for his wife. Certainly he ought to have and show godly affection and love toward his children and grandchildren. Yet his affection and love for his wife should abound so much more that all might clearly see her place of priority in his heart. In fact, such abounding love and affection toward his wife will serve as a strong foundation for the godly training of his children and for a godly influence upon his grandchildren. Yea, such abounding love and affection toward his wife will serve as a powerful example to teach spiritual truth all by itself.

The husband must not allow tension with his wife's family to create division between him and his wife. The husband must develop the same honor and affection toward his wife's parents, as he ought to show toward his own parents. In addition, he must seek to dwell in peace, unity, and brotherly love with her extended family, just as with his own extended family. However, if any member of his wife's family mistreats her, he must take up the responsibility to protect her physically, mentally, emotionally, and spiritually from that mistreatment.

The husband must not allow his friendships with others to become a higher priority than his unity and friendship with his wife. He must remember that there is no divine requirement for him to spend time out with the fellows, but that there is a divine requirement for him to develop and maintain his relationship with his wife. Certainly the husband must never allow his acquaintance or friendship with another woman to create a division between him and his wife. He must ever take care over his own heart that it might not turn in the smallest degree away from his own wife toward another woman. He must also take every precaution within his power to prevent another woman from drawing too close in relationship unto him. If his wife expresses any level of concern about his relationship with another woman, he must not ignore her concern or condemn her for her concern, but must take every legitimate step within his power to relieve that concern.

The husband must take care concerning his job or profession that it or some aspect of it might not create a division between him and his wife. Certainly the husband is required of God to provide financially and materially for his family. According to 1 Timothy 5:8, if he neglects his responsibility in this regard, ***"he hath denied the faith, and is worse than an infidel."*** In order to walk aright before the Lord his God, the husband must work as he is able to provide for his family. Yet he must not allow this responsibility to become a tool in the devil's hand for destroying his one-flesh relationship with his wife. He must not allow his relationships with his coworkers to eclipse his relationship with his wife. He must not allow his love and affection for his profession to grow greater than his love and affection for his wife. He must not allow the job to become an escape from the responsibility to pursue and maintain his one-flesh relationship with his wife. He must not allow a desire for money, material things, and a higher standard of living to become more important than his one-flesh relationship with his wife.

In like manner, the husband must take care concerning his ministry responsibility in the ministry of the church that it or some aspect of it might not create a division between him and his wife. Certainly, according to 1 Corinthians 12:18, every child of God has been divinely appointed to a ministry responsibility in the body of Christ, the church. Yet the husband has also been divinely appointed to his marriage responsibility in his one-flesh relationship with his wife. As we have learned previously, in 1 Corinthians 7:32-33 the Lord our God Himself in His Holy Word recognizes that the responsibility of the marriage relationship will limit a husband's involvement in church ministry. Thus, in order to fulfill both his marriage responsibility and his ministry responsibility before the Lord his God, the husband must be guided by the Holy Spirit of God to maintain a spiritual balance between them.

Finally, the husband must take great care that no element of self-interest might create a division between him and his wife. He must never allow his affection for and his involvement in his own hobbies and recreational activities to eclipse his love for and his relationship with his wife. Furthermore, through the spiritual strength of the indwelling Holy Spirit he must wage spiritual warfare against any selfish attitude, such as selfish superiority, selfish anger, or selfish desire, and against any selfish actions, such as selfish words, selfish behavior, and selfish spending, lest they might divide, damage, and destroy his one-flesh relationship with his wife.

Appreciate His Wife

In the second place, in considering what it means for the husband to cleave unto his wife, we find that he is *to appreciate his wife as a good gift of our Lord's favor.* God's Holy Word declares in Proverbs 18:22, **"Whoso findeth a wife findeth a good thing, and obtaineth favour of the LORD."** From the parallelism in opening portion of this verse, we learn that a wife is "a good thing;" and from the latter portion of this verse, we learn that a wife is a gift that is given from our Lord out of His goodwill and favor. This verse teaches every husband that his own wife is a good gift of the Lord's favor toward him. The Lord our God has poured out His favor upon that man and has granted him the precious treasure of a wife. So then, if the husband is to cleave aright unto his wife, he must view her as such. Yea, he must *thank* the Lord *daily* for His good will and favor in granting unto him the *good gift* and *precious treasure* of his wife.

In Genesis 2:24 the word "cleave" means "to cling to, to hold closely and dearly, to follow hard after, to follow closely." Such is to be the way of a husband toward his wife. She is to be held closely and dearly to his heart. His heart attitude must not be one of murmuring and complaining against her, whether to her face, to others, or to himself in the thoughts of his own heart; and certainly his heart attitude must not be one of bitterness against her. In Colossians 3:19 God's Holy Word gives the command – **"Husbands, love your wives, and be not bitter against them."** In cleaving unto his wife, the attitude of the husband's heart must ever be one of *thanksgiving* and *appreciation,* first unto the Lord for His favor in giving the good gift of a wife and then unto his wife as that good and precious gift.

Love His Wife

In the third place, in considering what it means for the husband to cleave unto his wife, we find that he is *to love his wife even as our Lord Jesus Christ loved the church.* In Ephesians 5:25-27 the instruction is given, **"Husbands, love your wives, even as Christ also** *loved the church, and gave himself for it; that he might sanctify and cleanse it with the washing of water by the word, that he might present it to himself a glorious church, not having spot, or wrinkle, or any such thing; but that it should be holy and without blemish."* Now, we must take note that the opening words of this passage present a Biblical command to husbands. The Lord our God *commands* each individual husband to love his own wife. This is not at all a matter of "falling in love" or of "falling out of love." This is a matter of *purposeful obedience* to a *direct command* from the Lord our God. Furthermore, for a husband to say, "But I just do not love my wife any more," is not at all an acceptable excuse with the Lord. In fact, such a claim is simply an admission concerning the *sinful attitude* of that husband before the Lord and toward his wife. Therefore, let each husband take to heart this Biblical truth – To love his wife is to obey the Lord in this matter, and not to love his wife is to disobey the Lord in this matter. There is no middle ground. There is only obedience or disobedience. There is only righteousness or wickedness.

What then does it mean for a husband to love his own wife? The closing phrase of Ephesians 5:25 reveals the answer, saying, *"Even as Christ also loved the church, and gave himself for it."* The Lord our God has not simply commanded the husband to love his wife, but has commanded that husband to love his wife *to the same extent* as our Lord Jesus Christ loved the church. So then, to what extent did our Lord Jesus Christ love the church? He completely gave up His life for it. This was the mindset that was in Christ Jesus our Lord and Savior – *"Who, being in the form of God, thought it not robbery to be equal with God: but made himself of no reputation, and took upon him the form of a servant, and was made in the likeness of men: and being found in fashion as a man, he humbled himself, and became obedient unto death, even the death of the cross."* (Philippians 2:6-8) Even so, the Lord our God commands the husband to have the same mindset toward his wife – to give up his own life completely for her.

Yet this is not simply a matter of the husband's dying physically for his wife, or even of being willing to do so. Rather, this is a matter of the husband's daily giving up of himself in humility in order to *serve* his wife. Concerning the matter of true, godly love, Galatians 5:13 declares, *"For, brethren, ye have been called unto liberty; only use not liberty for an occasion to the flesh, but by love serve one another."* Herein we find a contrast to and a demonstration of true, godly love. On the one hand, the contrast to true, godly love for another is to follow after "an occasion to the flesh;" and the essence of the old man of our flesh is self, selfishness, and self-serving. Following after selfish and self-serving ways is the opposite of true, godly love toward another. On the other hand, the essence and demonstration of true, godly love for another is to give one's self in service to the other.

So then, for the husband to walk in true, godly love toward his wife, he must give up the ways of selfishness and self-serving and must give himself in service to his wife. On the ground of true, godly love, he must serve his wife. Every day and every moment he is to give up his time, his energy, his interests, his rights, etc. *in service to his wife*. He is to humble himself and take upon himself the form of a servant in his relationship with his wife. Lest the husband might claim that he cannot take upon himself the form of a servant in his relationship with his wife because he is divinely called as her head, let it be remembered that our Lord Jesus Christ humbled Himself and took upon Himself the form of a servant although He Himself is God the Son, the second Person of the eternal Godhead. So then, just as our Lord Jesus Christ loved the church and gave Himself for it, even so the husband is to love his wife and to give himself for her.

Furthermore, the husband is to give up himself, not only in service to his wife, but also *for the sake of his wife*. The purpose for which our Lord Jesus Christ gave up Himself for the church is given in Ephesians 5:26-27 – *"That he might sanctify and cleanse it with the washing of water by the word, that he might present it to himself a glorious church, not having spot, or wrinkle, or any such thing; but that it should be holy and without blemish."* In these two verses we find two purpose statements with the second progressing from the first. Why did Christ give Himself in love for the church? The first purpose statement gives answer – *"That he might sanctify and cleanse it with the washing of water by the word.*" Why then does Christ desire to sanctify and cleanse the church? The second purpose statement gives answer – "*That he might present it to himself a glorious church, not having spot, or wrinkle, or any such thing; but that it should be holy and without blemish.*" The ultimate reason for which our Lord and Savior Jesus Christ gave up Himself in love for the church is that He might bring it to the place where it is a glorious church, being completely holy and without any blemish whatsoever.

Since the Lord our God has commanded the husband to love his wife "even as Christ loved the church," the husband is then to love his wife, not only to the same extent as Christ loved the church, but also *for the same purpose* that our Lord Jesus Christ loved the church. He is to give himself in love for his wife's sake that she might be brought to the place of a glorious wife. The purpose of his love for her should be centered upon her *continuing growth* in spiritual, mental, and emotional maturity. Yea, the purpose of the husband's love for his wife should be centered upon her continuing growth in her personal relationship with the Lord, in her daily walk as a woman of God, in her success before the Lord as a wife and mother, and in her fruitfulness in the work of the Lord. He is to give himself in love for her sake that she might ever grow in her daily sanctification unto the Lord in obedience and in her daily cleansing from the sinfulness of her flesh. In true, godly love for his wife, he should be much concerned that she might become the best woman of God, wife, mother, and minister for the Lord that she might possibly be.

Nourish His Wife

In the fourth place, in considering what it means for the husband to cleave unto his wife, we find that he is *to nourish his wife even as our Lord Jesus Christ nourishes the church*. In Ephesians 5:28-31 the instruction continues, "*So ought men to love their wives as their own bodies. He that loveth his wife loveth himself. For no man ever yet hated his own flesh; but nourisheth and cherisheth it, even as the Lord the church: for we are members of his body, of his flesh, and of his bones. For this cause shall a man leave his father and mother, and shall be joined unto his wife, and they two shall be one flesh.*" The opening portion of verse 33 then adds, "*Nevertheless let every one of you in particular so love his wife even as himself.*"

This passage continues the instruction to the husbands. It begins with the explanatory adverb "so," a word that means "in this manner." A door of explanation is opened that the husband may find greater understanding concerning the manner in which he is to love his wife. In particular, verse 28 begins with the instruction that the husband ought to love his wife as his own body. Such is the obligation and responsibility placed upon him by the Lord our God when he takes a woman to be his wife. In addition, the closing half of verse 28 presents the motivational truth that when the husband demonstrates love to his wife, he is equally demonstrating love to himself. Such is built upon the principle that at the moment of marriage the husband and his wife enter into a one-flesh relationship. She is bone of his bones and flesh of his flesh. She is a very part of him.

Thus verses 29-30 continue the explanation, saying, "*For no man ever yet hated his own flesh; but nourisheth and cherisheth it, even as the Lord the church: for we are members of his body, of his flesh, and of his bones.*" As believers we are in spiritual union with our Lord and Savior Jesus Christ. Spiritually we are members of His body, the church. We are bone of His bones and flesh of His flesh; and because of this spiritual union, our Lord nourishes and cherishes His body, the church. In like manner, we humans naturally nourish and cherish our own selves. Even so, since his wife is one with him in the one-flesh relationship of the marriage, the husband should nourish and cherish her as his very own flesh, even as our Lord nourishes and cherishes His own body, the church. This should be an *on-going*, daily matter. Throughout every day of their marriage relationship a husband should seek to be nourishing and cherishing his wife.

What then does it mean for a husband to nourish his wife? The word "nourish" here has reference to cultivation. The husband is to cultivate his wife's growth in maturity just as an individual might cultivate a beautiful flower. He is to plant her in the best of soil (that is – in a relationship with a truly Spirit-filled husband). The "soil" in which a wife is planted is the husband himself. Her father has given her away into *his* hand. God her heavenly Father has joined her in a one-flesh relationship with *him*. She is now bone of *his* bone and flesh of *his* flesh. She is now a part of *him*. She is now *his* helpmeet. *He* is the "soil" in which she has now been planted; and for that "soil" to be the most nourishing to her growth, he must be a truly Spirit-filled husband. As the "soil" for his wife, he must bring forth the spiritual fruit of love, joy, peace, longsuffering, gentleness, goodness, faith, meekness, and temperance that she might be nourished thereby. (Galatians 5:22-23) Furthermore, the husband is to provide his wife with every other necessary ingredient for growth. In every way possible he is to cultivate his wife so that she might blossom into the most beautiful wife, mother, and woman of God possible. Even so, when a man's wife does not blossom into such beauty of godliness and maturity, it is often the fault of *his own failure* in nourishing her.

Cherish His Wife

In the fifth place, in considering what it means for the husband to cleave unto his wife, we find that he is *to cherish his wife even as our Lord Jesus Christ cherishes the church.* Not only does our Lord nourish His body, the church; but also He cherishes it. Not only does a man naturally nourish his own flesh, but also he cherishes it. Even so, not only should a husband nourish his wife, but also he should cherish her. What then does it mean for a husband to cherish his wife? The only other New Testament passage in which we find this word "cherish" might help us come to an understanding of the matter. In 1 Thessalonians 2:7-8 we read, ***"But we were gentle among you, even as a nurse cherisheth her children: so being affectionately desirous of you, we were willing to have imparted unto you, not the gospel of God only, but also our own souls, because ye were dear unto us."*** The Greek word that is translated "cherish" literally means "to keep warm." It was often used of the manner in which a mother might care for her newborn child, holding that child close in order to keep that child warm. Thus she held her child close to her heart, cherishing him. Even so, the apostle Paul employed this picture to illustrate his own relationship with

108

the believers at Thessalonica; and in relation to this illustration he presented four phrases of explanation.

First, the apostle indicated that he had been *gentle* among the believers at Thessalonica. Second, he indicated that he had been *affectionately desirous* of them. Third, he indicated that he had *imparted his own soul* unto them. Finally, he indicated that they were *dear* unto him. In like manner, the husband is to cherish his wife by being gentle toward her. He must not have a harsh and overbearing manner, but must have a kind and tender manner in relation to her. He must not have a contentious and selfish spirit, but must have a meek and loving spirit toward her. In his relationship with his wife, he is to be longsuffering, forbearing, forgiving, peaceable, merciful, easily entreated, courteous, considerate, gracious, compassionate, comforting, and encouraging. He is to be ever sensitive to his wife's physical, mental, emotional, and spiritual needs.

Now, each individual wife is different. Therefore, the specific application of this principle will be somewhat different in the particulars for any given marriage relationship. However, a couple of examples may be of help to our understanding. If a husband's wife needs regular expressions of love and affection, that husband ought to meet that need; and this he ought to do cheerfully, not grudgingly. Or, if a husband's wife upon occasion needs a break from the responsibilities of children and home, that husband ought to do his best to provide that opportunity. Oh, how far short we husbands often fall in this regard! Yet we are required by the Lord our God in His Holy Word to cherish our wives. We *must* learn to be gentle toward them and to be sensitive to their needs, especially to their emotional needs.

In addition, the husband must be affectionately desirous of his wife. Not only is the gentleness of his manner toward her to be a matter of outward behavior, but also it is to be rooted in the affection of his heart toward her. His own heart is to be open toward her and to be full of warm and tender feeling for her sake. The desire of his heart is to be directed to her best interest; and flowing out of this affectionate desire for his wife, in the third place, the husband must be willing and well pleased to impart his own soul unto her. He is not to live unto himself, but to give of himself and to give up himself for her sake. Yea, he is to give of his very heart and soul to and for her. Finally, the husband must hold his wife dear to his heart. He is to value her highly in love and to adore her deeply in love. She is to be his darling, his sweetheart, his precious treasure, his beloved. He is to cherish his wife as his own body, even as our Lord Jesus Christ cherishes His own body, the church.

Truth for Meditation

The husband is to cleave unto his wife –

1. By giving his relationship with his wife the place of priority over all other human relationships. (Gen. 2:24; Matt. 19:6)
2. By appreciating his wife as a good gift of our Lord's favor. (Prov. 18:22)
3. By loving his wife even as our Lord Jesus Christ loved the church. (Eph. 5:25-27)
4. By nourishing his wife even as our Lord Jesus Christ nourishes the church. (Eph. 5:28-31)
5. By cherishing his wife even as our Lord Jesus Christ cherishes the church. (Eph. 5:28-31)

The husband is to love his wife –

1. To the same extent as Christ loved the church, daily giving up of himself in service to his wife. (Eph. 5:25; Gal. 5:13)
2. For the same purpose that Christ loved the church, that his wife might grow daily in spiritual, mental, and emotional maturity. (Eph. 5:26-27)

The husband is to nourish his wife –

1. By bringing forth the fruit of the Spirit in his relationship with her. (Gal. 5:22-23)
2. By providing her with every necessary ingredient for continuing growth. (Eph. 5:29)

The husband is to cherish his wife –

1. By being gentle toward her. (1 Thess. 2:7)
2. By being affectionately desirous of her. (1 Thess. 2:8)
3. By imparting his own soul to her. (1 Thess. 2:8)
4. By holding her dear to his heart. (1 Thess. 2:8)

111

Verses for Memorization

Proverbs 18:22: Whoso findeth a wife findeth a good thing, and obtaineth favour of the LORD.

Ephesians 5:25: Husbands, love your wives, even as Christ loved the church, and gave himself for it.

Ephesians 5:28-29: So ought men to love their wives as their own bodies. He that loveth his wife loveth himself. For no man ever yet hated his own flesh; but nourisheth and cherisheth it, even as the Lord the church.

9

Cleaving unto Thy Wife
(Part 2)

In Genesis 2:24 the Lord our God delivered three foundational principles for a good marriage, saying, ***"Therefore shall a man leave his father and his mother, and shall cleave unto his wife; and they shall be one flesh."*** The second of these three foundational principles is that a husband is to cleave unto his wife. What does the Lord our God mean when He instructs a husband to cleave unto his wife? What all are the specific elements involved in a husband's cleaving unto his wife?

In the previous chapter, we began to consider the answer to these questions; and in so doing we found five Biblical truths concerning this matter. First, the husband is to give his relationship with his wife the place of priority over all other human relationships. Second, the husband is to appreciate his wife as a good gift of our Lord's favor. Third, the husband is to love his wife even as our Lord Jesus Christ loved the church. Fourth, the husband is to nourish his wife even as our Lord Jesus Christ nourishes the church. Fifth, the husband is to cherish his wife even as our Lord Jesus Christ cherishes the church. In this chapter we shall continue our study in God's Holy Word concerning this matter.

Dwell at Harmony with His Wife

In the sixth place, in considering what it means for the husband to cleave unto his wife, we find that he is *to dwell at harmony with his wife according to knowledge.* In the opening portion of 1 Peter 3:7, God's Holy Word gives instruction to husbands, saying, "***Likewise, ye husbands, dwell with them according to knowledge.***" The word "dwell" here means "to live in a home with another." When used in a context where the emphasis is less upon the location and more upon the relationship, as in the case of 1 Peter 3:7, the word conveys the idea of living *at* home with another. In our present day, we might think of this as living at *harmony* with another. Even so, the husband is to dwell with his wife. He is to live at harmony with her. He is to develop and maintain a unity of friendship and fellowship with her.

So then, upon what ground will the husband be able to develop and maintain this harmony, this unity of friendship and fellowship, with his wife? The prepositional phrase "according to knowledge" reveals the answer. The husband must come to *know* his own wife. Yea, he must put forth the effort and energy to know his own wife *as an individual* – to know her individual personality, to know her individual joys and burdens, to know her individual likes and dislikes, to know her individual delights and annoyances, to know her individual pleasures and pains, to know her individual strengths and weaknesses, to know her individual hopes and fears.

In addition, the husband must come to know how his own wife thinks and feels *differently from himself.* Certainly this will require that he lovingly, attentively, and faithfully *communicate with* his wife, and especially this will require that he carefully and considerately *listen to* his wife. Then as the husband comes to know these things, he must dwell in harmony with her in accord with that knowledge. When he comes to know that something bothers his wife, he should put forth every Biblically acceptable effort to avoid that thing; and when he comes to know that something pleases his wife, he should put forth every Biblically acceptable effort to pursue that thing. The husband must be considerate of his wife, considering her individual desires and needs and acting accordingly.

114

Give Honor unto His Wife

In the seventh place, in considering what it means for the husband to cleave unto his wife, we find that he is *specifically to give honor unto his wife*. The instruction of God's Word continues in 1 Peter 3:7, saying, **"Likewise, ye husbands, dwell with them according to knowledge, giving honour unto the wife."** Not only is the husband to give affection unto his wife, but also to give *honor* unto her. Now, his honor is not simply to be granted unto her upon a rare occasion or an assigned holiday. Rather, this honor is to be poured out daily unto her in specific, tangible ways. Each day throughout every step of the day the husband is to prize his wife as a precious treasure. In addition, this honor is not to be granted in a grudging manner. Rather, this honor is to be poured out from the fullness of the husband's heart in attitude, word, and action.

The husband is not to take his wife and her efforts for granted, nor is he to treat her as an unimportant inferior or as a worthless possession. Rather, as Romans 12:10 teaches, in honor he is to prefer her above himself. Furthermore, the husband is not to tear down or tear into his wife verbally. Rather, he is to bless her and praise her for the fruit of her hands and the faithfulness of her work. Finally, the husband is not to mistreat, misuse, marginalize, manipulate, malign, mock, menace, or manhandle his wife. Rather, he is to behave toward his wife in such a manner as to magnify her and minister unto her. In all, the husband should express and demonstrate respect and appreciation for his wife's thoughts, feelings, opinions, suggestions, time, efforts, labor, and submission.

Having presented the two-fold instruction for husbands to dwell at harmony with their wives and to give honor unto their wives, 1 Peter 3:7 then presents a two-fold reason for these instructions. There we read, **"Likewise, ye husbands, dwell with them according to knowledge, giving honour unto the wife, as unto the weaker vessel, and as being heirs together of the grace of life."** The first reason is that the wife is the weaker vessel. This does not indicate that the wife is somehow inferior to her husband and weaker than her husband in spiritual, mental, or emotional matters. Rather, the phrase "weaker vessel" refers to the natural weakness of the wife in physical matters. By both general observation and scientific study it is recognized that women on average are physically weaker than men. Thus women are generally more vulnerable in physical matters. Because of this the husband is to handle his wife with care and to honor her with consideration. He is not to take advantage of her as the weaker vessel. Rather, he is to bestow more abundant honor upon her as the weaker vessel. He is not to disregard her as the weaker vessel. Rather, he is to dwell at harmony with her as the weaker vessel.

Then the second reason for the two-fold instruction of 1 Peter 3:7 is that both the husband and his wife are "heirs *together* of the grace of life." Although the wife may be the weaker vessel in physical matters, both the husband and his wife are co-equals in the matters and blessings of life. In their one-flesh relationship they are joint-heirs of those gracious blessings that the Lord our God will pour out upon them and provide to them throughout this life. Therefore, the husband is to dwell at harmony with his wife and to give honor unto his wife in a manner that is worthy of her as his very own joint-heir to those life-graces.

Yet 1 Peter 3:7 not only provides a two-fold instruction to the husband and a two-fold reason for that instruction, but also it provides a warning to the husband who neglects or refuses to obey that instruction. In the closing line of the verse the husband is warned, **"*That your prayers be not hindered.*"** Now, the word "hindered" here portrays the picture of a tree that is cut into, even to the point of being cut down to the ground. When a husband either neglects or refuses to dwell at harmony with and give honor unto his wife, that husband's prayer life will become ineffective and unavailing. Yea, the Lord our God Himself will neglect and refuse to hear that husband's prayers. As we have previously learned from 1 Corinthians 11:3, the head of the wife is the husband, and the Head of the husband is the Lord. Therefore, when the husband does not treat his wife aright, his Head and Lord will hold that husband accountable and will reject his prayers. Oh, how important it is that the husband dwell at harmony with and give honor unto his wife!

Cheer Up and Please His Wife

In the eighth place, in considering what it means for the husband to cleave unto his wife, we find that he is *purposefully to cheer up and please his wife*. In Deuteronomy 24:5 the Law of Moses proscribed concerning a newly married husband, *"When a man hath taken a new wife, he shall not go out to war, neither shall he be charged with any business: but he shall be free at home one year, and shall cheer up his wife which he hath taken."* In the time of the Old Testament, the Lord our God directly forbade a newly married, Israelite husband to be gone from home for war or business during the entire first year of his marriage. Instead, that husband was to spend that first year of marriage with his new bride, purposefully cheering her up and making her happy. A husband's cheering up of his wife is so important to our Lord that He had a specific directive established in the Old Testament Law concerning the matter.

Now, certainly the Lord our God does not intend that a husband should cease all efforts to cheer up his wife after their first year of marriage. Rather, the husband is to put forth every Biblically acceptable effort to cheer up his wife and make her happy throughout the whole of their married life upon this earth. Even so, the New Testament passage of 1 Corinthians 7:33 reveals the responsibility of a husband to take care how he might please his wife. There we read, *"But he that is married careth for the things that belong to the world, how he may please his wife."* Thus, as much as is possible before the Lord, the husband must avoid those things in attitude, word, and action that would upset and annoy his wife. Also as much as is possible before the Lord, he must pursue those things in attitude, word, and action that would cheer up and please his wife.

Provide for His Wife

In the ninth place, in considering what it means for the husband to cleave unto his wife, we find that he is *to provide for his wife's needs, and even for her wants.* 1 Timothy 5:8 gives warning, saying, *"But if any provide not for his own, and especially for those of his own house, he hath denied the faith, and is worse than an infidel."* In

117

its immediate context, this verse concerns the matter of providing materially for one's widowed mother or some other widowed relative. In verse 4 the instruction is given, "***But if any widow have children or nephews, let them learn first to shew piety at home, and to requite their parents: for that is good and acceptable before God.***" Yet the principle of verse 8 extends further than provision for such widows. There we find that the man and husband of the home is to provide "for his own, and especially for those of his own house." Certainly, this would include his own wife. Yea, especially this would include his own wife, even above all others. Just as the husband is to cleave unto his wife and thus maintain a relationship with her above all others, even so the husband is to care and provide for his wife above all others.

Furthermore, in accord with the responsibility of the husband to love, nourish, cherish, dwell at harmony with, honor, and cheer up his wife, this provision should encompass *both* her basic needs and her extra wants. The word "provide" here carries the idea of considering ahead of time for the purpose of caring and providing for another. Thus the husband is to consider ahead of time the material needs and desires of his wife and to put forth every Biblically acceptable effort to provide for those needs and desires. Certainly this must be within Biblical reason and within practical possibility. If a husband were to provide for his wife's wants and desires when he did not truly have the means, then in some future time he would be unable to provide for her actual needs. Yet the husband must not hold back from his wife those things that she might need or desire simply out of his own stinginess or selfishness.

Pursue Companionship with His Wife

In the tenth place, in considering what it means for the husband to cleave unto his wife, we find that he is *to pursue a growing companionship with his wife*. In a previous chapter we learned that one of our Lord God's purposes in instituting and establishing the marriage relationship is to meet the need for human companionship. Even so, in the closing phrase of Malachi 2:14, the Lord our God speaks to the husband concerning his wife, saying, "***Yet is she thy*** *companion, and the wife of thy covenant.*" A husband's wife is to be his life-long companion and his closest human friend. He is to walk together with her throughout their days upon this earth in close friendship and intimate fellowship.

Yet such a friendship and fellowship will not just happen. It must be developed and maintained. Every day it must be pursued for growth and guarded against damage. Thus, as we have also already learned, to develop and maintain such a growing and guarded companionship with his wife, the husband must actively pursue open communication with her, emotional camaraderie with her, a faithful commitment to her, a caring compassion for her, and an intimate communion with her. The husband must not stand aloof from his wife, physically, emotionally, mentally, or spiritually. Rather, he must actively and purposefully relate to her as his dearest friend.

Live Joyfully with His Wife

In the eleventh place, in considering what it means for the husband to cleave unto his wife, we find that he is *ever to rejoice and live joyfully with his wife.* In Proverbs 5:18 the Lord our God gives commandment to the husband, saying, "***Let thy fountain be blessed: and rejoice with the wife of thy youth.***" Furthermore, Ecclesiastes 9:9 instructs the husband, saying, "***Live joyfully with the wife whom thou lovest all the days of the life of thy vanity, which he hath given thee under the sun, all the days of thy vanity: for that is thy portion in this life, and in thy labour which thou takest under the sun.***" Certainly the immediate context of Proverbs 5:18 concerns the matter of sexual relations. Thus, in keeping with the context, we understand that the husband is to rejoice and find joy in the sexual advances and pleasures of his own wife, and not in another. Yet the principle itself, that the husband is to rejoice with his wife, extends further than just the matter of sexual relations.

In *all* of the realms of their marriage relationship, the husband is to rejoice and find joy with, in, through, and concerning his wife. He must not be filled with annoyance over her troublesome attributes, but must be filled with joy over her endearing qualities. He must not be regularly complaining about her faults and failures, but must be ever rejoicing over her efforts and accomplishments. He must not seek to avoid her company as much as possible, but must choose to enjoy her company. Yea, the husband must seek to make their time together upon this earth as happy and enjoyable as possible. He must live joyfully with his wife *all* of the days of their life together. He must seek, as much as he is able, to create a happy, joyful, and enjoyable atmosphere within their marriage relationship, that he may find joy in and with his wife and that she may find joy in and with him. Let the husband then seek for ways to put a smile on his wife's face, a bounce in her step, and a song in her heart!

Be Ravished with His Wife's Love

In the twelfth and final place, in considering what it means for the husband to cleave unto his wife, we find that he is *always to be satisfied and ravished with his wife's love.* In Proverbs 5:19 the Lord our God gives additional commandment to the husband concerning his relationship with his wife, saying, "***Let her be as the loving hind and the pleasant roe; let her breasts satisfy thee at all times; and be thou ravished always with her love.***" Here, in accord with the immediate context, the focus is set upon the husband's physical and sexual relationship with his wife. In this regard the husband is commanded to be satisfied at all times with his wife's body and to be ravished always with her love.

Now, the verb "satisfy" here carries the idea of drinking to the full, of being satiated or saturated. At all times the husband is to drink to the full of his own wife's physical person, such that he is completely satiated and satisfied in her and such that he has no interest or desire for any other. The husband must not have hungering eyes or heart for any other woman. Rather, his own wife must be the apple of his eye, the center of his interest, and the full joy of his desire. Furthermore, the verb "ravished" here carries the idea of being led astray by intoxication. Usually the Hebrew word is employed with negative force in the Old Testament Scriptures of being led astray into error. However, in Proverbs 5:19 it is employed with positive force as a command of the Lord our God Himself to

120

the husband in his relationship with his wife. The husband must always be intoxicated and enraptured with his wife's love. He must always be taken in and taken over by his wife's love. He must always be conquered and carried away as by force through the force of his own wife's love and affection.

Truth for Meditation

The husband is to cleave unto his wife –

(*From Chapter 8*)

1. By giving his relationship with his wife the place of priority over all other human relationships. (Gen. 2:24; Matt. 19:6)

2. By appreciating his wife as a good gift of our Lord's favor. (Prov. 18:22)

3. By loving his wife even as our Lord Jesus Christ loved the church. (Eph. 5:25-27)

4. By nourishing his wife even as our Lord Jesus Christ nourishes the church. (Eph. 5:28-31)

5. By cherishing his wife even as our Lord Jesus Christ cherishes the church. (Eph. 5:28-31)

(*From Chapter 9*)

6. By dwelling at harmony with his wife according to knowledge. (1 Pet. 3:7)

7. By specifically giving honor unto his wife. (1 Pet. 3:7)

8. By purposefully cheering up and pleasing his wife. (Deut. 24:5; 1 Cor. 7:33)

9. By providing for his wife's needs, and even her wants. (1 Tim. 5:8)

10. By pursuing a growing companionship with his wife. (Mal. 2:14)

11. By ever rejoicing and living joyfully with his wife. (Prov. 5:18; Eccl. 9:9)

12. By always being satisfied and ravished with his wife's love. (Prov. 5:19)

Verses for Memorization

1 Peter 3:7: Likewise, ye husbands, dwell with them according to knowledge, giving honour unto the wife, as unto the weaker vessel, and as being heirs together of the grace of life; that your prayers be not hindered.

Proverbs 5:18-19: Let thy fountain be blessed: and rejoice with the wife of thy youth. Let her be as the loving hind and pleasant roe; let her breasts satisfy thee at all times; and be thou ravished always with her love.

10

An Help Meet for Him
(Part 1)

As we have noted many times throughout this study, with the institution of marriage at the time of the creation, the Lord our God delivered three foundational principles for a good marriage in Genesis 2:24 – *"Therefore shall a man leave his father and his mother, and shall cleave unto his wife; and they shall be one flesh."* Now, the first two of these foundational principles is directed toward the husband alone. Yet the third of these principles is directed toward both the husband and the wife. Thus we learn that both the husband and the wife are actively to pursue an intimate, one-flesh relationship with one another.

As we have learned, the essence of the husband's responsibility in this matter may be found in the words of the second foundational principle – that he is to "cleave unto his wife." With these words we find the first truth that the Lord our God Himself delivered concerning the relationship of a husband toward his wife. What then is the essence of the wife's responsibility in this matter? The answer is to be found in Genesis 2:18 – *"And the LORD God said, It is not good that the man should be alone; I will make him an help meet for him."*

With the closing words of this verse, we find the first description that the Lord our God gave for the wife and the first truth that the Lord our God Himself delivered concerning the relationship of a wife toward her husband. Even so, we learn the essence of the wife's responsibility in actively pursuing an intimate, one-flesh relationship with her husband – that she is to be "an help meet for him." What did the Lord our God mean when He divinely described the wife as a helper who is meet for her husband? What all are the specific elements involved in a wife's being a helper who is truly meet for her husband?

The Highest Calling of God

In the first place, a wife is *to view this responsibility toward her husband as the highest calling of God for her life.* As we have noted, the phrase "an help meet for him" was the very first description of the Lord our God for the first woman Eve. The Lord did not simply create her as the female half of the human race. Rather, He created her to be the wife of the first man Adam. Yet in His first mention of her, the Lord did not refer to her simply with the word "wife." Rather, in His first mention of her, He referred to her as a helper who would be meet for the first man Adam. In this manner the Lord our God revealed His own *definition* for a wife and His own *purpose* and *calling* in a wife's life – that she be a helper who is truly meet for her husband. To this day such remains the first and highest calling that the Lord our God has set before each and every wife – to be a helper who is *truly* meet for her husband.

Now, since this is the highest calling of the Lord her God for her life, the wife must pursue this relationship with and responsibility toward her husband as a higher priority than all other human relationships. Just as the principle and precept of Matthew 19:6 holds true for the husband, even so it holds true for the wife – "***Wherefore they are no more twain, but one flesh. What therefore God hath joined together, let not man put asunder.***" Just as the husband is not to allow any other human relationship to hinder his one-flesh relationship with his wife, even so the wife is not to allow any other human relationship to hinder her one-flesh relationship with her husband. Yea, just as the husband is not to allow any other human relationship to hinder him from cleaving unto his wife, even so the wife is not to allow any other human relationship to hinder her from being a helper who is truly meet for her husband.

The wife must not allow her motherly affection and responsibilities toward her children or her grandchildren to eclipse her wifely affection and responsibilities toward her husband. Certainly she ought to have godly affection toward her children and grandchildren, and certainly she ought to fulfill her God-given responsibilities to guide her children and grandchildren in the right way. Yet her affection for her husband should abound so much more that all might clearly see his place of priority in her heart. Furthermore, her guidance of the children should be handled, not simply as the responsibility of a mother, but as the responsibility of the helper of their father, ever focused upon *helping him* to "bring them up in the nurture and admonition of the Lord." In fact, such abounding affection and focused responsibility in her relationship toward her husband will serve as a strong foundation for the godly training of the children and for a godly influence on the grandchildren. Yea, such will serve as a powerful example to teach spiritual truth by itself.

The wife must not allow her affection and love toward her parents to eclipse her affection and love toward her husband. Furthermore, she must not allow her relationship to her parents to stir up strife and division in her relationship with her husband. Certainly she is required by the Lord her God to honor her parents and to have affection toward them. Yet she is to honor her husband and to have affection toward him all the more. In the realm of human relationships, her first love and loyalty is no longer to be toward her parents, but is to be toward her husband. Thus, if times of conflict might arise between her husband and her parents, when she might be required to choose either her husband or her parents, she must choose the side of her husband. Yes, she should seek the Lord's face in prayer for the spiritual discernment to honor both her husband and her parents, as she ought. Yet she must ever remember that her priority calling from the Lord is to stand with and to support her husband as a helper who is truly meet *for him.* In addition, the wife must never use her relationship with her parents as a means to manipulate her husband. She especially should not compare her husband with her father in a derogatory and damaging manner. Rather, she should ever seek, as much as she is able, to draw her husband and her parents into a growing relationship of love, peace, and unity with one another.

The wife must not allow her sisterly affection and relationship toward her brother(s), or sister(s), or other extended family to rise higher than her affection and relationship toward her husband. Certainly she ought to seek, as much as she is able, to dwell in peace, unity, and brotherly love with her brother(s), sister(s), and other extended family. Yet her unity and intimate communion with her husband should ever rise higher, extend further, and go deeper. She must especially take care that she not develop a closer relationship with a sister or another woman in her family than with her husband. Although the relationships between the female members of a family are important and even necessary, such relationships should never take priority over the marriage relationship between the wife and her husband. Furthermore, such relationships between the female members of the family ought never to involve occasions of husband bashing, either against the wife's own husband, or against the husbands of the others.

The wife must not allow tension with her husband's family to create division between her and her husband. Rather, she must develop the same honor and affection toward her husband's parents, as she ought to show toward her own parents. In addition, she must seek to dwell in peace, unity, and brotherly love with her husband's extended family, just as with her own extended family. Therefore, the wife must take great care not to create or contribute to any tensions or divisions with her husband's parents and family.

The wife must not allow her friendships with others to become a greater priority than her unity and friendship with her husband. Certainly the wife may receive great encouragement, comfort, and support from the friendships of other godly women. Yet she must always remember that the Lord our God has directly commanded her to develop and walk in one-flesh unity and friendship, not with her friends, but with her husband. She is to draw closer to him than to any other human companion or friend. Furthermore, the wife certainly must never allow her acquaintance or friendship with another man to create division between her and her husband. She must ever take care over her own heart that it not turn in the smallest degree away from her own husband toward another man. Even so, she must not demonstrate greater interest in or respect for another man. She must also take every precaution within her power to prevent another man from drawing too close in relationship to her. If her husband expresses any level of concern about her relationship with another man, she must not ignore his concern or condemn him for his concern, but must take every legitimate step within her power to relieve that concern.

The wife must take care that no work responsibilities might ever eclipse her relationship with her husband. According to God's Word the Lord our God holds the husband responsible to provide financially for the family. There is no command of God that the wife must work a job outside of the home, and there is certainly no command of God that the wife must pursue a profession. Therefore, the wife must never allow such things to become more important than her husband and her relationship with her husband. Furthermore, the wife must even take care that her responsibilities in the home might not become a ground for tension and division between her and her husband. Yes, according to Titus 2:5 the wife is required of God to be a keeper of the home. Yet the wife must understand that she is not called to keep the home in competition with her relationship to her husband, but as a very part of her calling to be a helper who is meet for him. She is not to keep the home simply for her own sake, but even more so for her husband's sake.

In like manner, the wife must take care concerning her ministry responsibility in the ministry of the church that it or some aspect of it might not create a division between her and her husband. Certainly, according to 1 Corinthians 12:18, every child of God has been divinely appointed to a ministry responsibility in the body of Christ, the church. Yet the wife has also been divinely appointed to her marriage responsibility in her one-flesh relationship with her husband to be a helper who is meet for him. As we have learned previously, in 1 Corinthians 7:32-33 the Lord our God Himself in His Holy Word recognizes that the responsibility of the marriage relationship will limit a wife's involvement in church ministry. Thus, in order to fulfill both her marriage responsibility and her ministry responsibility before the Lord her God, the wife must be guided by the Holy Spirit of God to maintain a spiritual balance between them. She must especially understand that even in this matter her greatest calling is to serve together with her husband as a helper who is meet for him in his ministry responsibility before the Lord.

Finally, the wife must take great care that no element of self-interest might create a division between her and her husband. She must never allow her affection for and her involvement in her own hobbies and recreational activities to eclipse her love for and her relationship with her husband. Furthermore, through the spiritual strength of the indwelling Holy Spirit she must wage spiritual warfare against any selfish attitude, such as selfish manipulation, selfish anger, or selfish desire, and against any selfish actions, such as selfish words, selfish behavior, and selfish spending, lest they might divide, damage, and destroy her one-flesh relationship with her husband.

Be a Crown for Her Husband

In the second place, in considering what it means for a wife to be a helper who is meet for her husband, we find that she is *to be a crown upon her husband's head and not as a cancer in his bones.* God's Word declares in Proverbs 12:4, "***A virtuous woman is a crown to her husband: but she that maketh ashamed is as rottenness in his bones.***" With this verse the Lord our God divides all of the wives of the world into two categories. On the one hand, there are the wives who are a crown to their husbands. On the other hand, there are the wives who are as rottenness in their husbands' bones. Yet what do these classifications mean?

A crown is foremost a symbol of honor, and sometimes also a symbol of authority. In like manner, the wife who is a crown to her husband is one who, through her character and behavior, ever seeks *to bring honor to her husband* and *to support his position of authority* in the home. According to Proverbs 12:4 it is the *virtuous* woman who will be such a crown to her husband. Even so, concerning the character of the virtuous woman, Proverbs 31:23 reveals, "***Her husband is known in the gates, when he sitteth among the elders of the land.***" When considered alone this verse may appear only to speak concerning the virtuous woman's husband, and not concerning her at all. Yet the whole context of Proverbs 31:10-31 is clearly about the character of the virtuous woman herself. Thus we understand that within this context verse 23 is intended as another commendation of the virtuous woman. It is specifically because of her virtuous character and behavior that "her husband is known in the gates." As a helper who is meet for her husband, the virtuous wife will enhance his reputation and will bring him respect among the general public and even among "the elders of the land." She will be a crown upon her husband's head, bringing glory unto him. In turn, this will be a glory unto the virtuous wife herself also; for a crown is itself glorious just as it reflects glory upon the one who wears it.

However, the wife "that maketh ashamed" is not so. She is the opposite of the virtuous wife. She does not bring honor to her husband and does not support his authority in the home. She does not enhance his reputation, nor bring him respect among others. Rather, through her character and behavior she brings shame upon him and brings him to shame. Thereby she is as a form of rottenness, such as cancer, in his very bones. The bones are the foundational strength of the human body, and rottenness in the bones will physically weaken an individual at the foundational level. In like manner, the wife "that maketh ashamed" will weaken her husband at the foundational level, ever eating away at the strength of his heart to move forward in his responsibilities. In addition, such a wife will weaken her husband's honor, authority, reputation, respect, and success at the foundational level. Such a wife certainly is not a helper who is meet for her husband. Rather, she is a rottenness that undermines him at the deepest level.

Submit unto Her Husband

In the third place, in considering what it means for a wife to be a helper who is meet for her husband, we find that she is *willingly to submit herself unto her husband's headship as unto the Lord.* In Ephesians 5:22-24 the instruction is given, **"Wives, submit yourselves unto your own husbands, as unto the Lord. For the husband is the head of the wife, even as Christ is the head of the church: and** *he is the saviour of the body. Therefore as the church is subject unto Christ, so let the wives be to their husbands in every thing.*" Again in Colossians 3:18 the instruction is given, "*Wives, submit yourselves unto your own husbands, as it is fit in the Lord.*" Yet again in 1 Peter 3:1-2 the instruction is given, "*Likewise, ye wives, be in subjection to your own husbands; that, if any obey not the word, they also may without the word be won by the conversation of the wives; while they behold your chaste conversation coupled with fear.*" Finally, in the closing portion of Titus 2:5, we learn that the older women of God are to teach the younger to be "*obedient to their own husbands, that the word of God be not blasphemed.*"

❖ From these passages it is clear that the Lord our God would have each individual wife to submit herself unto her own respective husband. Now, the words "submit" and "subject" in these verses mean "to arrange under authority." The Lord our God has commanded the wife to arrange herself under the leadership authority of her husband. In fact, this is the first reason revealed in these passages for the wife to submit herself unto her own husband – *because the Lord our God has set the husband in the headship and leadership role within the marriage and home.* Even so, Ephesians 5:23 declares, "*For the husband is the head of the wife, even as Christ is the head of the church: and he is the saviour of the body.*" To this 1 Corinthians 11:3 adds, "*But I would have you know, that the head of every man is Christ; and the head of the woman is the man; and the head of Christ is God.*"

This is not a matter of natural superiority or inferiority. Rather, this is a matter of the divinely established roles within the structure of the marriage and home for their proper function. Just as God the Son, the Lord Jesus Christ, is not inferior in deity to God the Father, even so the wife is not inferior as a person to the husband. Yet just as God the Father is the Head of God the Son in the proper function of the Godhead, even so the husband is the head of the wife in the proper function of the marriage. Because this is so, the Lord our God instructs the wife to submit herself unto her husband as her divinely appointed head.

❖ The second reason that we find in these passages for the wife to submit herself unto her own husband is *because it is proper and pleasing in the sight of the Lord.* Colossians 3:18 declares, *"**Wives, submit yourselves unto your own husbands, as it is fit in the Lord.**"* The Lord our God Himself established the institution of marriage, and He Himself set the husband in the role of headship and leadership within the marriage. Thus it is proper and pleasing in our Lord's sight when the wife submits herself unto the leadership of her husband, for in doing so she also submits herself unto the will of the Lord. If the wife desires, not only to have a proper marriage relationship with her husband, but also to have a proper Christian walk before her Lord, she must submit herself unto her own husband. Such may not be proper and pleasing in the sight of this world, but it most certainly is proper and pleasing in the sight of our Lord.

❖ The third reason that we find in these passages for the wife to submit herself unto her own husband is *because it is the divinely established means by which she may influence her husband toward the things of God.* 1 Peter 3:1-2 declares, *"**Likewise, ye wives, be in subjection to your own husbands; that, if any obey not the word, they also may without the word be won by the conversation of the wives; while they behold your chaste conversation coupled with fear.**"* Most often we believe that the way to influence others is by leading them and instructing them. Yet in the case of the wife's spiritual influence upon her husband, the Lord our God declares that the way of influence is by submitting herself to her husband's headship and leadership. In fact, in 1 Peter 3:1 this is presented as the means of the wife's influence upon her husband specifically when he is in direct disobedience to the Word of God, including even the gospel message. "Without the word" (that is – without words of instruction, correction, rebuke, or nagging) she is to win the heart of her husband unto obedience to the Lord through her faithful, submissive, pure, respectful behavior. This is her divinely established means of spiritual influence upon him.

❖ The fourth and final reason that we find in these passages for the wife to submit herself unto her own husband is *because an unsubmissive spirit will create an occasion for the Word of God to be blasphemed.* This is the warning that we find at the end of Titus 2:5 where we learn that the younger women are to be taught to be ***"obedient to their own husbands, that the word of God be not blasphemed."*** The people of this lost world are ever watching the behavior of those who claim to be God's own people. They are watching our behavior in public, on the job, in our recreation, in our family relationships, and in our marriage relationships. With regard to our marriage relationships, they are ever watching how those who claim to be men of God relate to their wives and how those who claim to be women of God relate to their husbands. Thus when the wife who claims to be a woman of God does not relate to her husband in the Biblical manner, it creates an occasion for the truth of God's Word as a whole to be slandered, disrespected, and rejected by this lost world. On the other hand, when the wife who claims to be a woman of God does relate to her husband in the Biblical manner, it creates an occasion for the truth of God's Word as a whole to be exalted, honored, and received by this lost world.

So then, in what manner and to what extent is the wife to submit herself unto her own husband?

❖ First, we find that the wife's submission is to be *with a willing spirit.* In Ephesians 5:22 we read, ***"Wives, submit yourselves unto your own husbands, as unto the Lord."*** Again in Colossians 3:18 we read, ***"Wives, submit yourselves unto your own husbands, as it is fit in the Lord."*** In both of these verses, the instruction is given to each wife herself to submit *herself* unto her own husband. This is not to be a submission that is forced upon her by her husband, but a submission that she *willingly* offers to her husband. She herself is willingly to arrange herself in both her attitude and her actions under her husband's headship and leadership authority.

❖ Second, we find that the wife's submission is to be *"as unto the Lord."* In Ephesians 5:22 we read, ***"Wives, submit yourselves unto your own husbands, as unto the Lord."*** Just as the wife would give respect and submission unto the Lord Himself, even so she should give such respect and submission unto her husband. Yet a wife might defend an unsubmissive spirit with the claim that her husband is not actually worthy of such a high level of respect and submission. However, the instruction of God's Holy Word does not give any such exception to the rule. The wife is to grant this respect and submission unto her husband, not because he himself is so worthy, but because the Lord Jesus Christ, who indeed is abundantly worthy, requires it.

❖ Third, we find that the wife's submission is to be *"in every thing."* In Ephesians 5:24 we read, ***"Therefore as the church is subject unto Christ, so let the wives be to their husbands in every thing."*** Yet immediately the question might be asked – What if the husband requires the wife to do something that is contrary to God's Word? Certainly if the husband requires his wife to do something that is *directly* contrary to a *specific* command of God's Holy Word, then the wife should follow the principle of Acts 5:17 – ***"We ought to obey God rather than men."*** Yet even in such a case the wife should apply this principle with ***"a meek and quiet spirit."*** (1 Peter 3:4)

In addition, the wife should never use this principle selfishly as a weapon against her husband to get her own way in a matter. Nor should she ever apply this principle to matters of her own formulation that are not specifically presented in God's Word. Such cases are to be subject only to the direct declaration of God's Word, and not to her own interpretations of right and wrong. Rather, in *everything* else except a case in which something is directly contrary to God's Word, the wife is to submit herself completely unto her own husband. Such submission "in every thing" not only includes submission to her husband's stated decisions, but also to her husband's unstated desires and direction.

Reverence Her Husband

In the fourth place, in considering what it means for a wife to be a helper who is meet for her husband, we find that she is *to reverence her husband's individual person and leadership position.* In Ephesians 5:22-33 we find a lengthy passage concerning the marriage relationship between the husband and the wife. In verses 22-24 we find the instruction to the wife to submit herself unto her own husband. In verses 25-32 we find the instruction to the husband to love his wife as Christ loved the church and in love to nourish and cherish his wife as Christ nourishes and cherishes the church. Finally, in verse 33 we come to the conclusion of this passage. There the instruction is given to both the husband and the wife, ***"Nevertheless let every one of you in particular so love his wife as himself; and the wife see that she reverence her husband."***

Now, this is not quite as we would expect. Certainly in the context of this passage, we would expect the final instruction to the husband to be a reminder that he ought to love his wife. Yet in the context of this passage, we would also expect the final instruction to the wife to be a reminder that she ought to submit herself unto her husband. However, this is not the case. Rather, in this conclusion we find an instruction to the wife to *reverence* her husband. Thus we understand that an attitude of reverence toward her husband is a part of Biblical submission. Her submission is not simply to be demonstrated in *acts of obedience*, but also in an *attitude of reverence*.

What then does it mean for the wife to reverence her husband? It means that she is to maintain a spirit and attitude of respect, esteem, and honor toward him. She is to hold him in an exalted place within her heart and to treat him with honor through her behavior. She is not to be critical of him, but to lift him up with honor. She is to adore him as her husband, to be attentive unto his thoughts and desires, and to be supportive of him and his pursuits. She is to be ever concerned to please him and to be ever cautious not to offend him. Although the wife will certainly be aware of her husband's weaknesses and unworthiness, yet in her submission unto him she is to maintain a spirit of reverence toward him "as unto the Lord."

Truth for Meditation

The wife is to be a helper who is truly meet for her husband –

1. By viewing this responsibility toward her husband as the highest calling of God for her life. (Gen. 2:18; Matt. 19:6)

2. By being a crown upon her husband's head and not as a cancer in his bones. (Prov. 12:4)

3. By submitting herself unto her husband's headship as unto the Lord. (Eph. 5:22-24; Col. 3:18; 1 Pet. 3:1-2; Tit. 2:5)

4. By reverencing her husband's individual person and leadership position. (Eph. 5:33)

The wife is to submit herself unto her own husband because –

1. The Lord our God has set the husband in the headship role within the marriage and home. (Eph. 5:23; 1 Cor. 11:3)

2. It is proper and pleasing in the sight of the Lord our God. (Col. 3:18)

3. It is the divinely established means by which she may influence her husband toward the things of God. (1 Pet. 3:1-2)

4. An unsubmissive spirit will create an occasion for the Word of God to be blasphemed. (Tit. 2:5)

The wife is to submit herself unto her own husband –

1. Willingly – with a willing spirit. (Eph. 5:22; Col. 3:18)

2. Respectfully – "as unto the Lord." (Eph. 5:22)

3. Completely – "in every thing." (Eph. 5:24)

135

Verses for Memorization

Proverbs 12:4: A virtuous woman is a crown to her husband: but she that maketh ashamed is as rottenness in his bones.

Ephesians 5:22: Wives, submit yourselves unto your own husbands, as unto the Lord.

Ephesians 5:24: Therefore as the church is subject unto Christ, so let the wives be to their own husbands in every thing.

Colossians 3:18: Wives, submit yourselves unto your own husbands, as it is fit in the Lord.

11

An Help Meet for Him
(Part 2)

The very first description that the Lord our God delivered concerning the relationship of the wife toward her husband is to be found in the closing words of Genesis 2:18 – "*And the LORD God said, It is not good that the man should be alone; I will make him an help meet for him.*" What did the Lord our God mean when He divinely described the wife as a helper who is meet for her husband? What all are the specific elements involved in a wife's being a helper who is truly meet for her husband?

In the previous chapter, we began to consider the answer to these questions; and in so doing we found four Biblical truths concerning this matter. First, the wife is to view this responsibility toward her husband as the highest calling of God for her life. Second, the wife is to be a crown upon her husband's head and not as a cancer in his bones. Third, the wife is willingly to submit herself unto her husband's headship as unto the Lord. Fourth, the wife is to reverence her husband's individual person and leadership position. In this chapter we shall continue our study in God's Holy Word concerning the matter.

Maintain Pure and Holy Behavior

In the fifth place, in considering what it means for a wife to be a helper who is meet for her husband, we find that she is *to maintain pure and holy behavior both at home and in public.* In 1 Peter 3:1-2 God's Holy Word gives instruction to wives concerning their relationship with their husbands, saying, "**Likewise, ye wives, be in subjection to your own husbands; that, if any obey not the word, they also may without the word be won by the conversation of the wives; while they behold your chaste conversation coupled with fear.**" Already in the previous chapter, we noted that a submissive spirit toward her husband's headship is the divinely established means by which the wife may influence her husband toward the things of God. In addition, we must take notice that this submissive spirit is to be demonstrated through the wife's "chaste conversation."

From the closing portion of verse 1 we learn that the wife must seek to win her husband unto obedience to God's Word "without the word" (that is – without words of instruction, correction, rebuke, or nagging), but by her "conversation." Then verse 2 reveals that this "conversation" is to be "chaste conversation." Now, this word "conversation" refers to the wife's behavior, to her entire manner of life. In the common usage of the word "conversation," we have narrowed its meaning to interaction through speaking. However, the foundational meaning of the word is "to live together." Thus the older usage of the word referred to an individual's entire manner of life and behavior. In addition, the word "chaste" refers to that which is pure, holy, and undefiled.

1 Peter 3:1-2 reveals that the husband may be won unto obedience to God's Word, not by *hearing* the wife's instructions, corrections, rebukes, and naggings, but by *beholding* her pure, holy, and undefiled manner of life, both in and out of the home. Even so, the wife serves as a helper who is truly meet for her husband as she maintains this pure, holy, and undefiled manner of life. Thus the opening words of Titus 2:5 indicate that the older women of God are to teach the younger "**to be discreet, chaste,**" etc. Purity in attitude, word, and action as the manner of her life is a necessary part of the wife's responsibility to be a helper who is meet for her husband.

How then might the wife maintain such purity in her manner of life? Proverbs 31:30, one of the concluding verses in the passage on the character of the virtuous woman, reveals the answer, saying, *"Favour is deceitful, and beauty is vain: but a woman that feareth the LORD, she shall be praised."* As the wife walks in the fear of the Lord, even so she will walk in purity of behavior. Her pure manner of life in attitude, word, and action will *flow directly out of* her daily, personal walk with the Lord her God. The first love and central focus of her heart must be upon the Lord Himself. As she abides in Him through humble dependence and surrendered obedience, then her manner of life in her marriage relationship, home responsibilities, and public behavior will be filled with the purity and holiness of the Lord Himself. Her "chaste conversation" in all things must be *rooted in* the fear of the Lord.

Furthermore, according to 1 Peter 3:2 the wife's "chaste conversation" specifically in relation to her husband must be coupled with the "fear" of her husband. *"While they behold your chaste conversation coupled with fear."* Now, the word "fear" here conveys the same idea as that of the "fear" of the Lord. It is not the fear of terror and trembling. Rather, it is the fear of respect and reverence. It is not the fear that causes one to flee from another. Rather, it is the fear that causes one to draw nigh unto another. The wife's pure behavior in her one-flesh relationship to her husband must be *accompanied by* and *rooted in* a spirit of respect and reverence toward him.

Be Adorned with a Meek and Quiet Spirit

In the sixth place, in considering what it means for a wife to be a helper who is meet for her husband, we find that she is *to be adorned with the rich and beautiful ornament of a meek and quiet spirit*. In 1 Peter 3:3-4 the instruction of God's Word continues, saying, *"Whose adorning let it not be that outward adorning of plaiting the hair, and of wearing of gold, or of putting on of apparel; but let it be the hidden man of the heart, in that which is not corruptible, even the ornament of a meek and quiet spirit, which is in the sight of God of great price."* Does this mean that the wife should never care for her hair, adorn herself with jewelry, or wear nice clothing? No, for these verses are presenting a contrast in priorities.

Certainly it is acceptable and even preferable for her husband's sake that the wife might maintain a nice, neat, and attractive appearance, and not be sloppy and slovenly in appearance. Yet the wife should not set her priority upon physical beauty or public favor. God's Holy Word declares in Proverbs 31:30, *"Favour is deceitful, and beauty is vain: but a woman that feareth the LORD, she shall be praised."* Rather, the wife should set her priority upon "the hidden man" of her heart. Public favor is deceitful; it may be here today, yet gone tomorrow. In addition, it may be given, not out of genuine respect, but out of selfish motivation. Physical beauty is vain; it does not require any real substance underneath. In addition, it can be taken away in a moment or will fade away with time. Yet true, spiritual character of heart is that which is *not corruptible*. Thus such a true, spiritual character of heart is that which the wife should pursue as her priority.

What then is the nature of this true, spiritual character of heart? The closing portion of 1 Peter 3:4 gives answer, saying, *"Even the ornament of a meek and quiet spirit, which is in the sight of God of great price."* "A meek and quiet spirit" – this is the ornament of true, incorruptible beauty. This is the adorning of "the hidden man of the heart." In addition, this ornament, this adorning of the heart, has the highest value set upon it. The Lord our God Himself considers this ornament of a meek and quiet spirit to be "of great price." Oh, how great, how glorious, how beautiful, how worthwhile is this ornament that the Lord our God Himself would value it so!

Yet what is a meek and quiet spirit? First, it is not simply an external show, but a true attitude of *heart*. Second, it is an attitude of heart that *governs* the external behavior of the life. Third, it is an attitude of *meekness* – not of selfish manipulation or abrasive demeanor, but of humble selflessness and patient gentleness. Fourth, it is an attitude of *quietness* – not self-assertive or contentious, but peaceable and harmonious. It is the spirit of one who is not pushing to get her own way, but who is ever giving up her own way for the sake of peace. It is the spirit of one who is not pushing herself forward to take the lead, but who is yielding herself to the lead of her husband. It is the spirit of one who speaks her mind less and serves her husband more. Does this mean that the wife is never permitted to express herself to and before her husband? Certainly not, for open communication is a necessary part of the one-flesh marriage relationship. Yet it does mean that when she expresses herself, she speaks, not with "*grievous words*" (Proverbs 15:1), but with "*the law of kindness*" (Proverbs 31:26).

Be Worthy of Her Husband's Trust

In the seventh place, in considering what it means for a wife to be a helper who is meet for her husband, we find that she is *to be worthy of her husband's whole-hearted trust.* Concerning the virtuous woman, Proverbs 31:10-12 proclaims, "*Who can find a virtuous woman? For her price is far above rubies. The heart of her husband doth safely trust in her, so that he shall have no need of spoil. She will do him good and not evil all the days of her life.*" In the opening half of verse 11, the key word is that word "safely." Not only does the husband of the virtuous woman trust in his wife, but he is able to do so *safely.* He is able to set his trust in his wife without any fear that his trust is unfounded. He is able to set his trust in his wife with the full assurance that she will indeed "do him good and not evil all the days of her life."

❖ First, the virtuous wife will be worthy of her husband's whole-hearted trust in the financial and material realm, "*so that he shall have no need of spoil.*" She will not overspend the money out from underneath her husband and family. Her husband will not find it continually necessary to come up with more money in order to pay the bills that she has accumulated. As a helper who is meet for her husband, she will understand his God-given responsibility to provide for the family and will help him, rather than hinder him, in this regard. The virtuous wife will willingly remain within the financial boundaries that her husband has established. Furthermore, she will not take for granted or mishandle their material possessions. She will take good care of those things that she views as "his," as well as those things that she views as "hers."

❖ Second, the virtuous wife will be worthy of her husband's whole-hearted trust with regard to their children. According to Ephesians 6:4 the father is the one who is primarily responsible for the training, discipline, and spiritual progress of the children. Yet the father is not able to be with the children every moment of the day. He is often required to entrust the care and even the correction of the children unto his wife, and the virtuous wife will truly be a helper who is meet for her husband in this realm. She will support his authority in the home and will faithfully help him to bring up their children "in the nurture and admonition of the Lord." Thus her husband will not find it necessary to counteract her ungodly, unbiblical, and undisciplined example and training of the children.

❖ Third, the virtuous wife will be worthy of her husband's whole-hearted trust in relation to her general behavior toward him. *"She will do him good and not evil all the days of her life."* She will *do good for* him and will *do good to* him from the time of their marriage until the time of death. She will be a blessing to him, and not a curse. She will not speak against him, but will speak *"alway with grace."* (Colossians 4:6) She will encourage her husband, not discourage him. She will build him up, not tear him down. She will give thanks for him, not complain against him. Her words will not be *"like the piercings of a sword"* (Proverbs 12:18), but will be *"as an honeycomb,"* sweet to her husband's soul and health to his bones (Proverbs 16:24). In addition, the virtuous wife will *stand by* her husband, submitting to him, supporting him, serving him, and seeking to be of one mind and one heart with him. She will show him affection and kindness. She will attend to his comforts and make the home to be a comfortable place for him. She will willingly and lovingly bestow much labor upon him. She will not seek her own, or be easily provoked, or think evil of her husband. (1 Corinthians 13:5) Rather, in honor she will prefer him above herself. (Romans 12:10) Even when her husband does her wrong (for every husband will), the virtuous wife will be longsuffering and forbearing toward him in love. (Ephesians 4:2) She will not be filled with *"bitterness, and wrath, and anger, and clamour, and evil speaking"* toward him, but will be kind, tenderhearted, and forgiving toward him. (Ephesians 4:31-32)

Maintain Affection toward Her Husband

In the eighth place, in considering what it means for a wife to be a helper who is meet for her husband, we find that she is *to maintain godly and supportive affection toward her husband.* In Titus 2:4 we learn, "***That they*** [the older women of God] ***may teach the young women to be sober, to love their husbands, to love their children.***" The word "love" here refers primarily to the love of affection and fellowship. Now, some might claim that it is natural and automatic for a wife to love her husband with emotional affection. Yet the very fact that this passage instructs the older women of God to *teach* the younger women of God to love their husbands thus would indicate otherwise. Yes, it is true that women are more naturally inclined to emotional affection. Yet through their sinful nature this emotional affection tends to be motivated by selfishness. For example – The wife may pursue romantic occasions with her husband, claiming that such is out of affection toward him, yet being far more centered upon how such occasions make her feel good, rather than upon how they make her husband feel. Rather, the wife must be taught and must learn to direct her affection *selflessly* toward her husband. She must be taught and must learn to direct her affection so as to support, encourage, respect, and honor her husband, his interests, and his pursuits. Yea, she must give herself to share in his interests and in his pursuits.

Be an Industrious Keeper of the Home

In the ninth place, in considering what it means for a wife to be a helper who is meet for her husband, we find that she is *to be an industrious keeper of the home.* In Titus 2:5 we learn that the older women of God are to teach the younger "***to be discreet, chaste, keepers at home, good, obedient to their husbands, that the word of God be not blasphemed.***" In this verse the phrase "keepers at home" indicates that the wife is to set the keeping of her home and household as a priority in her life. According to 1 Timothy 5:8 the husband is responsible for the providing of the household. According to Titus 2:5 the wife is responsible for the keeping of the home. Thus, in describing the character of the virtuous wife,

Proverbs 31:27 declares, *"She looketh well to the ways of her household, and eateth not the bread of idleness."* The wife who is a helper that is truly meet for her husband will take seriously her responsibility to keep the home and will fulfill this responsibility with diligence. She will not be idle in the matter, but will be industrious about the matter. She will ever be concerned that her husband and family have a comfortable, clean home environment.

Even so, in Proverbs 31:13-25 we read concerning the virtuous wife, *"She seeketh wool, and flax, and worketh willingly with her hands. She is like the merchants' ships; she bringeth her food from afar. She riseth also while it is yet night, and giveth meat to her household, and a portion to her maidens. She considereth a field, and buyeth it: with the fruit of her hands she planteth a vineyard. She girdeth her loins with strength, and strengtheneth her arms. She perceiveth that her merchandise is good: her candle goeth not out by night. She layeth her hands to the spindle, and her hands hold the distaff. She stretcheth out her hand to the poor; yea, she reacheth forth her hands to the needy. She is not afraid of the snow for her household: for all her household are clothed with scarlet. She maketh herself coverings of tapestry; her clothing is silk and purple. Her husband is known in the gates, when he sitteth among the elders of the land. She maketh fine linen, and selleth it; and delivereth girdles unto the merchant. Strength and honour are her clothing; and she shall rejoice in time to come."*

Be Wise, Prudent, and Discreet

In the tenth place, in considering what it means for a wife to be a helper who is meet for her husband, we find that she is *to be wise, prudent, and discreet in all her behavior.* Proverbs 14:1 declares, *"Every wise woman buildeth her own house: but the foolish plucketh it down with her hands."* To this Proverbs 19:14 adds, *"House and riches are the inheritance of fathers: and a prudent wife is from the LORD."* Finally, with the opening three words of Titus 2:5, we learn that the older women of God are to teach the younger *"to be discreet."* Now, the wisdom of which these verses speak is not the wisdom of this world. Rather, it is the wisdom that is from above. It is the wisdom of the Lord our God that He gives to those who walk after Him in righteousness. It is the wisdom, prudence, and discretion of God that He develops within those who faithfully read, study, meditate upon, delight in, and walk after His Word. It is the wisdom that will be *"first pure, then peaceable, gentle, and easy to be intreated, full of mercy and good fruits, without partiality, and without hypocrisy"* in its daily character and behavior. (James 3:17)

This is the wisdom, prudence, and discretion whereby the wife may build up her husband and her household. Yea, this is the wisdom, prudence, and discretion whereby the wife may truly be a helper who is meet for her husband and a precious inheritance from the hand of the Lord Himself to her husband. She will have good understanding and will exercise sound judgment in practical matters. In word and in deed she will not be careless or rash, but will be cautious and sensible. Especially in her speech, she will open her mouth with wisdom. (Proverbs 31:26) On the other hand, the foolish wife (the one who will not learn and follow the wisdom of the Lord and His Word) will tear down her husband and her household with her own character, words, and behavior. She herself will be a force of destruction in their midst. Oh, dear wives, how important it is for your husband's sake and your household's sake that you might walk in the wisdom of God!

Pursue Friendship with Her Husband

In the eleventh place, in considering what it means for a wife to be a helper who is meet for her husband, we find that she is *to pursue a growing friendship with her husband.* In a previous chapter we learned that one of our Lord God's purposes in the institution and establishment of the marriage relationship is to meet the need for human companionship. Even so, in the second half of the Song of Solomon 5:16, the wife declared concerning her beloved husband, *"This is my beloved, and this is my friend, O daughters of Jerusalem."* Just as the truth was presented concerning the husband's relationship with his wife, even so the truth is presented concerning the wife's relationship with her husband. A wife's husband is to

145

be her life-long companion and her closest human friend. She is to walk together with him throughout their days upon this earth in close friendship and intimate fellowship.

Yet such a friendship and fellowship will not just happen. It must be developed and maintained. Every day it must be pursued for growth and guarded against damage. Thus, as we have also previously learned, to develop and maintain such a growing and guarded companionship with her husband, the wife must actively pursue open communication with him, emotional camaraderie with him, a faithful commitment to him, a caring compassion for him, and an intimate communion with him. She must actively and purposefully relate to her husband as her dearest friend, spiritually, emotionally, mentally, and physically.

Take Delight in Her Husband's Advances

In the twelfth and final place, in considering what it means for a wife to be a helper who is meet for her husband, we find that she is *to take delight in her husband's loving advances toward her.* In the Song of Solomon 1:2 the wife proclaimed concerning her husband, ***"Let him kiss me with the kisses of his mouth: for thy love is better than wine."*** Again in verse 13 she proclaimed, ***"A bundle of myrrh is my wellbeloved unto me; he shall lie all night betwixt my breast."*** Yet again in the Song of Solomon 2:3 she proclaimed, ***"As the apple tree among the trees of the wood, so is my beloved among the sons. I sat down under his shadow with great delight, and his fruit was sweet to my taste."*** In the Song of Solomon 4:16, after her husband had described her as his beautiful garden, the wife offers herself to him, saying, ***"Awake, O north wind; and come, thou south; blow upon my garden, that the spices thereof may flow out. Let my beloved come into his garden, and eat his pleasant fruit."*** Finally, in the Song of Solomon 7:10-12 she offers herself to him, saying, ***"I am my beloved's, and his desire is toward me. Come, my beloved, let us go forth into the field; let us lodge in the villages. Let us get up early to the vineyards; let us see if the vine flourish, whether the tender grape appear, and the pomegranates bud forth: there will I give thee my loves."***

Truth for Meditation

The wife is to be a helper who is truly meet for her husband –

(From Chapter 10)

1. By viewing this responsibility toward her husband as the highest calling of God for her life. (Gen. 2:18; Matt. 19:6)

2. By being a crown upon her husband's head and not as a cancer in his bones. (Prov. 12:4)

3. By submitting herself unto her husband's headship as unto the Lord. (Eph. 5:22-24; Col. 3:18; 1 Pet. 3:1-2; Tit. 2:5)

4. By reverencing her husband's individual person and leadership position. (Eph. 5:33)

(From Chapter 11)

5. By maintaining pure and holy behavior both at home and in public. (1 Pet. 3:1-2; Tit. 2:5)

6. By being adorned with the rich and beautiful ornament of a meek and quiet spirit. (1 Pet. 3:3-4)

7. By being worthy of her husband's whole-hearted trust. (Prov. 31:10-12)

8. By maintaining godly and supportive affection toward her husband. (Tit. 2:4)

9. By being an industrious keeper of the home. (Tit. 2:5; Prov. 31:13-27)

10. By being wise, prudent, and discreet in all her behavior. (Prov. 14:1; 19:14; Tit. 2:5)

11. By pursuing a growing friendship with her husband. (Song 5:16)

12. By taking delight in her husband's loving advances toward her. (Song 1:2, 13; 2:3; 4:16; 7:10-12)

Verses for Memorization

1 Peter 3:4: But let it be the hidden man of the heart, in that which is not corruptible, even the ornament of a meek and quiet spirit, which is in the sight of God of great price.

Proverbs 31:10-12: Who can find a virtuous woman? For her price is far above rubies. The heart of her husband doth safely trust in her, so that he shall have no need of spoil. She will do him good and not evil all the days of her life.

Proverbs 14:1: Every wise woman buildeth her house: but the foolish plucketh it down with her hands.

12

A Christ Centered Marriage

In Ephesians 5:22-33 we find an extended instruction concerning the marriage relationship, and at the center of that instruction we find the Person of our Lord and Savior Jesus Christ. In verse 22 wives are instructed to submit themselves unto their own husbands *"as unto the Lord."* In verse 23 the truth is revealed that the husband has been divinely set in the role of headship over the wife, *"even as Christ is the head of the church."* To this the closing portion of verse 23 adds the truth that He, the Lord Jesus Christ, *"is the saviour of the body."* In verse 24 wives are instructed to submit themselves unto their own husbands in everything, even *"as the church is subject unto Christ."* In verses 25-27 husbands are instructed to love their wives, *"even as Christ also loved the church, and gave himself for it; that he might sanctify and cleanse it with the washing of water by the word, that he might present it to himself a glorious church, not having spot, or wrinkle, or any such thing; but that it should be holy and without blemish."* Finally, in verses 28-29 husbands are instructed to love their wives as their own bodies, nourishing and cherishing their wives, *"even as the Lord the church."*

Centered and Founded upon the Will of Christ

Furthermore, the immediate context of this instruction to wives and husbands reveals the need for a daily fellowship with our Lord Jesus Christ to be the foundation for a good, growing, godly marriage relationship. This immediate context begins with the instruction of verses 15-16 – "*See then that ye walk circumspectly, not as fools, but as wise, redeeming the time, because the days are evil.*" In all our daily walk, including all that involves the marriage relationship, we must proceed with great spiritual carefulness in accord with true, godly wisdom. Only by such spiritual carefulness and wisdom shall we redeem the time that we have been given from the evil of this spiritually dark world.

Yet how shall we find the true, godly wisdom necessary for such a careful walk? Verse 17 gives answer, saying, "*Wherefore be ye not unwise, but understanding what the will of the Lord is.*" This is our source of true, godly wisdom in all our daily walk, including all that is involved in the marriage relationship – *to understand and follow the will of our Lord.* Our Lord and His will must be the central and foundational element of all our daily living. Yea, such holds true for the marriage relationship, as well as for any other part of our daily living.

Guided and Empowered by the Spirit of Christ

Then to the instruction of verse 17 is added the instruction of verse 18 – "*And be not drunk with wine, wherein is excess; but be filled with the Spirit.*" In order to *understand* the will of our Lord, we need spiritual *guidance*; and in order to *follow* the will of our Lord, we need spiritual *strength.* Such spiritual guidance and spiritual strength is provided to us through the Holy Spirit of God, whom God our heavenly Father has sent forth to dwell within us as believers. (Galatians 4:6; 2 Corinthians 1:21-22; Romans 8:9; 1 Corinthians 6:19) Thus we are instructed to "be filled with the Spirit" (that is – to be under the guiding influence of the indwelling Holy Spirit of God). We must *yield* to His direction and *depend* upon His empowerment in order that we might understand and follow the will of our Lord in our daily walk.

Even so, in verses 19-21 we find the results of such yieldedness and dependence – "*Speaking to yourselves in psalms and hymns and spiritual songs, singing and making melody in your heart to*

150

the Lord; giving thanks always for all things unto God and the Father in the name of our Lord Jesus Christ; submitting yourselves one to another in the fear of God." The results of being under the guiding influence of the indwelling Holy Spirit is that we should be filled with a spirit of praise and thanksgiving toward the Lord our God and with a spirit of selflessness and submission toward one another. It is on this foundation that a good, godly marriage relationship is to be built – *centered upon our Lord and His will, guided and empowered by His Holy Spirit.*

Governed by the Word of Christ

In like manner, the immediate context of the instructions to wives and husbands in Colossians 3:18-19 also reveals the need for a Christ-centered marriage relationship. This context begins with the instructions of verses 1-3 – *"If ye then be risen with Christ, seek those things which are above, where Christ sitteth on the right hand of God. Set your affection on things above, not on things on the earth. For ye are dead, and your life is hid with Christ in God."* This context then closes with the instructions of verses 16-17 – *"Let the word of Christ dwell in you richly in all wisdom; teaching and admonishing one another in psalms and hymns and spiritual songs, singing with grace in your hearts to the Lord. And whatsoever ye do in word or deed, do all in the name of the Lord Jesus, giving thanks to God and the Father by him."*

From verses 1-3 we learn that our affections are to be "on things above" (that is – on the things of our Lord). Such indicates that the *affections* and *focus* of our hearts are to be *centered upon* the will and ways of our Lord Jesus Christ. Furthermore, from verse 16 we learn that we are to allow the Word of Christ to dwell in us richly as the governing principle of our hearts. Such indicates that the *direction* and *decisions* of our hearts are to be *governed by* the truth and wisdom of the Word of Christ. It is on this foundation that a good, godly marriage relationship is to be built – *centered upon our Lord's will, governed by His Word.*

Directed in and for the Name of Christ

Yet there is another truth. From verse 17 we learn that our entire behavior, whether in word or deed, is all to be done "in the name of the Lord Jesus Christ." Such indicates that the *words* and *actions* of our lives are to be done *with the endorsement* and *for the sake* of Christ's name. Yea, it is on this foundation that a good, godly marriage relationship is to be built – *centered upon our Lord's will, guided by His Spirit, governed by His Word, all for the glory of His name.*

Characterized by the Nature of Christ

In addition, this context includes a list of spiritual characteristics that should be a part of a Christ-centered walk, and thus also of a Christ-centered marriage relationship. In verses 12-15 we are instructed, *"Put on therefore, as the elect of God, holy and beloved, bowels of mercies, kindness, humbleness of mind, meekness, longsuffering; forbearing one another, and forgiving one another, if any man have a quarrel against any: even as Christ forgave you, so also do ye. And above all these things put on charity, which is the bond of perfectness. And let the peace of God rule in your hearts, to the which also ye are called in one body; and be ye thankful."* Just as these spiritual characteristics should be a part of our relationships with all others, even more so they should be a part of the marriage relationship.

The behavior of the husband and wife should be full of mercy and kindness toward one another, and the attitude of the husband and wife should be full of humility and meekness with regard to one another. A longsuffering spirit should rule in times of offense. Forbearance and forgiveness should be regularly and quickly granted. Godly love should encompass and fill every part of the marriage relationship, binding it together in one-flesh fellowship and unity. The peace of God should rule in the heart of the husband toward his wife and in the heart of the wife toward her husband in order that the peace of God might rule in the marriage relationship as a whole. Such is the character and atmosphere of a Christ-centered marriage – *characterized by the nature of Christ.*

In all, the Christ-centered marriage will be characterized by the mutual submission of Ephesians 5:21. In such a Christ-centered marriage, as the husband cleaves unto his wife and gives his relationship with her the place of priority, so the wife will give herself completely in service to him as a helper who is truly meet for him. Furthermore, in such a Christ-centered marriage, as the wife gives herself completely in service to her husband as a helper who is truly meet for him, so the husband will cleave unto her and give his relationship with her the place of priority. In such a Christ-centered marriage, as the husband demonstrates deep appreciation for his wife, so the wife will serve as a crown upon his head. Furthermore, in such a Christ-centered marriage, as the wife serves as a crown upon her husband's head, so the husband will demonstrate deep appreciation for her.

In such a Christ-centered marriage, as the husband loves his wife in self-sacrifice for her best benefit, so she will submit herself under his headship and leadership. Furthermore, in such a Christ-centered marriage, as the wife submits herself under her husband's headship and leadership, so he will love her in self-sacrifice for her best benefit. In such a Christ-centered marriage, as the husband nourishes and cherishes his wife, so she will reverence him with all of her heart. Furthermore, in such a Christ-centered marriage, as the wife gives reverence to her husband, so he will nourish and cherish her with all of his heart.

In such a Christ-centered marriage, as the husband seeks to know his wife as an individual and to dwell at harmony with her according to that knowledge, so she will adorn herself with a meek and quiet spirit toward him. Furthermore, in such a Christ-centered marriage, as the wife adorns herself with a meek and quiet spirit toward her husband, so he will seek to know her as an individual and to dwell at harmony with her according to that knowledge. In such a Christ-centered marriage, as the husband gives honor unto his wife, rejoices in her, and lives joyfully with her, so she will ever seek to maintain pure, wise, prudent, discreet behavior and thus to be worthy of her husband's whole-hearted trust. Furthermore, in

153

such a Christ-centered marriage, as the wife ever seeks to maintain pure, wise, prudent, discreet behavior and thus to be worthy of her husband's whole-hearted trust, so he will give honor unto her, rejoice in her, and live joyfully with her.

In such a Christ-centered marriage, as the husband purposefully seeks to cheer up and to please his wife, so she will maintain godly and supportive affection toward him. Furthermore, in such a Christ-centered marriage, as the wife maintains godly and supportive affection toward her husband, so he will purposefully seek to cheer up and to please her. In such a Christ-centered marriage, as the husband faithfully labors to provide for his wife's needs and even her wants, so the wife will faithfully labor to keep the home for his comfort. Furthermore, in such a Christ-centered marriage, as the wife faithfully labors to keep the home for her husband's comfort, so he will faithfully labor to provide for her needs and even for her wants. In such a Christ-centered marriage, as the husband remains always satisfied and ravished with his wife's love, so she will ever take delight in his loving advances toward her. Furthermore, in such a Christ-centered marriage, as the wife takes delight in her husband's loving advances toward her, so he will remain always satisfied and ravished with her love.

The Only Two Options

On the other hand, if the husband and the wife do not center their focus upon the Lord Jesus Christ, then their focus will be centered rather upon themselves. These are the only two options available – either a Christ-centered marriage relationship or a self-centered marriage relationship. Colossians 3:1-2 reveals the contrast, saying, **"If ye then be risen with Christ, seek those things which are above, where Christ sitteth on the right hand of God. Set your affection on things above, not on things on the earth."** In our daily living, including all that is involved in the marriage relationship, we seek after and set our affection either upon the things of our Lord Jesus Christ or upon the things of this world.

Now, the foundational characteristic of a focus upon the things of this world is revealed in 1 John 2:16 – *"For all that is in the world, the lust of the flesh, and the lust of the eyes, and the pride of life, is not of the Father, but is of the world."* Herein "the lust of the flesh" refers to the desire for personal pleasure; "the lust of the eyes" refers to the desire for personal possessions; and "the pride of life" refers to the desire for personal position. In a word such a focus is all about *self*.

Such a self-centered focus will only bring conflict into the marriage relationship. James 4:1 declares, *"From whence come wars and fightings among you? Come they not hence, even of your lusts that war in your members?"* Wars and fightings arise among us as the selfish desires of one individual come into conflict with the selfish desires of another individual. Yea, conflict and contention arise within a marriage relationship as the selfish desires of one spouse come into conflict with the selfish desires of the other. With such a self-centered focus the husband and the wife will strive against one another as each strives to get his or her own way. Anger and wrath will boil up with a burning heat again and again out of the husband's heart against his wife as things do not go his way and out of the wife's heart against her husband as things do not go her way. An attitude of bitterness will ever grow in the heart of each against the other; and biting, ungracious words will regularly add to the tension and division between them.

These are the two options before us. On the one hand, we can pursue a self-centered marriage relationship in which that very selfishness will be a force of contention and destruction within the relationship. On the other hand, we can pursue a Christ-centered marriage relationship in which the fellowship and character of Christ will be a force of peace and growing unity within the relationship.

Yet a Christ-centered marriage relationship can only begin as the husband and the wife each first receive God the Son, the Lord Jesus Christ, through faith for eternal salvation from sin. Each must recognize that he or she is indeed *a guilty sinner against God*. *"For all have sinned, and come short of the glory of God."*

155

(Romans 3:23) *"As it is written, There is none righteous, no, not one."* (Romans 3:10) Second, each must recognize that he or she indeed *deserves God's judgment*. *"For the wages of sin is death."* (Romans 6:23a) *"And whosoever was not found written in the book of life was cast into the lake of fire."* (Revelation 20:15) Third, each must recognize that he or she can indeed *do nothing to save himself or herself* from sin and its judgment. *"But we are all as an unclean thing, and all our righteousnesses are as filthy rags; and we all do fade as a leaf; and our iniquities, like the wind, have taken us away."* (Isaiah 64:6) *"Therefore by the deeds of the law there shall no flesh be justified in his sight: for by the law is the knowledge of sin."* (Romans 3:20)

Then each must recognize that God the Son, the Lord Jesus Christ, is *the one and only Way of eternal salvation from sin*. *"Jesus saith unto him, I am the way, the truth, and the life: no man cometh unto the Father, but by me."* (John 14:6) *"Neither is there salvation in any other: for there is none other name under heaven given among men, whereby we must be saved."* (Acts 4:12) Finally, each must *from his or her heart trust in God the Son, the Lord Jesus Christ*, calling upon Him for salvation from sin. *"For God so loved the world, that he gave his only begotten Son, that whosoever believeth in him should not perish, but have everlasting life."* (John 3:16) *"He that believeth on the Son hath everlasting life: and he that believeth not the Son shall not see life; but the wrath of God abideth on him."* (John 3:36) *"For whosoever shall call upon the name of the Lord shall be saved."* (Romans 10:13) *"For by grace are ye saved through faith; and that not of yourselves: it is the gift of God: not of works, lest any man should boast."* (Ephesians 2:8-9)

Truth for Meditation

In a Christ-centered marriage relationship, the hearts and lives of the husband and the wife are –

1. Centered and founded upon the will of Christ. (Eph. 5:15-17; Col. 3:1-3)

2. Guided and empowered by the Spirit of Christ. (Eph. 5:18)

3. Governed by the Word of Christ. (Col. 3:16)

4. Directed in and for the name of Christ. (Col. 3:17)

5. Characterized by the nature of Christ. (Col. 3:12-15; Eph. 5:21)

Verses for Memorization

Ephesians 5:17-18: Wherefore be ye not unwise, but understanding what the will of the Lord is. And be not drunk with wine, wherein is excess; but be filled with the Spirit.

Colossians 3:16-17: Let the word of Christ dwell in you richly in all wisdom; teaching and admonishing one another in psalms and hymns and spiritual songs, singing with grace in your hearts to the Lord. And whatsoever ye do in word or deed, do all in the name of the Lord Jesus, giving thanks to God and the Father by him.

Ephesians 5:21: Submitting yourselves one to another in the fear of God.

13

Love One Another

In Ephesians 5:25 the command is given, *"**Husbands, love your wives, even as Christ loved the church, and gave himself for it.**"* Again in the first half of verse 28, the instruction is given, *"**So ought men to love their wives as their own bodies.**"* Yet again in the first portion of verse 33, we find the instruction, *"**Nevertheless let every one of you in particular so love his wife even as himself.**"* Finally, in Colossians 3:19 we find the command, *"**Husbands, love your wives, and be not bitter against them.**"* In addition, from Titus 2:4 we find that the younger women of God are to be taught *"**to love their own husbands.**"* From these passages of Scripture, we learn that the marriage relationship is to be a relationship of love one to another. The husband is to maintain a sacrificial, cherishing, and nourishing love toward his wife; and the wife is to maintain a submissive, affectionate, and reverential love toward her husband.

A Command of the Lord our God

Now, it must first be understood that such a love to one another in the marriage relationship is a command of the Lord our God. For a husband to claim that he just does not love his wife any more is simply an indication that that husband is in disobedience against the Lord his God. In like manner, for a wife to claim that she just does not love her husband any more is simply an indication that that wife is in disobedience against the Lord her God.

159

This truth is confirmed by the general command of God's Word that each one of us should love his neighbor as himself. In Matthew 22:37-40 our Lord Jesus Christ presented this as the second greatest commandment of God's Law. There we read, "*Jesus saith unto him, Thou shalt love the Lord thy God with all thy heart, and with all thy soul, and with all thy mind. This is the first and great commandment. And the second is like unto it, Thou shalt love thy neighbor as thyself. On these two commandments hang all the law and the prophets.*" Furthermore, from Galatians 5:14 we learn that all of God's Law concerning our relationship with others is fulfilled in this one command. There we read, "*For all the law is fulfilled in one word, even in this; Thou shalt love thy neighbor as thyself.*" Since according to God's Holy Word the marriage relationship is a one-flesh relationship, it would be reasonable to conclude that there is no closer neighbor than one's own spouse.

So then, what all is involved in such a marriage relationship of love toward one another?

Motivated by Our Lord's First Love

In the first place, the love of the husband and of the wife toward the other is *to be motivated, not by the loveliness or worthiness of the other, but by our Lord's first love toward us.* In 1 John 4:9-11 the truth is revealed, "*In this was manifested the love of God toward us, because that God sent his only begotten Son into the world, that we might live through him. Herein is love, not that we loved God, but that he loved us, and sent his Son to be the propitiation for our sins. Beloved, if God so loved us, we ought also to love one another.*"

It is not because of his wife's love toward him that the husband is to love his wife, nor is it because of her husband's love toward her that the wife is to love her husband. Rather, it is because of *God the Father's first love* toward both that each spouse is to love the other. No, one's spouse may not always be lovely, loveable, or loving. No, one's spouse may not always behave in a manner that is worthy of love. Yet it is not the nature or behavior of the other

160

spouse that should motivate the love of each spouse for the other. Rather, the love of each spouse for the other should be motivated by God the Father's love in sending His only begotten Son to die for us sinners that we might receive eternal salvation and eternal life through faith in Him. This is our Lord God's infinite love toward us; and since the Lord our God and Savior so loved us, each spouse ought also to love the other. As long as God's infinite love remains, there is no legitimate defense for either spouse not to love the other.

Characterized by the Sacrifice of Self

In the second place, the love of the marriage relationship is *to be characterized by the sacrifice of self for the benefit of the other.* In 1 John 3:16 the truth is revealed and the instruction is given, **"Hereby perceive we the love of God, because he laid down his life for us: and we ought to lay down our lives for the brethren."** God the Son, the Lord Jesus Christ, laid down His own life upon the cross for us. In this we are able to perceive the reality of His love toward us. In like manner, the husband is able to demonstrate the reality of his love for his wife only as he lays down his life for her; and the wife is able to demonstrate the reality of her love for her husband only as she lays down her life for him. Yet this does not simply mean that each spouse must be willing to die for the other. Rather, this means that each spouse must be willing to *live* for the other. It means that each spouse must willingly sacrifice of personal interest, personal desire, personal means, personal possession, personal time, and personal effort for the sake of the other.

In this matter of love, talk is indeed cheap. Genuine love is not just about talking love. It is not just about saying, "I love you." Genuine love is also about *demonstrating* love. It is also about *sacrificing of self* in order to prove the sincerity of love. Even so, 1 John 3:17-18 continues, **"But whoso hath this world's good, and seeth his brother have need, and shutteth up his bowels of compassion from him, how dwelleth the love of God in him? My little children, let us not love in word, neither in tongue; but in deed and in truth."** As much as each is able, each spouse should give of self and lay down self to meet the needs and desires of the other.

161

Genuine love includes both an open heart of *compassion* and an open hand of *giving* toward the other. Yea, out of genuine, godly love the husband and the wife will each "very gladly spend" with an open hand of giving "and be spent" with an open heart of compassion for the other. Such is the example of love that is revealed to us in 2 Corinthians 12:15, where the apostle Paul declared unto the believers at Corinth, "*And I will very gladly spend and be spent for you; though the more abundantly I love you, the less I be loved.*" This is genuine, godly love. This is love "in deed and in truth." This is self-sacrificing love – spending and being spent for another, and continuing to do so more abundantly even when there is no return of love whatsoever. Such is the love that the husband and the wife should have and maintain for one another.

Characterized by a Longsuffering and Forbearing Spirit

In the third place, the love of the marriage relationship is *to be characterized by a longsuffering and forbearing spirit toward the other*. In the opening portion of 1 Corinthians 13:4, the truth is revealed, "*Charity suffereth long, and is kind.*" Now, the word "charity" here refers to genuine, godly love in relationship to others. In such genuine, godly love, the husband and the wife will each be longsuffering toward the other. In addition, the opening words of verse 7 teach us that charity "*beareth all things;*" and the closing words teach us that charity "*endureth all things.*"

Will friction occur within a marriage relationship at times? Will tensions and conflicts arise at times? Will the behavior of one spouse at times be annoying, aggravating, and offensive to the other? Will one spouse at times sin against the other, do wrong by the other, mistreat the other, and even be maliciously hurtful toward the other? Yes, such things will occur; for we all yield to the desires and ways of our selfish, sinful flesh at times. How then does genuine, godly love respond in such cases? It responds with a spirit of longsuffering. It will not be quick tempered and will not engage in any manner of retaliation. It will not return evil for evil. It will not return selfishness for selfishness. It will not return bad attitude for bad attitude. It will not return harsh, grievous words for harsh, grievous words. It will not return annoyance and aggravation for inconvenience. It will not return anger and retaliation for mistreatment. As 1 Corinthians 13:5 reveals, this genuine, godly love *"is not easily provoked."*

Rather, in love each spouse will bear inconveniences and mistreatments from the other with a humble, patient, sweet spirit. *"With all lowliness and meekness, with longsuffering,"* they will be *"forbearing one another in love."* (Ephesians 4:2) In genuine, godly love the husband and the wife will each restrain himself or herself from responding negatively toward the other, either in attitude, word, or action. In genuine, godly love each will refrain from taking offense at the other. In genuine, godly love each will overlook the annoyances, offenses, and wrongdoings of the other against himself or herself.

Even so, 1 Peter 4:8 gives instruction, saying, *"And above all these things have fervent charity among yourselves: for charity shall cover the multitude of sins."* In like manner, Proverbs 10:12 proclaims, *"Hatred stirreth up strifes: but love covereth all sins."* Now, this does not mean that such genuine, godly love will help another to get away with sin. Rather, this means that such genuine, godly love will cover over and not take offense at a multitude of sins *against itself.* Furthermore, this longsuffering and forbearing spirit is not just over a few, small, occasional sins against itself, but is over a *multitude* of sins against itself. Such genuine, godly love continues, enduring patiently and faithfully with humility and meekness and without anger and retaliation, although offenses may be repeated over, and over, and over again. Yea, such is the manner of one who is pursuing a loving relationship with another, even as the first portion of Proverbs 17:9 declares, *"He that covereth a transgression seeketh love."* Such is the love that the husband and the wife should have, maintain, and pursue one for another.

Characterized by Kindness

In the fourth place, the love of the marriage relationship is *to be characterized by kindness in attitude, word, and action toward the other.* Again in the opening portion of 1 Corinthians 13:4, the truth is revealed, *"Charity suffereth long, and is kind."* Day by day the husband and the wife should maintain a sweet and tender spirit toward one another. Out of that sweet and tender spirit, each should be inclined to say and do those things that would be beneficial and profitable for the sake of the other. According to Romans 13:10, *"Love worketh no ill to his neighbor."* Rather, it works only that which is good and helpful. Thus the husband and the wife should each be *sensitive and compassionate* to the interests, needs, and burdens of the other. Each should take to heart the heart concerns of the other, making them one's own.

Furthermore, the husband and the wife should each be *quick to help* the other. Each should have both a gracious spirit and a helping hand toward the other. Each should ever seek, not to serve and indulge self, but to give of self in order to serve and help the other. Even so, Galatians 5:13 presents the warning and instruction, *"For, brethren, ye have been called unto liberty; only use not liberty for an occasion to the flesh* [that is – for an occasion to self], *but by love serve one another."* In genuine, godly love the husband and the wife will each give up themselves in *service* to the other.

Finally, the husband and the wife should each *speak with kindness* to and about one another. As Ephesians 4:29 instructs, each should speak *"that which is good to the use of edifying, that it may minister grace"* unto the other. Each should speak unto the other gracious words and not grievous words, helpful words and not harsh words, encouraging words and not biting words. Each should speak words of gratitude and not words of selfishness. Each should speak with humility and meekness and not with pride and arrogance. Each should speak about the other words of honor and not words of criticism.

In addition, with a longsuffering and forbearing spirit, such kindness in attitude, word, and action should *continue* even when the other does *not* behave with kindness or respond with gratitude. In Matthew 5:44 our Lord Jesus Christ proclaimed, *"But I say unto you, love your enemies, bless them that curse you, do good to them that hate you, and pray for them which despitefully use you, and persecute you."* Now, if such loving kindness is necessary in relation to our enemies, then certainly it is necessary in the relationship of marriage.

In genuine, godly love the husband and the wife are each to speak blessing to the other even when the other speaks cursing against him or her. Each is to speak kind, gentle words even when the other speaks harsh, grievous words. In genuine, godly love the husband and the wife are each to do good to the other even when the other does evil to him or her. Each is to be kind and tenderhearted even when the other is unkind and mean spirited. In genuine, godly love the husband and the wife are each to pray for the grace and mercy of our Lord to be poured out upon the other even when the other spitefully mistreats him or her. With the longsuffering and forbearing spirit of genuine, godly love, each is to remain kind unto the other, even as our heavenly Father *"is kind unto the unthankful and to the evil."* (Luke 6:35) Such is the love that the husband and the wife should have and maintain one for another.

Characterized by Humility and Selflessness

In the fifth place, the love of the marriage relationship is *to be characterized by humility and selflessness rather than pride and selfishness.* From the negative perspective, the latter portion of 1 Corinthians 13:4 continues into verse 5, saying, *"Charity envieth not; charity vaunteth not itself, is not puffed up, doth not behave itself unseemly, seeketh not her own, is not easily provoked, thinketh no evil."* Here we find seven characteristics that are the opposite of genuine, godly love. Thus in genuine love for one another, the husband and the wife will resist and reject such characteristics in their relationship with one another.

❖ In genuine love the husband and the wife will not develop a spirit of envy concerning one another. Envy is the selfish desire to have what another has, whether it might be a possession, a position, popularity, praise, success, beauty, or ability. In time it will develop into the malicious desire that the other might lose what he or she has. It begins with the selfish attitude, "I want it." In time it develops into the bitter attitude, "If I cannot have it, then I do not want another to have it either." Yet godly love selflessly desires the best benefit of the other. Thus in genuine, godly love the husband and

165

the wife will not selfishly envy the progress and profit of the other, but will rejoice in it with the other.

❖ In genuine love the husband and the wife will not boast of self against the other. Just as genuine, godly love will not envy the other's progress and profit, so also it will not brag of its own progress and profit. Such boasting exalts self above the other. Yet genuine love selflessly prefers that the other receive the honor. Thus in genuine, godly love the husband and the wife will not each boast against the other of his or her own intellectual, educational, social, financial, or physical accomplishments, but will build up the honor of the other.

❖ In genuine love the husband and the wife will not be puffed up with pride against the other. Pride thinks of itself as being more important than the other. Yet in humbleness of mind, genuine love selflessly esteems the other to be better than self. Thus in genuine, godly love the husband and the wife will not walk in pride, but in lowliness and meekness in relation to one another.

❖ In genuine love the husband and the wife will not behave in an unseemly, insensitive, rude manner toward one another. Such behavior is rooted in selfishness, for the selfish are often so self-centered that they have no thought for the feelings and situations of others. They are inconsiderate because they are so self-absorbed that they have no time or energy to consider the case of others. They do not care enough about others to be courteous, nor do they care enough to recognize the offense of their lack of courtesy. They are not careful of the sensitivities of others because they are not full of care for others. Yet genuine love is kind. Thus in genuine, godly love the husband and the wife will not be insensitive and rude toward one another, but will take care to be considerate and courteous toward one another.

❖ In genuine love the husband and the wife will not selfishly seek for personal interests at the expense of the other's interests. Genuine love gives up self in service to the other. Thus in genuine, godly love the husband and the wife will each set his or her focus, not on the interests of self, but also on the interests of the other.

❖ In genuine love the husband and the wife will not be easily provoked in relation to the other. Being quick tempered and easily provoked to anger is also rooted in selfishness. When an individual is set on getting his or her own way, irritation and anger will quickly rise as things do not go his or her way. Yet in a spirit of self-sacrifice, genuine love is longsuffering and kind. Thus in genuine, godly love the husband and the wife will not each be set upon getting his or her own way and will not be easily provoked when he or she does not get it. Rather, in genuine, godly love the husband and the wife will be set upon self-sacrifice for the benefit of the other and will be patient, compassionate, and gentle toward the other.

❖ In genuine love the husband and the wife will not think evil thoughts concerning the other. Now, such evil thinking has two elements. On the one hand, such evil thinking begins with a meditation upon the annoyances and mistreatments that the other has committed against one's self. It keeps a mental record of such things and reviews over that record regularly. On the other hand, as such thinking upon these annoyances and mistreatments continues, one's thinking will turn to resentment, bitterness, and evil thinking against the other. In anger and bitterness it will devise ways of retaliation to get back at the other. Yet genuine love is kind, tenderhearted, and forgiving toward the other. Thus in genuine, godly love the husband and the wife will not dwell upon past offenses that the other has committed, will not develop a resentful attitude toward the other, and will not devise ways of retaliation against the other. Rather, in genuine, godly love the husband and the wife will seek to maintain, and even guard a tender spirit toward the other, *"forbearing one another, and forgiving one another."* (Colossians 3:13)

Characterized by Joy in Righteousness

In the sixth place, the love of the marriage relationship is *to be characterized by joy and rejoicing in righteousness and not in unrighteousness.* From 1 Corinthians 13:6 we learn that charity *"rejoiceth not in iniquity, but rejoiceth in the truth."* Genuine, godly love finds joy in that which is in accord with the truth of God's Holy Word. It finds joy in learning the truth of God's Word, in

167

meditating upon the truth of God's Word, and in following the truth of God's Word. In addition, it will rejoice in the growth and walk of another in the truth of God's Word. Genuine, godly love and God's holy truth are never in conflict, but always in perfect union.

In genuine, godly love for one another, the husband and the wife will not compromise God's truth for the sake of the relationship, but will ever seek to turn the relationship toward the righteousness of God's truth. Each will be quick to rejoice in and praise every step of righteousness that is taken by the other. Furthermore, each will seek to build up and encourage the other to continue in a daily walk of fellowship with our Lord. Even so, the closing line of 1 Corinthians 8:1 declares, "***Knowledge puffeth up, but charity edifieth.***" Thus each will honor the other's private time with the Lord in private prayer and Bible meditation. Finally, each will join in spiritual fellowship with the other that they might serve the Lord together. Each will pursue a relationship with the other in which they might pray together, praise the Lord together, grow in His truth together, pursue His will and righteousness together, and minister for the glory of His name together.

On the other hand, genuine, godly love never finds joy in that which contradicts God's Word and never rejoices in disobedience to God's Word, whether it might be the disobedience of self or of another. It never excuses, justifies, or glorifies any sin. It ever views any and all sin as a filthy, wicked, evil abomination and offense in the sight of the Lord our God; and it ever recognizes any and all sin as a destructive force in the life of any individual. Thus in genuine, godly love for one another, the husband and the wife will each be grieved by his or her own sinful influence and impact upon the other and will each be quick to express repentance thereof. Furthermore, each will be grieved by sin in the other, not out of concern for any offense against self, but out of concern for the offense against the Lord, out of concern for the other's spiritual departure from the Lord, and out of concern for the destruction that such sin will bring into the life of the other. Therefore, each will earnestly pray with deep burden of heart and with many tears that the other might repent and might enter into a faithful walk after the Lord in His truth.

Characterized by a Spirit of Trust and Hope

In the seventh place, the love of the marriage relationship is *to be characterized by a spirit of trust and hope toward the other*. In 1 Corinthians 13:7 we learn that charity *"beareth all things, believeth all things, hopeth all things, endureth all things."* In relation to the longsuffering and forbearing spirit of genuine, godly love, we have already considered the first and last of these four truths. Yet with the middle two truths we also find that genuine, godly love "believeth all things" and "hopeth all things."

In genuine, godly love for one another, the husband and the wife will maintain a spirit of trust toward one another. They will each resist a suspicious and cynical spirit toward the other. The husband will not expect the worst in his wife or believe the worst about his wife, and the wife will not expect the worst in her husband or believe the worst about her husband. If there is any uncertainty about the other's motivation or fault in a matter, each will believe the best possible option. In genuine, godly love each will not consider the other to be guilty until proven innocent, but to be innocent until proven guilty.

In addition, even when failure is demonstrated to be true, in genuine, godly love for one another the husband and the wife will continue to maintain hope for the future. The husband will not consider a failure in his wife to be the end of it all, nor will the wife consider a failure in her husband to be the end of it all. Rather, in genuine, godly love each will maintain a spiritual hope for the future repentance, change, and growth of the other.

Characterized by a Forgiving Spirit

In the eighth place, the love of the marriage relationship is *to be characterized by a forgiving spirit toward the other*. Concerning the matter of forgiveness, we read in 2 Corinthians 2:6-8, *"Sufficient unto the man is this punishment, which was inflicted of many. So that contrariwise ye ought rather to forgive him, and comfort him, lest perhaps such a one should be swallowed up with overmuch sorrow. Wherefore I beseech you that ye would confirm your love toward him."*

169

In the church at Corinth, a particular member had been found in sin. Biblical church discipline had been enacted upon him, and he had been separated from the fellowship of the church. This discipline had apparently been sufficient to bring this man unto repentance. Therefore, under the inspiration of God the Holy Spirit, the apostle Paul instructed them that they should no longer continue with the discipline, but should contrariwise forgive and comfort him. Then in verse 8 the apostle indicated that such forgiveness and comfort was the means by which they might confirm their love toward him. Thus we learn that a forgiving spirit and genuine, godly love are directly connected to one another. Yea, we learn that genuine, godly love is a forgiving love.

In genuine, godly love for one another, the husband and the wife will each maintain a forgiving spirit toward the other and will each confirm his or her love to the other through specific acts of forgiveness. Such loving forgiveness will graciously let go of the offense, not holding it on the record, not harboring any resentment, not taking it up again in the future, and not using it at any time as a weapon of attack against the other. Even so, Proverbs 17:9 presents the contrast, *"He that covereth a transgression seeketh love; but he that repeateth a matter separateth very friends."*

In addition, such forgiveness will graciously comfort the other by opening the way and by pursuing the process to fully reconcile the relationship with the other. Depending upon the severity of the offense, this process to fully reconcile the relationship may require some time and effort. Yet with the forgiving spirit of genuine, godly love, the offended spouse will freely open his or her heart toward the other and will fervently pursue the process of reconciliation with the other.

Characterized by an Affectionate Spirit

In the ninth place, the love of the marriage relationship is *to be characterized by an affectionate spirit toward the other.* In the opening portion of Romans 12:10, the instruction is given, *"Be kindly affectioned one to another with brotherly love."* Now, the idea of kind affection here refers to tender feeling for and warm interest in another. In genuine, godly love the husband and the wife will each develop and maintain a *fondness* and *tenderness* toward the other. Each will be held dear to the other's heart. Tenderness and affection will take root in the heart of each for the other and will ever become more deeply rooted therein. Furthermore, *displays* of tenderness and affection, in word, touch, smiles, courtesies, sensitivity, understanding, care, compassion, help, gifts, etc., will reach out from each to the other, ever knitting their hearts more tightly together in loving unity. A glow of emotional affection and tenderness will shine between them and around them, and a clear warmth of friendship and fellowship will ever grow in their relationship with one another.

Characterized by a Pure Heart and Fervent Spirit

In the tenth and final place, the love of the marriage relationship is *to be characterized by a pure heart and fervent spirit toward the other.* 1 Peter 1:22 gives the instruction, "***Seeing ye have purified your souls in obeying the truth through the Spirit unto unfeigned love of the brethren, see that ye love one another with a pure heart fervently.***" Yet again the opening portion of 1 Peter 4:8 gives the instruction, "***And above all things have fervent charity among yourselves.***" Finally, the opening portion of Romans 12:9 gives the instruction, "***Let love be without dissimulation.***" Now, the word "dissimulation" refers to that which is feigned and hypocritical. It is the opposite of a pure heart with pure, unselfish motivation. In genuine, godly love for one another, the husband and the wife will not put on a false show of love toward the other, but will maintain a pure heart and motivation of love for the other and a fervent and earnest spirit of love toward the other. Yea, each will fervently and earnestly from the heart pursue growth in all of the above characteristics of genuine, godly love.

Oh, the blessing of a marriage relationship that is founded upon, filled with, immersed in, and surrounded by genuine, godly love! It is far more valuable than material wealth and riches, even as Proverbs 15:17 proclaims, "***Better is a dinner of herbs where love is, than a stalled ox and hatred therewith.***" Yea, the closing portion of the Song of Solomon 8:7 declares, *"If a man would give all the substance of his house for love, it would utterly be contemned."* It is stronger than the tribulations and storms of life, even as the opening portion of the Song of Solomon 8:7 declares, *"Many waters cannot quench love, neither can the floods drown it."* Yea, the opening portion of 1 Corinthians 13:8 proclaims, *"Charity never faileth."* It is greater even than the virtues of faith and hope, even as 1 Corinthians 13:13 reveals, *"And now abideth faith, hope, charity, these three; but the greatest of these is charity."*

Oh, the spiritual importance for the husband and wife to walk in genuine, godly love one toward another! First, it is necessary for daily fellowship with the Lord our God, even as 1 John 4:7-8 teaches and warns – *"Beloved, let us love one another: for love is of God; and every one that loveth is born of God, and knoweth God. He that loveth not knoweth not God; for God is love."* Also the closing portion of 1 John 4:16 declares, *"God is love; and he that dwelleth in love dwelleth in God, and God in him."* Second, it is necessary for a daily walk in the light without stumbling, even as 1 John 2:9-10 warns and reveals – *"He that saith he is in the light, and hateth his brother, is in darkness even until now. He that loveth his brother abideth in the light, and there is none occasion of stumbling in him."*

Third, it is necessary for a good testimony unto the name of our Lord and Savior Jesus Christ, even as our Lord Himself declared in John 13:35, *"By this shall all men know that ye are My disciples, if ye have love one to another."* Finally, it is necessary for the spiritual profitableness of our ministry activities and family development, even as 1 Corinthians 13:1-3 proclaims – *"Though I speak with the tongues of men and of angels, and have not charity, I am become as a sounding brass, or a tinkling cymbal. And though I have the gift of prophecy, and understand all mysteries, and all knowledge; and though I have all faith, so that I could remove mountains, and have not charity, I am nothing. And though I bestow all my goods to feed the poor, and though I give my body to be burned, and have not charity, it profiteth me nothing."*

Therefore, let each husband and wife pray daily that our Lord might make them *"to increase and abound in love one toward another."* (1 Thessalonians 3:12) Then let them walk in the Spirit, yielding themselves to the guiding and empowering influence of the indwelling Holy Spirit, that He might shed abroad the love of God in their hearts and that He might produce the fruit of love through their lives. (Galatians 5:16, 22-23, 25; Romans 5:5)

Truth for Meditation

The love of the marriage relationship is to be –

1. Motivated by our Lord's first love toward us, and not by the other's loveliness or worthiness. (1 John 4:9-11)

2. Characterized by the sacrifice of self for the benefit of the other. (1 John 3:16-18; 2 Cor. 12:15)

3. Characterized by a longsuffering and forbearing spirit toward the other. (1 Cor. 13:4, 7; Eph. 4:2; 1 Pet. 4:8; Prov. 10:12; 17:9)

4. Characterized by kindness in attitude, word, and action toward the other. (1 Cor. 13:4; Rom. 13:10; Gal. 5:13; Eph. 4:29; Matt. 5:44)

5. Characterized by humility and selflessness rather than pride and selfishness. (1 Cor. 13:4-5)

6. Characterized by joy and rejoicing in righteousness and not in unrighteousness. (1 Cor. 13:6; 8:1)

7. Characterized by a spirit of trust and hope toward the other. (1 Cor. 13:7)

8. Characterized by a forgiving spirit toward the other. (2 Cor. 2:6-8; Prov. 17:9)

9. Characterized by an affectionate spirit toward the other. (Rom. 12:10)

10. Characterized by a pure heart and fervent spirit toward the other. (1 Pet. 1:22; 4:8)

Verses for Memorization

1 John 4:11: Beloved, if God so loved us, we ought also to love one another.

1 John 3:16-18: Hereby perceive we the love of God, because he laid down his life for us: and we ought to lay down our lives for the brethren. But whoso hath this world's good, and seeth his brother have need, and shutteth up his bowels of compassion from him, how dwelleth the love of God in him? My little children, let us not love in word, neither in tongue; but in deed and in truth.

1 Corinthians 13:4-7: Charity suffereth long, and is kind; charity envieth not; charity vaunteth not itself, is not puffed up, doth not behave itself unseemly, seeketh not her own, is not easily provoked, thinketh no evil; rejoiceth not in iniquity, but rejoiceth in the truth; beareth all things, believeth all things, hopeth all things, endureth all things.

1 Peter 4:8: And above all these things have fervent charity among yourselves: for charity shall cover the multitude of sins.

14

Affection One for Another

In considering how a husband is to cleave unto his wife, we learned from Ephesians 5:29 that he is to cherish her. Then through the example of the relationship of the apostle Paul to the believers at Thessalonica as presented in 1 Thessalonians 2:7-8, we learned that such cherishing includes gentleness toward his wife, an affectionate desire for his wife, the imparting of his own soul to his wife, and the holding of his wife dear to his heart. Furthermore, in considering how a wife is to be a helper who is meet for her husband, we learned from Titus 2:4 that she is to love her husband with emotional affection and intimate fellowship. Finally, in considering the nature of the love of the marriage relationship, we learned from Romans 12:10 that the husband and the wife are to *"be kindly affectioned one to another."*

A Daily Decision of the Heart

Such affection begins with the heart, *"for out of it are the issues of life."* (Proverbs 4:23) The husband and the wife must each purposefully open the affection of his or her heart to the other and must purposefully root the other therein. This is not just a matter of emotion and feeling. Although emotion and feeling will certainly be involved, this is something more. This is a *daily decision of the heart.* Day by day the husband and the wife must each decide from the heart to take the other and make the other as the dearly beloved of his or her own heart. Day by day each must allow the other to become more and more deeply rooted in the affection of his or her heart in order that the other might become more and more dearly beloved with each passing day.

Day by day the husband must purposefully set his heart affection upon his wife in order that he might ever view her as the husband of the Song of Solomon viewed his wife – as his love (1:9, 15; 2:2, 10, 13; 4:1, 7; 5:2; 6:4; 7:6), his beloved (1:16), his fair one (2:10, 13), and his dove (2:14; 5:2; 6:9). Day by day the wife must purposefully set her heart affection upon her husband in order that she might ever view him as the wife of the Song of Solomon viewed her husband – as her love (2:7; 3:5; 8:4), her beloved (1:13-14; 2:3, 8-10, 16-17; 4:16; 5:2, 4-6, 8, 10, 16; 6:2-3; 7:10-11, 13; 8:14), and the one whom her soul loved (1:7; 3:1-4).

A Tenderness of Heart

In the second place, affection one for another includes *tenderness of heart toward one another*. In Ephesians 4:32 we are instructed to be ***"kind one to another, tenderhearted."*** Now, a tender heart is the opposite of a hard heart. Such a tender heart will not push the other away. Rather, with such a tender heart the husband and the wife will each draw close to the other and will draw the other close. Each will entrust the fullness of his or her heart unto the consideration, compassion, and care of the other. Such a tender heart will not be harsh, abrasive, or contentious toward the other. Rather, with such a tender heart the husband and the wife will each be ***"peaceable, gentle, and easy to be entreated, full of mercy and good fruits"*** toward the other. (James 3:17) Each will be ***"gentle, shewing all meekness"*** unto the other (Titus 3:2) through ***"the meekness and gentleness of Christ"*** (2 Corinthians 10:1). Finally, such a tender heart will not be careless, inconsiderate, or insensitive toward the other. Rather, with such a tender heart the husband and the wife will each seek to learn and understand the individual sensitivities of the other and will be ever careful, as much as is possible, to honor those sensitivities. Each will purposefully remember, consider, and be sensitive to the other's individual sensitivities.

A Compassion of Heart

In the third place, affection one for another includes *compassion of heart toward one another*. In 1 Peter 3:8 we are instructed to be *"all of one mind, having compassion one of another."* Now, the word "compassion" basically means "suffering together in sorrow with another." The husband and the wife should each be touched in heart by the sufferings, sorrows, sensitivities, setbacks, weaknesses, and needs of the other. Each should become so knit in heart affection and unified in mindset with the other that the sufferings, sorrows, sensitivities, setbacks, weaknesses, and needs of the one become those of the other also. As Romans 12:15 indicates and instructs, each should rejoice with the other when he or she is brought to rejoicing and should weep with the other when he or she is brought to weeping. There we are instructed, *"Rejoice with them that do rejoice, and weep with them that weep."* This is "having compassion one of another" – to sympathize with the other, to be unified in feeling with the other, to be touched in heart with the feeling of the other's situation. Yea, the husband and the wife should have such heart affection for one another that each is *quick* to sympathize with the other.

Yet "having compassion one of another" includes something more than *sympathetic feeling*. It also includes *merciful action*. In Colossians 3:12 we are instructed to *"put on therefore, as the elect of God, holy and beloved, bowels of mercies."* Such feeling of sympathy and action of mercy is combined in the nature of the Lord our God, even as the closing line of James 5:11 declares, *"That the Lord is very pitiful, and of tender mercy."* Thus in Luke 6:36 the instruction is given, *"Be ye therefore merciful, as your Father also is merciful."* Yea, from James 3:17 we learn that *"the wisdom that is from above"* (the wisdom that is truly godly in nature) is *"full of mercy and good fruits."* The husband and the wife should be very compassionate toward one another, such that each is *moved* with compassion of heart to be *full* of mercy and good fruits toward the other. Each is *"to be ready to every good work"* toward the other. (Titus 3:1)

179

Now, this matter of compassionate mercy involves two elements. On the one hand, it involves the tenderness of heart to forbear and forgive the offenses that another might commit against us. This is illustrated by our Lord's parable of the unforgiving servant in Matthew 18:23-35. There we read, *"Therefore is the kingdom of heaven likened unto a certain king, which would take account of his servants. And when he had begun to reckon, one was brought unto him, which owed him ten thousand talents. But forasmuch as he had not to pay, his lord commanded him to be sold, and his wife, and children, and all that he had, and payment to be made. The servant therefore fell down, and worshipped him, saying, Lord, have patience with me, and I will pay thee all. Then the lord of that servant was moved with compassion, and loosed him, and forgave him the debt. But the same servant went out, and found one of his fellowservants, which owed him an hundred pence: and he laid hands on him, and took him by the throat, saying, Pay me that thou owest. And his fellowservant fell down at his feet, and besought him, saying, Have patience with me, and I will pay thee all. And he would not: but went and cast him into prison, till he should pay the debt. So when his fellowservants saw what was done, they were very sorry, and came and told unto their lord all that was done. Then his lord, after that he had called him, said unto him, O thou wicked servant, I forgave thee all that debt, because thou desiredst me: shouldest not thou also have had compassion on thy fellowservant, even as I had pity on thee? And his lord was wroth, and delivered him to the tormentors, till he should pay all that was due unto him. So likewise shall my heavenly Father do also unto you, if ye from your hearts forgive not every one his brother their trespasses."* A heart of compassion is a *forgiving* heart.

On the other hand, compassionate mercy involves the kindness of hand to help another in his or her time of need at our own expense. This is illustrated by our Lord's parable of the merciful Samaritan in Luke 10:30-37. There we read, *"And Jesus answering said, A certain man went down from Jerusalem to Jericho, and fell among thieves, which stripped him of his raiment, and wounded him, and departed, leaving him half dead. And by chance there came down a certain priest that way: and when he saw him, he passed by on the other side. And likewise a Levite, when he was at the place, came and looked on him, and passed by on the other side. But a certain Samaritan, as he journeyed, came where he was: and when he saw him, he had compassion on him, and went to him, and bound up his wounds, pouring in oil and wine, and set him on his own beast, and brought him to an inn, and took care of him. And on the morrow when he departed, he took out two pence, and gave them to the host, and said unto him, Take care of him; and whatsoever thou spendest more, when I come again, I will repay thee. Which now of these three, thinkest thou, was neighbour unto him that fell among the thieves? And he said, He that shewed mercy on him. Then said Jesus unto him, Go, and do thou likewise."* Such is also illlustrated by the rhetorical question of 1 John 3:17 – *"But whoso hath this world's good, and seeth his brother have need, and shutteth up his bowels of compassion from him, how dwelleth the love of God in him?"* A heart of compassion is a *freely giving* heart.

An Effort to Comfort

In the fourth place, affection one for another includes *an effort to comfort one another.* We are instructed in 1 Thessalonians 5:14, *"Now we exhort you, brethren, . . . comfort the feebleminded, support the weak, be patient toward all men."* In the ministry of comfort toward one another, the husband and the wife should each seek with loving compassion to strengthen and refresh the spirit of the other when it has been weakened, broken, and made faint by tribulation, sorrow, opposition, etc. Through a listening ear, a caring heart, a sympathetic understanding, an uplifting word, a cheering encouragement, and a helping hand, each should minister comfort to the other. In addition, each should support the other *with patience* until the other has recovered full strength in spirit. This ministry of comfort is not a momentary act, but a continuing process; and the objective of this ministry should be to edify the other – to build up the other in his or her daily walk with, joyful trust in, and faithful obedience to the Lord. In 1 Thessalonians 5:11 we are instructed, *"Wherefore comfort yourselves together, and edify one another, even as also ye do."*

Therefore, the ministry of the husband and the wife to comfort one another must find its source in God our heavenly Father. Concerning the ministry of comfort, 2 Corinthians 1:3-4 proclaims, "***Blessed be God, even the Father of our Lord Jesus Christ, the Father of mercies, and the God of all comfort; who comforteth us in all our tribulation, that we may be able to comfort them which are in any trouble, by the comfort wherewith we ourselves are comforted of God.***" God our heavenly Father is the Source of all true comfort; and in His tender mercy and compassion, He ministers that comfort to us in our times of trouble. Yet this is not simply for our own benefit. Rather, He desires that we each should then minister comfort to others in their times of trouble by the very comfort that we ourselves have received from Him. Even so, the husband and the wife should each patiently minister comfort to the other by the very comfort that he or she has received from the Lord our God, so as to encourage the other unto a closer walk with Him.

An Effort to Be Courteous

In the fifth place, affection one for another includes *an effort to be courteous toward the other*. We are instructed in 1 Peter 3:8, "***Finally, be ye all of one mind, having compassion one of another, love as brethren, be pitiful, be courteous.***" Such courtesy is simply a matter of kindness, and godly love is kind. The husband and the wife should each be courteous in manner, word, and behavior toward the other. Each should be considerate of the other and polite to the other. Each should speak words of honor, encouragement, and appreciation to the other. Each should be quick to give a helping hand to the other with a cheerful spirit. Each should be pleasant in relation to the other, rather than grouchy, cranky, snappy, irritable, disagreeable, moody, etc. Especially such courteous behavior should include regular, sincere expressions of gratitude and thanks to one another. Whether it be for special, unexpected gestures of love and kindness or for small, every day efforts and activities, each should specifically express gratitude and thanks to the other daily. Whatever efforts each may contribute to the progress of the marriage and family, whether great or small, the other should express gratitude and thanks.

A Yearning of Heart

In the sixth place, affection one for another includes *a yearning of heart toward the other*. Such yearning of heart may display itself in an earnest desire for the other's *companionship*. Even so, in 1 Thessalonians 3:6 the apostle Paul expressed his desire toward the believers at Thessalonica, saying, "***But now when Timotheus came from you unto us, and brought us good tidings of your faith and charity, and that ye have good remembrance of us always, desiring greatly to see us, as we also to see you.***" Even so also, in 2 Timothy 1:3-4 the apostle expressed his desire toward his "dearly beloved son" Timothy, saying, "***I thank God, whom I serve from my forefathers with pure conscience, that without ceasing I have remembrance of thee in my prayers night and day; greatly desiring to see thee, being mindful of thy tears, that I may be filled with joy.***" In like manner, the husband and the wife should maintain an earnest desire to be with one another and to enjoy one another's company.

In addition, such yearning of heart may display itself in an earnest desire for the other's *progress*. Even so, in 3 John 1:2 the apostle John expressed his desire concerning his well-beloved Gaius, saying, "***Beloved, I wish above all things that thou mayest prosper and be in health, even as thy soul prospereth.***" Even so also, in Philippians 4:1 the apostle Paul expressed his desire toward the believers at Philippi, saying, "***Therefore, my brethren dearly beloved and longed for, my joy and crown, so stand fast in the Lord, my dearly beloved.***" In like manner, the husband and the wife should each maintain an earnest desire that the other might prosper in his or her endeavors.

Finally, such yearning of heart may display itself with an earnest concern for the other's *burdens*. Even so, in Philippians 2:26 the concern of Epaphroditus for the believers at Philippi is revealed, "***For he longed after you all, and was full of heaviness, because that ye had heard that he had been sick.***" Even so also, in Philippians 1:8 the apostle Paul expressed his concern for them, saying, "***For God is my record, how greatly I long after you all in the bowels of Jesus Christ.***" In like manner, the husband and the wife should maintain a heart of compassion for one another.

183

Truth for Meditation

Affection for one another includes –

1. A decision of heart to make the other dearly beloved. (Prov. 4:23; Song 1:7, 9, 13-16; 2:2-3, 8-10, 13-14, 16-17; 3:1-5 4:1, 7, 16; 5:2, 4-6, 8, 10, 16; 6:2-4, 9; 7:6, 10-11, 13: 8:4, 14)

2. A tenderness of heart toward the other. (Eph. 4:32; Jam. 3:17)

3. A compassion of heart toward the other. (1 Pet. 3:8; Rom. 12:15; Col. 3:12; Luke 6:36; Jam. 3:17; Matt. 18:23-35; Luke 10:30-37; 1 John 3:17)

4. An effort to comfort the other. (1 Thess. 5:11, 14; 2 Cor. 1:3-4)

5. An effort to be courteous toward the other. (1 Pet. 3:8)

6. A yearning of heart toward the other. (1 Thess. 3:6; 2 Tim. 1:3-4; 3 John 1:2; Phil. 1:8; 2:26; 4:1)

Verses for Memorization

1 Peter 3:8: Finally, be ye all of one mind, having compassion one of another, love as brethren, be pitiful, be courteous.

1 Thessalonians 5:11: Wherefore comfort yourselves together, and edify one another, even as also ye do.

15

Communicate One with Another
(Part 1)

In considering the purpose of marriage, we learned that one reason for which the Lord our God instituted and established the marriage relationship was for human companionship. Then from Exodus 33:11 and Proverbs 27:6 & 9, we learned that open communication, including hearty counsel and loving rebuke, is necessary to develop and maintain an intimate companionship of friendship and fellowship. Furthermore, in considering how a husband is to cleave unto his wife, we learned from 1 Peter 3:7 that he is to dwell at harmony with her according to knowledge. The husband is to put forth the effort and energy to understand and be considerate of his own wife as an individual – to know her individual personality, interests, strengths, weaknesses, etc. and to be considerate thereof. Growth in such an understanding and consideration will require that he communicate with and listen to his wife. Finally, in considering how a wife is to be a helper who is meet for her husband, we learned from Proverbs 31:10-12 that she is to be worthy of his whole-hearted trust. Such trustworthiness will certainly include the manner in which she communicates to and about him.

Recognize the Power of Words

Yet the husband and the wife must take care concerning their communication with one another, for our words have a great power either to bless or to destroy. How then should they handle this matter of communication? In the first place, *they must recognize this very truth – that the words of their mouths have the power either to wonderfully develop or to utterly destroy the one-flesh unity of their marriage relationship.* The opening portion of Proverbs 18:21 declares, **"Death and life are in the power of the tongue."**

On the one hand, the words of our mouths have the power to produce *destruction and death.* In James 3:3-6 the truth is revealed, **"Behold, we put bits in the horses' mouths, that they may obey us; and we turn about their whole body. Behold also the ships, which though they be so great, and are driven of fierce winds, yet are they turned about with a very small helm, whithersoever the governor listeth. Even so the tongue is a little member, and boasteth great things. Behold, how great a matter a little fire kindleth! And the tongue is a fire, a world of iniquity: so is the tongue among our members, that it defileth the whole body, and setteth on fire the course of nature; and it is set on fire of hell."** Yes, the tongue is a little member; yet it has great power.

Just a few words of our mouths can kindle a fire that may grow into a raging inferno. Yea, the words of our mouths are able to defile our entire life upon this earth. Under the control of our sinful, selfish flesh, our tongues will be an instrument of unrighteousness and a very "world of iniquity." Furthermore, the words of our mouths are able to set on fire and burn with fierceness through every relationship of our lives. Under the control of our sinful, selfish flesh, our tongues will be a destroying fire that is ignited out of the very fires of hell. Therefore, the husband and the wife must take great care concerning their communication to and about one another, lest through corrupt, selfish words they kindle a consuming fire within their marriage relationship.

In addition, the words of our mouths have the power to pierce deeply as a weapon into the spirit of another. The opening half of Proverbs 12:18 states, **"There is that speaketh like the piercings of a sword."** Psalm 64:3 proclaims concerning those who speak bitter words, **"Who whet their tongue like a sword, and bend their bows to**

shoot their arrows, even bitter words." The closing half of Proverbs 15:4 describes a perverse, corrupt, selfish tongue as "***a breach in the spirit.***" Proverbs 18:8 describes the words of a talebearer, of those who talk negatively about others, saying, "***The words of a talebearer are as wounds, and they go down into the innermost parts of the belly.***" The closing half of Proverbs 10:11 states concerning wicked, selfish individuals, "***But violence covereth the mouth of the wicked.***" Psalm 52:4 speaks of "***all devouring words.***" Psalm 140:3 speaks concerning the deadly poison of corrupt, selfish communication, saying, "***They have sharpened their tongues like a serpent; adders' poison is under the lips. Selah.***" Oh, how violently harsh and deeply wounding our words can be!

Therefore, the warning is given in Galatians 5:15, "***But if ye bite and devour one another, take heed that ye be not consumed one of another.***" Oh, how the husband and the wife must each take great heed lest through the biting and devouring of their words, they consume one another and destroy their marriage relationship. Oh, how the husband and the wife must each take heed lest through grievous, selfish, biting words, he or she stir up anger, sow strife, and separate the one-flesh unity of their marriage relationship. Just as the closing half of Proverbs 11:11 warns that a city may be "***overthrown by the mouth of the wicked,***" even so a marriage may be overthrown by the grievous words of the husband and the wife.

On the other hand, the words of our mouths have the power to produce *life and growth*. The opening half of Proverbs 15:4 states, "***A wholesome tongue is a tree of life;***" and the opening half of Proverbs 10:11 adds, "***The mouth of the righteous man is a well of life.***" In like manner, the closing half of Proverbs 12:18 states, "***But the tongue of the wise is health;***" and Proverbs 16:24 adds, "***Pleasant words are as an honeycomb, sweet to the soul, and health to the bones.***" Thus in Proverbs 12:25 the truth is revealed, "***Heaviness in the heart of man maketh it stoop: but a good word maketh it glad;***" and the closing half of Proverbs 15:23 proclaims, "***And a word spoken in due season, how good is it!***" Oh, how wonderfully sweet and pleasantly helpful our words can be!

187

In addition, such wholesome, pleasant, wise words will help others to learn and grow, even as the closing half of Proverbs 16:21 reveals, *"And the sweetness of the lips increaseth learning."* In like manner, the opening half of Proverbs 15:7 declares, *"The lips of the wise disperse knowledge;"* and thereby the opening half of Proverbs 10:21 adds, *"The lips of the righteous feed many."* Furthermore, such wholesome, pleasant, wise words will deliver others from trouble, even as the closing half of Proverbs 12:6 reveals, *"But the mouth of the upright shall deliver them."* Thus Proverbs 20:15 proclaims, *"There is gold, and a multitude of rubies: but the lips of knowledge are a precious jewel."* Thus also the opening half of Proverbs 10:20 declares, *"The tongue of the just is as choice silver;"* and Proverbs 25:11 adds, *"A word fitly spoken is like apples of gold in pictures of silver."* Oh, how important it is that the husband and the wife each take heed to speak with such wise, wholesome, pleasant, gracious words. Oh, how important it is that each speak *"that which is good to the use of edifying"* in order that each may be used as a tool in the hand of the Lord our God to minister His own grace to the other. (Ephesians 5:29) Oh, how healthy and pleasant such a marriage relationship would be!

Recognize the Matter of the Heart

In the second place, concerning their communication with one another, *the husband and the wife must recognize that all communication is first a matter of the heart.* In Luke 6:45 our Lord Jesus Christ delivered the truth unto His disciples, saying, *"A good man out of the good treasure of his heart bringeth forth that which is good; and an evil man out of the evil treasure of his heart bringeth forth that which is evil: for of the abundance of the heart his mouth speaketh."* The words of our mouth, whether they are wholesome, pleasant, sweet, gracious, loving words or piercing, harsh, biting, grievous, selfish words, find their source in the character of hearts.

If the heart-treasury of the husband's and the wife's daily thoughts, desires, and motivations is *self-centered*, then the words of his or her mouth will be selfish and grievous in relation to the other. Even when fair words might be employed out of such a selfish heart, they will be used with deceit, being for a selfish purpose. Proverbs 26:24-25 gives the warning, *"He that hateth dissembleth with his lips, and layeth up deceit within him; when he speaketh fair, believe him not: for there are seven abominations in his heart."* Yes, fair words may be spoken; but the heart is far from graciousness and love. Yet if the heart-treasury of the husband's and the wife's daily thoughts, desire, and motivations is *selflessly loving*, then the words of his or her mouth will be loving and gracious in relation to the other.

On the one hand, concerning the communication of the individual with a proud heart, Psalm 10:7 declares, *"His mouth is full of cursing and deceit and fraud: under his tongue is mischief and vanity."* Out of the proud treasury of his or her heart, the mouth will speak harsh words, deceit, fraud, and hurtful mischief. Concerning those who *"imagine mischief in their heart,"* Psalm 140:3 reveals, *"They have sharpened their tongues like a serpent; adders' poison is under their lips. Selah."* Out of the mean-spirited treasury of his or her heart, the mouth will speak biting and poisonous words. Concerning *"a naughty person, a wicked man,"* Proverbs 6:12 states that he or she *"walketh with a froward mouth."* Then verse 14 adds, *"Frowardness is in his heart, he deviseth mischief continually; he soweth discord."* Out of the naughty and wicked treasury of his or her heart, the mouth will speak words of contention and discord. Concerning the ungodly man, the closing half of Proverbs 16:27 reveals the truth that *"in his lips there is as a burning fire."* Out of the ungodly, self-centered treasury of his or her heart, the mouth will speak grievous and angry words. Finally, concerning those who are evil, Proverbs 24:2 declares, *"For their heart studieth destruction, and their lips talk of mischief."* What his or her heart studies, his or her lips speak forth.

On the other hand, concerning the communication of the upright and righteous individual, who *"speaketh the truth in his heart,"* Psalm 15:3 declares that he *"backbiteth not with his tongue, nor doeth evil to his neighbor, nor taketh up a reproach against his neighbor."* Out of the righteous and upright treasury of his or her heart, the mouth will refuse to speak biting words to or about the other. Yet again concerning the righteous and just individual, Proverbs 10:11 reveals that the words of his or her mouth will be *"a well of life;"* verse 20 reveals that they will be *"as choice silver;"* and verse 21 reveals that they will *"feed many."* Out of the just, righteous, and upright treasury of his or her heart, the mouth will speak wholesome and helpful words. Concerning the individual whose heart is faithful in love toward another, Proverbs 11:13 states, *"A talebearer revealeth secrets: but he that is of a faithful spirit concealeth the matter."* Out of the faithful and loving treasury of his or her heart, the mouth will refuse to speak any manner of gossip. Finally, concerning the individual who *"loveth pureness of heart"* (Proverbs 22:11), the closing half of Proverbs 15:26 declares, *"But the words of the pure are pleasant words."* Out of the pure and godly treasury of his or her heart, the mouth will speak pleasant and gracious words.

The heart of the matter is the husband's heart and the wife's heart in the matter. If his or her heart attitude is right toward the Lord and toward the other, then his or her communication will be right toward the other. However, if his or her heart attitude is not right toward the Lord and toward the other, then his or her communication will also not be right toward the other. Yea, as much as the husband or the wife may attempt to conceal a wrong heart attitude toward the other, the tone of his or her communication will betray the true treasury of the heart.

Even so, the instruction is given in Proverbs 4:23, *"Keep thy heart with all diligence; for out of it are the issues of life."* Then verse 24 immediately adds the instruction, *"Put away from thee a froward* [stubborn, proud, selfish] *mouth, and perverse lips put far from thee."* As the husband and the wife each diligently guard his or her heart against any wrong attitude, and as each keep his or her heart in the way of a pure, upright, loving attitude toward the other, then and only then will each guard his or her communication against selfish and grievous words and keep it in the way of loving and gracious words toward the other. Thus in Psalm 19:14 David prayed that both the words of his mouth *and* the meditation of his heart might be acceptable in the sight of the Lord, for out of the meditation of our hearts springs forth the words of our mouths.

Yield the Tongue to the Lord

In the third place, concerning their communication with one another, *the husband and the wife must each yield his or her tongue to the Lord's control as an instrument of righteousness in His hand.* Considering that the words of our mouths have the power either for life or for death, it is necessary that the tongue be kept with a bridle under strict control. Yet such strict control of the tongue is not humanly possible. No human individual through personal ability and determination can control his or her own tongue. James 3:7-8 declares, *"For every kind of beasts, and of birds, and of serpents, and of things in the sea, is tamed, and hath been tamed of mankind: but the tongue can no man tame; it is an unruly evil, full of deadly poison."*

The tongue burns with a consuming fire that is ignited by the very fires of hell. It is "a world of iniquity." (James 3:6) The tongue is able to defile our lives and to destroy our relationships. It is "an *unruly* evil, full of deadly poison." No human individual can tame that unruly evil. Yet *"the things which are impossible with men are possible with God."* (Luke 18:27) *"With men it is impossible, but not with God; for with God all things are possible."* (Mark 10:27) Oh, what hope is this! Oh, what glorious hope is this that we may find in the Lord our God and Savior!

Certainly the husband and the wife should each join with the man of God David from Psalm 17:3 in saying, *"I am purposed that my mouth shall not transgress."* In fact, such a daily purpose of heart before the Lord our God is approved in His sight and is necessary for each to communicate aright with the other. Yet even as this daily purpose of heart is made, the husband and the wife must each recognize his or her *personal inability* to accomplish the task; for without abiding in our Lord Jesus Christ, we ourselves can do nothing. (John 15:5) Yet we *"can do all things through Christ"* when we trust in Him to strengthen us. (Philippians 4:13) Thus the husband and the wife must each join with David from Psalm 141:3 in praying each day, *"Set a watch, O LORD, before my mouth; keep the door of my lips."*

Every day, each must yield and entrust the words of his or her mouth into the Lord's hand. Every day, each must yield the powerful member of his or her tongue unto the Lord as an instrument of righteousness. (Romans 6:13) Every day, each must acknowledge the Lord and His will concerning all the ways of his or her communication, including all the words of his or her mouth and all the attitudes of his or her heart from which those words spring. (Proverbs 3:6) Yea, every day, each must join with David from Psalm 19:14 in praying – *"Let the words of my mouth, and the meditation of my heart, be acceptable in thy sight, O LORD, my strength, and my redeemer."*

Meditate upon the Truth of God's Word

In the fourth place, concerning their communication one with another, *the husband and the wife must meditate upon the truth and wisdom of God's Holy Word.* In Proverbs 8:4-8 the personified wisdom of God cries forth, *"Unto you, O men, I call; and my voice is to the sons of man. O ye simple, understand wisdom: and, ye fools, be ye of an understanding heart. Hear; for I will speak of excellent things; and the opening of my lips shall be right things. For my mouth shall speak truth; and wickedness is an abomination to my lips. All the words of my mouth are in righteousness; there is nothing froward or perverse in them."* Those who allow the truth of God's Holy Word to dwell in them richly, who make it their *"meditation all the day"* (Psalms 119:97) and choose it as the governing principle of their hearts, shall have the treasury of their hearts filled with the wisdom of God. Then out of this good treasury of God's wisdom, the mouth will speak excellent and right things and will refuse to speak froward or perverse thing. Such is the nature of God's pure and holy wisdom.

Thus the instruction is given in Proverbs 22:17, *"Bow down thine ear, and hear the words of the wise, and apply thine heart unto my knowledge."* Who then is more wise than the Lord our God, and whose words are more wise than those of His Holy Word? Oh, how every husband and wife should apply their hearts to the truth and wisdom of God's Word, and that every day! What then will be the result of such an application of the heart to the truth and wisdom of God's Word? In verse 18 the answer is revealed, *"For it is a pleasant thing if thou keep them within thee; they shall withal be fitted in thy lips.*" That to which the heart is applied will become the character of one's words. Even so, Proverbs 16:23 declares, "*The heart of the wise teacheth his mouth, and addeth learning to his lips.*" How then shall an individual find true wisdom? Proverbs 2:6 gives answer, "*For the LORD giveth wisdom: out of his mouth cometh knowledge and understanding.*" Thus Psalm 37:30 states, "*The mouth of the righteous speaketh wisdom, and his tongue talketh of judgment;*" and the opening half of verse 31 provides the reason, "*The law of his God is in his heart.*" Therefore, let the husband and the wife each set their delight in the truth and wisdom of God's Holy Word; and let each meditate therein day and night.

Truth for Meditation

In communicating with one another, the husband and the wife must –

1. Recognize the power of their words to develop or to destroy their marriage relationship. (Prov. 18:21; Jam. 3:3-6; Psa. 52:4; 64:3; 140:3; Prov. 10:11, 20-21; 11:11; 12:6, 18, 25; 15:4, 7, 23; 16:21, 24; 18:8; 20:15; 25:11; Gal. 5:15; Eph. 4:29)

2. Recognize that all communication is first a matter of the heart. (Luke 6:45; Psa. 10:7; 15:2-3; 19:14; 140:3; Prov. 4:23-24; 6:12, 14; 10:11; 20-21; 11:13; 15:26; 16:27; 22:11; 24:2; 26:24-25)

3. Yield his or her tongue to the Lord's control as an instrument of righteousness in His hand. (Jam. 3:7-8; Luke 18:27; Mark 10:27; John 15:5; Phil. 4:13; Psa. 141:3; Rom. 6:13; Prov. 3:6; Psa. 19:14)

4. Meditate upon the truth and wisdom of God's Holy Word. (Prov. 8:4-8; 22:17-18; 16:23; Psa. 37:30-31)

193

Verses for Memorization

Proverbs 18:21: Death and life are in the power of the tongue: and they that love it shall eat the fruit thereof.

Proverbs 12:18: There is that speaketh like the piercings of a sword: but the tongue of the wise is health.

Proverbs 15:4: A wholesome tongue is a tree of life: but perverseness therein is a breach in the spirit.

Proverbs 16:24: Pleasant words are as an honeycomb, sweet to the soul, and health to the bones.

Proverbs 25:11: A word fitly spoken is like apples of gold in pictures of silver.

Luke 6:45: A good man out of the good treasure of his heart bringeth forth that which is good; and an evil man out of the evil treasure of his heart bringeth forth that which is evil: for of the abundance of the heart his mouth speaketh.

Psalm 141:3: Set a watch, O LORD, before my mouth; keep the door of my lips.

Psalm 19:14: Let the words of my mouth, and the meditation of my heart, be acceptable in thy sight, O LORD, my strength and my redeemer.

16

Communicate One with Another
(Part 2)

Good communication between a husband and wife is necessary for them to develop and maintain the intimate companionship of their one-flesh relationship. Furthermore, good communication is necessary for the husband to know and understand his wife as an individual person in order that he might obey the Biblical command to dwell with her according to knowledge. Finally, good communication is necessary for the wife to be worthy of her husband's whole-hearted trust in order that she might be a helper who is truly meet for him.

Even so, in the previous chapter we considered four characteristics that should be a part of the husband's and wife's communication with one another. First, they must recognize the power of their words either to develop or to destroy their marriage relationship. Second, they must recognize that all communication is first a matter of the heart. Third, they each must yield his or her tongue unto the Lord's control as an instrument of righteousness in His hand. Fourth, they each must meditate upon the truth and wisdom of God's Holy Word. In this chapter we shall find a number of additional characteristics that should be a part of their communication with one another.

Be Quick to Listen

In the fifth place, concerning their communication with one another, *the husband and the wife must be quick to listen and pay attention to the other's thoughts, suggestion, concerns, and input.* In James 1:19 we are instructed, *"Wherefore, my beloved brethren, let every man be swift to hear, slow to speak, slow to wrath."* Generally we find it far easier in a conversation to express our own input than to listen to another's input. In addition, we find it far easier simply to ignore another's input than to listen with concentration and patience. Such behavior is rooted in our self-centered nature. Yet the Lord our God has commanded us to be *swift* to listen to the other's input and *slow* to express our own. Clearly in this matter of communication the Lord our God desires that we give priority to the practice of *listening* over the practice of *speaking.*

The opening half of Proverbs 15:28 states, *"The heart of the righteous studieth to answer."* The heart of the righteous is both wise concerning the matter of communication and considerate concerning the other's input. The heart of the righteous is diligent to listen, to understand, to consider, and *then* to respond, and that carefully, considerately, lovingly, and helpfully. The heart of the righteous is humble enough to recognize how little it really understands. Therefore, the heart of the righteous is slow to make judgment calls and express personal opinions and is more inclined to ask questions for better understanding.

Even so, Proverbs 18:13 gives the warning, *"He that answereth a matter before he heareth it, it is folly and shame unto him."* Responding before listening is the way of foolishness, whereas carefully and attentively listening before responding is the way of wisdom. Concerning the relationships of the home, Proverbs 24:3 reveals the truth, *"Through wisdom is an house builded; and by understanding it is established."* The godly wisdom of careful, attentive, and patient listening will be a necessary ingredient in developing and maintaining the one-flesh unity of the marriage relationship. However, through foolishness a marriage and household will be torn apart and destroyed; and the foolish practice of answering before listening will be a significant contributor to that destruction. Thus the husband and the wife should each be quick to listen and pay attention to the input of the other.

In fact, the husband and the wife should also be quick to seek counsel from each other, even as Proverbs 15:22 declares, *"Without counsel purposes are disappointed: but in the multitude of counsellors they are established."* In like manner, Proverbs 11:14 declares, *"Where no counsel is, the people fall: but in the multitude of counsellors there is safety."* Where a husband and wife will not seek and consider counsel from one another, their marriage relationship will be damaged. Yet in counsel with one another, the one-flesh unity of their marriage relationship may be better established and may find greater safety. Yea, Proverbs 12:15 proclaims, *"The way of a fool is right in his own eyes: but he that hearkeneth unto counsel is wise."*

Furthermore, the husband and the wife should each be easily entreated and open to correction, even as James 3:17 teaches that *"the wisdom that is from above is first pure, then peaceable, gentle, and easy to be entreated."* Even so, Proverbs 1:5 states, *"A wise man will hear, and will increase learning; and a man of understanding shall attain unto wise counsels."* Again Proverbs 15:31-32 states, *"The ear that heareth the reproof of life abideth among the wise. He that refuseth instruction despiseth his own soul: but he that heareth reproof getteth understanding."* Yet again Proverbs 10:17 adds, *"He is in the way of life that keepeth instruction: but he that refuseth reproof erreth."* Finally, Proverbs 13:18 warns, *"Poverty and shame shall be to him that refuseth instruction: but he that regardeth reproof shall be honoured."* Thus Proverbs 19:20 instructs, *"Hear counsel, and receive instruction, that thou mayest be wise in thy latter end."* Yes, the husband and the wife should each be quick to hear and receive the counsel, instruction, and even correction of the other.

Be Slow to Speak

In the sixth place, concerning their communication with one another, *the husband and the wife must be slow to speak his or her own thoughts, understandings, complaints, and opinions.* Again in James

197

1:19 we are instructed, *"Wherefore, my beloved brethren, let every man be swift to hear, slow to speak, slow to wrath."* Too often in the pride of our hearts, we think more highly of our own thoughts, understandings, complaints, and opinions than we ought to think. Too often in the pride of our hearts, we think that our thoughts must be revealed, that our understandings must be shared, that our complaints must be heard, and that our opinions must be spoken. Yet Proverbs 29:11 proclaims the truth, *"A fool uttereth all his mind: but a wise man keepeth it in till afterwards."* In like manner, the closing portion of Ecclesiastes 5:3 declares, *"And a fool's voice is known by multitude of words;"* and the opening portion of Ecclesiastes 10:14 adds, *"A fool also is full of words."* Even so, the warning is given in Proverbs 29:20, *"Seest thou a man that is hasty in his words? There is more hope of a fool than of him."*

Yet why is it so foolish to be so full of words, to be hasty in our words, and to utter all of our mind? In Proverbs 10:19 the answer is given, *"In the multitude of words there wanteth not sin: but he that refraineth his lips is wise."* Because (as we have learned in the previous chapter from James 3:6-8) the tongue is such a burning fire, such a world of iniquity, such an unruly evil, so full of deadly poison, a multitude of unbridled and hasty words will bring forth much sin and offense in the sight of the Lord our God and against others. So much of the sin that a husband and wife commit against one another involves their words and manner of communication. Therefore, they must each take great care concerning the words that they say to and about one another.

This is especially so when they express matters of anger, frustration, and complaint. Even so, the instruction of James 1:19 to be *"slow to speak"* is directly joined with the additional instruction to be *"slow to wrath."* In like manner, Proverbs 11:12 declares, *"He that is void of wisdom despiseth his neighbor: but a man of understanding holdeth his peace."* Yet again Proverbs 12:16 states, *"A fool's wrath is presently known: but a prudent man covereth shame."* A careful and considerate husband or wife will be far more inclined to hold his or her peace during such times of anger, frustration, and complaint. Whereas a foolish and selfish husband or wife will be

198

quick to express his or her anger, frustration, and complaints, and that with a despising and despiteful tone against the other. Oh, how damaging such hasty, unbridled, grievous words will be to that marriage relationship!

Proverbs 13:3 proclaims the truth, *"He that keepeth his mouth keepeth his life: but he that openeth wide his lips shall have destruction."* When the husband or the wife make it a practice to open wide his or her lips to speak all of his or her mind, such will bring much destruction into the marriage relationship. However, when the husband and the wife each keep a careful guard upon the words of his or her mouth, such will also provide a guard for their marriage relationship. In like manner, Proverbs 21:23 proclaims, *"Whoso keepeth his mouth and his tongue keepeth his soul from troubles."* Yea, the husband and the wife that carefully guard the words of his or her mouth will guard their marriage from many troubles.

Yet being "slow to speak" is not the same as being never to speak. Certainly the wise husband or wife will be slow and careful about his or her words. Yet the wise husband or wife will also speak the right words at the right times so as to *minister God's grace* unto the other. Proverbs 29:11 states, *"A fool uttereth all his mind: but a wise man keepeth it in till afterwards."* Yes, uttering *all* of one's mind is the way of the foolish. Yet there is a time *afterward* when the wise may speak the *appropriate* word. In like manner, Proverbs 15:2 declares, *"The tongue of the wise useth knowledge aright: but the mouth of fools poureth out foolishness."* Thus Proverbs 15:23 exclaims, *"A man hath joy by the answer of his mouth: and a word spoken in due season, how good is it!"* To this Proverbs 25:11 adds, *"A word fitly spoken is like apples of gold in pictures of silver."* Finally, Proverbs 24:26 states, *"Every man shall kiss his lips that giveth a right answer."*

Do Not Speak with Corrupt Communication

In the seventh place, concerning their communication one with another, *the husband and the wife must not speak with any corrupt communication toward the other.* In the opening portion of Ephesians

199

4:29 we are instructed, *"Let no corrupt communication proceed out of your mouth."* So then, what all is encompassed under the category of "corrupt communication"? The term "corrupt" simply refers to that which is not of good use, to that which is worthless, offensive, or even harmful.

Certainly taking the name of the Lord our God in vain and speaking reproachfully against the Lord our God would be included therein. Concerning the wicked Psalm 139:20 states, *"For they speak against thee wickedly, and thine enemies take thy name in vain."* Such not only is a sinful offense against the Lord our God, but also a spiritual hindrance to those who hear. In addition, the filthy communication of vulgar and obscene language would be included therein. In Colossians 3:8 the instruction is given, *"But now ye also put off all these; anger, wrath, malice, blasphemy, filthy communication out of your mouth."*

Cursing and bitter words against another would also be a part of corrupt communication, even as Romans 3:13-14 reveals, *"Their throat is an open sepulchre; with their tongues they have used deceit; the poison of asps is under their lips: whose mouth is full of cursing and bitterness."* The words of pride, haughtiness, and boasting would also be in this category. Psalm 73:8 describes the speech of the corrupt and wicked, saying, *"They are corrupt, and speak wickedly concerning oppression: they speak loftily."* To this the opening half of Proverbs 14:3 adds, *"In the mouth of the foolish is a rod of pride."* Thus in Psalm 12:3 the judgment is pronounced, *"The LORD shall cut off all flattering lips, and the tongue that speaketh proud things."*

Grievous words that are harsh, hurtful and stir up anger (Proverbs 15:1), contentious words that produce strife and discord (Proverbs 6:14, 19; 16:28; 18:6), froward and perverse words that are selfish, willful, stubborn, and contrary to the truth and righteousness of God (Proverbs 2:12-15; 4:24; 6:12; 8:13; 10:32; 15:4, 28; 16:30; 17:20; 19:1; 24:1-2), piercing words that are harsh, biting, malicious, and violent (Psalm 57:4; 64:2-4; Proverbs 10:11; 12:6, 18; 16:27; Galatians 5:15; 3 John 1:10), foolish words that are to no profit, but only for the sake of attention (Proverbs 10:8, 14; 12:23; 14:7; 15:2; Ephesians 5:4), jesting words that are cutting, discouraging, and dishonoring (Ephesians 5:4) – All of these are to be classified as corrupt communication. No such corrupt communication is to have any place in the relationship of the husband and the wife with one another. Yea, no such corrupt communication is ever to proceed out of the mouth of either one against the other.

Do Not Speak with Backbiting Communication

In the eighth place, concerning their communication with one another, *the husband and the wife must not speak with any backbiting communication about one another.* This also is a form of corrupt communication. Yet it is not corrupt communication that is spoken to the other. Rather, it is corrupt communication and evil speaking that is spoken *about* the other. In 1 Peter 2:1 we are instructed to be *"laying aside all malice, and all guile, and hypocrisies, and envies, and all evil speakings."* In like manner, Ephesians 4:31 gives the instruction, *"Let all bitterness, and wrath, and anger, and clamour, and evil speaking, be put away from you, with all malice."*

Oh, how destructive a backbiting tongue can be to the one-flesh unity of a marriage relationship, even as Proverbs 16:28 warns, *"A froward man soweth strife: and a whisperer separateth chief friends."* Yea, a whispering, backbiting tongue will even separate the chief union of a marriage. Oh, how deeply the husband or the wife might wound the spirit of the other through backbiting words, even as Proverbs 26:22 warns, *"The words of a talebearer are as wounds, and they go down into the innermost parts of the belly."* Oh, how much strife is kindled and stirred up in a marriage relationship through the backbiting of one against the other, even as Proverbs 26:20 reveals, *"Where no wood is, there the fire goeth out: so where there is no talebearer, the strife ceaseth."* Yet as each additional piece of wood will intensify the fire, so each additional word of backbiting will increase the strife.

On the other hand, the faithful, prudent, loving husband and wife will each refrain from any form of backbiting about the other. Proverbs

11:13 declares, *"A talebearer revealeth secrets: but he that is faithful concealeth the matter."* Again Proverbs 12:23 reveals, *"A prudent man concealeth knowledge: but the heart of fools proclaimeth foolishness."* Yet again Proverbs 17:9 proclaims, *"He that covereth a transgression seeketh love; but he that repeateth a matter separateth very friends."* Repeating negative matters of frustration and complaint about the other to someone else will only separate the one-flesh relationship of the marriage. Thus in faithful love and prudent consideration toward one another, the husband and the wife should conceal and cover over such negative matters. Yea, such matters must remain the secrets of *a loving heart*, rather than the substance of *a backbiting tongue*.

Do Not Speak with Dishonest Communication

In the ninth place, concerning their communication with one another, *the husband and the wife must not speak with any dishonest communication to or about the other*. In Ephesians 4:25 we are instructed, *"Wherefore putting away lying, speak every man truth with his neighbor: for we are members one of another."* Yea, in the context of the marriage relationship, let the husband and the wife speak truth with one another for they are *one-flesh* with one another. In like manner, 1 Peter 3:10 proclaims, *"For he that will love life, and see good days, let him refrain his tongue from evil, and his lips that they speak no guile."* Yea, the husband and the wife that will love their marriage relationship and see good days therein, let them also refrain their tongues from evil and see that they speak no guile. Thus in the closing portion of Proverbs 24:28 the instruction is given, *"And deceive not with thy lips."*

Deceitfulness and lying is the way of the wicked. The opening portion of Psalm 10:5 describes the mouth of the wicked, saying, *"His mouth is full of cursing and deceit and fraud."* Again the opening portion of Psalm 36:3 describes the words of the wicked, saying, *"The words of his mouth are iniquity and deceit."* Yet again Psalm 50:19 gives rebuke to the wicked, saying, *"Thou givest thy mouth to evil, and thy tongue frameth deceit."* Finally, the opening half of Proverbs 12:20 declares, *"Deceit is in the heart of them that imagine evil."*

Even when such individuals employ fair and flattering words, they cannot be trusted; for they employ these fair and flattering words with a double heart. Their words may appear to be with loving-kindness, yet they are actually with benefit to self and with damage to the other. In Psalm 12:2 the wicked are described, *"They speak vanity every one with his neighbor: with flattering lips and with a double heart do they speak."* Thus Proverbs 26:24-25 gives warning, *"He that hateth dissembleth with his lips, and layeth up deceit within him; when he speaketh fair, believe him not: for there are seven abominations in his heart."* To this the closing half of Proverbs 27:6 adds, *"But the kisses of an enemy are deceitful."*

Certainly such is not the way of a loving and faithful husband and wife who are ever seeking to strengthen their one-flesh relationship together. Yea, Proverbs 26:28 reveals that deceitfulness, lying, and flattery are the way of hatred, not of love, and the way to ruin a marriage relationship, not to strengthen it. There we read, *"A lying tongue hateth those that are afflicted by it; and a flattering mouth worketh ruin."* In like manner, Psalm 52:2-4 describes deceitfulness as sharp and devouring, saying, *"Thy tongue deviseth mischief; like a sharp razor, working deceitfully. Thou lovest evil more than good; and lying rather than to speak righteousness. Selah. Thou lovest all devouring words, O thou deceitful tongue."* Again Proverbs 25:18 proclaims, *"A man that beareth false witness against his neighbor is a maul, and a sword, and a sharp arrow."* Yet again the opening half of Proverbs 11:9 states, *"An hypocrite with his mouth destroyeth his neighbor."* Oh, how much damage might a husband or wife do unto the other through lying and deceitfulness! Oh, how much destruction might they bring upon their marriage relationship!

Even so, the wrath and judgment of the Lord our God will be poured out upon all such corrupt communication and deceitfulness. From Proverbs 6:16-19 we learn that a lying tongue, a false witness, and one that sows discord within a relationship are a hateful abomination in the sight of the Lord our God. In like manner, Proverbs 12:22 proclaims, *"Lying lips are abomination to the LORD: but they that deal truly are his delight."* Concerning those who are deceitful,

203

Psalm 5:6 declares, *"Thou shalt destroy them that speak leasing* [falsehood]*: the LORD will abhor the bloody and deceitful man."* Yea, to those of a deceitful tongue, Psalm 52:5 gives warning, *"God shall likewise destroy thee for ever, he shall take thee away, and pluck thee out of thy dwelling place, and root thee out of the land of the living. Selah."* Thus Proverbs 19:5 warns, *"A false witness shall not be unpunished, and he that speaketh lies shall not escape;"* and Proverbs 12:19 adds, *"The lip of truth shall be established for ever: but a lying tongue is but for a moment."*

Furthermore, Psalm 12:3-4 proclaims, *"The LORD shall cut off all flattering lips, and the tongue that speaketh proud things: who have said, With our tongue will we prevail; our lips are our own: who is lord over us?"* In like manner, Proverbs 22:12 declares, *"The eyes of the LORD preserve knowledge, and he overthroweth the words of the transgressor."* Concerning the froward and perverse tongue, Proverbs 17:20 warns, *"He that hath a froward heart findeth no good: and he that hath a perverse tongue falleth into mischief."* The closing half of Proverbs 10:31 adds, *"But the froward tongue shall be cut out."* Concerning those who shoot forth bitter words like piercing arrows, Psalm 64:7-8 proclaims, *"But God shall shoot at them with an arrow; suddenly shall they be wounded. So they shall make their own tongue to fall upon themselves: all that see them shall flee away."* Even so, the opening half of Proverbs 12:13 declares, *"The wicked is snared by the transgression of his lips."*

Now, from such judgments there can be no escape; for the Lord our God hears and knows every word that we speak. Yea, Psalm 139:4 reveals the truth, saying, *"For there is not a word in my tongue, but, lo, O LORD, thou knowest it altogether."* In addition, our Lord Jesus Christ gave warning in Matthew 12:36, *"But I say unto you, That every idle word that men shall speak, they shall give account thereof in the day of judgment."* Therefore, concerning every word of corrupt communication that has proceeded out of our mouths, we should join with the prophet Isaiah in brokenhearted confession and repentance, saying, *"Woe is me! For I am undone; because I am a man of unclean lips."* (Isaiah 6:5) Yea, the husband and the wife must acknowledge all corrupt communication and deceitfulness as the sinful abomination that it is in the sight of the Lord our God. They each must seek His forgiveness and cleansing thereof, and they each must seek the forgiveness of the other for any corrupt communication spoken against the other.

Speak Edifying Words that Minister God's Grace

In the tenth and final place, concerning their communication with one another, *the husband and the wife must speak edifying words that minister God's grace to the other.* In Ephesians 4:29 we are instructed, **"Let no corrupt communication proceed out of your mouth, but that which is good to the use of edifying, that it may minister grace to the hearers."** So then, what all is encompassed under the category of "good to the use of edifying"? Good communication is that which is useful for edifying, for building up the other spiritually. It is that which draws the other closer to the Lord our God and that which ministers our Lord God's grace to the other.

First, exalting the name of our Lord, praising the works of our Lord, and honoring the truth of our Lord would be included therein. The man of God David expressed his commitment in Psalm 34:1-2, saying, **"I will bless the LORD at all times: his praise shall continually be in my mouth. My soul shall make her boast in the LORD: the humble shall hear thereof, and be glad."** Again in Psalm 145:5 he expressed his commitment, **"I will speak of the glorious honour of thy majesty, and of thy wondrous works."** In Psalm 89:1 the psalmist Ethan expressed his commitment, saying, **"I will sing of the mercies of the LORD for ever: with my mouth will I make known thy faithfulness to all generations."** In Psalm 71:15-16 the commitment is expressed, **"My mouth shall shew forth thy righteousness and thy salvation all the day; for I know not the numbers thereof. I will go in the strength of the Lord GOD: I will make mention of thy righteousness, even of thine only."** Yet again in Psalm 119:172 the commitment is expressed, **"My tongue shall speak of thy word: for all thy commandments are righteousness."**

Gracious words that are motivated by a loving, gracious spirit and that minister grace unto the other's spirit would also be a part of good communication. Colossians 4:6 gives the instruction, "***Let your speech be alway with grace, seasoned with salt, that ye may know how ye ought to answer every man.***" Such is the character of the wise man's words, even as the opening portion of Ecclesiastes 10:12 reveals, "***The words of a wise man's mouth are gracious.***" Pleasant words that are rooted in purity and that encourage the other's spirit are a part thereof. Proverbs 15:26 declares, "***The thoughts of the wicked are an abomination to the LORD: but the words of the pure are pleasant words.***" Again Proverbs 16:24 proclaims, "***Pleasant words are as an honeycomb, sweet to the soul, and health to the bones.***"

Soft, gentle words that turn away anger and promote peace (Proverbs 12:20; 15:1; 31:26), sweet words that enhance and encourage learning (Proverbs 16:21), wholesome words that comfort and encourage (Proverbs 12:25; 15:4), wise words that counsel and guide according to God's truth and wisdom (Psalm 37:30-31; Proverbs 10:13, 31; 31:26), truthful words that are without lying or deceit (Proverbs 12:17, 19, 22; 13:5; 14:5) – All of these are to be classified as a part of good communication. Finally, such good communication would include hearty counsel and loving correction. Even so, Proverbs 27:9 declares, "***Ointment and perfume rejoice the heart: so doth the sweetness of a man's friend by hearty counsel.***" Furthermore, Proverbs 27:5 states, "***Open rebuke is better than secret love;***" and the opening half of verse 6 adds, "***Faithful are the wounds of a friend.***" Such is the manner of communication that is *always* to proceed out of the mouth of the husband and the wife toward one another.

Truth for Meditation

In communicating with one another, the husband and the wife must –

(From Chapter 15)

1. Recognize the power of their words to develop or to destroy their marriage relationship. (Prov. 18:21; Jam. 3:3-6; Psa. 52:4; 64:3; 140:3; Prov. 10:11, 20-21; 11:11; 12:6, 18, 25; 15:4, 7, 23; 16:21, 24; 18:8; 20:15; 25:11; Gal. 5:15; Eph. 4:29)

2. Recognize that all communication is first a matter of the heart. (Luke 6:45; Psa. 10:7; 15:2-3; 19:14; 140:3; Prov. 4:23-24; 6:12, 14; 10:11; 20-21; 11:13; 15:26; 16:27; 22:11; 24:2; 26:24-25)

3. Yield his or her tongue to the Lord's control as an instrument of righteousness in His hand. (Jam. 3:7-8; Luke 18:27; Mark 10:27; John 15:5; Phil. 4:13; Psa. 141:3; Rom. 6:13; Prov. 3:6; Psa. 19:14)

4. Meditate upon the truth and wisdom of God's Holy Word. (Prov. 8:4-8; 22:17-18; 16:23; Psa. 37:30-31)

(From Chapter 16)

5. Be quick to listen and pay attention to the other's thoughts, suggestions, concerns, and input. (Jam. 1:19; 3:17; Prov. 1:5; 10:17; 11:14; 12:15; 13:18; 15:22, 28, 31-32; 18:13; 19:20)

6. Be slow to speak his or her own thoughts, understandings, complaints, and opinions. (Jam. 1:19; Prov. 11:12; 12:16; 13:3; 15:2; 21:23; 29:11, 20; Eccl. 5:3; 10:14)

7. Not speak with any corrupt communication toward the other. (Eph. 4:29; Psa. 12:3; 57:4; 64:2-4; 73:8; 139:20; Prov. 2:12-15; 4:24; 6:12, 14, 19; 8:13; 10:8, 11, 14, 32; 12:6, 18, 23; 14:3, 7; 15:1-2, 4, 28; 16:27-28, 30; 17:20; 18:6; 19:1; 24:1-2; Rom. 3:13-14; Gal. 5:15; Eph. 5:4; Col. 3:8; 3 John 1:10)

8. Not speak with any backbiting communication about the other. (Eph. 4:31; 1 Pet. 2:1; Prov. 11:13; 12:23; 17:9; 16:28; 26:20, 22)

207

9. Not speak with any dishonest communication to or about the other. (Eph. 5:25; 1 Pet. 3:10; Psa. 10:5; 12:2; 36:3; 50:19; 52:2-4; Prov. 11:9; 12:20; 24:28; 25:18; 26:24-25, 28; 27:6)

10. Speak edifying words that minister God's grace to the other. (Eph. 4:29; Psa. 34:1-2; 37:30-31; 71:15-16; 89:1; 119:172; 145:5; Prov. 10:13, 31; 12:17, 19-20, 22, 25; 13:5; 14:5; 15:1, 4, 26; 16:21, 24; 27:5-6, 9; 31:26; Eccl. 10:12; Col. 4:6)

Verses for Memorization

James 1:19: Wherefore, my beloved brethren, let every man be swift to hear, slow to speak, slow to wrath.

Proverbs 18:13: He that answereth a matter before he heareth it, it is folly and shame unto him.

Proverbs 10:19: In the multitude of words there wanteth not sin: but he that refraineth his lips is wise.

Ephesians 4:29: Let no corrupt communication proceed out of your mouth, but that which is good to the use of edifying, that it may minister grace unto the hearers.

Proverbs 17:9: He that covereth a transgression seeketh love; but he that repeateth a matter separateth very friends.

Psalm 34:1: I will bless the LORD at all times: his praise shall continually be in my mouth.

Psalm 119:172: My tongue shall speak of thy word: for all thy commandments are righteousness.

Colossians 4:6: Let your speech be alway with grace, seasoned with salt, that ye may know how ye ought to answer every man.

17

Confess One to Another

In considering the responsibility that the Lord our God has set before each husband and wife in their relationship together, it is to be recognized that failure will occur. In fact, the husband and the wife who honestly and humbly examine themselves in accord with our Lord's standard will find that they often fall short and fail in their responsibility toward one another. Furthermore, it must be recognized that such falling short and failure is a sin against our Lord and against the other; for disobedience to any command of our Lord is sin.

What then is to be done about this sinful failure? The answer of God's Holy Word is the practice of *confession*. Concerning sin against the Lord our God, 1 John 1:9 reveals the provision and the promise, *"If we confess our sins, he is faithful and just to forgive us our sins, and to cleanse us from all unrighteousness."* In addition, concerning sin against one another, the opening portion of James 5:16 instructs, *"Confess your faults one to another."* Thus in their marriage relationship the husband and the wife are to confess the sinful failures that they have committed against one another – first to the Lord our God for His forgiveness and cleansing and then to one another for the forgiveness of the other and for reconciliation with the other. In fact, our Lord has even set confession and reconciliation as a higher priority than public worship. In Matthew 5:23-24 He declared, *"Therefore if thou bring thy gift to the altar* [an act of worship], *and there rememberest that thy brother hath ought against thee; leave there thy gift before the altar, and go thy way; first be reconciled to thy brother, and then come and offer thy gift."*

What then is involved in this matter of confession?

Be Open and Humble to Receive Correction

In the first place, the husband and the wife *must be open and humble in heart to receive conviction and correction.* The Biblical truth is that there is no one upon this earth who does not commit sin against God and against others. (1 Kings 8:46; Ecclesiastes 7:20) In fact, James 3:2 reveals that only a perfect individual does not commit sin with the words of his or her mouth. Even so, if we make the claim that we have not and do not commit sin, 1 John 1:8 declares that *"we deceive ourselves, and the truth is not in us."* Yes, we all regularly commit sin in attitude, word, and action against God and against others. Thus we all should humbly maintain an open ear to the counsels and corrections of others and an open heart to the conviction of the indwelling Holy Spirit through the truth of God's Holy Word. More specifically each husband and wife regularly commits sin in attitude, word, and action against God and against each other. Thus each husband and wife should humbly maintain an open ear to the counsels and corrections of the other and an open heart to the convictions of the indwelling Holy Spirit through the truth of God's Holy Word.

It is the spiritual fool who refuses to consider counsel and correction. In pride of heart, he or she believes that his or her way is certainly right and cannot possibly be wrong. Thus in the pride of his or her heart, the spiritual fool does not recognize any need for outside counsel or correction. On the other hand, the opening portion of Proverbs 1:5 proclaims, *"A wise man will hear, and will increase learning."* In humility of heart, the spiritually wise individual recognizes that he or she has not yet attained unto perfect understanding, perfect maturity, or perfect righteousness. In humility of heart, he or she recognizes how little is actually known and understood and how much growth in maturity and righteousness is yet necessary. Thus the spiritually wise individual is ever pursuing growth and is ever open to hear and consider any counsel or correction that might aid in such growth. Even so, Proverbs 12:15 informs us, saying, *"The way of a fool is right in his own eyes: but he that hearkeneth unto counsel is wise."* In addition, Proverbs 26:12 warns, *"Seest thou a man wise in his own conceit? There is more hope of a fool than of him."* Specifically then, in humility of heart the spiritually wise husband or wife will be open to receive the counsels and corrections of the other. Whereas the Lord our God defines a husband or wife who refuses such counsel and correction as an arrogant fool.

Furthermore, an individual's response to the corrections of God's Word and the convictions of God's Spirit will determine that individual's daily fellowship with our Lord Himself. According to 2 Timothy 3:16 the Lord our God has given us His Holy Word to be profitable unto us *"for doctrine"* – to teach us what is right, *"for reproof"* – to convict us where we are not right, *"for correction"* – to reveal how we might make things right, and *"for instruction in righteousness"* – to train us up in living right. Then according to verse 17 all of this doctrine, reproof, correction, and instruction is for the purpose that the man or woman of God might be brought to perfect spiritual maturity and might be completely developed in the practice of every good work.

In addition, Hebrews 4:12 speaks concerning the convicting work of God's Word, saying, *"For the word of God is quick, and powerful, and sharper than any twoedged sword, piercing even to the dividing asunder of soul and spirit, and of the joints and marrow, and is a discerner of the thoughts and intents of the heart."* As employed by God's Holy Spirit, the Spirit of truth, God's Holy Word is able to pierce us to the very depths of our hearts, discerning the character of our very thoughts, desires, motivations, and priorities. Now, all of this holds true for the husband and the wife in their marriage relationship as well as in any other area of their lives. If they will humbly receive it, the conviction and correction of God's true and holy Word will help the husband and the wife to grow in their relationship with God and with one another.

211

Thus Proverbs 3:11-12 gives the instruction, *"My son, despise not the chastening of the LORD; neither be weary of his correction: for whom the LORD loveth he correcteth; even as a father the son in whom he delighteth."* Even so, the personified wisdom of God cries forth in Proverbs 1:23, saying, *"Turn you at my reproof: behold, I will pour out my spirit unto you, I will make known my words unto you."* If we will hear and heed the reproofs of God's Word and wisdom, we will learn and be filled with that Word and wisdom.

To those who refuse the counsel and reject the reproofs of that Word and wisdom, verses 24-31 give warning, *"Because I have called, and ye refused; I have stretched out my hand, and no man regarded; but ye have set at nought all my counsel, and would none of my reproof: I also will laugh at your calamity; I will mock when your fear cometh; when your fear cometh as desolation, and your destruction cometh as a whirlwind; when distress and anguish cometh upon you. Then shall they call upon me, but I will not answer; they shall seek me early, but they shall not find me: for that they hated knowledge, and did not choose the fear of the LORD: they would none of my counsel: they despised all my reproof. Therefore shall they eat of the fruit of their own way, and be filled with their own devices."*

On the other hand, to those who will receive the counsel and reproofs of God's Word and wisdom, the promise is given in verse 33, *"But whoso heakeneth unto me shall dwell safely, and shall be quiet from fear of evil."* In like manner, Proverbs 8:33-35 pronounces the blessing, *"Hear instruction, and be wise, and refuse it not. Blessed is the man that heareth me, watching daily at my gates, waiting at the posts of my doors. For whoso findeth me findeth life, and shall obtain favour of the LORD."*

Thus Proverbs 10:17 states, *"He is in the way of life that keepeth instruction: but he that refuseth reproof erreth."* More specifically the husband and the wife who are open and humble in heart to receive conviction and correction shall have a good, godly, growing marriage relationship. Yet a husband or wife who refuses conviction and correction shall move his or her marriage down the path of error and destruction. In addition, Proverbs 12:1 proclaims, *"**Whoso loveth instruction loveth knowledge: but he that hateth reproof is brutish.**"* More specifically the husband and the wife who are open and humble in heart, not only to receive, but also to seek for and delight in the wisdom of conviction and correction, reveal their desire to grow in a right relationship with one another. Yet a husband or wife who rejects and resists conviction and correction reveals that he or she is utterly foolish and completely ignorant concerning a good marriage relationship.

In like manner, Proverbs 15:31-32 declares, *"**The ear that heareth the reproof of life abideth among the wise. He that refuseth instruction despiseth his own soul: but he that heareth reproof getteth understanding.**"* To this Proverbs 13:18 adds, *"**Poverty and shame shall be to him that refuseth instruction: but he that regardeth reproof shall be honoured.**"* More specifically the husband and the wife who are open and humble in heart to receive conviction and correction shall develop understanding in their relationship with one another and shall build a marriage relationship that is honored by God and others. However, a husband or wife who refuses conviction and correction despises his or her own marriage relationship and shall bring it to shame. Finally, Proverbs 29:1 warns, *"**He, that being often reproved hardeneth his neck, shall suddenly be destroyed, and that without remedy.**"* Such a husband or wife shall bring severe destruction upon his or her marriage relationship.

Acknowledge the Reality and Wickedness of Your Sin

In the second place, the husband and the wife *must acknowledge the reality and wickedness of their sin against one another*. In 1 John 1:9 and James 5:16 the verb "confess" basically means "to say the same thing." Concerning the confession of our sin unto the Lord our God, it means that we must come to full agreement with Him that a given attitude, word, or action was indeed a sin against Him and was a wicked abomination in His sight. Concerning the confession of our sin unto one another, it means that we must fully acknowledge to the other that a given attitude, word, or action was indeed a sin against him or her and was a harmful offense to him or her.

In the opening portion of Isaiah 1:18 the Lord instructed His people Israel concerning their sin, saying, *"Come now, and let us reason together, saith the LORD."* They were to come together and reason together with the Lord until He and they had come to an agreement about their sin. Now, since the Lord our God always abides on the ground of absolute truth and will never compromise that truth, coming to an agreement with Him means coming to *His perspective* against our sin. It means *joining with Him in accusation* against the wicked, evil offense and abomination of our sin. Thus in the opening portion of Psalm 32:5, David confessed unto the Lord, *"I acknowledge my sin unto thee, and mine iniquity have I not hid."* He would no longer seek to ignore the truth of his sin or seek to hide it with excuses and deceptions. Rather, he acknowledged his sin and the iniquity thereof.

In Psalm 106:6 the psalmist confessed unto the Lord concerning himself and his people, saying, *"We have sinned with our fathers, we have committed iniquity, we have done wickedly."* Again in Jeremiah 14:20 the prophet Jeremiah confessed, *"We acknowledge, O LORD, our wickedness, and the iniquity of our fathers: for we have sinned against thee."* Yet again in Nehemiah 1:6-7 the man of God Nehemiah confessed, *"Let thine ear now be attentive, and thine eyes open, that thou mayest hear the prayer of thy servant, which I pray before thee now, day and night, for the children of Israel thy servants, and confess the sins of the children of Israel, which we have sinned against thee: both I and my father's house have sinned. We have dealt very corruptly against thee, and have not kept the commandments, nor the statutes, nor the judgments, which thou commandedst thy servant Moses."* Finally, in Daniel 9:5 the man of God Daniel confessed, *"We have sinned, and have committed iniquity, and have done wickedly, and have rebelled, even by departing from thy precepts and from thy judgments."*

No matter how great or small a matter it may be in the view of man, any and all departure from the precepts and principles, statutes and standards, commands and counsels of God's Holy Word must be acknowledged as sin, and that *specifically*. We are not simply to confess our sinfulness generally, but to confess our sins specifically –

each one in particular. In addition, such Biblical confession is not simply an acknowledgement of wrongdoing, but is also a humble acknowledgement of *the sinfulness, unrighteousness, wickedness, evil, and rebellion* of that wrongdoing.

In like manner, the husband and the wife should confess their faults one to another. Just as they are required to acknowledge unto the Lord each specific sin committed against Him, even so they each are required to acknowledge unto the other each specific sin committed against the other. No matter how great or small a matter it may be in the view of man, any attitude, word, or action that God's Word defines as sin and that impacts the other must be confessed to the other as sin. Just as the prodigal son confessed unto his father in Luke 15:21, **"I have sinned against heaven, and in thy sight,"** even so each is to acknowledge unto the other that he or she has sinned against God and against the other in that specific attitude, word, or action.

Furthermore, in this confession there must be an honest, humble acknowledgement of the offensiveness, hurtfulness, wickedness, and harmfulness of that sin against the other. This is *not* an expression of sorrow that the *other* was somehow offended. Such would *not* be an acknowledgement of one's *own* sin against the other, but would actually be a subtle *accusation* that the other should not have become offended. Yet if a sin was indeed committed against the other, then the other had the right to be offended thereby. Even more *the Lord our God Himself* was offended by that sin. Thus the husband himself or the wife herself must make a clear acknowledgement to the other that he or she did indeed commit a wicked, harmful sin against the other.

Accept Full Responsibility for Your Sin

In the third place, the husband and the wife *must accept the full responsibility for any sin committed against the other.* Biblical confession does not allow for the shifting of the blame or responsibility. Yes, others may influence one to sin and may be involved in one's sins. Yes, circumstances may create and contribute to moments of temptation. Yet in Biblical confession the husband and the wife will not shift the blame or responsibility for their own sinful choices upon those others or those circumstances. Rather, they will acknowledge the truth of God's Word that every temptation to sin is the drawing away of one's *own* desires. (James 1:14)

In Biblical confession the husband and the wife will each *accept the full responsibility for his or her own sinful attitudes, words, and actions*, regardless of the influences or involvements of others and regardless of the circumstances. In Psalm 51:3 David confessed, *"For I acknowledge my transgression: and my sin is ever before me."* The personal responsibility for his sin was ever acknowledged in his thoughts. He faced that responsibility fully and did not seek to shift any part of it out of sight. His heart was broken over the sin that he himself had committed. Even so, in verse 17 he proclaimed, *"The sacrifices of God are a broken spirit: a broken and a contrite heart, O God, thou wilt not despise."*

In like manner, the prophet Isaiah cried out with a broken heart in the opening portion of Isaiah 6:5, *"Then said I, Woe is me! For I am undone; because I am a man of unclean lips."* Again the prophet Jeremiah cried out in Lamentations 5:16, *"The crown is fallen from our head: woe unto us, that we have sinned!"* In addition, the prophet Isaiah confessed in Isaiah 59:12, *"For our transgressions are multiplied before thee, and our sins testify against us: for our transgressions are with us; and as for our iniquities, we know them."* Again the prophet Jeremiah confessed in Jeremiah 3:25, *"We lie down in our shame, and our confusion covereth us: for we have sinned against the LORD our God, we and our fathers, from our youth even unto this day, and have not obeyed the voice of the LORD our God."* Yet again in Ezra 9:6 the man of God Ezra confessed, *"O my God, I am ashamed and blush to lift up my face to thee, my God: for our iniquities are increased over our head, and our trespass is grown up unto the heavens."* Finally, in Daniel 9:8 the man of God Daniel confessed, *"O Lord, to us belongeth confusion of face, to our kings, to our princes, and to our fathers, because we have sinned against thee."* Acceptance of full responsibility, brokenness of heart, honest and humble shame and sorrow – Such is the spirit of Biblical confession both toward the Lord and toward one another.

216

Furthermore, in accepting full responsibility for any sin committed against the other, the husband and the wife must also *patiently accept whatever punishments or consequences may result from the sin.* When instructing His people Israel through His servant Moses concerning the matter of confession, the Lord God stated in the closing portion of Leviticus 26:41, "*If then their uncircumcised hearts be humbled, and they then accept of the punishment of their iniquity.*" Even so, in the opening portion of Micah 7:9 the prophet Micah represented the repentant among God's people Israel as saying, "*I will bear the indignation of the LORD, because I have sinned against him.*"

Yea, in accepting full responsibility for any sin committed against the other, the husband and the wife must *recognize that any punishments and consequences are fully deserved.* In Daniel 9:14 the man of God Daniel confessed, "*Therefore hath the LORD watched upon the evil* [that is – the painful, grievous work of chastening and punishment], *and brought it upon us: for the LORD our God is righteous in all his works which he doeth: for we obeyed not his voice.*" In like manner, the Levites confessed in Nehemiah 9:33, "*Howbeit thou art just in all that is brought upon us; for thou hast done right, but we have done wickedly.*" Yes, the Lord our God is righteous in His work of chastening and punishment upon us for our sins. Yet the Lord our God is also merciful. In Ezra 9:13 the man of God Ezra stated, "*And after all that is come upon us for our evil deeds, and for our great trespass, seeing that thou our God hast punished us less than our iniquities deserve, and hast given us such deliverance as this.*"

Even when repentance has been made and forgiveness has been requested and received, it must be recognized that the Biblical principle still applies – "*Whatsoever a man soweth, that shall he also reap.*" (Galatians 6:7) It must be recognized that even after the Lord our God has forgiven us of our sins, He may yet maintain negative circumstances in our lives. This He may do in order to vindicate and honor the righteousness of His name (2 Samuel 12:13-14) and in order to train us in the way of resistance to temptation and of faithful obedience to His will (2 Chronicles 12:5-8). Also in relation to one another, even after being forgiven of a sinful fault, it may be necessary for the husband or wife diligently to rebuild trustworthiness before

217

the other and humbly to follow a set of boundaries and accountabilities to help prevent a repetition of the sinful fault.

Finally, in accord with the nature of the sinful fault, it may be necessary to make some form of restitution. In Numbers 5:7 the Lord our God instructed His people Israel, saying, *"Then they shall confess their sin which they have done: and he shall recompense his trespass with the principal thereof, and add unto it the fifth part thereof, and give it unto him against whom he hath trespassed."* Yet the husband or wife who has truly come to repentance and who truly seeks after reconciliation will willingly accept such consequences as a part of his or her full responsibility in the sinful fault.

Humbly Request Forgiveness for Your Sin

In the fourth place, the husband and the wife *must humbly request forgiveness from God and from the other*. In Psalm 51:1 David made request of the Lord, *"Have mercy upon me, O God, according to thy lovingkindness: according unto the multitude of thy tender mercies blot out my transgressions;"* and again in verse 9, *"Hide thy face from my sins, and blot out all mine iniquities."* Here David was asking God to forgive him of his sins. Furthermore, David made his request with a humble recognition that he himself was undeserving thereof. He did not ask for forgiveness according to his own worthiness, but according to the multitude of the Lord's tender mercies and loving kindness.

In like manner, the husband and the wife must ask God to forgive them of the sins that they have committed against one another. All sin is first and foremost sin against the Lord our God. Thus confession must be made to Him, and forgiveness must be requested from Him. That request must be made with deep humility, recognizing his or her own wickedness and unworthiness, and recognizing that forgiveness is wholly according to our Lord's gracious and merciful nature. In addition, the husband and the wife must each ask the other to forgive the sins that he or she has committed against the other. Again that request must be made with sincere humility, recognizing that such forgiveness is wholly according to the other's grace and mercy.

Seek to Change Your Sinful Behavior

In the fifth and final place, the husband and the wife *must seek to change their behavior so as not to repeat the sinful fault.* In Psalm 51:10 David prayed unto the Lord, *"Create in me a clean heart, O God; and renew a right spirit within me."* Not only did he desire forgiveness of his sins, but he also desired change of heart so as not to repeat such sins. In like manner, the husband and the wife must not only seek for forgiveness, but also seek to change. Certainly the process of change in behavior may take time, and the sinful fault may yet be repeated. However, the husband or wife who is truly repentant will ever be striving after genuine change and will be quick to confess any repetition of the sinful fault. Yea, in this desire for genuine change, he or she will even be grateful for the chastening, consequences, and accountabilities that aid in such change. In Psalm 119:67 the psalmist stated, *"Before I was afflicted I went astray: but now have I kept thy word,"* and then added in verse 71, *"It is good for me that I have been afflicted; that I might learn thy statutes."* Although the chastening and negative consequences themselves will not be joyous, but grievous, afterward they will yield *"the peaceable fruit of righteousness unto them which are exercised thereby."* (Hebrews 12:11) For this the truly repentant individual will be grateful.

Yet what if the husband or wife stubbornly hardens his or her heart and refuses to confess his or her sins unto the Lord and unto the other? Proverbs 28:13-14 gives answer, *"He that covereth his sins shall not prosper: but whoso confesseth and forsaketh them shall have mercy. Happy is the man that feareth alway: but he that hardeneth his heart shall fall into mischief."* The Lord our God has promised to grant mercy and forgiveness unto those who humbly confess their sins. Oh, how blessed is the individual who receives such mercy and whose sins are thus forgiven! (Psalm 32:1-2) Yet the individual who hardens his or her heart and refuses to confess his or her sins shall fall under the heavy hand of God's chastening. Concerning that time when he himself hardened his heart in refusing to confess his sins, David reported in Psalm 32:3-4, *"When I kept silence, my bones waxed old through my roaring all the day long. For day and night thy hand was heavy upon me: my moisture is turned into the drought of summer. Selah.*" Yea, in Proverbs 29:1 the warning is given, *"He, that being often reproved hardeneth his neck, shall suddenly be destroyed, and that without remedy."* Let each then be quick to confess his or her sins in humility with a broken heart unto the Lord our God and unto the other.

Truth for Meditation

Concerning the confession of sin to one another, the husband and the wife must –

1. Be open and humble in heart to receive conviction and correction. (Prov. 1:5, 23-31, 33; 3:11-12; 8:33-35; 10:17; 12:1, 15; 13:18; 15:31-32; 26:12; 29:1)

2. Acknowledge the reality and wickedness of their sin against one another. (1 John 1:9; Jam. 5:16; Isa. 1:18; Psa. 32:5; 106:6; Jer. 14:20; Neh. 1:6-7; Dan. 9:5; Luke 15:21)

3. Accept the full responsibility for any sin committed against the other. (Jam. 1:14; Psa. 51:3, 17; Isa. 6:5; 59:12; Jer. 3:25; Lam. 5:16; Dan. 9:14; Neh. 9:33; Ezra 9:13 Gal. 6:7; 2 Sam. 12:13-14; 2 Chron. 12:5-8; Numb. 5:7)

4. Request forgiveness from God and from the other. (Psa. 51:1, 9)

5. Seek to change their behavior so as not to repeat the sinful fault. (Psa. 51:10; 119:67, 71)

Verses for Memorization

1 John 1:9: If we confess our sins, he is faithful and just to forgive us our sins, and to cleanse us from all unrighteousness.

Proverbs 3:11-12: My son, despise not the chastening of the LORD; neither be weary of his correction: for whom the LORD loveth he correcteth; even as a father the son in whom he delighteth.

Proverbs 15:31-32: The ear that heareth the reproof of life abideth among the wise. He that refuseth instruction despiseth his own soul: but he that heareth reproof getteth understanding.

Psalm 51:17: The sacrifices of God are a broken spirit: a broken and a contrite heart, O God, thou wilt not despise.

Psalm 51:1: Have mercy upon me, O God, according to thy lovingkindness: according unto the multitude of thy tender mercies blot out my transgressions.

Proverbs 28:13: He that covereth his sins shall not prosper: but whoso confesseth and forsaketh them shall have mercy.

18

Forgiving One Another

In the previous chapter we considered the truth that the husband and the wife must each confess to one another those sinful faults that he or she commits against the other. In this chapter we come to the other side of the matter – that the husband and the wife are to forgive one another. In Ephesians 4:32 we are commanded, "*And be ye kind one to another, tenderhearted, forgiving one another, even as God for Christ's sake hath forgiven you.*" Again in Colossians 3:12-13 the instruction is given, "*Put on therefore, as the elect of God, holy and beloved, bowels of mercies, kindness, humbleness of mind, meekness, longsuffering; forbearing one another, and forgiving one another, if any man have a quarrel against any; even as Christ forgave you, so also do ye.*" Furthermore, we learn from 2 Corinthians 2:7-8 that forgiveness is a necessary part of love one toward another – "*So that contrariwise ye ought rather to forgive him, and comfort him, lest perhaps such a one should be swallowed up with overmuch sorrow. Wherefore I beseech you that ye would confirm your love toward him.*"

The Meaning of Forgiveness

What then does it mean to forgive one another? The basic meaning of the word "forgive" has two parts. The first part relates to the offense itself, and the second part relates to the offender. On the one hand, it means "to let go of an offense committed or debt accrued by another." On the other hand, it means "to freely grant reconciliation with and favor to another." It is not a matter of feelings, but a matter of decision. The husband and the wife must each *decide* to let go of the offense that the other has committed. They must each *decide* to release the other graciously and freely from the requirement to suffer some form of punishment for the offense. They must each *decide* to pursue reconciliation with the other. They must each *decide* to grant favor toward the other regardless of the offense.

Biblical forgiveness is a willful decision by the husband or wife that he or she will not hold the offense of the other's sinful fault on record against him or her. It is a willful decision that he or she will not require payment from the other in order for the other to earn a restoration of love and favor. It is a willful decision that he or she will not dwell upon the offense and will not harbor resentment about the offense. It is a willful decision that he or she will not bring up the offense in the future as a weapon of attack and will not report the offense to others in a negative light. It is a willful decision that he or she will not allow the offense of the other's sinful fault to prevent or hinder growth in their marriage relationship. Resentment in attitude, retaliation in word and action, revenge in purpose, plan, and pursuit, resistance to full reconciliation – None of these are a part of Biblical forgiveness. Rather, in Biblical forgiveness the husband and the wife will each cast the other's offense away from his or her thoughts and will heartily pursue reconciliation.

This is the manner of our Lord's forgiveness toward us. When we sin against Him, we stand guilty of an offense in His sight; and our sin separates between us and Him. (Isaiah 59:2) Yet when He forgives our sins, He removes the guilt of our offense from His sight and renews us to the place of fellowship. In the closing portion of Jeremiah 31:34, our Lord proclaims, ***"For I will forgive their iniquity, and I will remember their sin no more."*** It is not that our Lord ceases to be all-knowing, but that He will cease to be mindful of the offense of our sins. He will no longer consider us to be guilty of the offense and will no longer allow the offense of our sins to separate between us and Him. Thus David prayed unto the Lord in Psalm 51:9, ***"Hide thy face from my sins, and blot out all mine*** *iniquities.*" In addition, David declared with gratitude in Psalm 103:12, "*As far as the east is from the west, so far hath he removed our transgressions from us.*" Whereas the offense of our sins had been His focus and had kindled His anger against us, now He hides His face from the offense of our sins and pours out His gracious favor upon us. Whereas the guilt of our sins had separated us from Him, now He separates us from the guilt of our sins. In like manner, the husband and the wife are to forgive one another.

Now, such Biblical forgiveness does *not* prohibit the possibility of boundaries or accountabilities for the future. In the case of David's sin of adultery with Bath-sheba and murder of Uriah her husband, when David confessed his sin with a broken and contrite heart, the Lord forgave him of his sin and cleansed him of his unrighteousness. (2 Samuel 12:13; Psalm 32:5) Yet in order *to vindicate the honor of His name*, which David's sin had profaned before the Lord's enemies, the Lord still established a consequence of accountability with regard to David's sin. In 2 Samuel 12:14 the consequence was pronounced, "*Howbeit, because by this deed thou hast given great occasion to the enemies of the LORD to blaspheme, the child also that is born unto thee shall surely die.*" This consequence was not given as punishment for David's sin in order to make him pay somewhat for the offense and guilt of his sin against the Lord. The Lord had fully forgiven him of that offense and guilt. Rather, this consequence was intended *to teach* David and others *not to follow the path of sin and rebellion against the Lord in the future.*

In like manner, when King Rehoboam and the princes of Judah forsook the Lord their God and His Word, the Lord empowered Shishak king of Egypt to conquer and destroy them. Yet when King Rehoboam and the princes of Judah humbled themselves before the Lord over their sin, He forgave them and granted them deliverance. (2 Chronicles 12:6-7) However, in order *to teach them to serve Him more faithfully in the future*, the Lord established a consequence of accountability upon Rehoboam and Judah. This consequence was pronounced in 2 Chronicles 12:8 – "*Nevertheless they shall be his* [Shishak's] *servants; that they may know my service, and the service of the kingdom's of the countries.*" The

Lord allowed Shishak to hold Rehoboam and Judah under the service of tribute in order that Rehoboam and Judah might learn the service of the Lord. Again this consequence was not punishment for the offense and guilt of their sin. The Lord had forgiven them of that offense and guilt. Rather, this consequence was intended as *a boundary and accountability for the future*.

Even so, when the husband or the wife forgives the other according to the Biblical standard, he or she may yet request and require a set of boundaries and accountabilities in order to help the other in preventing a repetition of the sin in the future. These boundaries and accountabilities will be related to the individual nature of the sin and situation. In some cases they may be long term; in others they may be short term; and in others they may not be necessary at all. Furthermore, in the spirit of Biblical forgiveness, these boundaries and accountabilities must not be motivated by a desire to retaliate, to punish, or to make the other somehow pay for his or her sin. Rather, in the spirit of Biblical forgiveness and love, these boundaries and accountabilities must be motivated by a desire to help the other in spiritual growth and victory.

The Motivation for Forgiveness

Yet why should the husband and the wife grant such forgiveness to one another? What should motivate them to be in the practice of forgiving one another? Certainly the very command of the Lord our God should move us to obedience. Yet the Lord our God has provided another ground for motivation. It is the truth concerning *His own gracious forgiveness* of the *infinite* offense and guilt of our own sins *against Him*. Because He has *first* forgiven us, we should forgive one another. The instruction is given at the close of Ephesians 4:32, "***Forgiving one another, even as God for Christ's sake hath forgiven you.***" Again it is given at the close of Colossians 3:13, "***Even as Christ forgave you, so also do ye.***" Because God the Son, the Lord Jesus Christ, provided for our forgiveness of sins through His death on the cross, we should forgive one another. Because God the Father grants eternal forgiveness to all who believe on His Son as eternal Savior, we should forgive one another.

If the husband and the wife have each received God's forgiveness through faith in the Lord Jesus Christ His Son, then they should be moved and motivated *thereby* to forgive one another. Even so, the Lord our God views any refusal to forgive as a direct disregard of His eternal forgiveness. In the parable of the unforgiving servant, our Lord Jesus Christ presented the rebuke of the lord (who represents the Lord our God) against the servant who would not forgive his fellow servant – "***Then his lord, after that he had called him, said unto him, O thou wicked servant, I forgave thee all that debt, because thou desiredst me: shouldest not thou also have had compassion on thy fellowservant, even as I had pity on thee?***" (Matthew 18:32-33) Yea, if the husband or wife refuses to forgive the other, the Lord our God will give the same rebuke and report – "O thou wicked servant!"

The Manner of Forgiveness

What then is the manner by which the husband and the wife should forgive one another? Such forgiveness should be expressed directly to one another. Just as the confession of sins should be specifically communicated, even so the forgiveness of sins should be *specifically* communicated. Responding to the other's repentance and confession of sin with such comments as – "It's no big deal;" "Don't worry about it;" "Everything is fine" – is not a genuine expression of forgiveness. If sin has truly been committed, then everything is *not* fine – not in the sight of the Lord our God. It *is* a "big deal," at least in the sight of the Lord our God. The other *should* be concerned about his or her sin and *should* express repentance over it. In turn, the forgiveness should be *clearly* and *directly* expressed concerning that sin – "I forgive you." Such is necessary for the process of reconciliation to have a certain foundation.

The Measure of Forgiveness

Yet how often must the husband and the wife forgive one another? Is there any limitation at which forgiveness is no longer necessary? Are there any sins that are so great that forgiveness is not required? What is the measure of Biblical forgiveness to one another? In Matthew 18:21 the apostle Peter asked a question along this very line – "*Then came Peter to him, and said, Lord, how oft shall my brother sin against me, and I forgive him? Till seven times?*" In verse 22 we find our Lord's response – "*Jesus saith unto him, I say not unto thee, Until seven times: but, Until seventy times seven.*" To the majority in this world, granting forgiveness for the first and second offense would be reasonable; and granting forgiveness for the third and fourth offense would be quite generous. However, as a chosen servant of the Lord Jesus Christ, Peter understood the need to go beyond the majority opinion. Thus Peter suggested a number that would go above and beyond the world's call of duty and generosity, a number that was often employed in the Old Testament Scriptures to represent perfection – "Till seven times?" Yet our Lord Jesus Christ very emphatically denied Peter's technique of counting offenses and forgivenesses. Rather, He replaced it with multiplication upon multiplication – "Until seventy times seven." Our Lord took Peter's number of perfection, seven, and multiplied it by a multiple of the number of perfection, seventy. Yea, He took perfection, multiplied it by perfection, and then multiplied it yet the more, not in order to set an extremely high standard for count keeping, but in order to represent God's own infinite perfection as our standard.

This then is the measure by which the husband and the wife are called to forgive one another – *the infinite perfection of God's own forgiveness toward them.* Such is illustrated by our Lord's parable of the unforgiving servant in Matthew 18:23-35. First, in verses 23-27 we find the case of the servant's debt unto his lord – "*Therefore is the kingdom of heaven likened unto a certain king, which would take account of his servants. And when he had begun to reckon, one was brought unto him, which owed him ten thousand talents. But forasmuch as he had not to pay, his lord commanded him to be sold, and his wife, and children, and all that he had, and payment to be made. The servant therefore fell down, and worshipped him, saying, Lord, have patience with me, and I will pay thee all. Then the lord of that servant was moved with compassion, and loosed him, and forgave him the debt.*"

This servant owed his lord a debt of ten thousand talents, an amount equal to multiplied millions of dollars, and possibly reaching to hundreds of millions of dollars. Yet upon this servant's humble plea, the lord of the parable had compassion upon him "and forgave him the debt." Now, the lord of this parable represents God our heavenly Father. Furthermore, the debt of the servant represents the *infinite* debt of sin that each of us sinners owes to the Lord our God. Finally, the forgiveness of the lord represents the *eternal* forgiveness and *eternal* salvation that the Lord our God and heavenly Father will graciously grant to each and every one of us who receives His Son the Lord Jesus Christ through faith as Savior. Oh, the immeasurable abundance of the riches of God's grace, compassion, and forgiveness toward us in our eternal salvation!

Yet the parable continues in verses 28-33 – *"But the same servant went out, and found one of his fellowservants, which owed him an hundred pence: and he laid hands on him, and took him by the throat, saying, Pay me that thou owest. And his fellowservant fell down at his feet, and besought him, saying, Have patience with me, and I will pay thee all. And he would not: but went and cast him into prison, till he should pay the debt. So when his fellowservants saw what was done, they were very sorry, and came and told unto their lord all that was done. Then his lord, after that he had called him, said unto him, O thou wicked servant, I forgave thee all that debt, because thou desiredst me: shouldest not thou also have had compassion on thy fellow-servant, even as I had pity on thee?"*

The fellow servant owed the forgiven servant a debt of one hundred pence, a very small sum compared to the debt that the forgiven servant had owed to his lord. Yet the forgiven servant had no spirit of compassion and forgiveness whatsoever. He did not simply challenge his fellow servant to pay the debt, but took him by the neck. He would not hear the plea of his fellow servant, "but went and cast him into prison." Thus the lord of the parable confronted him with these opening words, "O thou wicked servant." In addition, the lord rebuked this servant on the grounds that he should have been compassionate and granted forgiveness to his fellow servant *even as* (that is – just because) his lord had been compassionate and granted forgiveness to him.

229

Now, the relationship of this servant toward his fellow servant represents our relationship toward those who sin against us. No matter how great the sin may be that another has sinned against us, it does not even come close to be compared with the infinite offense of our own sin against the Lord our God. Yet through faith in His Son the Lord Jesus Christ, He has graciously forgiven us all that offense. Should not then the husband and the wife each have compassion upon the other to forgive him or her for his or her trespass? Yes, they should grant forgiveness to one another *just because* God has granted forgiveness to them. Yea, they should continue to do so until the level of their forgiveness toward one another reaches the fullness of the immeasurably abundant forgiveness of the Lord our God toward them.

Yet what is to be done if the other commits the very same sin over, and over, and over again in the very same day? In Luke 17:3-4 our Lord Jesus Christ gave instruction, saying, *"Take heed to yourselves: If thy brother trespass against thee, rebuke him; and if he repent, forgive him. And if he trespass against thee seven times in a day, and seven times in a day turn again to thee, saying, I repent; thou shalt forgive him."* Even in such cases forgiveness is required. Yea, how many times have we ourselves committed the very same sin over, and over, and over again against the Lord our God? Yet He is faithful to forgive us our sins whenever we repent. Even so, the husband and the wife must each take heed unto themselves. Each must be very attentive to grant forgiveness unto the other over, and over, and over again.

The Spirit of Forgiveness

Yet what is to be done if the other does not express any repentance concerning his or her trespass? Even in this case the husband and the wife must each take heed to maintain a *spirit* of forgiveness toward the other. We are called to forgive even as Christ forgave us (Colossians 3:13) and even as God the Father for Christ's sake hath forgiven us (Ephesians 4:32). Now, the Lord our God Himself does *not* grant forgiveness to those who will not repent. Yet He *does* maintain a spirit of forgiveness toward them. He is ever *grieved* in the destruction of the wicked and is ever *desirous* that the wicked might repent and thereby be delivered from destruction. In the opening portion of Ezekiel 33:11, He proclaimed, "*Say unto them, As I live, saith the Lord GOD, I have no pleasure in the death of the wicked; but that the wicked turn from his way and live.*" In addition, He is full of compassion, great in kindness, slow to anger, abundant in grace, plenteous in mercy, and ever ready to forgive at the very moment of repentance. In Psalm 86:5 David declared with assurance, "*For thou, Lord, art good, and ready to forgive; and plenteous in mercy unto all them that call upon thee.*" Yea, from Micah 7:18 we learn that "*He retaineth not his anger for ever, because he delighteth in mercy;*" and from Daniel 9:9 we learn that "*to the Lord our God belong mercies and forgivenesses*" as a very part of His glorious nature.

In like manner, the husband and the wife are to maintain such a spirit of forgiveness toward one another; and such a spirit of forgiveness includes three particular elements. Each of these three elements is specifically connected to the instruction of forgiveness in the New Testament and is presented as foundational ground for the practice of forgiveness.

❖ The first element of such a spirit of forgiveness is *a forbearing spirit*. In Colossians 3:13 the instruction is delivered, "*Forbearing one another, and forgiving one another, if any man have a quarrel against any; even as Christ forgave you, so also do ye.*" Even if the other does not express repentance concerning his or her trespass, the husband and the wife must each restrain himself or herself from responding negatively toward the other in attitude, word, or action. In the spirit of forgiveness, each must not take hold of the offense of the other's trespass, but must overlook that offense against himself or herself. Each must be slow to anger and not engage in any manner of retaliation, not returning evil for evil, or selfishness for selfishness, or bad attitude for bad attitude, or harsh words for harsh words. Yea, in the spirit of forgiveness, even if the other has not yet expressed repentance, each must continue enduring patiently and faithfully with humility and meekness and without anger and retaliation.

231

❖ The second element of such a spirit of forgiveness is *a tender heart*. In Ephesians 4:32 the instruction is delivered, *"And be ye kind one to another, tenderhearted, forgiving one another, even as God for Christ's sake hath forgiven you."* Even if the other does not express repentance concerning his or her trespass, the husband and the wife must not become hard hearted toward the other. Rather, in the spirit of forgiveness, each must maintain a sweet, gentle, and peaceable heart-attitude toward the other. Each must not push the other away, but must ever pursue after reconciliation. Yea, in the spirit of forgiveness, each must ever delight in mercy and must ever be ready to forgive.

❖ The third element of such a spirit of forgiveness is *a kind behavior*. Again in Ephesians 4:32 the instruction is delivered, *"And be ye kind one to another, tenderhearted, forgiving one another, even as God for Christ's sake hath forgiven you."* Even if the other does not express repentance concerning his or her trespass, the husband and the wife must each say and do those things that would be beneficial and profitable for the other's sake. In the spirit of forgiveness, each must continue to be compassionate toward the other, considerate of the other, and caring for the other. Yea, in the spirit of forgiveness, even if the other has not yet expressed repentance, each must be quick to help the other, to give up self in order to help and serve the other. Each must also continue to speak gracious, helpful, and encouraging words to the other. In the spirit of forgiveness, each must continue to speak with meekness and honor to and about the other, and not with biting and criticism.

The Refusal to Forgive

So then, what will happen if a husband or wife refuses to forgive the other or to maintain a spirit of forgiveness toward the other? The Word of God gives answer with a seven-fold warning.

❖ First, if one will not forgive the other or maintain a spirit of forgiveness toward the other, *then the Lord our God will view him or her as a wicked servant*. As we have previously noted, in our Lord's parable of the unforgiving servant, the lord of that servant rebuked him in Matthew 18:32-33, saying, *"O thou wicked servant, I forgave thee all that debt, because thou desiredst me: shouldest not thou also have had compassion on thy fellowservant, even as I had pity on thee?"* Even so, God our heavenly Father will rebuke the one who will not forgive the other, saying, "O thou *wicked* servant!" It is a wicked, evil thing in the sight of the Lord our God for a husband or wife not to forgive the other.

❖ Second, if one will not forgive the other or maintain a spirit of forgiveness toward the other, *then the Lord our God's anger will be kindled against him or her.* Our Lord concluded the parable of the unforgiving servant in Matthew 18:34-35, saying, *"And his* [the unforgiving servant's] *lord was wroth, and delivered him to the tormentors, till he should pay all that was due unto him. So likewise shall my heavenly Father do also unto you, if ye from your hearts forgive not every one his brother their trespasses."* Just as the lord of the parable was wroth with his unforgiving servant, even so the Lord our God and heavenly Father will be wroth with the one who will not forgive the other. Oh, how fearful a thing it is to have the wrath of almighty God kindled against us! *"For,"* as Hebrews 12:29 proclaims, *"our God is a consuming fire."* Yea, the opening portion of Nahum 1:6 warns, *"Who can stand before his indignation? And who can abide in the fierceness of his anger?"*

❖ Third, if one will not forgive the other or maintain a spirit of forgiveness toward the other, *then the Lord our God will chasten him or her with troubles and tribulations.* Again we consider our Lord's conclusion to the parable of the unforgiving servant in Matthew 18:34-35 – *"And his lord was wroth, and delivered him to the tormentors, till he should pay all that was due unto him. So likewise shall my heavenly Father do also unto you, if ye from your hearts forgive not every one his brother their trespasses."* Just as the lord of the parable delivered his servant unto the tormentors, even so the Lord our God and heavenly Father will chasten with torments the one who will not forgive. Even so, David described his own experience with the chastening torments of our Lord God's hot displeasure in Psalm 38:1-6, saying, *"O LORD, rebuke me not in thy wrath: neither chasten me in thy hot displeasure. For thine*

233

arrows stick fast in me, and thy hand presseth me sore. There is no soundness in my flesh because of thine anger; neither is there any rest in my bones because of my sin. For mine iniquities are gone over mine head: as an heavy burden they are too heavy for me. My wounds stink and are corrupt because of my foolishness. I am troubled; I am bowed down greatly; I go mourning all the day long."

❖ Fourth, if one will not forgive the other or maintain a spirit of forgiveness toward the other, *then the Lord our God will not forgive his or her daily trespasses against Him.* In Matthew 6:14-15 our Lord Jesus Christ proclaimed, *"For if ye forgive men their trespasses, your heavenly Father will also forgive you: but if ye forgive not men their trespasses, neither will your Father forgive your trespasses."* When we commit sin against the Lord our God from day to day, that sin breaks our fellowship with Him. The only means by which we might return to our walk of daily fellowship with our Lord is that through our humble and contrite confession of that sin, He would forgive us our sin and cleanse us from our unrighteousness. Yet if an individual will not forgive another of his or her trespasses, then the Lord our God will not forgive that individual of his or her daily trespasses; and if the Lord our God will not forgive that individual, then that individual cannot be restored to daily fellowship with the Lord. Yea, as long as a husband or wife refuses to forgive the other or refuses to maintain a spirit of forgiveness toward the other, it is spiritually *impossible* for that husband or wife to walk in daily fellowship with the Lord. Thus, as long as this unforgiving spirit continues, it is also spiritually *impossible* for that husband or wife to be guided or blessed by the Lord.

❖ Fifth, if one will not forgive the other or maintain a spirit of forgiveness toward the other, *then the effectiveness of his or her prayers will be hindered.* In Mark 11:25-26 our Lord Jesus Christ instructed and warned, *"And when ye stand praying, forgive, if ye have ought against any: that your Father also which is in heaven may forgive you your trespasses. But if ye do not forgive, neither will your Father which is in heaven forgive your trespasses."* A forgiving spirit is a necessary ingredient for an effective prayer life.

234

Yet if one will not forgive the other, it will be an iniquity regarded in the heart; and in Psalm 66:18 the truth is revealed, *"If I regard iniquity in my heart, the Lord will not hear me."* Furthermore, Isaiah 59:1-2 declares, *"Behold, the LORD's hand is not shortened, that it cannot save; neither his ear heavy, that it cannot hear: but your iniquities have separated between you and your God, and your sins have hid his face from you, that he will not hear."*

❖ Sixth, if one will not forgive the other or maintain a spirit of forgiveness toward the other, *then bitterness will overtake his or her heart and life.* In Ephesians 4:31-32 we find that a spirit of bitterness and a spirit of forgiveness are opposites of one another. There we read, *"Let all bitterness, and wrath, and anger, and clamour, and evil speaking, be put away from you, with all malice: and be ye kind one to another, tenderhearted, forgiving one another, even as God for Christ's sake hath forgiven you."* There are only two opposite directions in which the husband and the wife may travel on this matter, either in the direction of bitterness or in the direction of forgiveness. If one does not forgive the other, that one *will* be overtaken by bitterness; and that bitterness *will* be a destructive force in his or her life.

Even so, Hebrews 12:15 gives the warning, *"Looking diligently lest any man fail of the grace of God; lest any root of bitterness springing up trouble you, and thereby many be defiled."* To "fail of the grace of God" means to fall short of that place where God's daily grace might be granted. The husband or wife who is overtaken by bitterness *will not find God's daily grace* available *"to help in time of need"* (Hebrews 4:16), either for spiritual strength or for spiritual service. Furthermore, the husband or wife who is overtaken by bitterness *will be overwhelmed by trouble* in the character of his or her own heart and life. Finally, the husband or wife who is overtaken by bitterness *will defile the relationships* in which he or she has a part. Oh, how very many shall be defiled! Oh, how that marriage and home shall be defiled!

❖ Seventh, if one will not forgive the other or maintain a spirit of forgiveness toward the other, *then Satan will get an advantage over him or her.* In 2 Corinthians 2:7-10 the apostle Paul instructed the believers at Corinth concerning the matter of forgiveness. Then in verse 11 he delivered a warning under the inspiration of God the Holy Spirit, saying, ***"Lest Satan should get an advantage of us: for we are not ignorant of his devices."*** Forgiving others prevents Satan from getting an advantage over us. However, refusing to forgive opens the door wide for him to get an advantage over us and thereby to devour our daily Christian lives. In 1 Peter 5:8-9 we are warned and instructed, ***"Be sober, be vigilant; because your adversary the devil, as a roaring lion, walketh about, seeking whom he may devour: whom resist steadfast in the faith, knowing that the same afflictions are accomplished in your brethren that are in the world."*** Yet the one who is overtaken by bitterness will lack the spiritual strength to resist the attacks of our adversary the devil. Such a bitter individual will not be able to withstand the wiles of the devil (Ephesians 6:10-13) and will be spiritually pierced and burned by his fiery darts (Ephesians 6:16). Yea, day after day through the bitterness of an unforgiving spirit, our adversary the devil will have an advantage over that husband's or wife's life.

Truth for Meditation

Concerning the practice of forgiving one another, the husband and the wife must understand –

1. The meaning of forgiveness: To let go of the offense committed by the other and to freely grant reconciliation with and favor to the other. (Jer. 31:34; Psa. 51:9; 103:12)

2. The motivation for forgiveness: God the Father's gracious forgiveness through Christ of the infinite offense and guilt of their sin against Him. (Eph. 4:32; Col. 3:13; Matt. 18:32-33)

3. The manner of forgiveness: To express forgiveness specifically and directly unto the other.

4. The measure of forgiveness: God the Father's immeasurable forgiveness toward them. (Matt. 18:21-33; Luke 17:3-4)

Even if the other does not express repentance, the husband and the wife must maintain a spirit of forgiveness toward the other, which includes –

1. A forbearing spirit. (Col. 3:13)

2. A tender heart. (Eph. 4:32)

3. A kind behavior. (Eph. 4:32)

If a husband or wife refuses to forgive the other or to maintain a spirit of forgiveness toward the other –

1. The Lord our God will view him or her as a wicked servant. (Matt. 18:32)

2. The Lord our God's anger will be kindled against him or her. (Matt. 18:34-35; Heb. 12:29; Nah. 1:6)

3. The Lord our God will chasten him or her with troubles and tribulations. (Matt. 18:34-35; Psa. 38:1-6)

4. The Lord our God will not forgive his or her daily trespasses against Him. (Matt. 6:14-15)

5. The effectiveness of his or her prayers will be hindered. (Mark 11:25-26; Psa. 66:18; Isa. 59:1-2)

6. Bitterness will overtake his or her heart and life. (Eph. 4:31-32; Heb. 12:15)

7. Satan will get an advantage over him or her. (2 Cor. 2:11; 1 Pet. 5:8-9)

Verses for Memorization

Ephesians 4:32: And be ye kind one to another, tenderhearted, forgiving one another, even as God for Christ's sake hath forgiven you.

Colossians 3:13: Forbearing one another, and forgiving one another, if any have a quarrel against any; even as Christ forgave you, so also do ye.

Luke 7:4: And if he trespass against thee seven times in a day, and seven times in a day turn again to thee, saying, I repent; thou shalt forgive him.

Matthew 6:14-15: For if ye forgive men their trespasses, your heavenly Father will also forgive you: but if ye forgive not men their trespasses, neither will your Father forgive your trespasses.

19

Correcting One Another

In considering how the husband and wife are to love one another, we learned that genuine, godly love *"rejoiceth not in iniquity, but rejoiceth in the truth."* (1 Corinthian 13:6) Genuine, godly love will never find joy in that which contradicts God's Word, but will ever find joy in that which is in accord with God's Word. Thus in genuine, godly love for one another, the husband and the wife will be grieved by sin in the other, not out of concern for any offense against self, but out of concern for the other's offense against the Lord, out of concern for the other's spiritual departure from the Lord, and out of concern for the destruction that such sin will bring into the other's life. Furthermore, in genuine, godly love for one another, the husband and the wife will desire that the other might be corrected of such sin and might be brought to walk in the way of righteousness. Yea, in genuine, godly love he or she might take opportunity according to the guidance of God the Holy Spirit to express correction to the other. Even so, Proverbs 27:5 states, *"Open rebuke is better than secret love."*

In addition, in considering how the husband and the wife are to communicate with one another, we learned from Ephesians 4:29 that they are always to speak *"that which is good to the use of edifying, that it may minister grace unto the hearers."* Good communication is that which is useful for building up the other spiritually. It is that which draws the other closer to the Lord our God and that which ministers our Lord God's grace to the other. Furthermore, we learned that such good communication will include hearty counsel and loving correction. Even so, the opening portion of Proverbs 27:6 indicates, *"Faithful are the wounds of a friend;"* and Proverbs 27:9 declares, *"Ointment and perfume rejoice the heart: so doth the sweetness of a man's friend by hearty counsel."* Also we learned that the husband and the wife should each be open to hear and to receive the counsels and corrections of the other. Even so, Proverbs 15:31-32 proclaims, *"The ear that heareth the reproof of life abideth among the wise. He that refuseth instruction despiseth his own soul: but he that heareth reproof getteth understanding."*

Avoid a Judgmental Spirit

However, there is a right way and a wrong way for a husband and wife to express correction unto one another. In the first place, in the process of correcting one another, the husband and the wife *must avoid a judgmental spirit toward the other.* In Matthew 7:1-2 our Lord Jesus Christ gave the warning, *"Judge not, that ye be not judged. For with what judgment ye judge, ye shall be judged: and with what measure ye mete, it shall be measured to you again."* Now, this warning does not prohibit any form of spiritual discernment or loving correction concerning another's behavior. In fact, within the very same context we are granted permission in verse 5, after first correcting our own sinful faults, *"to cast out the mote out of thy brother's eye."* Such would require spiritual discernment to see "the mote" in the other's life, and such would require loving correction to help the other remove "the mote" from his or her life.

Yet our Lord's warning not to judge does mean that each is not to have a *judgmental spirit* toward the other. The husband and the wife must not be always *looking for* faults in the other. In addition, they must not be always *looking down upon* the other for his or her faults. Each must avoid a critical and condemning spirit toward the other. Such a judgmental spirit is not the way of a loving heart and kind manner, but is the way of a biting tongue and devouring manner. (Galatians 5:14-15) Yea, in many cases a loving spirit will graciously overlook faults against itself without becoming angry and without pursuing confrontation. (Proverbs 10:12; 17:9; Ephesians 4:2; 1 Peter 4:8)

Included with our Lord's instruction in Matthew 7:1 not to judge is also His warning in verse 2 – "*For with what judgment ye judge, ye shall be judged: and with what measure ye mete, it shall be measured to you again.*" Whatever measure of a judgmental spirit the husband or wife might mete out to the other, he or she shall *receive back* the same measure, whether from the other, or from still others, or from the Lord Himself. If the husband or wife regularly metes out criticizing and condemning against the other, he or she shall receive back much criticizing and condemning against himself or herself. If the husband or wife follows the way of biting and devouring the other, he or she shall receive back biting and devouring against himself or herself. Sowing in a judgmental spirit reaps back a judgmental spirit. "*Judge not, that ye be not judged.*"

Correct One's Own Sinful Faults

In the second place, in the process of correcting one another, the husband and the wife *must first correct his or her own sinful faults.* In Matthew 7:3-5 our Lord Jesus Christ gave the warning and instruction, "*And why beholdest thou the mote that is in thy brother's eye, but considerest not the beam that is in thine own eye? Or how wilt thou say to thy brother, Let me pull out the mote out of thine eye; and, behold, a beam is in thine own eye? Thou hypocrite, first cast out the beam out of thine own eye; and then shalt thou see clearly to cast out the mote out of thy brother's eye.*"

A mote is a small speck of wood, whereas a beam is a much larger log of wood. What spiritual right would a husband or wife have to point out the small speck of wood that is in the other's eye while he or she is ignoring the log of wood that is in his or her own eye? Yea, how could such a husband or wife even be able to see straight to help remove the small speck of wood from the other's eye while that log of wood remains in his or her own eye? Even so, a husband or wife has *no spiritual grounds* for confronting and correcting the faults of the other *while overlooking* the faults in his or her own life. Yea, our Lord rebukes such with the words, "Thou hypocrite." Thus the husband or wife must *first* cast the log of wood out of his or her own eye in order to see clearly to cast the speck of wood out of the other's eye.

241

❖ First, each must consider the faults in his or her own heart and life as the greater problem. Our natural view is to consider the faults of our own hearts and lives as small matters in comparison to the much greater faults in others' lives. Yet our Lord describes the case in the opposite manner. He indicates that our own faults are the *log* of wood and that in comparison the other's faults are the *speck* of wood. This is the manner in which our Lord desires for the husband and the wife to view his or her own faults in comparison to faults of the other. Each is to consider the faults of his or her own heart and life as the greater problem in the relationship.

❖ Second, each must correct the faults in his or her own heart and life through Biblical confession. As we have learned previously, each must humbly acknowledge the reality and wickedness of his or her own sinful fault against God and against the other. Each must accept the full responsibility for his or her own sinful fault against God and against the other. Each must request forgiveness from God and from the other for his or her own sinful fault. Finally, each must pursue change in his or her own life concerning the fault.

❖ Third, each may then clearly see to help the other correct the faults in his or her life. Each must recognize that unconfessed, uncorrected sin, whether in attitude, word, or action, distorts and damages one's own spiritual discernment. While in such a spiritual condition, an individual is under the influence of his or her own sinful flesh; and in our sinful flesh there dwells no good thing. (Romans 7:18) While under the influence of our sinful flesh, we are guided, not by the spiritual wisdom of God, but by the selfish wisdom of this world. Even so, the husband and the wife must each recognize that he or she cannot be of spiritual help to the other while his or her own spiritual discernment is distorted and damaged by his or her own sinful fault. Each must first deal with the faults of his or her own life, and then may they each "see clearly" to deal with the faults in the other's life.

Earnestly Pray for the Other's Repentance

In the third place, in the process of correcting one another, the husband and the wife *must earnestly pray for the other's repentance*. In the opening portion of 1 John 5:16 we find the instruction, "*If any man see his brother sin a sin which is not unto death, he shall ask, and he shall give him life for them that sin not unto death.*" "A sin which is not unto death" is any sinful behavior that is not certain to bring the chastening of physical death from the hand of the Lord our God. Indeed, most sinful behavior is not sin that is unto death. Concerning any such sin in the other's life, the husband and the wife are to pray that the Lord might give the other life. This is not a prayer for the other to receive regeneration life, for in the context of the verse the one sinning is already a fellow brother or sister in Christ. Nor is this a prayer for the other to receive physical life, for the other has not sinned a sin that is unto physical death. Rather, this is a prayer for the other to receive restoration unto spiritually abundant life.

Any sin, whether in attitude, word, or action, destroys the spiritually abundant life of a believer. In order for a sinning believer to be restored unto such spiritually abundant life, that believer must come to Biblical confession and repentance and must be forgiven and cleansed by the Lord. Thus praying for the other to receive spiritually abundant life is essentially praying for the Lord to bring the other unto the place of Biblical confession and repentance whereby He might restore the other to that spiritually abundant life.

Even so, if a husband or wife sees the other in a sinful fault that is not unto death, he or she is to pray that the Lord might bring the other unto repentance and might thereby restore the other unto spiritually abundant life. Such prayer is to be lifted up with the humble recognition that *only* the Lord our God can reach to the heart of the other so as to produce correction and transformation in the other's heart and life. Certainly that husband or wife may be used as an instrument in the Lord's hand to help in the process of correction. Yet it is not the forcefulness or skillfulness of that husband's or wife's confrontation that will bring conviction to bear upon the other's heart. Rather, it is *God the Holy Spirit* who must bring conviction to bear in the other's heart. It is *the Word of God as employed by the Spirit of God* that must pierce unto the heart, discerning and convicting "*the thoughts and intents of the heart.*" (Hebrews 4:12) Therefore, the husband and the wife must each concentrate far more upon *praying* for the Lord to convict and correct the other's heart through His Word by His Spirit rather than upon trying to *force* conviction and correction through personal confrontation or manipulation.

Be under the Guidance of the Holy Spirit

In the fourth place, in the process of correcting one another, the husband and the wife *must be under the guiding influence of the Holy Spirit.* In Galatians 6:1 the instruction and warning is given, ***"Brethren, if a man be overtaken in a fault, ye which are spiritual, restore such an one in the spirit of meekness; considering thyself, lest thou also be tempted."*** According to this Biblical instruction, it is not just anyone who is qualified to correct a fault in another's life. Rather, the responsibility to correct is entrusted only to those who are *spiritual.* What then does it mean to be spiritual? The answer is revealed in the earlier context of Galatians 5:13-26. In Galatians 5:16 the instruction is given, ***"This I say then, Walk in the Spirit, and ye shall not fulfil the lust of the flesh."*** Again in verse 25 the instruction is given, ***"If we live in the Spirit, let us also walk in the Spirit."*** Being spiritual means walking under the guiding influence of God the Holy Spirit.

Furthermore, the result of such a walk in the Spirit is revealed in verses 22-23 – ***"But the fruit of the Spirit is love, joy, peace, longsuffering, gentleness, goodness, faith, meekness, temperance: against such there is no law."*** Being spiritual means bringing forth this fruit of the Spirit in one's daily attitude, speech, and behavior through the guiding influence of the Holy Spirit. When a husband or wife approaches the other for the purpose of correction, he or she must be walking under the guiding influence of the Holy Spirit and must be displaying the spiritual fruit of love, longsuffering, gentleness, and meekness in attitude.

Finally, we learn that such a walk in the Spirit is the opposite of walking in and after the ways of our selfish, sinful flesh. In verse 16 we find, not only the instruction, but also the promise, ***"This I say then, Walk in the Spirit, and ye shall not fulfil the lust of the flesh."***

In verse 13 granting an occasion to our selfish flesh is set in contrast to serving others in love. In verses 14-15 loving one another is set in contrast to the fleshly ways of biting and devouring one another. In verses 19-23 the works of the flesh, including such things as wrath, strife, envy, etc., are set in contrast to the fruit of the Spirit. In verses 25-26 walking in the Spirit is set in contrast to the fleshly attitude of being *"desirous of vain glory, provoking one another, envying one another."* Thus being spiritual means not yielding to and following after the selfish ways of one's sinful flesh. When a husband or wife approaches the other for the purpose of correction, he or she must not be under the influence of any selfish motivation or attitude. Selfish pride, selfish anger, selfish manipulation, and selfish goals – None of these are the ways of those who are spiritual.

Be Filled with a Spirit of Meekness

In the fifth place, in the process of correcting one another, the husband and the wife *must be filled with a spirit of meekness*. In Galatians 6:1 we again find the instruction, *"Brethren, if a man be overtaken in a fault, ye which are spiritual, restore such an one in the spirit of meekness; considering thyself, lest thou also be tempted."* This spirit of meekness is an attitude of *humility* concerning self and *gentleness* concerning the other. Describing His own character in Matthew 11:29, our Lord Jesus Christ joined meekness and humility, saying, *"Take my yoke upon you, and learn of me; for I am meek and lowly of heart: and ye shall find rest unto your souls."* Again meekness and humility are joined in Ephesians 4:2 where the instruction is given, *"With all lowliness and meekness, with longsuffering, forbearing one another in love."* Furthermore, we find meekness and gentleness joined in Titus 3:2 where we are instructed, *"To speak evil of no man, to be no brawlers, but gentle, shewing all meekness unto all men."* Finally, in Galatians 6:1 itself this spirit of meekness is defined by the phrase, *"Considering thyself, lest thou also be tempted."*

In the process of correction, a husband or wife must not approach the other with a spirit of pride, thinking and acting as if he or she were spiritually superior to the other. Each must not approach the other in self-righteousness or with self-exaltation. Each also must not approach the other in a grievous, contentious, striving, impatient manner. Rather, each must approach the other with a spirit of Biblical humility as a fellow sinner in daily need of God's delivering and empowering grace. In addition, each must approach the other with a spirit of gentle love, wholly motivated for the other's best spiritual good.

Sincerely Seek after Understanding

In the sixth place, in the process of correcting one another, the husband and the wife *must sincerely seek after understanding*. In Proverbs 18:13 the warning is given, *"**He that answereth a matter before he heareth it, it is folly and shame unto him.**"* Often when one approaches another for the purpose of correction, some important details of the case are yet unknown. Such might be circumstantial details, motivational details, relational details, spiritual details, etc. In some cases, when these details are known, the initial accusation is found to be *invalid*. Thus the correction is found to be *unnecessary*. In other cases a deeper need of the heart may be revealed. Thus the correction may become *more helpful* for the other's *spiritual growth*.

In still other cases it may be revealed that the *corrector* is also in some manner at fault and has thereby contributed to the case. Thus the process of correction may be used by our Lord to convict and correct the faults *of both*. Thus also the process of correction may result in a *more full* reconciliation and strengthening of the marriage relationship. Even so, such a sincere desire to seek after understanding will require a willingness to listen unto and be considerate of the other's perspective. It does not necessarily mean that an actual fault of the other will be excused through understanding. Rather, it means that the correction of any such fault will be made more substantial, helpful, and complete.

Speak the Truth of God in Love

In the seventh place, in the process of correcting one another, the husband and the wife *must speak the truth of God in Biblical love*.

In Ephesians 4:15 the instruction is given, *"But speaking the truth in love, may grow up into him in all things, which is the head, even Christ."* In addition, the opening portion of Proverbs 27:6 declares, *"Faithful are the wounds of a friend."* In the process of correction, the standard by which a husband or wife should determine what is actually a sinful fault in the other's life must be the truth of God's Word. It must not be the subjective standard of human perceptions and feelings, but must be the objective standard of God's precepts and principles as revealed in His Word.

Furthermore, in the process of correction, a husband or wife must be truly motivated by genuine, godly love for the other. The motivation must be spiritual, not selfish. It must be to serve the other in self-sacrifice for the other's best spiritual good. Even so, all of the principles of good communication must be employed in the process in order that the correction might truly build up the other spiritually and minister God's grace to the other. In addition, all of the elements of genuine, godly love must be employed in the process in order that the wounds of correction may be truly faithful and not destructive.

Confront for the Purpose of Restoration

In the eighth place, in the process of correcting one another, the husband and the wife *must confront for the purpose of restoration.* Yet again in Galatians 6:1 we find the instruction, *"Brethren, if a man be overtaken in a fault, ye which are spiritual, restore such an one in the spirit of meekness; considering thyself, lest thou also be tempted."* Any sinful fault in an individual's heart and life causes spiritual separation between that individual and the Lord. Thus the ultimate purpose of correction must be to restore that individual unto a renewed fellowship with the Lord our God. When a husband or wife approaches the other in correction, the ultimate purpose must not be to remove some annoyance from self or to relieve some tension in the marriage. Certainly such elements may have some part in the matter. Yet the ultimate and primary purpose must be to restore the other unto a right relationship with the Lord.

Confront for the Purpose of Reconciliation

In the ninth place, in the process of correcting one another, the husband and the wife *must confront for the purpose of reconciliation.* In Matthew 18:15 our Lord Jesus Christ instructed, "*Moreover if thy brother shall trespass against thee, go and tell him his fault between thee and him alone: if he shall hear thee, thou hast gained thy brother.*" Correction must not be employed for the purpose of attacking the other or of getting some advantage over the other. Rather, when a husband or wife approaches the other in correction, he or she should maintain the purpose of *gaining* the other – not of gaining *over* the other, but of gaining a renewed relationship *with* the other. Each must maintain the purpose of reconciling the relationship and restoring its unity and fellowship.

Discern When to Refrain from Confrontation

In the tenth and final place, in the process of correcting one another, the husband and the wife *must discern when to refrain from confrontation.* Proverbs 9:7 reveals the truth, "*He that reproveth a scorner getteth to himself shame: and he that rebuketh a wicked man getteth himself a blot.*" Sometimes the one in need of correction clearly reveals that he or she is stubbornly opposed to correction concerning a matter. In such cases the other must have the spiritual discernment to refrain or back away from expressing correction. Instead, he or she must earnestly commit the case unto the Lord in prayer, trusting in and waiting on the Lord to bring forth conviction and correction in the other's heart.

In addition, 1 Peter 3:1-4 specifically instructs wives in such cases, saying, "*Likewise, ye wives, be in subjection to your own husbands; that, if any obey not the word, they also may without the word be won by the conversation of the wives; while they behold your chaste conversation, coupled with fear. Whose adorning let it not be that outward adorning of plaiting the hair, and of wearing gold, or of putting on of apparel; but let it be the hidden man of the heart, in that which is not corruptible, even the ornament of a meek and quiet spirit, which is in the sight of God of great price.*" If the husband reveals in some manner that he is opposed to his wife's correction, then she must quietly and continually pray unto the Lord for her husband. Furthermore, she must concentrate on abiding in respectful submission to him with a meek and quiet spirit and with a pure and Spirit-filled behavior. Yet she specifically must *not* continue to confront him with the word of rebuke, reproof, and correction.

Also 1 Peter 3:7 specifically instructs husbands in such cases, saying, *"Likewise, ye husbands, dwell with them according to knowledge, giving honour unto the wife, as unto the weaker vessel, and as being heirs together of the grace of life; that your prayers be not hindered."* If the wife reveals in some manner that she is opposed to her husband's correction, then he must quietly and continually pray unto the Lord for his wife. Furthermore, he must concentrate on abiding in peace and harmony with her as much as is Biblically permitted, being sensitive and considerate toward her, giving honor unto her, and continuing to nourish and cherish her. Although the husband, as the head of his wife, retains the authority and responsibility to pursue correction, in such cases he must patiently concentrate more upon honoring, nourishing, and cherishing his wife and less upon rebuking, reproving, and correcting her.

In conclusion, a warning must be submitted concerning this matter of correction in the marriage relationship. Although correctives may proceed in both directions, the process of correction does not cancel out the divinely established roles in the marriage relationship. The wife must never employ correction in an unsubmissive manner to gain authority over her husband, and the husband must never employ correction in an unloving manner to lord it over his wife.

Truth for Meditation

Concerning the practice of correcting one another, the husband and the wife must –

1. Avoid a judgmental spirit toward the other. (Matt. 7:1-2; Gal. 5:14-15; Prov. 10:12; 17:9; Eph. 4:2; 1 Pet. 4:8)

2. First correct his or her own sinful faults. (Matt. 7:3-5)

3. Earnestly pray for the other's repentance. (1 John 5:16)

4. Be under the guiding influence of the Holy Spirit. (Gal. 6:1; 5:13-26)

5. Be filled with a spirit of meekness. (Gal. 6:1)

6. Sincerely seek after understanding. (Prov. 18:13)

7. Speak the truth of God in Biblical love. (Eph. 4:15; Prov. 27:6)

8. Confront for the purpose of restoration. (Gal. 6:1)

9. Confront for the purpose of reconciliation. (Matt. 18:15)

10. Know when to refrain from confrontation. (Prov. 9:7; 1 Pet. 3:1-4, 7)

In first correcting his or her own faults before seeking to correct the other's faults, the husband and the wife –

1. Must consider the faults in his or her own heart and life as the greater problem.

2. Must correct the faults in his or her own heart and life through Biblical confession.

3. May then clearly see to help the other correct the faults in his or her life.

Verses for Memorization

Matthew 7:1-2: Judge not, that ye be not judged. For with what judgment ye judge, ye shall be judged: and with what measure ye mete, it shall be measured to you again.

Matthew 7:5: Thou hypocrite, first cast out the beam out of thine own eye; and then shalt thou see clearly to cast out the mote out of thy brother's eye.

Galatians 6:1: Brethren, if a man be overtaken in a fault, ye which are spiritual, restore such an one in the spirit of meekness, considering thyself, lest thou also be tempted.

20

Be Not Bitter

In Ephesians 4:31-32 we all are instructed, *"Let all bitterness, and wrath, and anger, and clamour, and evil speaking, be put away from you, with all malice: and be ye kind one to another, tenderhearted, forgiving one another, even as God for Christ's sake hath forgiven you."* Furthermore, in Hebrews 12:15 we all are warned, *"Looking diligently lest any man fail of the grace of God; lest any root of bitterness springing up trouble you, and thereby many be defiled."* We learn through this Biblical instruction and warning that it is spiritually necessary for both the husband and the wife to put away from their hearts any form of bitterness against the other and to be on their guard against any form of bitterness springing up within their hearts against the other.

Yea, in Colossians 3:19 the instruction and warning is specifically delivered to husbands, saying, *"Husbands, love your wives, and be not bitter against them."* In fact, this is the only passage of God's Word wherein a specific group of individuals is warned against bitterness toward another specific group of individuals. Certainly we all are to take heed lest we become bitter against any other individual or group of individuals. Wives are to take heed lest they become bitter against their husbands. Husbands are to take heed lest they become bitter against their wives. Children are to take heed lest they become bitter against their parents. Parents are to take heed lest they become bitter against their children. Brothers and sisters are to take heed lest they become bitter against one another. However, through the more specific warning of Colossians 3:19, it appears that a husband will be more tempted toward the sin of bitterness against his wife than any other individual will be tempted concerning any other relationship. Therefore, the husband must especially take heed lest he become bitter against his wife.

The Definition of Bitterness

What then is the sin of bitterness? How is it to be defined? The basic meaning of bitterness is an attitude of anger and resentment against another individual that has become rooted in one's heart. Often in God's Word we find water described as bitter water. This bitter water is set in contrast to sweet water. For example, James 3:11 asks the rhetorical question, *"Doth a fountain send forth at the same place sweet water and bitter?"* Such bitter water would be sharp, harsh, biting, and unpleasant to the taste. It would be the opposite of fresh, clean, wholesome water. In fact, such bitter water might even be poisonous and deadly. In Revelation 8:11 we read, *"And the name of the star is called Wormwood: and the third part of the waters became wormwood; and many men died of the waters, because they were made bitter."* In like manner, the attitude and spirit of bitterness is the opposite of a sweet, gentle, loving spirit, the opposite of a tenderhearted spirit. Rather, it is a sharp, harsh, and biting spirit, a spirit of anger, annoyance, resentment, and hard heartedness.

Yet the sin of bitterness does not encompass every attitude of annoyance and anger. Rather, it encompasses any spirit of anger or resentment that becomes *rooted* in an individual's heart. In Hebrews 12:15 we are warned against "any *root* of bitterness springing up" in our hearts. Herein bitterness is described as a growing root, as an attitude that is ever growing more rooted in our hearts. Thus bitterness is an attitude of anger and resentment that is ever *growing deeper* into our hearts and that is ever taking *a tighter grasp* upon our hearts.

However, bitterness includes more than attitudes of anger or resentment that are *deeply* rooted in our hearts. Rather, it includes

254

any spirit of anger or resentment that becomes rooted in our hearts, no matter how great or small that root may be. Again in Hebrews 12:15 we are warned against "*any* root of bitterness springing up" in our hearts. Certainly a spirit of bitterness may be more easily detected after it has become deeply rooted in an individual's heart. Yet the sin of bitterness began when anger or resentment first began to take root and grow as the smallest root in that individual's heart. Therefore, the husband and the wife must each be diligently on his or her guard lest *any* root of bitterness might begin to grow in his or her heart against the other.

The Development of Bitterness

How then does such a root of bitterness develop? Since the husband and the wife are each to be diligently on guard concerning any root of bitterness growing against the other, it is necessary that they understand the manner by which any such root of bitterness might develop. In Hebrews 12:15 God's Word describes bitterness as a root, and in nature a root springs forth from a seed after that seed has germinated. What then is the seed from which the root of bitterness springs forth? Since bitterness is a spirit of anger or resentment that has taken root, the seed of bitterness is to be defined as the initial attitude of anger or annoyance.

At this beginning point the anger or annoyance is not yet a root of bitterness, but only the seed. In nature each seed has a set period for germination whereby the root springs forth and begins to grow. What then is the germination period for the seed of anger or annoyance to become a root of bitterness? We find the answer in God's Holy Word through the instruction and warning of Ephesians 4:26 – "***Be ye angry, and sin not: let not the sun go down upon your wrath.***" If a husband or wife allows an attitude of anger or annoyance to linger in his or her heart against the other from one day into the next, then the seed will germinate. Yea, then a root of bitterness will spring forth and begin to grow.

At the first this root of bitterness will grow unseen within the heart, even as in nature a root first grows unseen within the ground before its plant grows upward above the ground. The root of bitterness will grow more deeply *into* the heart and take a stronger grasp *upon* the heart before it displays itself more outwardly. Yet this root of bitterness will not remain hidden indefinitely. No matter how hard a husband or wife may try to hide a spirit of bitterness against the other, it *will* grow outwardly and *will* bring forth fruit in his or her outward attitudes, words, and actions.

The Destructiveness of Bitterness

As the root of bitterness ever grows deeper into a husband's or wife's heart, it will *fill* the treasury of his or her heart. Then out of that evil treasury, he or she will indeed bring forth evil things in outward attitude, word, and action. In Luke 6:45 our Lord Jesus Christ proclaimed, "*A good man out of the good treasure of his heart bringeth forth that which is good: and an evil man out of the evil treasure of his heart bringeth forth that which is evil: for of the abundance of the heart his mouth speaketh.*" The root of bitterness will eventually bring forth outbursts of wrath and anger in outward attitude, grievous and biting words in speech, and strife and maliciousness in action. (Ephesians 4:31; Romans 3:14; James 3:14)

Even so, Hebrews 12:15 warns us concerning the destructiveness of the sin of bitterness, saying, "*Looking diligently lest any man fail of the grace of God; lest any root of bitterness springing up trouble you, and thereby many be defiled.*" Here we find a two-fold manner in which the sin of bitterness will bring destruction. First, it will be troubling and damaging to the spirit and life of the bitter individual. Second, it will bring defilement to those relationships in which the bitter individual takes part.

Concerning the destructive effect of bitterness upon the bitter one himself or herself, his or her spirit and life will become sour and spoiled. As the opening portion of Hebrews 12:15 reveals, such a bitter individual will "*fail of the grace of God.*" This does not mean that he or she will fall out of God's eternal, saving grace. Rather, it means that he or she will fall short of God's daily, helping grace. It means that a bitter individual will miss that place spiritually where he or she might find God's grace to help in time of need (Hebrews 4:16), whether it be spiritual need, mental and emotional need, physical need, relational need, circumstantial need, or ministry need. Through the sin of bitterness, he or she will be separated from the blessing of our Lord's daily fellowship and thereby from abundant spiritual living. He or she will not find or know the unspeakable and glorious joy of our Lord, and his or her heart and mind will not be guarded by *"the peace of God, which passeth all understanding."* (Philippians 4:7) Rather, he or she will be troubled in heart, continually struggling with discouragement, depression, and even despair.

Furthermore, concerning the destructive effect of bitterness upon others, the harsh attitudes, words, and actions that a bitter spirit will bring forth will sour and spoil those relationships in which a bitter individual takes part. In particular, the husband's or the wife's bitter spirit against the other will defile, damage, and divide the marriage relationship, even to the point of divorce. In addition, his or her bitter spirit will defile the life of the family, undercutting the joy and peace of the home and hindering the godly upbringing of the children. Finally, his or her bitter spirit will even defile other extended relationships, including those with extended family, those on the job, those with neighbors, those in the church, etc.

The Deliverance from Bitterness

Yet what if a husband or wife has already yielded to the spirit of bitterness? What if the spirit of bitterness is already growing within? Is there any deliverance? Yes, there is deliverance in and through our Lord Jesus Christ. First, that husband or wife must *acknowledge* his or her internal, heart attitude of anger and resentment toward the other as the *sin* of bitterness. This is more than acknowledging the sinfulness of the various outward displays of harsh attitudes, words, and actions that are brought forth by a spirit of bitterness. Bitterness is a root *in the heart*. It must be plucked out of the heart *by the root* and must be cast away, *root and all*. If we only deal with the outward displays of bitterness while leaving the inward spirit of bitterness untouched, it will be like cutting off a weed at ground level while leaving the root in the ground. Such will not kill the weed. In fact, the roots of that weed will only grow deeper into the ground; and the weed will grow upward with greater strength.

In like manner, if we only deal with our outward displays of bitterness, the inward root of bitterness will only grow deeper into our hearts and will bring forth even greater outward displays the next time. Therefore, the bitter husband or wife must acknowledge and confess the harbored, nourished, rooted, inward *spirit* of bitterness as the sin that it is, both against the Lord our God and against the other. (1 John 1:9; James 5:16) Yea, the bitter husband or wife must acknowledge the sinfulness of the continuing *thoughts* of anger and resentment by which that spirit of bitterness is nourished. In Ephesians 4:31 we are instructed to put away *all* bitterness from us, not only the outward displays thereof, but even more so the inward spirit thereof.

Second, that husband or wife must *pray* for God's grace to *transform* the spirit and thinking of his or her mind toward the other. A root of bitterness begins when we are annoyed or angered at some perceived offense by the other and when we allow that annoyance or anger to linger in our hearts. As the root of bitterness grows, our thoughts continue to dwell upon that offense and to accumulate a list of additional offenses. In order to find deliverance from the spirit of bitterness, one must have the spirit of his or her mind *renewed* and have the thoughts of his or her mind *redirected*. Yet such renewal and redirection is not possible in one's own strength. Thus each must pray for God's grace that *He* might accomplish *His* work of transformation, removing the hard heart of bitterness and replacing it with the tender heart of genuine, godly love. Thereby each must seek to develop a forbearing and forgiving spirit toward the other, and thereby each must pursue a kind and gracious behavior toward the other.

Ephesians 4:31-32 sets the spirit of bitterness in direct contrast to a kind, tenderhearted, forgiving spirit – "*Let all bitterness, and wrath, and anger, and clamour, and evil speaking be put away from you, with all malice. And be ye kind one to another, tenderhearted, forgiving one another, even as God for Christ's sake hath forgiven*

258

you." Certainly the deeper that a root of bitterness has grown in a husband's or wife's heart, the more difficult it will be to transform the spirit of his or her heart. Yet our Lord through His Word by His Spirit is *more than able* to create in us a clean heart and to renew in us a right spirit. (Psalm 51:10) Praise Him for His transforming grace!

The Defense against Bitterness

Yet we need more than to learn how to be *delivered from* the spirit of bitterness. We need also to learn how to *defend against* the spirit of bitterness. Whereas Ephesians 4:31 instructs us to put away all of the bitterness that is *already* within our hearts, Hebrews 12:15 instructs us to guard diligently against any bitterness from *entering* into our hearts – "*Looking diligently lest any man fail of the grace of God; lest any root of bitterness springing up trouble you, and thereby many be defiled.*" This need for a defense is either that we might not yield to bitterness initially or that we might not return to that bitterness from which we have been delivered.

❖ First, the husband and the wife *must each be ever diligent to watch for and guard against any root of bitterness that might seek to enter into his or her heart against the other.* The opening two words of Hebrews 12:15 present the instruction, "*Looking diligently.*" Time and time again each will commit offenses against the other. At such times each will be tempted to fleshly annoyance and anger, and in turn each will be tempted to allow that annoyance and anger to linger and germinate into a root of bitterness. Thus each must be watching continually for and guarding diligently against this temptation. Each must learn to quickly recognize and diligently resist the attack of this temptation.

❖ Second, the husband and the wife *must each be quick to settle any attitude of annoyance or anger that it might not linger into the next day.* In Ephesians 4:26-27 the instruction is given, "*Be ye angry, and sin not: let not the sun go down upon your wrath: neither give place to the devil.*" When offenses occur, attitudes of annoyance and anger quickly rise up within our hearts. Yet most often these attitudes spring forth from our selfish, sinful flesh. Thus the closing portion of James 1:19 warns us to be *"**slow to wrath;**"* and verse 20 reveals the reason for the warning, explaining, *"**For the wrath of man worketh not the righteousness of God.**"* If a husband or wife dwells upon such an attitude of annoyance or anger and allows it to linger into the next day, this seed will germinate into a root of bitterness. Thereby he or she will depart from the way of God's righteousness and will grant the devil a place in his or her life.

Therefore, when attitudes of annoyance or anger rise up, they must be settled quickly before the sun goes down and the day passes. On the one hand, these fleshly attitudes must be confessed to the Lord as sin and must be replaced by the power of the indwelling Holy Spirit with loving forbearance and tenderhearted kindness. On the other hand, it may also be necessary to confront the other's offense and to pursue reconciliation. Yet however these attitudes may be settled in the husband's or the wife's own heart, the closing counsel of Ephesians 4:26 must be heeded – *"**Let not the sun go down upon your wrath.**"*

❖ Third, the husband and the wife *must each maintain a spirit of loving forbearance and Biblical forgiveness toward the other.* As we have noted already, Ephesians 4:31-32 sets the spirit of bitterness in direct contrast to a kind, tenderhearted, forgiving spirit. Thus we must take heed to the instruction of Ephesians 4:32 if we would find a defense against bitterness – *"**And be ye kind one to another, tenderhearted, forgiving one another, even as God for Christ's sake hath forgiven you.**"* The practice of Biblical forgiveness is a necessary ingredient in this defense. In addition, Colossians 3:13 instructs, *"**Forbearing one another, and forgiving one another, if any have a quarrel against any; even as Christ forgave you, so also do ye.**"*

❖ Fourth, the husband and the wife *must each maintain and practice tenderhearted loving kindness toward the other.* Again we come to the instruction of Ephesians 4:32 – *"**And be ye kind one to another, tenderhearted, forgiving one another, even as God for Christ's sake hath forgiven you.**"* As offenses and mistreatments arise, each must purposefully choose not to dwell upon thoughts of harshness toward the other, but upon thoughts of tenderness toward the other. Each must purposefully choose not to dwell upon the offenses and mistreatments against self, but upon the sacrifice of self in genuine love for the other. In addition, with such tenderhearted and loving thoughts toward the other, each must purposefully seek opportunities to show kindness and do good unto the other.

In Matthew 5:44 our Lord Jesus Christ gave instruction concerning those who oppose us, mistreat us, and hate us, saying, *"But I say unto you, Love your enemies, bless them that curse you, do good to them that hate you, and pray for them which despitefully use you, and persecute you."* In genuine, godly love each is purposefully to bless the other with his or her words and to do good unto the other with his or her behavior. Thereby each will resist yielding to the spirit of bitterness against the other. Yea, thereby each will find a defense against the evil of bitterness and will overcome evil with good. Even so, Romans 12:20-21 gives the instruction, *"Therefore if thine enemy hunger, feed him; if he thirst, give him drink: for in so doing thou shalt heap coals of fire on his head. Be not overcome of evil, but overcome evil with good."*

❖ Fifth, the husband and the wife *must each pray fervently and faithfully for the good of the other*. Again we consider the instruction of our Lord Jesus Christ in Matthew 5:44 – *"But I say unto you, Love your enemies, bless them that curse you, do good to them that hate you, and pray for them which despitefully use you, and persecute you."* Instead of dwelling on the offenses and mistreatments of the other against self, each is to be praying unto the Lord for the good of the other. Yea, even if the offenses and mistreatments may be classified as spiteful malice and hateful persecution, even then each is to pray for the good of the other.

❖ Sixth, the husband and the wife *must each walk daily under the guiding influence of the Holy Spirit*. The above-mentioned elements of defense against the spirit of bitterness – the love, the forbearance, the longsuffering, the tenderheartedness, the kindness, the goodness – all of these are a part of the fruit of the Spirit. Galatians 5:22-23 declares, *"But the fruit of the Spirit is love, joy, peace, longsuffering, gentleness, goodness, faith, meekness, temperance, against such there is no law.*" Yet a believer cannot "work up" this fruit from within himself or herself. Rather, this fruit must be *produced* through him or her *by the indwelling Holy Spirit.* He or she must walk under the guiding influence of the Spirit in order to bring forth this fruit of the Spirit.

Even so, Galatians 5:16 presents the instruction, *"This I say then, Walk in the Spirit, and ye shall not fulfil the lust of the flesh."* The spirit of bitterness is of the works and ways of our selfish, sinful flesh. According to Galatians 5:16 each must walk in the Spirit in order to defend against such ways of the flesh. The opposite spirit, the spirit of tenderheartedness, forbearance, kindness, and forgiveness, is of the godly fruit of the Holy Spirit. Therefore, each must walk in the Spirit in order to bring forth such godly fruit in direct contrast to the spirit of bitterness.

❖ Seventh, the husband and the wife *must each commit any case of mistreatment into God's hand, trusting Him to deal with it according to His righteous will.* In 1 Peter 2:21-23 our Lord Jesus Christ is presented as our perfect example in suffering mistreatment. There we read, *"For even hereunto were ye called: because Christ also suffered for us, leaving us an example, that ye should follow his steps: who did no sin, neither was guile found in his mouth: who, when he was reviled, reviled not again; when he suffered, he threatened not; but committed himself to him that judgeth righteously."* On the one hand, our Lord Jesus Christ did not respond to such mistreatment with bitterness and retaliation. On the other hand, He committed Himself and the case into the hand of God the Father as the One who judges righteously.

The husband and the wife should each "follow His steps." Instead of yielding to bitterness at such times, each should set his or her trust in God. Each should commit himself or herself into the loving care of the Lord our God and should trust wholly in Him to deal with the matter in His time, in His way, and according to His righteousness. Even so, in Romans 12:19 the instruction is given, *"Dearly beloved, avenge not yourselves, but rather give place unto wrath: for it is written, Vengeance is mine; I will repay, saith the Lord."*

❖ Eighth, the husband and the wife *must each rejoice continually in the Lord and in all His bountiful benefits toward him or her.* In Philippians 4:4 we are instructed, *"Rejoice in the Lord alway: and again I say, Rejoice."* Even so, David expressed his commitment in Psalm 13:6, saying, *"I will sing unto the LORD, because he hath dealt bountifully with me."* Again in Psalm 103:1-2 he expressed His commitment, saying, *"Bless the LORD, O my soul: and all that is within me, bless his holy name. Bless the LORD, O my soul, and forget not all his benefits."* At times of offense and mistreatment, we are quick to develop a complaining spirit. With such a complaining spirit, we dwell upon the offense and mistreatment and thereby nourish a spirit of anger and bitterness. The opposite of such a complaining spirit is a *rejoicing* spirit. Rather than focus upon the complaint, the husband or wife must focus upon rejoicing in the Lord and in all of His bountiful benefits toward him or her. No matter how great the offense and mistreatment may be, the bountiful benefits of the Lord are *multiplied times greater.* Yea, they are *"more than can be numbered."* (Psalm 40:5) Developing and maintaining such a focus upon rejoicing in the Lord will thus serve as a defense against a complaining and bitter spirit. Be not bitter against one another, but rejoice evermore in the Lord.

Truth for Meditation

Concerning the sin of bitterness toward one anther, the husband and the wife must understand –

1. The definition of bitterness: An attitude of anger and resentment that has become rooted in his or her heart against the other. (Jam. 3:11; Rev. 8:11; Heb. 12:15)

2. The development of bitterness: Allowing an attitude of anger or annoyance to linger from one day into the next whereby it will ever grow deeper and stronger within his or her heart and will eventually display itself in his or her outward attitudes, words, and actions. (Eph. 4:26; Luke 6:45; Eph. 4:31; Rom. 3:14; Jam. 3:14)

3. The destructiveness of bitterness: Troubling the spirit and life of the bitter one himself or herself and defiling those relationships in which he or she takes part. (Heb. 12:15)

4. The deliverance from bitterness: Acknowledging and confessing the spirit of bitterness as sin and praying for the Lord to transform the spirit and thinking of his or her mind. (1 John 1:9; Jam. 5:16; Eph. 4:31-32; Psa. 51:10)

To defend against a spirit of bitterness toward the other, the husband and the wife must –

1. Be ever diligent to watch for and guard against any root of bitterness that might seek to enter into his or her heart against the other. (Heb. 12:15)

2. Be quick to settle any attitude of annoyance or anger that it might not linger into the next day. (Eph. 4:26-27)

3. Maintain a spirit of loving forbearance and Biblical forgiveness toward the other. (Eph. 4:31; Col. 3:13)

4. Maintain and practice tenderhearted loving kindness toward the other. (Eph. 4:31; Matt. 5:44; Rom. 12:20-21)

5. Pray fervently and faithfully for the good of the other. (Matt. 5:44)

6. Walk daily under the guiding influence of the Holy Spirit. (Gal. 5:16, 22-23)

7. Commit any case of mistreatment into God's hand, trusting Him to deal with it according to His righteous will. (1 Pet. 2:21-23; Rom. 12:19)

8. Rejoice continually in the Lord and in all His bountiful benefits toward him or her. (Phil. 4:4; Psa. 13:6; 40:5; 103:1-2)

Verses for Memorization

Hebrews 12:15: Looking diligently lest any man fail of the grace of God; lest any root of bitterness springing up trouble you, and many be defiled.

Ephesians 4:26-27: Be ye angry, and sin not: let not the sun go down upon your wrath: neither give place to the devil.

James 1:20: For the wrath of man worketh not the righteousness of God.

Matthew 5:44: But I say unto you, Love your enemies, bless them that curse you, do good to them that hate you, and pray for them which despitefully use you, and persecute you.

Galatians 5:22-23: But the fruit of the Spirit is love, joy, peace, longsuffering, gentleness, goodness, faith, meekness, temperance, against such there is no law.

Philippians 4:4: Rejoice in the Lord alway: and again I say, Rejoice.

Psalm 13:6: I will sing unto the LORD, because he hath dealt bountifully with me.

21

Be Not Contentious

In Proverbs 17:1 the truth is revealed, *"Better is a dry morsel, and quietness therewith, than an house full of sacrifices with strife."* A home "full of sacrifices" is one that has much financial provision and much earthly goods. On the other hand, a home with only a dry morsel is one that is quite poor in financial provision and earthly goods. Yet it is far better to live in a financially poor home that is full of peace and quietness than to live in a financially full home that is also full of strife and contention. Thus in Romans 12:18 the instruction is given, *"If it be possible, as much as lieth in you, live peaceably with all men."* More specifically, with as much earnestness and effort as he is spiritually able, the husband is to live peaceably with his wife; and with as much earnestness and effort as she is spiritually able, the wife is to live peaceably with her husband. As much as is possible, each is to pursue peace with the other. The opening portion of Hebrews 12:14 declares, *"Follow peace with all men;"* and the closing half of Psalm 34:14 adds, *"Seek peace, and pursue it."*

Yet in Proverbs 26:21 the warning is given, *"As coals are to burning coals, and wood to fire; so is a contentious man to kindle strife."* Again in the opening half of Proverbs 16:28, the warning is given, *"A froward man soweth strife."* Yet again in Proverbs 29:22 the warning is given, *"An angry man stirreth up strife, and a furious man aboundeth in transgression."* Certainly these verses serve as a warning to every young lady not to seek after such a man to marry.

Even so, Proverbs 22:24 instructs, *"Make no friendship with an angry man; and with a furious man thou shalt not go."* However, these verses also serve as a warning to every husband that he should not *be* a man of such character lest he stir up strife within his marriage and home relationships.

In addition, the warning is given in the closing half of Proverbs 19:13, *"And the contentions of a wife are a continual dropping."* Again in Proverbs 27:15 the warning is given, *"A continual dropping in a very rainy day and a contentious woman are alike."* Yet again the warning is given in Proverbs 21:9, *"It is better to dwell in a corner of the housetop, than with a brawling woman in a wide house."* Finally, the warning is given in Proverbs 21:19, *"It is better to dwell in the wilderness, than with a contentious and an angry woman."* Certainly these verses serve as a warning to every young man not to seek after such a woman to marry. However, they also serve as a warning to every wife that she should not *be* a woman of such character lest she drive away the hearts of her husband and family from her and lest thereby she become a force of destruction within her marriage and home relationships.

The Pursuit of Peace

As we have previously learned, in the marriage relationship the husband and the wife are called into a relationship of one-flesh unity. Such is the desire and intent of the Lord our God – that the husband and the wife develop and dwell together in one-flesh unity. This one-flesh unity is to be developed and strengthened through the binding glue of peace. Even so, Ephesians 4:3 instructs, *"Endeavouring to keep the unity of the Spirit in the bond of peace."* The husband and the wife must each allow the peace of God to rule in their hearts (Colossians 3:15) in order that such peace might also rule in their marriage relationship and in their home life.

Thereby the fruit of righteousness will be sown in their marriage and home, even as James 3:18 reveals, *"And the fruit of righteousness is sown in peace of them that make peace."* Thereby the blessing of God will be poured out upon their marriage and home, even as our Lord Jesus Christ proclaimed in Matthew 5:9, *"Blessed are the peacemakers: for they shall be called the children of God."* In addition, 1 Peter 3:10-12 states, *"For he that will love life, and see good days, let him refrain his tongue from evil, and his lips that they speak no guile: let him eschew evil, and do good; let him seek peace, and ensue it. For the eyes of the Lord are over the righteous, and his ears are open unto their prayers: but the face of the Lord is against them that do evil."* To seek peace and pursue it is the way of the righteous, and the Lord our God looks with favor upon the righteous and opens His ears unto their prayers. Oh, what a blessing is this! Finally, thereby the atmosphere of joy and gladness will saturate their marriage and home, even as the latter half of Proverbs 12:20 declares, *"But to the counselors of peace is joy."* Yea, by seeking and pursuing peace together, the husband and the wife shall enjoy their marriage relationship and home life and shall see many good days therein.

On the other hand, a continuing atmosphere of contention and strife will create an ever-growing division within the marriage relationship. Now, it is likely that every marriage will experience contention, strife, and division at times. Yet this contention, strife, and division must be quickly resolved; and the one-flesh unity of the marriage relationship must be quickly reconciled and restored in peace. If such contention, strife, and division is allowed to linger and to grow, it will bring that marriage and home to desolation and destruction. In Matthew 12:25 our Lord Jesus Christ proclaimed, *"Every kingdom divided against itself is brought to desolation; and every city or house divided against itself shall not stand."* By the biting and devouring ways of contention, strife, and division, that marriage will consume itself and the members of that household. (Galatians 5:15)

The Source of Contention

What then is the source of contention, strife, and division within a marriage relationship? From a statistical perspective we could refer to various and sundry categories in which contention, strife, and division might arise within a marriage relationship. Yet such would only reveal the outward symptoms of the matter. The source itself is something deeper in the heart. The source of *all* such contention, strife, and division is the *selfishness* of our hearts. James 4:1 poses the question and reveals the answer, saying, *"From whence come wars and fightings among you? Come they not hence, even of your lusts that war in your members."* The selfish desires of our hearts will ever rise up in contention with any one or any thing that prevents us from acquiring what we want; and when the husband and the wife both selfishly engage in conflict with one another, the contention will multiply in intensity. The longer that they continue to engage with selfishness in the conflict, the greater the intensity of the contention will multiply.

The source of a contentious spirit is the selfishness of our hearts; and that selfishness is rooted in our selfish, sinful flesh. In Galatians 5:20 hatred (enmity, hostility), variance (contention, quarreling), emulations (selfish rivalry), wrath, strife, and seditions (divisions, dissension) are all included as works of the flesh. Also in 1 Corinthians 3:3 the apostle Paul, under the inspiration of God the Holy Spirit, rebuked the believers at Corinth, saying, *"For ye are yet carnal* [after the flesh]*: for whereas there is among you envying, and strife, and divisions, are ye not carnal* [after the flesh]*, and walk as men?"* The envying, strife, and divisions of these believers, being works of the flesh, served as unmistakable evidence that they were walking after their selfish, sinful flesh.

In like manner, when the husband or the wife possesses a contentious spirit, it clearly reveals that he or she is walking after his or her selfish, sinful flesh at that particular time. Thus each must confront his or her own contentious spirit as the sin that it is – against the Lord our God, against the other spouse, and against the other members of the family. Yea, each must confess and correct that contentious spirit accordingly.

The Seeds of Contention

Furthermore, each must confront, confess, and correct the seeds of contention that are produced out of his or her own contentious spirit and that are sent forth to sow and nourish contention and strife within the marriage and home. These seeds of contention are the various expressions of a contentious spirit through outward attitudes, words, and actions. They are the means by which one's contentious spirit makes an impact upon the spirit of others and upon the relationship with others. These seeds of contention include the following:

❖ *A proud heart.* The opening half of Proverbs 13:10 reveals the truth, *"Only by pride cometh contention."* The opening half of Proverbs 28:25 adds, *"He that is of a proud heart stirreth up strife."* A proud heart believes that it deserves to get its own way and to be in first place, and a proud heart will not yield its own way or acknowledge any fault on its own part. Thus a proud heart will contend and strive with any one that prevents it from getting its own way, that gets between it and first place, or that corrects it of any fault. Such a proud heart must be Biblically confessed as sin.

❖ *An angry demeanor.* Proverbs 15:18 declares, *"A wrathful man stirreth up strife: but he that is slow to anger appeaseth strife."* Proverbs 29:22 adds, *"An angry man stirreth up strife, and a furious man aboundeth in transgression."* This angry demeanor includes crankiness, snappiness, sulkiness, impatience, unkindness, harshness, bitterness, etc. Thereby an angry demeanor strikes out against others and stirs up within them an angry response. Such an angry demeanor in any of its manifestations must be Biblically confessed as sin.

❖ *Grievous words.* Proverbs 15:1 declares, *"A soft answer turneth away wrath: but grievous words stir up anger."* Such would include harsh, piercing, and biting words. Such would include proud, haughty, and boasting words. Such would include selfish, willful, and stubborn words. Such would include foolish, discouraging, and dishonoring words. Such would include deceitful or complaining words. All such grievous words must be Biblically confessed as sin.

❖ *Backbiting words.* Proverbs 16:28 declares, *"A froward man soweth strife: and a whisperer separateth chief friends."* Proverbs 26:20 adds, *"Where no wood is, there the fire goeth out: so where there is no talebearer, the strife ceaseth."* Backbiting is to be defined

271

as repeating negative matters of frustration and complaint about another to someone else. All such backbiting words must be Biblically confessed as sin.

❖ *Intentional aggravation.* Proverbs 30:33 declares, *"Surely the churning of the milk bringeth forth butter, and the wringing of the nose bringeth forth blood: so the forcing of wrath bringeth forth strife."* Certainly an individual may annoy and aggravate another unintentionally, without knowing. Yet such annoyances and aggravations against another are often rooted in inconsiderateness, selfishness, or maliciousness. All such aggravation must be Biblically confessed as sin.

❖ *An argumentative demeanor.* Proverbs 26:21 declares, *"As coals are to burning coals, and wood to fire: so is a contentious man to kindle strife."* Arguing in order to get one's own way, arguing in order to exalt one's own self, arguing in order to get one's own opinion heard, arguing in order to win over the other, arguing in order not to acknowledge one's own fault, etc. – Such manifestations of an argumentative demeanor must be Biblically confessed as sin.

❖ *Foolish meddling.* Proverbs 20:3 declares, *"It is an honour for a man to cease from strife: but every fool will be meddling."* Proverbs 18:6 adds, *"A fool's lips enter into contention, and his mouth calleth for strokes."* All too often we insert our opinion where we should remain uninvolved. All too often we spout forth when we should remain silent. All too often we boldly press forward when we should quietly back away. All too often we speak up at an unwise time, in an unwise place, with an unwise manner, without Biblical wisdom. Contention and strife is the result. All such foolish meddling must be Biblically confessed as sin.

❖ *Bitter hatred.* Proverbs 10:12 declares, *"Hatred stirreth up strifes: but love covereth all sins."* James 3:14-16 warns, *"But if ye have bitter envying and strife in your hearts, glory not, and lie not against the truth. This wisdom descendeth not from above, but is earthly, sensual* [of the flesh]*, devilish. For where envying and strife is, there is confusion and every evil work."* Such bitter hatred and envying (resentment) will ever look to defend itself against any perceived attack and to attack any one with whom it stands in conflict. It will often express itself with an angry and argumentative demeanor, with grievous and backbiting words, and with intentional and even malicious aggravation. Such bitter hatred must be Biblically confessed as sin.

❖ *A scornful demeanor.* Proverbs 22:10 declares, *"Cast out the scorner, and contention shall go out; yea, strife and reproach shall cease."* Proverbs 29:8 adds, *"Scornful men bring a city into a snare: but wise men turn away wrath."* A scornful demeanor will show great contempt and even indignation against others on a whim. It will strike out in any given direction at any given time, primarily with harsh, grievous, scoffing words. It will especially strike out against those in authority and against the boundaries of authority. It will fiercely oppose any form of correction, and it will often strike out against those who are in a weaker position than itself. This scornful demeanor and its scornful attacks must be Biblically confessed as sin.

❖ *A froward character.* Proverbs 6:12-14 declares, *"A naughty person, a wicked man, walketh with a froward mouth. He winketh with his eyes, he speaketh with his feet, he teacheth with his fingers; frowardness is in his heart, he deviseth mischief continually; he soweth discord."* Proverbs 16:28 adds, *"A froward man soweth strife: and a whisperer separateth chief friends."* A froward individual is one who is naughty, mischievous, perverted, deceitful, willful, stubborn, and contrary to the truth and righteousness of God. Such ways will often produce contention and strife. Yea, such a froward individual will even find perverse pleasure in stirring up contention and strife. This froward character and its ways must be Biblically confessed as sin.

The Guard against Contention

What then might the husband and the wife do to guard against a contentious spirit and against contention within their marriage relationship? What might they do to promote peace therein?

273

❖ First, they each *must walk daily under the guiding influence of the Holy Spirit*. The spirit and seeds of contention are rooted in the desires of our selfish, sinful flesh. It is through humbly surrendering ourselves to walk after the guidance of the Holy Spirit that we overcome the desires of our selfish, sinful flesh. Galatians 5:16 proclaims, ***"This I say then, Walk in the Spirit, and ye shall not fulfil the lust of the flesh."*** In addition, the spiritual fruit that the Holy Spirit will produce in and through us as we humbly surrender ourselves to His guidance is the very opposite of a contentious spirit. Galatians 5:22-23 states, ***"But the fruit of the Spirit is love, joy, peace, longsuffering, gentleness, goodness, faith, meekness, temperance: against such there is no law."*** In like manner, James 3:17-18 states, ***"But the wisdom that is from above*** [that is – the wisdom that is from the Holy Spirit] ***is first pure, then peaceable, gentle, and easy to be entreated, full of mercy and good fruits, without partiality, and without hypocrisy. And the fruit of righteousness is sown in peace of them that make peace."*** Walking daily after the guiding influence of the Holy Spirit will both deliver the husband and the wife from a selfishly contentious spirit and develop in the husband and the wife a spiritually peaceable spirit.

❖ Second, they each *must walk daily in humbleness of mind*. In Philippians 2:3-4 the instruction is given, ***"Let nothing be done through strife or vainglory; but in lowliness of mind let each esteem other better than themselves. Look not every man on his own things, but every man also on the things of others."*** In these verses the contentious spirit of strife and vainglory is set in direct contrast to a humble spirit. With genuine, godly humility in heart and mind, we will avoid strife and pursue peace. With genuine, godly humility in heart and mind, we will not seek after self-glory, but will esteem others more highly than self. With genuine, godly humility in heart and mind, we will not walk in selfishness, but will walk in service to others.

Even so, Philippians 2:5 continues with the instruction, ***"Let this mind be in you, which was also in Christ Jesus."*** What then was the mindset of our Lord Jesus Christ? Verses 6-7 give answer, ***"Who, being in the form of God, thought it not robbery to be equal with***

God: but made himself of no reputation, and took upon him the form of a servant, and was made in the likeness of men." Our Lord Jesus Christ willingly gave up His rightful place in glory on high and humbled Himself to the place of a servant. In like manner, the husband and the wife must do *nothing* with a contentious, self-serving, self-glorying spirit, but must do *everything* with a humble-minded and servant-minded spirit.

❖ Third, they each *must walk daily in genuine, godly love.* In Galatians 5:13-15 the warning is given, "*For, brethren, ye have been called unto liberty; only use not liberty for an occasion to the flesh* [that is – for an occasion to selfishness], *but by love serve one another. For all the law is fulfilled in one word, even in this; Thou shalt love thy neighbor as thyself. But if ye bite and devour one another, take heed that ye be not consumed one of another.*" In these verses a loving spirit toward one another is set in direct contrast to the contentious spirit of biting and devouring one another. Such backbiting is rooted in our selfish, sinful flesh. Yet genuine, godly love will not serve self at the expense of the other. Rather, it will sacrifice self in service to the other. Furthermore, genuine, godly love will not bite at the other to advance self over the other. Rather, it will forbear the faults of the other at the expense of self. Proverbs 10:12 declares, "*Hatred stirreth us strifes: but love covereth all sins.*" Even so, the husband and the wife must not bite at one another, but must lovingly serve one another and forbear one another.

❖ Fourth, they each *must speak with gentle, gracious words.* In Proverbs 15:1 the truth is given, "*A soft answer turneth away wrath: but grievous words stir up anger.*" Selfish, unkind, harsh, grievous words will produce anger, contention, and strife where none previously existed. On the other hand, loving, gentle, considerate, gracious words will turn away anger and promote peace where contention and strife has already entered in. Thus we learn that when a husband and wife will speak with gentle, gracious words, they will not only prevent contention and strife from entering into their relationship, but will also prevail over contention and strife that is already in their relationship.

❖ Fifth, they each *must be slow to annoyance and anger.* In Proverbs 15:18 the truth is given, *"A wrathful man stirreth up strife: but he that is slow to anger appeaseth strife."* A spirit of anger nourishes contention and strife. As a spirit of anger grows in a relationship, so grows contention and strife in that relationship. On the other hand, as the spirit of anger passes away, so the contention and strife will pass away with it. When a husband and wife will be slow to annoyance and anger, they will not only prevent contention and strife from entering into their relationship, but will also prevail over contention and strife that is already in their relationship.

❖ Sixth, they each *must refuse to engage in contention and strife.* In Proverbs 17:14 the warning is given, *"The beginning of strife is as when one letteth out water: therefore leave off contention, before it be meddled with."* Just as a small hole in a dam of water will continue to grow into a destructive torrent of water, even so the beginning of contention and strife will continue to grow until it is a destructive force in a relationship. Thus it is best for the husband and the wife to "leave off" contention and strife, even from its very beginning. They should not press forward in selfish contention, but should back away in loving submission. Even so, the opening half of Proverbs 20:3 proclaims, *"It is an honour for a man to cease from strife."*

❖ Seventh, they each *must not retaliate, but return good for evil in word and in action.* In Romans 12:18-21 the instruction is given, *"If it be possible, as much as lieth in you, live peaceably with all men. Dearly beloved, avenge not yourselves, but rather give place unto wrath: for it is written, Vengeance is mine; I will repay, saith the Lord. Therefore if thine enemy hunger, feed him; if he thirst, give him drink: for in so doing thou shalt heap coals of fire on his head. Be not overcome of evil, but overcome evil with good."* In the midst of contention and strife, our selfish, sinful flesh finds satisfaction in retaliation. Yet such retaliation only nourishes the contention and strife. Retaliation from one only leads to further retaliation from the other.

Therefore, the Lord our God has specifically commanded us not to respond with retaliation. Rather, we are to back away from the contention and strife and to give place unto our Lord's judgment and wrath in the matter. Vengeance is the Lord's. It is not our rightful place to retaliate. It is our Lord's place, and He has promised to do so according to His righteous will. In Proverbs 20:22 the instruction is given, ***"Say not thou, I will recompense evil; but wait on the LORD, and he shall save thee."*** On the other hand, the Lord our God has commanded us to pursue peace by returning good for evil in word and in action. The husband and the wife must, as much as each is able, live peaceably with one another. In times of contention and strife each must specifically speak blessing and do good unto the other. Thereby the evil of contention and strife will be overcome with good through the grace of our Lord.

Truth for Meditation

The source of contention within a marriage relationship is –

❖ The selfish desires of the husband's and the wife's selfish, sinful flesh.

The seeds of contention whereby contention and strife is sown and nourished within a marriage relationship include –

1. A proud heart. (Prov. 13:10; 28:25)

2. An angry demeanor. (Prov. 15:18; 29:22)

3. Grievous words. (Prov. 15:1)

4. Backbiting words. (Prov. 16:28; 26:20)

5. Intentional aggravation. (Prov. 30:33)

6. An argumentative demeanor. (Prov. 26:21)

7. Foolish meddling. (Prov. 20:3; 18:6)

8. Bitter hatred. (Prov. 10:12; Jam. 3:14-16)

9. A scornful demeanor. (Prov. 22:10; 29:8)

10. A froward character. (Prov. 6:12-14; 16:28)

To guard against contention and promote peace within their marriage relationship, the husband and the wife must –

1. Walk daily after the guidance of the Holy Spirit. (Gal. 5:16, 22-23; Jam. 3:17-18)

2. Walk daily in humbleness of mind. (Phil. 2:3-7)

3. Walk daily in genuine, godly love. (Gal. 5:13-15; Prov. 10:12)

4. Speak with gentle, gracious words. (Prov. 15:1)

5. Be slow to annoyance and anger. (Prov. 15:18)

6. Refuse to engage in contention and strife. (Prov. 17:14; 20:3)

7. Not retaliate, but return good for evil in word and action. (Rom. 12:18-21; Prov. 20:22)

Verses for Memorization

Proverbs 17:1: Better is a dry morsel, and quietness therewith, than an house full of sacrifices with strife.

Romans 12:18: If it be possible, as much as lieth in you, live peaceably with all men.

James 3:17-18: But the wisdom that is from above is first pure, then peaceable, gentle, and easy to be entreated, full of mercy and good fruits, without partiality, and without hypocrisy. And the fruit of righteousness is sown in peace of them that make peace.

Proverbs 15:1: A soft answer turneth away wrath: but grievous words stir up anger.

Proverbs 15:18: A wrathful man stirreth up strife: but he that is slow to anger appeaseth strife.

22

Providing for the Home
(Part 1)

In 1 Timothy 5:8 we find the following principle of God's truth – *"But if any provide not for his own, and specially for those of his own house, he hath denied the faith, and is worse than an infidel."* The immediate context of this principle concerns the matter of materially providing for one's widowed mother or some other widowed relative. In verse 4 we read, *"But if any widow have children or nephews, let them learn first to shew piety at home, and to requite their parents: for that is good and acceptable before God."* Yet the principle itself concerns more than this matter. If one's widowed mother is to be considered of his own house, then certainly his own wife and children are also to be considered of his own house. If a man has been given the responsibility before God to provide materially for his widowed mother as one of his own house, then certainly he has also been given the responsibility to provide materially for his own wife and children. Yea, according to the principle of God's Holy Word, he is responsible before God to provide *"specially* for those of his own house."

Furthermore, this principle is of a very serious nature and of great spiritual significance. God's Holy Word declares that if a man who is a believer does not fulfill his responsibility to provide for his own household, he has thereby *"denied the faith, and is worse than an*

281

infidel." By such irresponsibility he publicly denies and dishonors the transforming power of the gospel and the glorious name of his Savior, Jesus Christ. By such irresponsibility he behaves in a manner that is worse than this spiritually lost world, lost in spiritual darkness and sin. Oh, how much such irresponsibility must damage the testimony of Christ! Oh, how deeply such irresponsibility must grieve the heart of our Lord and Savior!

Now, this responsibility to provide materially for the home is first and foremost laid upon the man of the home. The opening portion of Proverbs 19:14 states, "***House and riches are the inheritance of fathers.***" Certainly as a helper who is meet for her husband, the wife is to help him in whatever Biblically appropriate way is necessary. In addition, if for some reason the man of the home is unavailable or incapacitated, it may be necessary for the woman of the home to carry the weight of this responsibility. Yet the foundational intent of the Lord our God is that the man of the home, the husband, the father, be primarily responsible to provide for his household. How then is the man of the home to fulfill this responsibility aright?

Set His Household's Priority on Serving the Lord Their God

In the first place, *he must set his own and his household's priority on serving the Lord their God, not on acquiring the things of this world.* In Matthew 6:19-21 our Lord Jesus Christ expressed the warning, "***Lay not up for yourselves treasures upon earth, where moth and rust doth corrupt, and where thieves break through and steal: but lay up for yourselves treasures in heaven, where neither moth nor rust doth corrupt, and where thieves do not break through nor steal: for where your treasure is, there will your heart be also.***" In verse 24 our Lord added the warning, "***No man can serve two masters: for either he will hate the one, and love the other; or else he will hold to the one, and despise the other. Ye cannot serve God and mammon*** [the things of this world]."

It is not spiritually possible for a man to love and serve the Lord his God and the things of this world at the same time. It is not spiritually possible for a man to lead his household in faithful love and service toward the Lord their God and the things of this world at the same time. No man and no household can serve these two masters at the same time. A choice of priority must be made. A man must choose whether he will set the priority of his own heart and his household's focus on laying up treasures in heaven through faithful love and service to the Lord their God or on laying up treasures upon earth through acquiring and accumulating the things of this world.

Setting the priority of his own heart and his household's focus on laying up treasures upon the earth is the *empty* choice. The things and treasures of this world *do not last*. They vanish away far more quickly than they were acquired. Even so, Proverbs 23:4-5 warns, *"Labour not to be rich: cease from thine own wisdom. Wilt thou set thine eyes upon that which is not? For riches certainly make themselves wings; they fly away as an eagle toward heaven."* Furthermore, the things and treasures of this world *do not satisfy*. Those whose priority is ever set on getting what they want ever want more than they get. Even so, Ecclesiastes 5:10 warns, *"He that loveth silver shall not be satisfied with silver; nor he that loveth abundance with increase: this is also vanity."* Finally, the things and treasures of this world will be *of no benefit* whatsoever in the day of judgment before the Lord our God. Even so, Proverbs 11:4 warns, *"Riches profit not in the day of wrath: but righteousness delivereth from death."*

In like manner, we find the warning of our Lord Jesus Christ in Luke 12:15-21 – *"And he said unto them, Take heed, and beware of covetousness: for a man's life consisteth not in the abundance of the things which he possesseth. And he spake a parable unto them, saying, The ground of a certain rich man brought forth plentifully: and he thought within himself, saying, What shall I do, because I have no room where to bestow my fruits? And he said, This will I do: I will pull down my barns, and build greater; and there will I bestow all my fruits and my goods. And I will say to my soul, Soul, thou hast much goods laid up for many years; take thine ease, eat, drink, and be merry. But God said unto him, Thou fool, this night thy soul shall be required of thee: then whose shall those things be, which thou hast provided? So is he that layeth up treasure for himself, and is not rich toward God."*

Spending one's personal and household life on acquiring and accumulating the things of this world will result only in an empty and wasted life. Thus our Lord Jesus Christ proclaimed in Luke 9:25, *"For what is a man advantaged, if he gain the whole world, and lose himself, or be cast away?"* Yea, we might add – What is the man of a home advantaged, if he gain the whole world for his household, while the members of his household themselves be lost or cast away?

In contrast, setting the priority of his own heart and his household's focus on laying up treasure in heaven is the *eternal* choice. Such treasures in heaven *shall eternally endure*. They shall never fade away or be stolen away. In Hebrews 10:34 the divinely inspired author of Hebrews commended and encouraged the Hebrew believers, saying, *"For ye had compassion of me in my bonds, and took joyfully the spoiling of your goods, knowing in yourselves that ye have in heaven a better and an enduring substance."* Furthermore, such treasures in heaven are *of eternal value*. In 1 Corinthians 9:25 the apostle Paul revealed that those who faithfully love and serve the Lord in this life shall receive an incorruptible reward and crown in the life to come. Finally, such treasures in heaven *will be awarded* from the hand of the Lord our God Himself at the day of judgment. In 2 Timothy 4:7-8 the apostle proclaimed, *"I have fought a good fight, I have finished my course, I have kept the faith: henceforth there is laid up for me a crown of righteousness, which the Lord, the righteous judge, shall give me at that day: and not to me only, but unto all them also that love His appearing."* Investing one's personal and household life in love and service to the Lord will result in eternal returns and rewards. In 1 Corinthians 15:18 the instruction and assurance is given, *"Therefore, my beloved brethren, be ye stedfast, unmoveable, always abounding in the work of the Lord, forasmuch as ye know that your labour is not in vain in the Lord."*

Direct His Household's Trust in the Lord for Provision

Yet the man of the home *is* responsible before the Lord his God to provide materially for his household. How can he set his priority on serving the Lord and also fulfill this responsibility? The answer to this question brings us to the second truth. In the second place, *he must direct his own and his household's trust in the Lord to grant the means and strength for him to provide adequately for his household.*

In Matthew 6:25-33 our Lord Jesus Christ declared, *"Therefore I say unto you, Take no thought for your life, what ye shall eat, or what ye shall drink; nor yet for your body, what ye shall put on. Is not the life more than meat, and the body than raiment? Behold the fowls of the air: for they sow not, neither do they reap, nor gather into barns; yet your heavenly Father feedeth them. Are ye not much better than they? Which of you by taking thought can add one cubit unto his stature? And why take ye thought for raiment? Consider the lilies of the field, how they grow; they toil not, neither do they spin: and yet I say unto you, That even Solomon in all his glory was not arrayed like one of these. Wherefore, if God so clothe the grass of the field, which to day is, and to morrow is cast into the oven, shall he not much more clothe you, O ye of little faith? Therefore take no thought, saying, What shall we eat? or, What shall we drink? or, Wherewithal shall we be clothed? (For after all these things do the Gentiles seek:) for your heavenly Father knoweth that ye have need of all these things. But seek ye first the kingdom of God, and his righteousness; and all these things shall be added unto you."*

God our heavenly Father knows our every need and knows how best to meet our every need. In addition, God our heavenly Father cares for us and will take care to meet our needs. He takes care to feed the birds of the air. He takes care to clothe the grass of the field. How much more shall He take care to meet the needs of His own dear children? Therefore, we who are His dear children should not be filled with a spirit of worry over our needs and should not set our priority on acquiring the material goods to meet our needs. Rather, we should set our priority on serving the Lord our God, on "the kingdom of God and His righteousness," and should trust Him to grant the means and strength for daily provision. This is His certain promise – *"And all these things shall be added unto you."*

Yes, the man of the home has the responsibility to provide materially for his household. Yea, God Himself has given him that responsibility.

Yet he should not be filled with worry over that responsibility and should not set his priority on acquiring material goods. Rather, he should set his own and his household's priority on serving the Lord their God. Then he should set his own and his household's trust in the Lord their God to grant the means and strength for daily provision according to His faithful promise and His righteous will. Yes, (as we shall consider in the next chapter) the man of the home must labor diligently to provide for his household. Yet he must never set his trust in his own strength and skills to acquire that provision. Rather, he must ever recognize and remember that it is the Lord his God who gives him that ability.

Even so, the man of God Moses warned God's people in Deuteronomy 8:11-14, saying, *"Beware that thou forget not the LORD thy God, in not keeping his commandments, and his judgments, and his statutes, which I command thee this day: lest when thou hast eaten and art full, and hast built goodly houses, and dwelt therein; and when thy herds and thy flocks multiply, and thy silver and thy gold is multiplied, and all that thou hast is multiplied; then thine heart be lifted up, and thou forget the LORD thy God, which brought thee forth out of the land of Egypt, from the house of bondage."* To this he added in verse 17, *"And thou say in thine heart, My power and the might of mine hand hath gotten me this wealth."* Material success brings with it the temptation to be lifted up with pride in heart. In addition, out of this pride of heart flows the temptation to forget the priority of serving the Lord our God and the temptation to credit our own strength and skills for that success. Such temptation must be resisted.

On the other hand, Moses instructed God's people in the opening portion of Deuteronomy 8:18, saying, *"But thou shalt remember the LORD thy God: for it is he that giveth thee power to get wealth."* Even so, Psalm 145:15 declares, *"The eyes of all wait upon thee; and thou givest them their meat in due season. Thou openest thy hand, and satisfiest the desire of every living thing."* Our provision of food is in His hand. Again Psalm 75:6-7 declares, *"For promotion cometh neither from the east, nor from the west, nor from the south. But God is the judge: he putteth down one, and setteth up another."*

Our promotion or decline is in His hand. Yet again in 1 Samuel 2:6-7 Hannah praised the Lord in her prayer, saying, *"The LORD killeth, and maketh alive: he bringeth down to the grave, and bringeth up. The LORD maketh poor, and maketh rich: he bringeth low, and lifteth up."* Our profit or loss in wealth is in His hand. And yet again in Deuteronomy 32:39 the Lord our God declared, *"See now that I, even I, am he, and there is no god with me: I kill, and I make alive: I wound, and I heal: neither is there any that can deliver out of my hand."* Our physical health and strength is in His hand. Finally, in Job 12:10 the man of God Job declared concerning the Lord, *"In whose hand is the soul of every living thing, and the breath of all mankind."* Our personal breath and life is in His hand. Yes, we must ever remember that it is the Lord our God who grants the ability to acquire material provision.

Thus the man of the home must lead his household to set their trust in the Lord their God and not in their own strength and skills. Yea, Jeremiah 17:5-8 pronounces the curse and the blessing, *"Thus saith the LORD; Cursed be the man that trusteth in man, and maketh flesh his arm, and whose heart departeth from the LORD. For he shall be like the heath in the desert, and shall not see when good cometh; but shall inhabit the parched places in the wilderness, in a salt land and not inhabited. Blessed is the man that trusteth in the LORD, and whose hope the LORD is. For he shall be as a tree planted by the waters, and that spreadeth out her roots by the river, and shall not see when heat cometh, but her leaf shall be green; and shall not be careful in the year of drought, neither shall cease from yielding fruit."* In like manner, Proverbs 10:3 pronounces the promise and the warning, *"The LORD will not suffer the soul of the righteous to famish: but he casteth away the substance of the wicked."* Finally, Proverbs 10:22 delivers the assurance, *"The blessing of the LORD, it maketh rich, and he addeth no sorrow with it."*

Let the man of the home then lead his household to found their lives upon and to follow the precepts, principles, and promises of God's Holy Word concerning material provision:

Psalm 34:8-10 – "*O taste and see that the LORD is good: blessed is the man [and the household] that trusteth in him. O fear the LORD, ye his saints: for there is no want to them that fear him. The young lions do lack, and suffer hunger: but they that seek the LORD shall not want any good thing.*" Psalm 84:11-12 – "*For the LORD God is a sun and shield: the LORD will give grace and glory: no good thing will he withhold from them that walk uprightly. O LORD of hosts, blessed is the man* [and the household] *that trusteth in thee.*" Psalm 37:3-5 – "*Trust in the LORD, and do good; so shalt thou dwell in the land, and verily thou shalt be fed. Delight thyself also in the LORD; and he shall give thee the desires of thine heart. Commit thy way unto the LORD; trust also in him; and he shall bring it to pass.*" Psalm 37:25 – "*I have been young, and now am old; yet have I not seen the righteous forsaken, nor his seed begging bread.*" Philippians 4:19 – "*But my God shall supply all your need according to his riches in glory by Christ Jesus.*" Matthew 6:9-11 – "*After this manner therefore pray ye: Our Father which art in heaven, Hallowed by thy name. Thy kingdom come. Thy will be done in earth, as it is in heaven. Give us this day our daily bread.*" Psalm 33:18-22 – "*Behold, the eye of the LORD is upon them that fear him, upon them that hope in his mercy; to deliver their soul from death, and to keep them alive in famine. Our soul waiteth for the LORD: he is our help and our shield. For our heart shall rejoice in him, because we have trusted in his holy name. Let thy mercy, O LORD, be upon us, according as we hope in thee.*"

Lead His Household to Thank the Lord for Every Provision

In the third place, concerning the man's responsibility to provide for his household, *he must lead his household to bless and thank the Lord their God for every provision and possession, no matter how great or small.* In Deuteronomy 8:10 the man of God Moses instructed the people of God, saying, "*When thou hast eaten and art full, then thou shalt bless the LORD thy God for the good land which he hath given thee.*" In like manner, in Psalm 103:1-5 the man of God David revealed the commitment of his own heart, saying, "*Bless the LORD, O my soul: and all that is within me, bless his holy name. Bless the LORD, O my soul, and forget not all his benefits: who forgiveth all thine iniquity; who healeth all thy diseases; who redeemeth thy life from destruction; who crowneth thee with lovingkindness and tender mercies; who satisfieth thy mouth with good things; so that thy youth is renewed like the eagle's."* Every good benefit and gift comes to us from the gracious and merciful hand of the Lord our God. Therefore, we should bless and thank Him for every one of these good benefits and gifts, whether it is spiritual, physical, or material. Certainly we should not take such benefits for granted. In like manner, the man of the home must ever lead his household to bless and thank the Lord for every benefit and provision that is provided. Even when the provision has come through the labors of the members of the household, the man of the home must ever lead his household to remember that it is the Lord our God who gave them the means, the strength, and the skills to get that provision and that wealth. (Deuteronomy 8:17-18)

In particular, concerning our provision of food, the closing portion of 1 Timothy 4:3 teaches us that the Lord our God has created meats and other foods *"to be received with thanksgiving of them which believe and know the truth."* To this verses 4-5 add, *"For every creature of God is good, and nothing to be refused, if it be received with thanksgiving: for it is sanctified by the word of God and prayer."* We are to receive our food with thanksgiving unto the Lord our God for His mercy in providing it to us. Just as our Lord instructed us to pray unto God our heavenly Father for our daily food (Matthew 6:11), even so we are to thank God our heavenly Father for the provision of our daily food.

Even so, in Matthew 14:19 we learn that at the miracle of the feeding of the five thousand, before He divided the food unto His disciples to distribute unto the multitude, first our Lord Jesus Christ looked up to heaven and blessed the food. Again in Matthew 15:36 we learn that at the miracle of the feeding of the four thousand, He first gave thanks unto the Father for the food before He divided it unto His disciples to distribute unto the multitude. Yet again in Luke 24:30 we learn that when our Lord Jesus Christ sat down to eat with two of His disciples in the village of Emmaus, *"He took the bread, and blessed it, and brake, and give it to them."* Finally, in Acts 27:35 we

289

learn that when the apostle Paul encouraged the shipmen and soldiers to eat just before their shipwreck at the island of Mileta, *"He took bread, and gave thanks to God in presence of them all: and when He had broken it, he began to eat."* In like manner, the man of the home should lead his household to give thanks unto the Lord their God before each meal for their daily food, whether it is a small morsel or a bountiful feast.

Govern His Household to Honor the Lord with Their Substance

In the fourth place, concerning the man's responsibility to provide for his household, *he must govern his household by the principle to honor the Lord their God with their substance and the first fruits of all their increase.* In Proverbs 3:9-10 the instruction and promise is given, *"Honour the LORD with thy substance, and with the firstfruits of all thine increase: so shall thy barns be filled with plenty, and thy presses shall burst out with new wine."* As we have learned, all of our substance and all of our increase is a gracious gift from the hand of the Lord our God. Yet it is more than a gift. It is also a *stewardship.* Yes, our gracious and merciful Lord God *"giveth us richly all things to enjoy."* (1 Timothy 6:17) Yet He does not give us these things to consume them selfishly upon our own lusts. (James 4:3) Rather, He desires and instructs that we should handle all of our substance and increase for the glory and honor of His name.

In fact, all that we possess and acquire is not truly our own. All of these things are truly owned by the Creator God and Sovereign Lord of all. Psalm 24:1proclaims, *"The earth is the LORD's, and the fullness thereof; the world, and they that dwell therein."* The Lord our God is the true Owner of the planet earth itself. The Lord our God is the true Owner of all the fullness of the earth, including that which He has graciously granted to us and entrusted into our care. Yea, the Lord our God is even the true Owner of us who are the inhabitants of this earth. Even so, having given a significant offering for the building of the temple, the man of God David declared unto the Lord in 1 Chronicles 29:14, *"But who am I, and what is my people, that we should be able to offer so willingly after this sort? For all things come of thee, and of thine own have we given thee."*

290

David understood that all of his substance and increase came from the gracious hand of the Lord. He further understood that it all remained the Lord's possession and that it was given only in trust as a stewardship. Thus David understood that when he gave an offering unto the Lord, he was giving unto the Lord that which was *already* His. In like manner, the man of the home should govern his household by the principle that *all* of their substance is truly the Lord's possession and is *graciously* given to them as a stewardship from the Lord, ever to be used unto the honor of His holy name.

In addition, the man of the home should lead his household to honor the Lord their God with the first fruits of all their increase. In *honor* to the Lord our God, we are to give in offering unto Him the first fruits of all our material and financial increase. It is no honor unto Him when we give what is left over after we have used the rest for ourselves. In 1 Corinthians 16:2 the principle is given, *"Upon the first day of the week let every one of you lay by him in store, as God hath prospered him, that there be no gatherings when I come."* The man of the home should lead his household each Sunday, as they assemble with God's people for worship, to honor the Lord in giving to the Lord's work and ministry the *first fruits* of the increase by which He graciously prospered them throughout the previous week. Furthermore, the man of the home should lead his household to give *bountifully* and *cheerfully*. In 2 Corinthians 9:6-7 the truth and principle is revealed, *"But this I say, He which soweth sparingly shall reap also sparingly; and he which soweth bountifully shall reap also bountifully. Every man according as he purposeth in his heart, so let him give; not grudgingly, or of necessity: for God loveth a cheerful giver."*

In particular, the man of the home should lead his household to honor the Lord with their first fruits through *tithes and offerings*. Throughout God's Word the most basic form of giving in honor to the Lord is the tithe (a tenth of the increase). After the Lord had graciously granted him victory over Chedorlaomer king of Elam and the kings that were with him, in order to deliver his nephew Lot and the people of Sodom and Gomorrah, the man of God Abraham gave tithes of all the spoil in honor of the Lord his God unto

Melchizedek king of Salem, the priest of the most High God. (Genesis 14:18-20) After the Lord spoke with him in his dream at Bethel and promised to bless him, provide for him, and protect him, Jacob pronounced his commitment unto the Lord in Genesis 28:20-22 – "*And Jacob vowed a vow, saying, If God will be with me, and will keep me in this way that I go, and will give me bread to eat, and raiment to put on, so that I come again to my father's house in peace; then shall the LORD be my God: and this stone, which I have set for a pillar, shall be God's house: and of all that thou shalt give me I will surely give the tenth unto thee.*"

In Leviticus 27:30 the Lord gave commandment to His people Israel through His servant Moses, saying, "*And all the tithe of the land, whether of the seed of the land, or of the fruit of the tree, is the LORD's: it is holy unto the LORD.*" Yet again He gave commandment in verse 32, "*And concerning the tithe of the herd, or of the flock, even of whatsoever passeth under the rod, the tenth shall be holy unto the LORD.*" Now, some might contend that the command to give the tithe is not specifically repeated in the New Testament for God's people today and that it was strictly a matter of the Old Testament Law for the nation of Israel. Yet the principle to honor the Lord our God with the first fruits of all the increase with which our Lord has graciously prospered us certainly applies for us today. In addition, hundreds of years before the Old Testament Law was given through Moses, both Abraham and Jacob understood that the most basic form of giving in honor unto the Lord our God is the tithe (a tenth of the increase).

Even so, in Malachi 3:8-9 the rebuke and chastening of the Lord our God was pronounced against His people Israel, "*Will a man rob God? Yet ye have robbed me. But ye say, Wherein have we robbed Thee? In tithes and offerings. Ye are cursed with a curse: for ye have robbed me, even this whole nation.*" To hold back from giving our tithes and offerings unto the Lord's work and ministry is to rob the Lord our God of the honor that is due unto Him in our giving. Furthermore, to rob the Lord our God in this manner is to bring down the curse of His chastening hand upon one's self and one's household. Yet in verse 10 the Lord our God graciously proclaimed His instruction and promise, "***Bring ye all the tithes into the storehouse, that there may be meat in mine house, and prove me now herewith, saith the LORD of hosts, if I will not open you the windows of heaven, and pour you out a blessing, that there shall not be room enough to receive it.***"

The Lord our God loves those who give cheerfully and bountifully in honor unto His name. (2 Corinthians 9:7) Thus His principle and promise is established in 2 Corinthians 9:6, "***But this I say, He which soweth sparingly shall reap also sparingly; and he which soweth bountifully shall reap also bountifully.***" Yea, 2 Corinthians 9:8-11 adds, "***And God is able to make all grace abound toward you; that ye, always having all sufficiency in all things, may abound to every good work: (As it is written, He hath dispersed abroad; he hath given to the poor: his righteousness remaineth for ever. Now he that ministereth seed to the sower both minister bread for your food, and multiply your seed sown, and increase the fruits of your righteousness;) being enriched in every thing to all bountifulness, which causeth through us thanksgiving to God.***"

When the man of the home leads his household to give cheerfully and bountifully unto the work and ministry of the Lord their God in honor to Him, the Lord will abound in His grace toward that household. He will minister provision for their food; He will multiply the progress of their efforts; and He will increase the fruits of their righteousness. Yea, the Lord our God will enrich that household in every good thing in order that they might have sufficiency in all things and may abound to every good work for the glory of His name.

In like manner, the apostle Paul commended the believers at Philippi for giving unto his needs for the Lord's work and ministry in honor unto the Lord. In Philippians 4:18 he declared, "***But I have all, and abound: I am full, having received of Epaphroditus the things which were sent from you, an odour of a sweet smell, a sacrifice acceptable, wellpleasing to God.***" Such cheerful and bountiful giving in honor to the Lord is received by the Lord our God like a sweet perfume. It is acceptable and well pleasing in His sight. Even so, to those who will honor the Lord with such giving, the promise of

Philippians 4:19 is established – *"But my God shall supply all your need according to his riches in glory by Christ Jesus."* Let the man of the home then lead his household to seek God's supply for their needs. Let him govern his household by the principle to honor the Lord their God with their substance and with the first fruits of all their increase.

Truth for Meditation

To provide for his household aright, the man of the home must –

1. Set his own and his household's priority on serving the Lord their God, not on acquiring the things of this world. (Matt. 6:19-21, 24; Prov. 11:4; 23:4-5; Eccl. 5:10; Luke 9:25; 12:15-21; Heb. 10:34; 1 Cor. 9:25; 15:18; 2 Tim. 4:7-8)

2. Direct his own and his household's trust in the Lord to grant the means and strength for him to provide adequately for his household. (Matt. 6:25-33; Deut. 8:11-14, 17-18; 32:39; Psa. 75:6-7; 145:15; 1 Sam. 2:6-7; Job 12:10; Jer. 17:5-8; Prov. 10:3, 22; Psa. 33:18-22; 34:8-10; 37:3-5, 25; 84:11-12; Phil. 4:19)

3. Lead his household to bless and thank the Lord their God for every provision and possession, no matter how great or small. (Deut. 8:10, 17-18; Psa. 103:1-5; 1 Tim. 4:3-5; Matt. 14:19; 15:36; Luke 24:30; Acts 27:35)

4. Govern his household by the principle to honor the Lord their God with their substance and the first fruits of all their increase. (Prov. 3:9-10; Psa. 24:1; 1 Chron. 29:14; 1 Cor. 16:2; 2 Cor. 9:6-11; Gen. 14:18-20; 28:20-22; Lev. 27:30, 32; Mal. 3:8-10; Phil. 4:18-19)

Verses for Memorization

Matthew 6:19-21: Lay not up for yourselves treasures upon earth, where moth and rust doth corrupt, and where thieves break through and steal: but lay up for yourselves treasures in heaven, where neither moth nor rust doth corrupt, and where thieves do not break through nor steal: for where your treasure is, there will your heart be also.

Luke 12:15: And he said unto them, Take heed, and beware of covetousness: for a man's life consisteth not in the abundance of the things which he possesseth.

Matthew 6:33: But seek ye first the kingdom of God, and his righteousness; and all these things shall be added unto you.

Deuteronomy 8:10: When thou hast eaten and art full, then thou shalt bless the LORD thy God for the good land which he hath given thee.

Proverbs 3:9-10: Honour the LORD with thy substance, and with the firstfruits of all thine increase: so shall thy barns be filled with plenty, and thy presses shall burst out with new wine.

2 Corinthians 9:6-7: But this I say, He which soweth sparingly shall reap also sparingly; and he which soweth bountifully shall reap also bountifully. Every man according as he purposeth in his heart, so let him give; not grudgingly, or of necessity: for God loveth a cheerful giver.

23

Providing for the Home
(Part 2)

According to the principle of God's Holy Word, the man of the home is responsible before God to provide materially for his household. Yea, 1 Timothy 5:8 proclaims, *"But if any provide not for his own, and specially for those of his own house, he hath denied the faith, and is worse than an infidel."* How then is the man of the home to fulfill this responsibility aright? In the previous chapter we considered four Biblical principles concerning this matter. First, he must set his own and his household's priority on serving the Lord their God, not on acquiring the things of this world. Second, he must direct his own and his household's trust in the Lord to grant the means and strength for him to provide adequately for his household. Third, he must lead his household to bless and thank the Lord their God for every provision and possession, no matter how great or small. Fourth, he must govern his household by the principle to honor the Lord their God with their substance and the first fruits of all their increase. In this chapter we shall consider six additional principles by which the man of the home may fulfill his responsibility aright to provide materially for his household.

Be Diligent to Labor for the Sake of His Household

In the fifth place, *he must be diligent to labor for the sake of his household with the strength and skills that the Lord our God has given him.* In Romans 12:11 the three-fold instruction is given, *"Not slothful in business; fervent in spirit; serving the Lord."* In this context the word "business" refers to the responsibilities that the Lord our God has placed before us. Even so, the man of the home should not be slothful in fulfilling his God-given responsibility to provide materially for his household. Rather, he should put forth all fervent energy and effort therein. Furthermore, he should be motivated to such fervent energy and effort, not simply by the needs of his household, but more so as a faithful servant of the Lord his God. The Lord our God Himself has placed this responsibility into his hand. In obedient and faithful service to the Lord, the man of the home must seek to fulfill that responsibility with all his might. (Ecclesiastes 9:10)

Even so, the opening half of Proverbs 21:5 declares, *"The thoughts of the diligent tend only to plenteousness."* Yea, his diligence tends to plenteousness for both himself and his household. In like manner, the opening half of Proverbs 28:19 declares, *"He that tilleth his land shall have plenty of bread."* Yea, he shall have plenty of bread both for himself and for his household. On the other hand, Proverbs 19:15 warns, *"Slothfulness casteth into a deep sleep; and an idle soul shall suffer hunger."* Again Proverbs 20:4 warns, *"The sluggard will not plow by reason of the cold; therefore shall he beg in harvest, and have nothing."* Yet again Proverbs 6:9-11 warns, *"How long wilt thou sleep, O sluggard? When wilt thou arise out of thy sleep? Yet a little sleep, a little slumber, a little folding of the hands to sleep: so shall thy poverty come as one that travelleth, and thy want as an armed man."* Oh, how troubled is that home where the man of the home will not be diligent to labor for its provision! Even so, Proverbs 10:4 presents the warning and the principle, *"He becometh poor that dealeth with a slack hand: but the hand of the diligent maketh rich."* To this Proverbs 13:4 adds, *"The soul of the sluggard desireth, and hath nothing: but the soul of the diligent shall be made fat."* Yea, the man who deals with a slack hand will bring poverty upon his household; but the man who deals with a diligent hand will bring much provision upon his household.

Guide His Household to Pursue the More Valuable Treasures

In the sixth place, concerning the man's responsibility to provide for his household, *he must guide his household to pursue diligently after those treasures that are more valuable than material wealth and possessions.* While the man of the home is responsible to provide materially for his household, he is also responsible to provide a godly and wholesome home life for them. Just as our Lord Jesus Christ declared in Luke 12:15 that "*a man's life consisteth not in the abundance of the things which he possesseth,*" even so a wholesome household consisteth not in the abundance of the material things which that household possesses. In fact, there are various attributes that are far more valuable to a wholesome home life than is the abundance of material wealth and possessions.

❖ The first of these more valuable treasures is *the wisdom of God.* Proverbs 3:13-18 declares, "*Happy is the man that findeth wisdom, and the man that getteth understanding. For the merchandise of it is better than the merchandise of silver, and the gain thereof than fine gold. She is more precious than rubies: and all the things thou canst desire are not to be compared unto her. Length of days is in her right hand; and in her left hand riches and honour. Her ways are the ways of pleasantness, and all her paths are peace. She is a tree of life to them that lay hold upon her: and happy is every one that retaineth her.*" Thus Proverbs 4:7-9 instructs, "*Wisdom is the principal thing; therefore get wisdom: and with all thy getting get understanding. Exalt her, and she shall promote thee: she shall bring thee to honour, when thou doest embrace her. She shall give to thine head an ornament of grace: a crown of glory shall she deliver to thee.*" Yea, Proverbs 16:16 exclaims, "*How much better is it to get wisdom than gold! And to get understanding rather to be chosen than silver!*" Even so, the man of the home should ever guide his household to value God's wisdom above all material wealth and to seek after it diligently.

❖ The second of these more valuable treasures is *the instruction of God's Word* (by which we acquire the wisdom of God). Psalm 19:7-10 declares, "*The law of the LORD is perfect, converting the soul: the testimony of the LORD is sure, making wise the simple. The statutes of the LORD are right, rejoicing the heart: the commandment of the LORD is pure, enlightening the eyes. The fear of the LORD is clean, enduring for ever: the judgments of the LORD are true and righteous altogether. More to be desired are they than gold, yea than much fine gold: sweeter also than honey and the honeycomb."* Thus in Psalm 119:14 the psalmist expressed the direction of his heart, saying, *"I have rejoiced in the way of thy testimonies, as much as in all riches."* Yet again in verse 72 he proclaimed, *"The law of thy mouth is better unto me than thousands of gold and silver."* Finally, in verse 127 he declared, *"Therefore I love thy commandments above gold; yea, above fine gold."* Even so, the man of the home should ever guide his household to value the precepts and principles, commandments and counsels, statutes and standards of God's Word above all material wealth and to follow it faithfully.

❖ The third of these more valuable treasures is *the fear of the Lord* (which is the foundation for acquiring the wisdom of God). Proverbs 15:16 declares, *"Better is little with the fear of the LORD than great treasure and trouble therewith."* The fear of the Lord is that heart attitude of reverence, respect, and awe for His glorious greatness wherein we humbly bow before His authority, surrender to His will, honor His name, seek His righteousness, rejoice in His fellowship, depend upon His strength, trust in His faithfulness, hope in His mercy, tremble at His judgment, and flee all that would bring Him displeasure. Let the man of the home then ever guide his household to value this heart attitude of the fear of the Lord above all material wealth and to walk therein daily.

❖ The fourth of these more valuable treasures is *an atmosphere of love and peace* (as opposed to contention, strife, and hatred). Proverbs 15:17 declares, *"Better is a dinner of herbs where love is, than a stalled ox and hatred therewith."* Again Proverbs 17:1 declares, *"Better is a dry morsel, and quietness therewith, than an house full of sacrifices with strife."* Let the man of the home then ever guide his household to value such love and peace in relation with one another above all material wealth and to pursue it fervently.

❖ The fifth of these more valuable treasures is *a character of righteousness and integrity* (as opposed to wickedness and dishonesty). Proverbs 16:8 declares, *"Better is a little with righteousness than great revenues without right."* Again Proverbs 19:1 proclaims, *"Better is the poor that walketh in his integrity, than he that is perverse in his lips, and is a fool;"* and the closing half of verse 22 adds, *"And a poor man is better than a liar."* Yet again Proverbs 28:6 states, *"Better is the poor that walketh in his uprightness, than he that is perverse in his ways, though he be rich."* And yet again Psalm 37:16-17 warns and promises, *"A little that a righteous man hath is better than the riches of many wicked. For the arms of the wicked shall be broken: but the LORD upholdeth the righteous."* Finally, Proverbs 22:1 gives the report, *"A good name* [that is – a reputation for righteousness and integrity] *is rather to be chosen than great riches, and loving favour rather than silver and gold."* Let the man of the home then ever guide his household to value such a character of righteousness and integrity above all material wealth and to grow therein earnestly.

❖ The sixth of these more valuable treasures is *a spirit of humility* (as opposed to pride and arrogance). Proverbs 16:18-19 warns and declares, *"Pride goeth before destruction, and an haughty spirit before a fall. Better it is to be of an humble spirit with the lowly, than to divide the spoil with the proud."* Let the man of the home then ever guide his household to value a spirit of Biblical humility above all material wealth and to abide therein continually.

Manage the Material Affairs of His Home with Wisdom

In the seventh place, concerning the man's responsibility to provide for his household, *he must manage the material affairs of his home according to the principles of God's wisdom for the best good of his household.* Proverbs 24:3-5 reveals the truth, *"Through wisdom is an house builded; and by understanding it is established: and by knowledge shall the chambers be filled with all precious and pleasant riches. A wise man is strong; yea, a man of knowledge increaseth strength."* Certainly the wife, as a helper who is meet for her husband, may help him in this matter. Yet the man of the home should remain primarily responsible. He may delegate some aspects of this management to his wife. Yet he himself should take up the primary burden of the responsibility to manage the material affairs of the household.

❖ The first of these principles is that the man of the home *should be personally aware of the financial condition of his household.* In Proverbs 27:23 God's Word gives the counsel, *"Be thou diligent to know the state of thy flocks, and look well to thy herds."*

❖ The second of these principles is that the man of the home *should plan and save ahead for the material welfare of his household.* In the opening portion of Proverbs 13:22 God's Word reveals the truth, *"A good man leaveth an inheritance to his children's children."* Yea, a good man will even consider the consequences of his financial decisions upon future generations.

❖ The third of these principles is that the man of the home *should guard his household from foolish and indulgent spending.* In Proverbs 21:17 God's Word gives the warning, *"He that loveth pleasure shall be a poor man: he that loveth wine and oil shall not be rich."* Then verse 20 adds, *"There is treasure to be desired and oil in the dwelling of the wise; but a foolish man spendeth it up."*

❖ The fourth of these principles is that the man of the home *should guard his household from the bondage of credit spending and debt.* In the closing half of Proverbs 22:7, God's Word reveals the principle, *"And the borrower is servant to the lender."* This principle does not absolutely forbid any and all borrowing. Yet it does challenge us to borrow or spend on credit as little as possible, and it does warn us not to be careless or indulgent in credit spending. In addition, Proverbs 3:27-28 instruct us to pay our debts as quickly as possible, saying, *"Withhold not good from them to whom it is due, when it is in the power of thine hand to do it. Say not unto thy neighbour, Go, and come again, and to morrow I will give; when thou hast it by thee."*

Teach His Household to Be Content with the Lord's Provision

In the eighth place, concerning the man's responsibility to provide for his household, *he must teach his household by his example to be content with the things that the Lord their God grants, and not to be greedy of gain.* Hebrews 13:5 instructs, *"Let your conversation* [that is – manner of life] *be without covetousness; and be content with such things as ye have: for he hath said, I will never leave thee, nor forsake thee."* Because our Lord is ever faithful to be present with us and to provide for us, we should not be covetous for more of the things of this world, but should be content with the things that He has graciously provided. Yea, 1 Timothy 6:6-8 proclaims, *"But godliness with contentment is great gain. For we brought nothing into this world, and it is certain we can carry nothing out. And having food and raiment let us be therewith content."* The things of this world possess no eternal existence, and thus they possess no eternal value. Yet godliness (a daily walk with and for the Lord our God) with contentment (a daily trust in the faithful presence and provision of the Lord our God) is of great benefit both for this present life and for the life to come. (1 Timothy 4:8)

On the other hand, 1 Timothy 6:9-10 presents the serious and sobering warning, *"But they that will be rich fall into temptation and a snare, and into many foolish and hurtful lusts, which drown men in destruction and perdition. For the love of money is the root of all evil: which while some coveted after, they have erred from the faith, and pierced themselves through with many sorrows."* The spirit of covetousness, desiring to be rich, being greedy of gain, having a love for money, will cause an individual to "fall into temptation and a snare." It will cause an individual to fall "into many foolish and hurtful lusts." It will drown an individual "in destruction and perdition." It will cause an individual to err and be turned aside from a faithful walk in God's truth. It will cause an individual to be pierced through "with many sorrows."

When the man of the home pursues this way, he will not only bring such trouble and ruin upon himself, but also upon his household. The opening half of Proverbs 15:27 declares, *"He that is greedy of*

303

gain troubleth his own house." To this Proverbs 28:22 adds, *"He that hasteth to be rich hath an evil eye, and considereth not that poverty shall come upon him."* While striving after more and more material wealth, he shall cause both himself and his household to be impoverished of the more valuable treasures to a wholesome life. In addition, since *"riches certainly make themselves wings"* and *"fly away as an eagle toward heaven"* (Proverbs 23:5), his pursuit of material wealth may come to failure and will thus plunge his household into material poverty as well.

Furthermore, the spirit of covetousness, desiring to be rich, being greedy of gain, having a love for money, will produce the fruit of all evil and unrighteousness. Proverbs 28:20 declares, *"A faithful man shall abound with blessings: but he that maketh haste to be rich shall not be innocent." "For the love of money is the root of all evil."* The spirit of covetousness is rooted in the heart-soil of selfishness. It is the selfish desire to get and to have whatever one wants, and in time it will grow into the selfish desire to get and to have what one wants *at the expense of others.* This is the "evil eye" of which Proverbs 28:22 speaks – *"He that hasteth to be rich hath an evil eye."* Out of this "evil eye" of selfishness and covetousness will flow the evil and unrighteous ways of deception, cheating, oppression, and even violence.

Even so, Proverbs 1:10-19 gives the warning, *"My son, if sinners entice thee, consent thou not. If they say, Come with us, let us lay wait for blood, let us lurk privily for the innocent without cause: let us swallow them up alive as the grave; and whole, as those that go down into the pit: we shall find all precious substance, we shall fill our houses with spoil: cast in thy lot among us; let us all have one purse: my son, walk not thou in the way with them; refrain thy foot from their path: for their feet run to evil, and make haste to shed blood. Surely in vain the net is spread in the sight of any bird. And they lay wait for their own blood; they lurk privily for their own lives. So are the ways of every one that is greedy of gain; which taketh away the life of the owners thereof."* Such are the evil ways of those who are greedy of gain, who have a love for money, who desire to be rich, who are filled with the spirit of covetousness. They will lurk privately to take advantage of the innocent. They will swallow up others in order to fill their own houses with material things. Their feet will run to evil and will make haste to destroy the lives of others for their own selfish gain.

Yet the anger of the Lord our God will be kindled against them. He will pour out His judgment upon them. He will turn their evil and oppressive ways against them so that they themselves are destroyed thereby. Proverbs 11:1 reveals the truth, *"A false balance* [that is – a balance of deception] *is abomination to the LORD: but a just weight is his delight."* No matter how the culture may accept it, deception and cheating in business and financial matters is a hateful offense in the sight of the Lord our God. It may bring financial profit at the first, but it will also bring the wrath of God in the end. Thus Proverbs 21:6 warns, *"The getting of treasure by a lying tongue is a vanity tossed to and fro of them that seek death."* To this Proverbs 13:11 adds, *"Wealth gotten by vanity* [that is – by unrighteous ways] *shall be diminished: but he that gathereth by labour shall increase."* Furthermore, Proverbs 22:16 reveals the truth, *"He that oppresseth the poor to increase his riches, and he that giveth to the rich, shall surely come to want."* Again verses 22-23 give the warning, *"Rob not the poor, because he is poor: neither oppress the afflicted in the gate: for the LORD will plead their cause, and spoil the soul of those that spoiled them."* Yea, Proverbs 10:2-3 declares, *"Treasures of wickedness profit nothing: but righteousness delivereth from death. The LORD will not suffer the soul of the righteous to famish: but he casteth away the substance of the wicked."* Such ways of selfishness and covetousness will not profit a home, but will only bring destruction upon it.

Train His Household Not to Be Proud of or Trust in Wealth

In the ninth place, concerning the man's responsibility to provide for his household, *he must train his household by his example to enjoy the things that the Lord their God grants, but not to be proud of or trust in those things.* In 1 Timothy 6:17 the charge is given for those who have been blessed with material things in this world – *"Charge them that are rich in this world, that they be not highminded, nor*

305

trust in uncertain riches, but in the living God, who giveth us richly all things to enjoy." The Lord our God is abundant in grace and rich in goodness toward us; and out of the abundance of His grace and the riches of His goodness, He gives us various things richly beyond our basic needs for us to enjoy. Let us then give thanks unto the Lord our God for the abundance of His grace to us, and let us then enjoy and rejoice in the riches of His goodness to us. In Ecclesiastes 5:18-19 the truth is revealed, "*Behold that which I have seen: it is good and comely for one to eat and to drink, and to enjoy the good of all his labour that he taketh under the sun all the days of his life, which God giveth him: for it is his portion. Every man also to whom God hath given riches and wealth, and hath given him power to eat thereof, and to take his portion, and to rejoice in his labour; this is the gift of God.*"

On the other hand, let us never become proud and high-minded about the material blessings that the Lord our God has given us, thinking more highly of ourselves than of others because we have more material things than those others have. Even so, the opening line of 1 Timothy 6:17 states, "*Charge them that are rich in this world, that they be not highminded.*" As we have previously learned, all of our material blessings are given to us by the grace and goodness of the Lord our God. We have not received them because we ourselves are so great and good, but because *He* is so gracious and good. *All* of the praise and honor for these blessings should be offered unto *His* glory, and not unto our own. However, if an individual's heart becomes lifted up with pride over these material blessings, then he will bring judgment and destruction upon himself and his household. Proverbs 16:5 declares, "*Every one that is proud in heart is an abomination to the LORD: though hand join in hand, he shall not be unpunished.*" In addition, Proverbs 16:18 proclaims, "*Pride goeth before destruction, and an haughty spirit before a fall.*" Finally, the opening half of Proverbs 15:25 warns, "*The LORD will destroy the house of the proud.*"

Furthermore, Moses the servant of the Lord instructed and warned the people of God Israel in Deuteronomy 8:10-14, saying, "*When thou hast eaten and art full, then thou shalt bless the LORD thy God for the good land which he hath given thee. Beware that thou forget not the LORD thy God, in not keeping his commandments, and his judgments, and his statutes, which I command thee this day; lest when thou hast eaten and art full, and hast built goodly houses, and dwelt therein; and when thy herds and thy flocks multiply, and thy silver and thy gold is multiplied, and all that thou hast is multiplied; then thine heart be lifted up, and thou forget the LORD thy God, which brought thee forth out of the land of Egypt, from the house of bondage."* If our hearts become lifted up with pride over our material blessings, we *will* forget and forsake the Lord our God and His ways of righteousness. Our focus will be set upon our material blessings rather than upon our Lord who has so graciously blessed us, and that focus will turn our hearts away from our Lord and His ways. We *cannot* love and serve *both* the Lord our God and the material things of this world.

In like manner, let us never set our trust in the material blessings that the Lord our God has given us, believing that they can satisfy our hearts and supply our needs. Even so, 1 Timothy 6:17 continues, saying, *"Charge them that are rich in this world, that they be not highminded, nor trust in uncertain riches, but in the living God, who giveth us all things richly to enjoy."* Material wealth is uncertain, and it *cannot* satisfy our hearts. Yet the Lord our God and Savior, the one true and living God of heaven and earth, He alone *can* satisfy our thirsting hearts and supply our every need. Thus Proverbs 11:28 gives the report, *"He that trusteth in his riches shall fall: but the righteous* [the one who trusts in and follows after the Lord*] shall flourish as a branch."* Yea, the household who sets their trust in material blessings shall fall; but the household who sets their trust in the Lord their God to follow after Him in all their ways shall flourish and be fruitful.

Cultivate within His Household a Spirit of Generosity

In the tenth and final place, concerning the man's responsibility to provide for his household, *he must cultivate within his own and his household's hearts a spirit of generosity in giving to help those who are poor and needy.* To those who have been blessed with material things in this world, 1 Timothy 6:18-19 continues the charge, *"That they do good, that they be rich in good works, ready to distribute, willing to communicate* [to share]*; laying up in store for themselves a good foundation against the time to come, that they may lay hold on eternal life."* The spirit of our hearts should be such that we are ever ready and willing to distribute out of our own material blessings in order to help others who are in material need. In such a generous spirit the Lord our God is well pleased; for Hebrews 13:16 declares, *"But to do good and to communicate* [to share] *forget not: for with such sacrifices God is well pleased."* Yea, the good and righteous man is described in Psalm 112:9, *"He hath dispersed, he hath given to the poor; his righteousness endureth for ever; his horn shall be exalted with honour."* To this Psalm 37:21 adds, *"The wicked borroweth, and payeth not again: but the righteous sheweth mercy, and giveth."* Furthermore, the virtuous woman is described in Proverbs 31:20 – *"She stretcheth out her hand to the poor; yea, she reacheth forth her hands to the needy."* Finally, Proverbs 14:31 proclaims, *"He that oppresseth the poor reproacheth his Maker: but he that honoureth him hath mercy on the poor."*

That man and household who give willingly and generously unto the poor and needy shall be blessed abundantly by the Lord our God. Proverbs 19:17 gives the promise, *"He that hath pity upon the poor lendeth unto the LORD; and that which he hath given will he pay him again."* On the other hand, Proverbs 21:13 gives the warning, *"Whoso stoppeth his ears at the cry of the poor, he also shall cry himself, but shall not be heard."* Thus Proverbs 11:24-25 gives the report, *"There is that scattereth, and yet increaseth; and there is that withholdeth more than is meet, but it tendeth to poverty. The liberal* [generous] *soul shall be made fat: and he that watereth shall be watered also himself."* Yet again Proverbs 28:27 reveals the truth, *"He that giveth unto the poor shall not lack: but he that hideth his eyes shall have many a curse."* Finally, Proverbs 22:9 states, *"He that hath a bountiful eye shall be blessed; for he giveth of his bread to the poor."*

Truth for Meditation

To provide for his household aright, the man of the home must –

(From Chapter 22)

1. Set his own and his household's priority on serving the Lord their God, not on acquiring the things of this world. (Matt. 6:19-21, 24; Prov. 11:4; 23:4-5; Eccl. 5:10; Luke 9:25; 12:15-21; Heb. 10:34; 1 Cor. 9:25; 15:18; 2 Tim. 4:7-8)

2. Direct his own and his household's trust in the Lord to grant the means and strength for him to provide adequately for his household. (Matt. 6:25-33; Deut. 8:11-14, 17-18; 32:39; Psa. 75:6-7; 145:15; 1 Sam. 2:6-7; Job 12:10; Jer. 17:5-8; Prov. 10:3, 22; Psa. 33:18-22; 34:8-10; 37:3-5, 25; 84:11-12; Phil. 4:19)

3. Lead his household to bless and thank the Lord their God for every provision and possession, no matter how great or small. (Deut. 8:10, 17-18; Psa. 103:1-5; 1 Tim. 4:3-5; Matt. 14:19; 15:36; Luke 24:30; Acts 27:35)

(From Chapter 23)

5. Be diligent to labor for the sake of his household with the strength and skills that the Lord our God has given him. (Rom. 12:11; Eccl. 9:10; Prov. 6:9-11; 10:4; 13:4; 19:15; 20:4; 21:5; 28:19)

6. Guide his household to pursue diligently after those treasures that are more valuable than material wealth and possessions. (Prov. 3:13-18; 4:7-9; 16:16; Psa. 19:7-10; 119:14, 72, 127; Prov. 15:16; Prov. 15:17; 17:1; Psa. 37:16-17; Prov. 16:8, 19:1, 22; 22:1; 28:6; Prov. 16:18-19)

7. Manage the material affairs of his home according to the principles of God's wisdom for the best good of his household. (Prov. 24:3-5; Prov. 27:23; Prov. 13:22; Prov. 21:17, 20; Prov. 22:7)

8. Teach his household by his example to be content with the things that the Lord their God grants, and not to be greedy of gain. (Heb. 13:5; 1 Tim. 6:6-10; Prov. 1:10-19; 10:2-3; 11:1; 13:11; 15:27; 21:6; 22:16, 22-23; 28:20, 22)

9. Train his household by his example to enjoy the things that the Lord their God grants, but not to be proud of or trust in those things. (1 Tim. 6:17; Eccl. 5:18-19; Prov. 15:25; 16:5, 18; Deut. 8:10-14; Prov. 11:28)

10. Cultivate within his own and his household's hearts a spirit of generosity in giving to help those who are poor and needy. (1 Tim. 6:18-19; Heb. 13:16; Psa. 37:21; 112:9; Prov. 11:24-25; 14:31; 19:17; 21:13; 22:9; 28:27; 31:20)

Those treasures that are more valuable to a wholesome home life than material wealth are –

1. The wisdom of God. (Prov. 3:13-18; 4:7-9; 16:16)

2. The instruction of God's Word. (Psa. 19:7-10; 119:14, 72, 127)

3. The fear of the Lord. (Prov. 15:16)

4. An atmosphere of love and peace. (Prov. 15:17; 17:1)

5. A character of righteousness and integrity. (Prov. 16:8; 19:1, 22; 22:1; 28:6; Psa. 37:16-17)

6. A spirit of humility. (Prov. 16:18-19)

The principles of God's wisdom whereby the man of the home is to manage the material affairs of his home are that –

1. He should be personally aware of the financial condition of his household. (Prov. 27:23)

2. He should plan and save ahead for the material welfare of his household. (Prov. 13:22)

3. He should guard his household from foolish and indulgent spending. (Prov. 21:17, 20)

4. He should guard his household from the bondage of credit spending and debt. (Prov. 3:27-28; 22:7)

Verses for Memorization

1 Timothy 5:8: But if any provide not for his own, and specially for those of his own house, he hath denied the faith, and is worse than an infidel.

Proverbs 16:16: How much better is it to get wisdom than gold! And to get understanding rather to be chosen than silver!

Psalm 119:72: The law of thy mouth is better unto me than thousands of gold and silver.

Hebrews 13:5: Let your conversation be without covetousness; and be content with such things as ye have: for he hath said, I will never leave thee, nor forsake thee.

1 Timothy 6:6: But godliness with contentment is great gain.

1 Timothy 6:9-10: But they that will be rich fall into temptation and a snare, and into many foolish and hurtful lusts, which drown men in destruction and perdition. For the love of money is the root of all evil: which while some coveted after, they have erred from the faith, and pierced themselves through with many sorrows.

1 Timothy 6:17: Charge them that are rich in this world, that they be not highminded, nor trust in uncertain riches, but in the living God, who giveth us richly all things to enjoy.

Proverbs 11:28: He that trusteth in his riches shall fall: but the righteous shall flourish as a branch.

Hebrews 13:16: But to do good and to communicate forget not: for with such sacrifices God is well pleased.

Proverbs 19:17: He that hath pity upon the poor lendeth unto the LORD; and that which he hath given will he pay him again.

24

Keeping of the Home

In Titus 2:3-5 we find that the older women of God are to maintain a daily behavior that is in unity with holiness and godliness in order that they might then teach the younger women of God also to behave in such a holy and godly manner. *"The aged women likewise, that they be in behaviour as becometh holiness, not false accusers, not given to much wine, teachers of good things; that they may teach the young women to be sober, to love their husbands, to love their children, to be discreet, chaste, keepers at home, good, obedient to their own husbands, that the word of God be not blasphemed."*

One of these godly characteristics that the older women of God are to teach unto the younger is to be "keepers at home." Now, in this context the focus of this phrase is not upon the preposition "at." The intent of this characteristic is not that a godly wife must always remain *at* home and may never leave the home. It does not even indicate that a godly wife may never minister or work outside the home. Rather, in this context the focus of this phrase is upon the words "keepers" and "home." The intent of this characteristic is that a godly wife must learn to set her *priority* upon being *a keeper of her home and household.* This means that a godly wife will be like a watchman in and for the home, ever watching and seeking to meet the needs of the various members of her household and ever working and laboring to provide a comfortable, clean home environment for her household. She will view her household (not the material possessions, but the individual members) as a precious treasure from the hand of the Lord her God; and she will give herself to watch out for them with care, compassion, and commitment.

Although at times she may be called to minister or work outside the home, the priority and focus of a godly wife's heart and life will ever be upon the care and progress of her household. Even so, Proverbs 31:10 sets our attention upon the virtuous woman and wife, saying, *"Who can find a virtuous woman? For her price is far above rubies."* Then in describing the virtuous woman and wife, Proverbs 31:27 reveals, *"She looketh well to the ways of her household, and eateth not the bread of idleness."* The godly woman and wife will not set her priority upon some profession outside the home, some position outside the home, some pursuit outside the home, or some popularity outside the home. Rather, as the wise woman of Proverbs 14:1, her priority will be to look well unto the ways of her household and to build up the members of her household.

Yea, after warning the younger women in 1 Timothy 5:13 against being idle busybodies, the apostle Paul instructed them in verse 14 under the inspiration of God the Holy Spirit, saying, *"I will therefore that the younger women marry, bear children, guide the house, give none occasion to the adversary to speak reproachfully."* The focus and priority of a godly woman and wife should not be outside the home, but inside the home. Her focus and priority should be upon the members and the management of her household. This is the will of the Lord our God for her life. This is the calling and responsibility that the Lord our God Himself has set before her, and the godly woman and wife will fulfill that calling and responsibility as a priority of her heart and life. How then is the godly woman and wife to fulfill this responsibility aright?

Be a Keeper of Her Home for the Sake of the Lord

In the first place, she *must be a keeper of her household and home for the sake of the Lord.* Having stated in Proverbs 31:27 that the virtuous woman and wife *"looketh well to the ways of her household, and eateth not the bread of idleness,"* God's Holy Word then speaks in verses 28-29 of the praise that her family will bestow upon her, saying, *"Her children rise up, and call her blessed; her husband also, and he praiseth her. Many daughters have done virtuously, but thou excellest them all."* In addition, verse 31 speaks of the praise that her own virtuous works, primarily in the care of her household, will bring to her, saying, *"Give her of the fruit of her hands; and let her own works praise her in the gates."* Yet verse 30 reveals the central reason that the virtuous woman and wife is worthy of such praise – *"Favour is deceitful, and beauty is vain: but a woman that feareth the LORD, she shall be praised."* She is not worthy of such praise because she is popular in the public eye. She is not worthy of such praise because she is beautiful to the physical eye. Rather, she is worthy of such praise because she walks in the fear of the Lord her God and Savior.

Yea, she behaves in the virtuous manner of looking well to the ways of her household, such that she is brought to praise by her household and her works, *specifically because* she walks in the fear of the Lord. It is all done for *His* sake. It is all done because *He* has called her to the responsibility. It is all done because she *loves* the Lord her God and desires to please *Him* and honor *Him*. It is all done that God's Word of truth might be honored and accepted, and not be blasphemed in the sight of the world around her. Even so, having presented the list of godly characteristics that the older woman of God are to teach the younger, including the characteristic that they must be "keepers at home," Titus 2:5 closes with the reason – *"That the word of God be not blasphemed."* This is the primary motivation of the virtuous woman and wife to look well unto the ways of her household – not for honor among the public or even for the love of her family, but *for the love of her Lord and for the honor of His Word.*

Be a Keeper of Her Home for the Sake of Her Husband

In the second place, the godly woman and wife *must be a keeper of her household and home for the sake of her husband.* Having exclaimed in Proverbs 31:10 that the virtuous woman and wife is far more valuable than rubies, verses 11-12 then speak immediately of her relationship toward her husband. There we read, *"The heart of her husband doth safely trust in her, so that he shall have no need of spoil. She will do him good and not evil all the days of her life.*" Just below her Lord stands her husband as the priority relationship of her life, and the highest calling in her life from the Lord her God is that she be a helper who is truly meet for her husband. Therefore, the wife's motive for keeping the home should not primarily be her love for cleanliness and orderliness, but much more should be *her love and honor for her husband.*

She should ever seek to "do him good and not evil all the days of her life" in the keeping of the home, as well as in every other area of her life. Yea, the wife must ever seek to keep the home in such a manner that her husband might find it to be a welcoming, refreshing, and comforting haven. She will be a keeper of the home and the household for *his* good. She will not keep the home in such a manner that her husband feels out of place in the home. Rather, she will keep the home in such a manner that her husband is *honored* in the home. Furthermore, she will not set her focus upon how much her husband helps her out in the housekeeping. (Certainly in loving, cherishing, nourishing, and honoring his wife, the husband should be courteous enough to pick up after himself and to help out around the house.) Rather, the wife will set her focus upon helping out her husband through the keeping of the home and the household.

Be a Keeper of Her Home for the Sake of Her Children

In the third place, the godly woman and wife *must be a keeper of her household and home for the sake of her children.* Concerning the virtuous woman and wife, Proverbs 31:15 states, "*She riseth also while it is yet night, and giveth meat to her household, and a portion to her maidens.*" She rises up early before the morning light and puts forth this effort for the sake of her entire household – for the sake of both her husband *and* her children. Again verse 19 states, "*She layeth her hands to the spindle, and her hands hold the distaff;*" and verse 21 adds, "*She is not afraid of the snow for her household: for all her household are clothed with scarlet.*" Again we see that the virtuous woman and wife puts forth this effort for the sake of her entire household – for the sake of her husband *and* her children. Yet again verse 27 states, *"She looketh well to the ways of her household, and eateth not the bread of idleness."*

Her priority and focus is ever upon the care of her entire household – upon the care of both her husband *and* her children. She will keep the home in such a manner that her children may grow up in a peaceful and encouraging atmosphere and that they may be brought up "in the nurture and admonition of the Lord." She will not seek to avoid the care of her children or to shift that responsibility unto others, but will ever concentrate upon their care with commitment and spiritual joy. Even so, when the time for praise comes, the opening line of Proverbs 31:28 will be found to be true – *"Her children arise up, and call her blessed."*

Be a Keeper of Her Home with a Willing Heart

In the fourth place, the godly woman and wife *must be a keeper of her household and home with a willing heart.* In describing the virtuous woman and wife, Proverbs 31:13 states, *"She seeketh wool and flax, and worketh willingly with her hands."* The godly woman and wife is ever working and laboring with her own hands for the sake of her household, and she does so *willingly.* Yes, it often seems that a woman's work in the home is never done. Day after day the meals must be prepared. Day after day the laundry must be laundered. Day after day the cleaning must be done. Day after day the chores continue to pile up, and it all seems to continue day after day after day with no end in sight.

After a while such seemingly endless chores can become troublesome and discouraging to the woman of the home, and she may find herself doing the work of the home day after day with a grudging and grumbling attitude. She may even find herself looking for reasons to neglect these household chores. Yet the godly woman and wife will not allow herself to develop such a bad attitude toward the keeping of her household and home. Rather, she will enter into these household chores day after day with a willing and wholehearted attitude. Yea, she will actually do these household chores with delight, not because the chores themselves are so delightful, but because she is doing them out of love for the sake of her beloved Lord, her beloved husband, and her beloved children.

Be a Keeper of Her Home with a Diligent Hand

In the fifth place, the godly woman and wife *must be a keeper of her household and home with a diligent hand.* In describing the virtuous woman and wife, Proverbs 31:14-19 states, *"She is like the merchants' ships; she bringeth her food from afar. She riseth also while it is yet night, and giveth meat to her household, and a portion to her maidens. She considereth a field, and buyeth it: with the fruit of her hands she planteth a vineyard. She girdeth her loins with strength, and strengtheneth her arms. She perceiveth that her merchandise is good: her candle goeth not out by night. She layeth her hands to the spindle, and her hands hold the distaff."* The godly woman and wife is ever working with her hands. Yea, she is ever strengthening herself for the purpose of work. She is willing to go to the farthest extent in order to meet her God-given responsibility in the keeping of her household and home. "She bringeth her food *from afar.*" She will go the distance to meet the needs of her household.

The godly woman and wife is a hard and diligent worker. "She eateth *not* the bread of idleness." She will not seek after reasons to neglect her responsibilities in the keeping of the household and home. Rather, she will do whatever it takes to fulfill her God-given responsibilities in a good and faithful manner. She does not convince herself that she has reasons and excuses not to do the work of keeping her home. Rather, she disciplines herself to do the work with diligence; and this she does out of love for her beloved Lord, her beloved husband, and her beloved children.

Be a Keeper of Her Home with a Sacrificial Spirit

In the sixth place, the godly woman and wife *must be a keeper of her household and home with a sacrificial spirit.* In describing the virtuous woman and wife, Proverbs 31:15 states, *"She riseth also while it is yet night, and giveth meat to her household, and a portion to her maidens."* Yet again verse 18 states, *"She perceiveth that her merchandise is good: her candle goeth not out by night.*" The godly woman and wife is willing to get up early in the morning and to stay up late into the night in order to fulfill her responsibility in the keeping of her household and home. She is willing to give up and sacrifice of self in order to fulfill her God-given responsibilities in the home. She does not pursue after her own desires, preferences, finances, pleasures, etc. Rather, she is willing to make whatever personal sacrifice is necessary to fulfill her responsibilities toward her household in a good and faithful manner; and again she makes this sacrifice of self out of love for the sake of her beloved Lord, her beloved husband, and her beloved children.

Be a Keeper of Her Home with a Prudent Wisdom

In the seventh place, the godly woman and wife *must be a keeper of her household and home with a prudent wisdom.* In describing the virtuous woman and wife, Proverbs 31:16 states, "*She considereth a field, and buyeth it: with the fruit of her hands she planteth a vineyard.*" She did not simply buy this field on a whim. Rather, she *carefully considered* the field – the true value of the field, the financial expense of purchasing the field, the investment prospects of the field, the time and effort necessary to make the field profitable, etc. The godly woman and wife will ever be careful about her use of time, money, and effort. She will not be wasteful and will not waste time, money, and effort on worthless or useless things. If something will not truly benefit and build up her husband and her household, then she will not expend her time, money, or effort therein.

Yea, the truth is given in Proverbs 14:1, "*Every wise woman buildeth her house: but the foolish plucketh it down with her hands.*" The wise woman and wife is prudent and careful in the keeping and building up of her household. She is not hasty in judgment and in making decisions. Rather, she carefully considers the best possible use of time, the best possible use of money, and the best possible use of her effort. Furthermore, when she finds the best possible way, then she gives herself diligently to the success of that best way. As 1 Timothy 5:14 instructs her to "guide the house," even so she will serve her household by guiding and managing the affairs of her household with wisdom and prudence. Finally, when all is done, she will find that her use of time, money, and effort will indeed be good for the benefit and best of her household. Even so, concerning the virtuous woman the opening half of Proverbs 31:18 reveals, *"She perceiveth that her merchandise is good."*

Be a Keeper of Her Home with an Effective Effort

In the eighth and final place, the godly woman and wife *must be a keeper of her household and home with an effective effort.* In describing the virtuous woman and wife, Proverbs 31:21-25 states, *"She is not afraid of the snow for her household: for all her household are clothed with scarlet. She maketh herself coverings of tapestry; her clothing is silk and purple. Her husband is known in the gates, when he sitteth among the elders of the land. She maketh fine linen, and selleth it; and delivereth girdles unto the merchant. Strength and honour are her clothing; and she shall rejoice in time to come."* By working prudently for the sake of her household, the godly woman and wife will also be working effectively for their sake. Her time and effort will not be wasted on emptiness, but will bring forth good fruit. Thus she will have no need to fear for her household because she will know that she has fulfilled her God-given responsibilities toward them in the best possible manner.

Yea, she herself will be such an effective wife and mother in the keeping of her household and home that it will be a public tribute unto her husband. Not only will her household be blessed, benefited, and built up by her effective efforts; but also her effective efforts will be noticed by the public and will bring honor unto her husband's name. Just as she will have no fear for her household, even so also her husband will have no fear for the household because of the effectiveness of her diligent, sacrificial, and prudent efforts. When he departs from the home in order to fulfill his responsibilities outside the home, he will have no need for fear because he will have the assurance that his godly, virtuous wife will be keeping and managing the household and home aright. Truly she will be a crown of joy and rejoicing upon her husband's head!

Truth for Meditation

To keep her household and home aright, the woman of the home must –

1. Be a keeper of her household and home for the sake of the Lord. (Prov. 31:27-31; Tit. 2:4-5)

2. Be a keeper of her household and home for the sake of her husband. (Prov. 31:11-12)

3. Be a keeper of her household and home for the sake of her children. (Prov. 31:15, 21, 27-28)

4. Be a keeper of her household and home with a willing heart. (Prov. 31:13)

5. Be a keeper of her household and home with a diligent hand. (Prov. 31:14-19)

6. Be a keeper of her household and home with a sacrificial spirit. (Prov. 31:15, 18)

7. Be a keeper of her household and home with a prudent wisdom. (Prov. 31:16, 18; 14:1; 1 Tim. 5:14)

8. Be a keeper of her household and home with an effective effort. (Prov. 31:21-25)

Verses for Memorization

Titus 2:4-5: That they may teach the young women to be sober, to love their husbands, to love their children, to be discreet, chaste, keepers at home, good, obedient to their own husbands, that the word of God be not blasphemed.

Proverbs 31:27: She looketh well to the ways of her household, and eateth not the bread of idleness.

Proverbs 31:30: Favour is deceitful, and beauty is vain: but a woman that feareth the LORD, she shall be praised.

25

Render Due Benevolence

In 1 Corinthians 7:1-5 God's Holy Word speaks of the physical relationship between a husband and wife, saying, *"Now concerning the things whereof ye wrote unto me: It is good for a man not to touch a woman. Nevertheless, to avoid fornication, let every man have his own wife, and let every woman have her own husband. Let the husband render unto the wife due benevolence: and likewise also the wife unto the husband. The wife hath not power of her own body, but the husband: and likewise also the husband hath not power of his own body, but the wife. Defraud ye not one another, except it be with consent for a time, that ye may give yourselves to fasting and prayer; and come together again, that Satan tempt you not for your incontinency."*

Yes, the true and holy Word of God does indeed speak concerning the physical relationship between a husband and wife. No, it does not speak in a physiological manner (that is – it does not present a discourse on the physical mechanics of the matter). In addition, God's Holy Word certainly does not speak in a pornographic manner (that is – in a manner to stir up sensual lust). Rather, God's Holy Word speaks in a *principled* manner. It presents a number of principles to guide and govern the physical relationship between a husband and wife.

The Command of the Lord

In the first place, we find the truth and principle that *the Lord our God directly commands the husband and wife to engage in a physical relationship together.*

In 1 Corinthians 6:13-20, the passage just before 1 Corinthians 7:1-5, God's Word warns us concerning the sinful relationship of fornication – *"Meats for the belly, and the belly for meats: but God shall destroy both it and them. Now the body is not for fornication, but for the Lord; and the Lord for the body. And God hath both raised up the Lord, and will also raise up us by his own power. Know ye not that your bodies are the members of Christ? Shall I then take the members of Christ, and make them the members of an harlot? God forbid. What? Know ye not that he which is joined to an harlot is one body? For two, saith he, shall be one flesh. But he that is joined unto the Lord is one spirit. Flee fornication. Every sin that a man doeth is without the body; but he that committeth fornication sinneth against his own body. What? Know ye not that your body is the temple of the Holy Ghost which is in you, which ye have of God, and ye are not your own? For ye are bought with a price: therefore glorify God in your body, and in your spirit, which are God's."* Therein we find a direct reference to the physical body eight times. Therein we are commanded to "flee fornication." Therein we are informed that our individual bodies are each purchased and owned by the Lord our God as the temple of His Holy Spirit. Finally, therein we are instructed to glorify the Lord our God both in our body and in our spirit because they are not our own, but are God's.

Then, having warned us against the sin of fornication and having instructed us to glorify the Lord our God in both our body and spirit, God's Holy Word speaks in 1 Corinthians 7:1-5 concerning physical, sexual relations within the marriage. First, we are informed in verse 2 that the marriage relationship is a divinely ordained defense against the sin of fornication – *"Nevertheless, to avoid fornication, let every man have his own wife, and let every woman have her own husband."* Then to the husband and the wife the Lord our God delivers His command in verse 3, *"Let the husband render unto the*

wife due benevolence: and likewise also the wife unto the husband."
This is not simply divine counsel; this is divine *command*. The
physical relationship between a husband and wife is indeed a matter
of importance unto the Lord our God. He desires that the husband
and wife should walk together in one-flesh unity, and He has
ordained that the physical relationship between the husband and
wife is an important element of that one-flesh unity. Thus the Lord
our God directly commands the husband and the wife to render the
due benevolence of physical relations one to another, and for the
husband and wife to disobey this command is to sin against the
Lord our God.

The Definition of the Lord

In the second place, we find the truth and principle that *the Lord our
God defines the physical relationship between a husband and wife
as "due benevolence."* Again we consider our Lord's command
from 1 Corinthians 7:3 – *"**Let the husband render unto the wife
due benevolence: and likewise also the wife unto the husband.**"*
This is the definition of the Lord our God Himself for the physical
relationship between the husband and the wife – *due benevolence*.
Now, from this divine definition we may learn a number of truths.

❖ First, we learn that the physical relationship between the husband
and the wife is *a matter of responsibility* within the marriage
relationship. God's Holy Word indicates that it is a benevolence
that is *due* from the husband unto his wife and likewise also from
the wife unto her husband. Literally, the physical relationship is a
debt of benevolence that the husband and the wife each *owe* unto
the other. Yea, it is a God-ordained responsibility that the husband
and the wife are each to fulfill for the sake of the other.

❖ Second, we learn that the physical relationship between the
husband and the wife is *an act of loving-kindness* toward one another.
God's Holy Word indicates that it is a *benevolence*. The physical
relationship between the husband and the wife is to be motivated
by love and good will toward the other. It is not to be an activity
of selfish taking, but an activity of *selfless giving*. In their physical

325

relationship with one another, the husband and the wife are each to focus upon *the pleasure of the other*. Even so, 1 Corinthians 7:4 indicates that within the physical relationship the physical bodies of each spouse are each to be used, not for the gratification of self, but for the gratification of the other. There the principle is given in the context of the physical relationship, *"The wife hath not power of her own body, but the husband: and likewise also the husband hath not power of his own body, but the wife."*

One area of application for this principle concerns the matter of frequency. Often in a marriage relationship one spouse desires physical relations more often than the other. This principle of loving-kindness, of selfless giving, would indicate that each spouse should give up of self-desire for the sake of the other; and as each gives up for the sake of the other, a loving and workable compromise may be found. Another area of application for this principle concerns the matter of activity. Although each spouse should be willing to experiment for the gratification of the other, the activities within the physical relationship should not include anything that would offend either spouse or make either spouse uncomfortable.

❖ Third, we learn that the physical relationship between the husband and the wife is *a gift of pleasure* for one another. The Biblical truth that the physical relationship between the husband and the wife is to be an act of benevolence one toward the other reveals that the Lord our God Himself intends it to be for *the benefit and happiness of the other*. It reveals that the Lord our God Himself intends that in the physical relationship each spouse should strive to grant the other the greatest possible level of *satisfaction and enjoyment*. Even so, in the marriage relationship the physical relationship is to be a pleasant and pleasurable gift granted from each spouse to the other.

❖ Fourth, we learn that the physical relationship between the husband and the wife is *a blessing for gratitude* unto one another. As we have learned, the physical relationship between a husband and wife is to be an act of loving-kindness toward one another. Now, just as Biblical courtesy would require an attitude and expression of gratitude for any other act of loving-kindness, even so Biblical courtesy would require an attitude and expression of gratitude from the husband and the wife toward one another for the benevolence and blessing of the physical relationship. They should never take this gift of benevolence and blessing from the other for granted, but should always receive it with *a heart of gratitude*. The husband and wife should ever give thanks and express gratitude unto the Lord their God for this wonderful gift of pleasure that they may enjoy together, and each should ever give thanks and express gratitude unto the other for the loving-kindness involved in granting this gift of pleasure to one another.

The Direction to the Husband

In the third place, we find the truth and principle that *the Lord our God directs the husband to take the lead in rendering this due benevolence unto his wife*. The order is significant in the two-fold command of 1 Corinthians 7:3 – *"Let the husband render unto the wife due benevolence: and likewise also the wife unto the husband."* *First* the husband is instructed to render this due benevolence unto his wife; *then* the wife is instructed likewise also to do so unto her husband. Furthermore, the husband's responsibility in the matter is presented as the foundation for the relationship; and the wife's responsibility in the matter is presented as that which grows out of and is built upon that foundation. This is revealed in the grammatical structure of the two-fold command. The first instruction is directed unto the husband to render this due benevolence unto his wife. Then the second instruction, the one to the wife, begins with the words "and likewise also." In addition, the verb and object of the command, "render due benevolence," is simply assumed in the command to the wife out of the command to the husband.

Herein the Lord our God through His Holy Word designates the husband as the leader in the responsibility to render this due benevolence unto one another. Far too often in the selfishness of sinful human nature, husbands take physical gratification and pleasure to themselves without any consideration for the gratification and pleasure of their wives. Far too often husbands, even among believers, enter into the physical relationship with a selfish focus and thus use their wives selfishly for their own gratification. Yet this is contrary to the intent and instruction of the Lord our God. This is SIN! Rather, the husband is *first* to focus upon the physical gratification and pleasure of his wife and is to take the lead in *first* rendering due benevolence unto his wife.

The Prohibition of the Lord

In the fourth place, we find the truth and principle that *the Lord our God directly forbids the husband and the wife from defrauding one another in this matter.* The instruction of God's Word continues in 1 Corinthians 7:5, saying, *"Defraud ye not one the other, except it be with consent for a time, that ye may give yourselves to fasting and prayer; and come together again, that Satan tempt you not for your incontinency."* The verb "defraud" means "to hold back unjustly or to cheat out of that which is another's by right." Just as the Lord our God has designated that the benevolence of the physical relationship is *due* from each spouse to the other, even so for either spouse to withhold this due benevolence from the other is to *defraud* the other in the sight of the Lord our God. Thus the due benevolence of the physical relationship should not be withheld by one spouse from the other out of neglect (which neglect is a lack of benevolence). In addition, this due benevolence should certainly never be withheld as a weapon of manipulation in order to get one's own way. This is contrary to the intent and instruction of the Lord our God. This is SIN!

In fact, the only Biblically acceptable reason for a spouse to withhold the due benevolence of the physical relationship for a significant period of time is to give one's self unto fasting and prayer. Yet even in such a case, this withdrawal from the physical relationship by either spouse must be agreed upon by the *mutual consent* of both the husband and the wife, and the period of time for this withdrawal from the physical relationship must be *specifically designated* by mutual consent in advance. Furthermore, God's Holy Word instructs that when this specifically and previously designated period of time for fasting and prayer is complete, then the husband and wife *must immediately* come together again in the physical relationship. This is the proscribed will of the Lord our God, and any disobedience thereto is sin against the will of the Lord our God. Finally, our Lord has established these precepts and principles in order that Satan, our great spiritual adversary, might not acquire an avenue for temptation through our lack of self-control sexually. Thus we may understand that a Biblically healthy, physical relationship between a husband and wife can be just as spiritually beneficial as the practice of fasting and prayer. In addition, we may understand the spiritual importance of the command to the husband and wife, *"Defraud ye not one the other."*

The Honor of the Lord

In the fifth place, we find the truth and principle that *the Lord our God describes the physical relationship between a husband and wife as being worthy of honor.* In Hebrews 13:4 God's Holy Word reports both the commendation and condemnation of the Lord our God concerning the matter of sexual relations. There we read, *"Marriage is honourable in all, and the bed undefiled: but whoremongers and adulterers God will judge."* Clearly in the closing portion of this verse, the Lord our God expresses His judgment against those who engage in fornication and adultery. Such is the truth of God's Holy Word. All who engage in sexual activity outside the marriage relationship are in wickedness and sin against God and under the condemnation and judgment of God.

On the other hand, in the opening portion of this verse the Lord our God expresses His approval for sexual activity within the marriage relationship. The opening line of this verse in itself is a general statement – *"Marriage is honourable in all."* Yet that statement is made within a context that concerns the matter of sexual activity. This is revealed by the reference to "the bed" of marriage in the second line of the verse and to the "whoremongers and adulterers" in the closing portion of the verse. Thus in this context the truth that "marriage is honourable in all" may be applied specifically to the physical, sexual relationship between a husband and wife. The Lord our God describes such a healthy physical relationship as being worthy of honor.

329

Yes, the Lord our God views such sexual activity as highly precious and highly valuable; and that which is highly honored in our Lord's sight ought also to be highly honored in our sight. Furthermore, God's Holy Word declares that this physical, sexual relationship between a husband and wife is undefiled. *"Marriage is honourable in all, and the bed undefiled."* In the estimation of the Lord our God, the physical relationship between a husband and wife is *not* defiled. It is *not* filthy. It is *not* sinful or unrighteous. It is *not* ungodly or unholy. Rather, in the estimation of the Lord our God, a healthy physical relationship between a husband and wife is pure and clean; for He created it. It is good and righteous, for He commands it. It is godly and holy, for He commends it. Therefore, to be honored of our Lord a husband and wife *must remain pure* from every form of fornication and adultery and *must not be prudes* in their physical, sexual relationship with one another.

The Desire of the Lord

In the sixth place, we find the truth and principle that *the Lord our God desires that the husband and wife enjoy and find pleasure in their physical relationship together.* In Proverbs 5:18-19 God's Word gives instruction to the husband, saying, *"Let thy fountain be blessed: and rejoice with the wife of thy youth. Let her be as the loving hind and pleasant roe; let her breasts satisfy thee at all times; and be thou ravished always with her love."* Herein the husband is instructed to rejoice with his wife, to treasure his relationship with his wife, to be satisfied always with his wife's breasts, and to be ravished always with his wife's love. Now, this instruction is presented in the context of sexual relations. In verses 3-14 and 20-23, the husband is warned against the sin of fornication and adultery with a woman who is not his wife. Yea, in verse 20 a direct contrast is made between the instruction of verses 18-19 and the warning against fornication and adultery; for there the question is asked, *"And why wilt thou, my son, be ravished with a strange woman, and embrace the bosom of a stranger?"*

In both the instruction of verse 19 and the warning of verse 20, we find the word "ravished." In verse 19 the husband is instructed to

330

be "ravished always" with his wife's love. Yet in verse 20 the husband is warned against being "ravished" with a woman who is not his wife. In this context this word "ravished" means "to be carried away with intoxication." Certainly the husband is never to be physically intoxicated in a sexual relationship with another woman. Yet he is *always* to be physically intoxicated with his own wife's love in his physical, sexual relationship with her. The love that she bestows upon him in giving herself physically to him should overcome him with intoxicating pleasure. Yea, in their physical relationship together the husband is to be satisfied (even, satiated) at all times with his wife's breasts and physical body. In all he is to rejoice and find joy in the sexual advances and pleasures of his own wife. This is the instruction and desire of the Lord our God.

Furthermore, we find that the Lord our God included and inspired an entire book in His Word concerning the romantic and physical relationship between a husband and wife. This book is the Song of Solomon. The opening verse of this book gives the title, "*The song of songs, which is Solomon's.*" What a high recommendation is this that God the Holy Spirit has placed upon the character and contents of this song – "The song of songs."

Yet the character and contents of this song are not prudish and reserved. Rather, in this song we find a beautifully poetic and boldly open celebration of the romantic and sensual pleasure that a husband and wife may find in their physical relationship with one another. Thereby the Lord our God reveals His own intent and desire concerning the passion and pleasure of the physical relationship between a husband and wife. The character and contents of this "song of songs" is equally as inspired by God the Holy Spirit as any other portion of God's true and holy Word. Yea, this "song of songs" is God's own revelation concerning the physical relationship within marriage; and as an inspired part of God's Holy Word, this song's character and contents are themselves pure and holy.

Now, although this "song of songs" presents both the husband's and the wife's perspective on the passion and pleasure of their physical relationship together, the greater portion of the song is from the wife's perspective, expressing her desire for and pleasure in that relationship. Yea, with the opening line of the song, she expressed her desire for the kisses and physical advances of her husband. Also in the second verse of the first chapter she declared, *"Let him kiss me with the kisses of his mouth: for thy love is better than wine."*

In the opening five verses of chapter three, she sought after her husband and aggressively initiated and pursued sexual relations with him – *"By night on my bed I sought him whom my soul loveth: I sought him, but I found him not. I will rise now, and go about the city in the streets, and in the broad ways I will seek him whom my soul loveth: I sought him, but I found him not. The watchmen that go about the city found me: to whom I said, Saw ye him whom my soul loveth? It was but a little that I passed from them, but I found him whom my soul loveth: I held him, and would not let him go, until I had brought him into my mother's house, and into the chamber of her that conceived me. I charge you, O ye daughters of Jerusalem, by the roes, and by the hinds of the field, that ye stir not up, nor awake my love, till he please."*

In the last verse of chapter four (verse 16), she expressed her desire that her body might be aroused for her husband and that he might enjoy the pleasures of her body. There she declared, *"Awake, O north wind; and come, thou south; blow upon my garden, that the spices thereof may flow out. Let my beloved come into his garden, and eat his pleasant fruits."* In the previous four verses the husband had poetically described his wife's body as a luscious, private garden. Then in verse 16 the wife expressed her desire that "the spices" of the garden of her body might "flow out" and that her husband might "eat his pleasant fruits" out of that garden.

Furthermore, in the last seven verses of chapter five (verses 10-16), she poetically described her pleasure in her husband's physical body – *"My beloved is white and ruddy, the chiefest among ten thousand. His head is as the most fine gold, his locks are bushy, and black as a raven. His eyes are as the eyes of doves by the rivers of waters, washed with milk, and fitly set. His cheeks are as a bed of spices, as sweet flowers: his lips like lilies, dropping sweet smelling myrrh.*

His hands are as gold rings set with the beryl: his belly is as bright ivory overlaid with sapphires. His legs are as pillars of marble, set upon sockets of fine gold: his countenance is as Lebanon, excellent as the cedars. His mouth is most sweet: yea, he is altogether lovely. This is my beloved, and this is my friend, O daughters of Jerusalem." Here we learn that her pleasure in her husband is rooted to the fact that he is *both* her beloved husband *and* her beloved friend.

In verse ten of chapter seven, after her husband had declared his delight in and desire for her in the previous nine verses, the wife expressed her delight in his desire, saying, *"I am my beloved's, and his desire is toward me."* Then in the next three verses she invited him to herself and offered herself to him, saying, *"Come, my beloved, let us go forth into the field; let us lodge in the villages. Let us get up early to the vineyards; let us see if the vine flourish, whether the tender grape appear, and the pomegranates bud forth: there will I give thee my loves. The mandrakes give a smell, and at our gates are all manner of pleasant fruits, new and old, which I have laid up for thee, O my beloved."* Finally, in the last verse of this song (8:14), she invited her husband to join her quickly, saying, *"Make haste, my beloved, and be thou like to a roe or to a young hart upon the mountains of spices."* Clearly this wife finds great enjoyment and much pleasure in her physical relationship with her husband; and as revealed by this book of God's Holy Word, this is just the attitude that our Lord desires for a wife to have toward her husband.

In addition, in this "song of songs" we find the husband's delight in and desire for his wife. In the last three verses of chapter one (verses 15-17), he declared, *"Behold, thou art fair, my love; behold, thou art fair; thou hast doves' eyes. Behold, thou art fair, my beloved, yea, pleasant: also our bed is green. The beams of our house are cedar, and our rafters of fir."*

In the first fifteen verses of chapter four, he poetically described his delight in the beauty and pleasure of her body, saying, *"Behold, thou art fair, my love; behold, thou art fair; thou hast doves' eyes within thy locks: thy hair is as a flock of goats, that appear from mount Gilead. Thy teeth are like a flock of sheep that are even*

333

shorn, which came up from the washing; whereof every one bear twins, and none is barren among them. Thy lips are like a thread of scarlet, and thy speech is comely: thy temples are like a piece of a pomegranate within thy locks. Thy neck is like the tower of David builded for an armoury, whereon there hang a thousand bucklers, all shields of mighty men. Thy two breasts are like two young roes that are twins, which feed among the lilies. Until the day break, and the shadows flee away, I will get me to the mountain of myrrh, and to the hill of frankincense. Thou art all fair, my love; there is no spot in thee. Come with me from Lebanon, my spouse, with me from Lebanon: look from the top of Amana, from the top of Shenir and Hermon, from the lions' dens, from the mountains of the leopards. Thou hast ravished my heart, my sister, my spouse; thou hast ravished my heart with one of thine eyes, with one chain of thy neck. How fair is thy love, my sister, my spouse! How much better is thy love than wine! And the smell of thine ointments than all spices! Thy lips, O my spouse, drop as the honeycomb: honey and milk are under thy tongue; and the smell of thy garments is like the smell of Lebanon. A garden inclosed is my sister, my spouse; a spring shut up, a fountain sealed. Thy plants are an orchard of pomegranates, with pleasant fruits; camphire, with spikenard, spikenard and saffron; calamus and cinnamon, with all trees of frankincense; myrrh and aloes, with all the chief spices: a fountain of gardens, a well of living waters, and streams from Lebanon." Truly he was excited by her and intoxicated with her.

Yet again in verses four through seven of chapter six, he poetically described his delight in her, saying, *"Thou art beautiful, O my love, as Tirzah, comely as Jerusalem, terrible as an army with banners. Turn away thine eyes from me, for they have overcome me: thy hair is as a flock of goats that appear from Gilead. Thy teeth are as a flock of sheep which go up from the washing, whereof every one beareth twins, and there is not one barren among them. As a piece of a pomegranate are thy temples within thy locks."*

Finally, in the first nine verses of chapter seven he exclaimed, *"How beautiful are thy feet with shoes, O prince's daughter! The joints of thy thighs are like jewels, the work of the hands of a cunning workman. Thy navel is like a round goblet, which wanteth not liquor: thy belly is like an heap of wheat set about with lilies. Thy two breasts are like two young roes that are twins. Thy neck is as a tower of ivory; thine eyes like the fishpools in Heshbon, by the gate of Bathrabbim: thy nose is as the tower of Lebanon which looketh toward Damascus. Thine head upon thee is like Carmel, and the hair of thine head like purple; the king is held in the galleries. How fair and how pleasant art thou, O love, for delights! This thy stature is like to a palm tree, and thy breasts to clusters of grapes. I said, I will go up to the palm tree, I will take hold of the boughs thereof: now also thy breasts shall be as clusters of the vine, and the smell of thy nose like apples; and the roof of thy mouth like the best wine for my beloved, that goeth down sweetly, causing the lips of those that are asleep to speak."* Clearly this husband had a passionate delight in his wife's physical body; and as revealed by this book of God's Holy Word, this is just the attitude that our Lord desires for a husband to have toward his wife.

Truth for Meditation

Concerning the physical relationship between a husband and wife –

1. The Lord our God directly commands the husband and wife to engage in a physical relationship together. (1 Cor. 7:2-3)
2. The Lord our God defines the physical relationship between a husband and wife as "due benevolence." (1 Cor. 7:3-4)
3. The Lord our God directs the husband to take the lead in rendering this due benevolence unto his wife. (1 Cor. 7:3)
4. The Lord our God directly forbids the husband and the wife from defrauding one another in this matter. (1 Cor. 7:5)
5. The Lord our God describes the physical relationship between a husband and wife as being worthy of honor. (Heb. 13:4)
6. The Lord our God desires that the husband and wife enjoy and find pleasure in their physical relationship together. (Prov. 5:18-19; Song of Solomon)

The truth that our Lord defines the physical relationship between a husband and wife as "due benevolence" teaches us that –

1. The physical relationship between the husband and the wife is *a matter of responsibility* within the marriage relationship.
2. The physical relationship between the husband and the wife is *an act of loving-kindness* toward one another.
3. The physical relationship between the husband and the wife is *a gift of pleasure* for one another.
4. The physical relationship between the husband and the wife is *a blessing for gratitude* unto one another.

Verses for Memorization

1 Corinthians 7:3: Let the husband render unto the wife due benevolence: and likewise also the wife unto the husband.

Hebrews 13:4: Marriage is honourable in all, and the bed undefiled: but whoremongers and adulterers God will judge.

26

Flee Fornication
(Part 1)

As we have learned in the previous chapter, the physical, sexual relationship within marriage is highly honored in our Lord's sight. However, any sexual relationship outside the marriage bond is a wicked abomination in His sight. This contrast is clearly revealed in Hebrews 13:4 where we find both the commendation and condemnation – *"Marriage is honourable in all, and the bed undefiled: but whoremongers and adulterers God will judge."*

Even so, concerning the sin of adultery and fornication, God's Word instructs us in 1 Corinthians 6:18, *"Flee fornication."* We are not simply to resist or reject this sin of adultery and fornication. We are to run from it. We are not to stand and fight against it with determination. We are to turn and flee away from it with all motivation. Certainly we are not to approach unto it, ponder upon it, provide for it, play with it, pursue after it, or approve of it. Rather, we are to flee – to *flee* away with all enthusiastic motivation and energetic commitment of heart – to *FLEE* away as from a ravenous, wild beast.

Because Our Lord Commands Us

Now, in His Holy Word the Lord our God has given us various reasons that should move us to flee this sin of adultery and fornication with all of our heart. In the first place, we must flee this sin *because the*

Lord our God commands us to avoid any involvement in this sin. The seventh of the Ten Commandments that the Lord our God delivered unto the nation of Israel in Exodus 20 is just this – *"Thou shalt not commit adultery."* (Exodus 20:14) Again in Leviticus 18:20 the Lord our God instructed the nation of Israel, saying, *"Moreover thou shalt not lie carnally with thy neighbor's wife, to defile thyself with her."*

Furthermore, in the New Testament passage of Romans 13:12-13, God's Holy Word gives the instruction, *"The night is far spent, the day is at hand: let us therefore cast off the works of darkness, and let us put on the armour of light. Let us walk honestly, as in the day; not in rioting and drunkenness, not in chambering and wantonness, not in strife and envying."* In this passage we find three couplets that describe "the works of darkness" which we are to "cast off." The second of these couplets indicates that we are not to walk "in chambering and wantonness." In this context the word "chambering" refers to sinful activities of the bedchamber, and the word "wantonness" refers to unbridled sexual lust.

Yet again, referring to the sin of God's people in the time of the Old Testament, 1 Corinthians 10:8 warns us now in this time of the New Testament, saying, *"Nether let us commit fornication, as some of them committed, and fell in one day three and twenty thousand."* Yea, in Ephesians 5:3 we are warned, *"But fornication, and all uncleanness, let it not be once named among you, as becometh saints."* Finally, in 1 Thessalonians 4:3-4 the proclamation is given, *"This is the will of God, even your sanctification, that ye should abstain from fornication: that every one of you should know how to possess his vessel in sanctification and honour."*

Because Our Bodies Are Not Our Own

In the second place, we must flee the sin of adultery and fornication *because our bodies are not our own possession, but are the members of Christ.* In the closing portion of 1 Corinthians 6:13, the truth is revealed, *"Now the body is not for fornication, but for the Lord; and the Lord for the body."* The Lord our God did not give us our physical bodies with the intention that we should use them in order to commit the physical sin of fornication and adultery. Rather, the Lord our God gave us our physical bodies with the intention that we should use them in order to serve the righteous will of our Lord Himself. Our bodies exist for our Lord's sake and for righteousness' sake, not for sin's sake and fornication's sake.

Furthermore, 1 Corinthians 6:15-17 presents the question, *"Know ye not that your bodies are the members of Christ? Shall I then take the members of Christ, and make them the members of an harlot? God forbid. What? Know ye not that he which is joined to an harlot is one body? For two, saith he, shall be one flesh. But he that is joined unto the Lord is one spirit."* Through faith in Christ for eternal salvation from sin, every believer is spiritually joined unto the Lord Jesus Christ in spiritual union. In this spiritual union the body of each believer is spiritually made a member of Christ's spiritual body in this world. How then can we use our bodies, as the very members of Christ's body, to engage in the sin of fornication and adultery? How then can we enter a very part of Christ's body into the wicked corruption of fornication and adultery? Through salvation our bodies are sanctified unto Christ as instruments of righteousness and are no longer to be involved in sin as instruments of unrighteousness.

Finally, in 1 Corinthians 6:18-20 the proclamation is made, *"Flee fornication. Every sin that a man doeth is without the body; but he that committeth fornication sinneth against his own body. What? Know ye not that your body is the temple of the Holy Ghost which is in you, which ye have of God, and ye are not your own? For ye are bought with a price: therefore glorify God in your body, and in your spirit, which are God's."* In salvation we are "bought with a price" – with the price of Christ's shed blood and sacrificial death. Our lives and our bodies are not our own possession. They are the purchased possession of God our heavenly Father. In addition, God our heavenly Father has sent forth His Holy Spirit to dwell within us. Our bodies are now the sanctified temple of the indwelling Holy Spirit. Even so, to commit the sin of fornication and adultery, and thereby to sin against one's own body, is actually to sin against the purchased possession of God the Father and to sin against the sanctified temple of God the Holy Spirit. God forbid!

339

Our bodies are not our own possession to be corrupted in the sin of fornication and adultery as we please. Rather, our bodies are the temple of the Holy Spirit to be filled with His purity and are the possession of God to be used for His glory.

Because Fornication Will Bring Forth Corruption

In the third place, we must flee the sin of adultery and fornication *because this sin will bring forth the corruption and destruction of one's life.* In Galatians 5:19 we find that the works of our sinful flesh include adultery, fornication, uncleanness, and lasciviousness (or, unbridled sexual lust). Then in Galatians 6:7 the warning is given, *"Be not deceived; God is not mocked: for whatsoever a man soweth, that shall he also reap;"* and the opening half of verse 8 adds, *"For he that soweth to his flesh shall of the flesh reap corruption."* This is the absolute principle of God for our lives – If we sow to the fleshly works of adultery, fornication, and sexual lust, we shall reap the fruit of spiritual corruption. Certainly our sinful flesh will attempt to convince us that we can escape the consequences and corruption of our sin. Yet God's Holy Word cries forth the warning – *"Be not deceived."* The righteous Lord God will not be mocked in this matter.

Furthermore, speaking of the adulterous woman in warning to the young man, Proverbs 2:18-19 declares, *"For her house inclineth unto death, and her paths unto the dead. None that go unto her return again, neither take they hold of the paths of life."* The path of adultery, fornication, and sexual lust is the path of death. It is the path of spiritual darkness and destruction. Flee away! Again in Proverbs 6:27-29 the warning is given, *"Can a man take fire in his bosom, and his clothes not be burned? Can one go upon hot coals, and his feet not be burned? So he that goeth in to his neighbor's wife; whosoever toucheth her shall not be innocent."* To this verse 32 adds, *"But whoso committeth adultery with a woman lacketh understanding: he that doeth it destroyeth his own soul."* Flee, flee away!

Yet again, concerning the foolish man who is ensnared by the adulterous woman, Proverbs 7:22-23 givest the report, *"He goeth after her straightway, as an ox goeth to the slaughter, or as a fool to the correction of the stocks; till a dart strike through his liver; as a bird hasteth to the snare, and knoweth not that it is for his life.*" To this verses 24-27 add the general warning to all, saying, "*Hearken unto me now therefore, O ye children, and attend to the words of my mouth. Let not thine heart decline to her ways, go not astray in her paths. For she hath cast down many wounded: yea, many strong men have been slain by her. Her house is the way to hell, going down to the chambers of death.*" Flee fast away! Yea, Proverbs 23:27-28 proclaims, "*For a whore is a deep ditch; and a strange woman is a narrow pit. She also lieth in wait as for a prey, and increaseth the transgressors among men.*" Flee far away!

Finally, in Proverbs 5:3-14 the extended warning is delivered, "*For the lips of a strange woman drop as an honeycomb, and her mouth is smoother than oil: but her end is bitter as wormwood, sharp as a twoedged sword. Her feet go down to death; her steps take hold on hell. Lest thou shouldest ponder the path of life, her ways are moveable, that thou canst not know them. Hear me now therefore, O ye children, and depart not from the words of my mouth. Remove thy way far from her, and come not nigh the door of her house: lest thou give thine honour unto others, and thy years unto the cruel: lest strangers be filled with thy wealth; and thy labours be in the house of a stranger; and thou mourn at the last, when thy flesh and thy body are consumed, and say, How have I hated instruction, and my heart despised reproof; and have not obeyed the voice of my teachers, nor inclined mine ear to them that instructed me! I was almost in all evil in the midst of the congregation and assembly.*" The pathway of adultery, fornication, and sexual lust is a way of bitterness and piercing trouble. It is a way of deception and worthless living. It is a way of dishonor and sorrowful grief. It is truly the destruction of one's own soul.

Because Fornication Will Hold Fast and Lead Astray

In the fourth place, we must flee the sin of adultery and fornication *because this sin will hold one fast in spiritual captivity and lead one astray into greater iniquity.* In Proverbs 5:20-23 the young man is warned, *"And why wilt thou, my son, be ravished with a strange woman, and embrace the bosom of a stranger? For the ways of man are before the eyes of the LORD, and he pondereth all his goings. His own iniquities shall take the wicked himself, and he shall be holden with the cords of his sins. He shall die without instruction; and in the greatness of his folly he shall go astray."* The wicked individual's own iniquities and sins will serve as the very spiritual cords that bind him; and the particular sin of this context is that of adultery, fornication, and sexual lust. Thus we are brought to understand that this sin of adultery, fornication, and sexual lust will take captive and hold fast an individual's character. This sin is not one from which there is an easy escape. Rather, the great folly of this sin will cause an individual to go yet further and further astray into greater foolishness and deeper iniquity. The end thereof will be a wasted spiritual life without any spiritual value.

Because Fornication is Treachery against Marriage

In the fifth place, we must flee the sin of adultery and fornication *because this sin is treachery against our Lord's intent for the exclusive relationship of marriage.* In the previous chapter we learned that the Lord our God intends for the physical, sexual relationship between a man and woman to be exclusive to the marriage relationship. This is revealed in the contrasting truths of Hebrews 13:4 – *"Marriage is honourable in all, and the bed undefiled: but whoremongers and adulterers God will judge."* Within marriage the physical, sexual relationship is worthy of honor in our Lord's sight; but outside marriage the physical, sexual relationship is worthy of judgment in His sight. Thus the sin of fornication and adultery is treachery against our Lord God's intent for the exclusiveness of the marriage relationship. It is a betrayal of trust before our Lord. It is an act of treason against the exclusive marriage relationship.

❖ First, the sin of fornication and adultery is treachery *against one's own spouse and against one's own marriage.* In Malachi 2:13-14 the Lord our God pronounced His judgment against the men of Israel in that day, saying, *"And this have ye done again, covering the altar of the LORD with tears, with weeping, and with crying out, insomuch that he regardeth not the offering any more, or receiveth it with good will at your hand. Yet ye say, Wherefore? Because the LORD hath been witness between thee and the wife of thy youth, against whom thou hast dealt treacherously: yet is she thy companion, and the wife of thy covenant.*" According to the context, these men of Israel were leaving their own wives and marriages for other women. Thus the Lord our God proclaimed that each of them was dealing treacherously against the wife of his youth. They were betraying the trust of their marriage covenant before the Lord and were acting with treason against the exclusive companionship of their wives. In like manner, the opening portion of Jeremiah 3:20 indicates that such treachery is also committed by a wife who departs from her husband for another man, saying, "*Surely as a wife treacherously departeth from her husband.*"

❖ Second, the sin of fornication and adultery is treachery *against one's neighbor and against his or her marriage.* In 1 Thessalonians 4:3-6 the truth is given, "*For this is the will of God, even your sanctification, that ye should abstain from fornication: that every one of you should know how to possess his vessel in sanctification and honour; not in the lust of concupiscence, even as the Gentiles which know not God: that no man go beyond and defraud his brother in any matter: because that the Lord is the avenger of all such, as we also have forewarned you and testified.*" Certainly the instruction not to defraud another "in any matter" encompasses any and all manner of cheating another. Yet the one specific sin mentioned in this passage is the sin of fornication. To commit the sin of fornication and adultery with another individual's spouse is to defraud (or, cheat) that individual out of the divinely ordained exclusiveness of his or her marriage relationship. Even if the individual with whom this sin is committed is not married at the time, this sin defrauds some future spouse out of the exclusiveness of the physical, sexual relationship that the Lord our God intended for the marriage relationship. This is treachery. Yea, this is the reason that Proverbs 6:34-35 declares concerning the sin of fornication and adultery, "*For jealousy is the rage of a man: therefore he will not spare in the day of vengeance. He will not regard any ransom; neither will he rest content, though thou givest many gifts.*"

Because Fornication Will Bring Spiritual Reproach

In the sixth place, we must flee the sin of adultery and fornication *because this sin will bring a spiritual reproach upon one's life that will not be wiped away.* In Proverbs 6:30-35 the warning is proclaimed, *"Men do not despise a thief, if he steal to satisfy his soul when he is hungry; but if he be found, he shall restore sevenfold; he shall give all the substance of his house. But whoso committeth adultery with a woman lacketh understanding: he that doeth it destroyeth his own soul. A wound and dishonour shall he get; and his reproach shall not be wiped away. For jealousy is the rage of a man: therefore he will not spare in the day of vengeance. He will not regard any ransom; neither will he rest content, though thou givest many gifts."* It is truly not possible to pay back a man or woman for committing adultery with his or her spouse. A thief can make restitution for his crime, even if it costs him all of his substance; but restitution can never truly be made for the sin of adultery. Rather, a scar of dishonor and disgrace shall ever abide upon the adulterer's name.

Because Fornication Will Give Occasion to the Lord's Enemies

In the seventh place, we must flee the sin of adultery and fornication *because this sin will give a great occasion for the enemies of our Lord to blaspheme His holy name.* In 2 Samuel 11 we find the account of King David's sin of adultery with Bath-sheba, of his attempt to cover up that sin, and of his murder of Bath-sheba's husband, Uriah the Hittite, through the sword of the children of Ammon. The closing phrase of this chapter gives the report, *"But the thing that David had done displeased the LORD."* Thus at the beginning of chapter 12 we find that the Lord sent the prophet Nathan to confront David for his sin. Involved in this confrontation, the prophet Nathan stated in the opening portion of 2 Samuel 12:14, *"Howbeit, because by this deed thou hast given great occasion to the enemies of the LORD to blaspheme."* In like manner, by the sin of adultery and fornication, we who are the children of God today would also give such a great occasion for the enemies of our Lord to blaspheme His holy name. Oh, how important it is for the sake of our Lord's holy name that we flee away!

344

Because Fornication is a Hateful Abomination before Our Lord

In the eighth place, we must flee the sin of adultery and fornication *because this sin is a hateful abomination before our Lord that brings spiritual defilement.* At the opening of Leviticus 18, the Lord our God warned His people, the children of Israel, not to walk after the sinful doings of the people of the land of Egypt or of the people of the land of Canaan. Rather, He instructed them to walk after His statutes, judgments, and ordinances. Then in verses 6-23 the Lord provided a list of specific sins that the children of Israel were to avoid, and all but one of those sins are sexually related sins. Among this list is included the sin of adultery; for verse 20 declares, *"Also thou shalt not lie carnally with thy neighbor's wife, to defile thyself with her."*

Finally, in the closing seven verses of the chapter (verses 24-30), our Lord proclaimed, *"Defile not ye yourselves in any of these things: for in all these the nations are defiled which I cast out before you: and the land is defiled: therefore I do visit the iniquity thereof upon it, and the land itself vomiteth out her inhabitants. Ye shall therefore keep my statutes and my judgments, and shall not commit any of these abominations; neither any of your own nation, nor any stranger that sojourneth among you: (For all these abominations have the men of the land done, which were before you, and the land is defiled;) that the land spue not you out also, when ye defile it, as it spued out the nations that were before you. For whosoever shall commit any of these abominations, even the souls that commit them shall be cut off from among their people. Therefore shall ye keep mine ordinance, that ye commit not any one of these abominable customs, which were committed before you, and that ye defile not yourselves therein: I am the LORD your God."*

Four times in this passage the Lord our God indicates that these sexually related sins, including the sin of fornication and adultery, are a hateful abomination in His sight. Furthermore, six times in this passage the Lord our God indicates that these sexually related sins, including the sin of fornication and adultery, are a spiritual defilement in His sight. First, He reveals that such sexual sin defiles the individuals who are involved therein. Then He reveals

345

that such sexual sin defiles the very land in which these individuals dwell. Finally, our Lord indicates that the defiled land itself will seek to vomit out the wicked inhabitants that so defile it.

Because Fornication Will Bring the Lord's Judgment

In the ninth place, we must flee the sin of adultery and fornication *because this sin will bring down the judgment of the Lord our God upon one's life.* In Jeremiah 5:7-9 the Lord our God pronounced His judgment upon the nation of Israel, saying, *"How shall I pardon thee for this? Thy children have forsaken me, and sworn by them that are no gods: when I had fed them to the full, they then committed adultery, and assembled themselves by troops in the harlots' houses. They were as fed horses in the morning: every one neighed after his neighbour's wife. Shall I not visit for these things? saith the LORD: and shall not my soul be avenged on such a nation as this?"* Also in the New Testament passage of Hebrews 13:4, the truth is declared, *"Marriage is honourable in all, and the bed undefiled: but whoremongers and adulterers God will judge."* Be sure that the vengeance of God's judgment will indeed be poured out in this life upon those who commit this sin.

Because Fornication Will Bring Material Grief

In the tenth and final place, we must flee the sin of adultery and fornication *because this sin will bring one to material and financial grief and devastation.* Proverbs 5:7-10 gives the warning concerning the adulterous woman, saying, *"Hear me now therefore, O ye children, and depart not from the words of my mouth. Remove thy way far from her, and come not nigh the door of her house: lest thou give thine honour unto others, and thy years unto the cruel: lest strangers be filled with thy wealth; and thy labours be in the house of a stranger."* Again the warning is given in the opening half of Proverbs 6:26, *"For by means of a whorish woman a man is brought to a piece of bread."* Yet again Proverbs 29:3 declares, *"Whoso loveth wisdom rejoiceth his father: but he that keepeth company with harlots spendeth his substance."*

346

Truth for Meditation

The Biblical reasons that we should flee fast and far away with all of our heart from the sin of adultery and fornication is because –

1. The Lord our God commands us to avoid any involvement in this sin. (Exo. 20:14; Lev. 18:20; Rom. 13:12-13; 1 Cor. 10:8; Eph. 5:3; 1 Thess. 4:3-4)

2. Our bodies are not our own possession, but are the members of Christ. (1 Cor. 6:13-20)

3. This sin will bring forth the corruption and destruction of one's life. (Gal. 6:7-8; Prov. 2:18-19; 5:3-14; 6:27-29, 32; 7:22-27; 23:27-28)

4. This sin will hold one fast in spiritual captivity and lead one astray into greater iniquity. (Prov. 5:20-23)

5. This sin is treachery against our Lord's intent for the exclusive relationship of marriage. (Mal. 2:13-14; Jer. 3:20; 1 Thess. 4:3-6; Prov. 6:34-35)

6. This sin will bring a spiritual reproach upon one's life that will not be wiped away. (Prov. 6:30-35)

7. This sin will give a great occasion for the enemies of our Lord to blaspheme His holy name. (2 Sam. 12:14)

8. This sin is a hateful abomination before our Lord that brings spiritual defilement. (Lev. 18:24-30)

9. This sin will bring down the judgment of the Lord our God upon one's life. (Jer. 5:7-9; Heb. 13:4)

10. This sin will bring one to material and financial grief and devastation. (Prov. 5:7-10; 6:26; 29:3)

Verses for Memorization

1 Corinthians 6:19-20: What? Know ye not that your body is the temple of the Holy Ghost which is in you, which ye have of God, and ye are not your own? For ye are bought with a price: therefore glorify God in your body, and in your spirit, which are God's.

1 Thessalonians 4:3-4: This is the will of God, even your sanctification, that ye abstain from fornication: that every one of you should know how to possess his vessel in sanctification and honour.

Proverbs 6:32: But whoso committeth adultery with a woman lacketh understanding: he that doeth it destroyeth his own soul.

27

Flee Fornication
(Part 2)

I n the previous chapter we considered the command of our Lord from 1 Corinthians 6:18 that we are to flee the sin of adultery and fornication. In addition, we considered ten reasons that the Lord our God provides in His Holy Word to move us and motivate us to flee this sin with all of our heart. Now in this chapter let us consider the means that the Lord our God has given us by which we may flee away and find victory over the temptation and sin of adultery and fornication.

Receive the Lord Jesus Christ through Faith as Savior

In the first place, *we must be eternally saved from the power of darkness through faith in the Lord Jesus Christ as our eternal Savior.* Every other principle in this chapter *hinges* upon this one, for no other principle of the chapter can be put into practice *correctly* without this one. In Ephesians 2:1-3 we find the spiritual condition, character, and conduct of those who do not yet possess eternal life and new spiritual birth. There we read, *"And you hath he quickened, who were dead in trespasses and sins; wherein in time past ye walked according to the course of this world, according to the prince of the power of the air, the spirit that now worketh in the children of disobedience: among whom also we all had our conversation in times past in the lusts of our flesh, fulfilling the desires of the flesh and of the mind; and were by nature the children of wrath, even as others."*

Before any individual is made alive (quickened) spiritually by God's grace and power through eternal salvation and new birth, that individual is spiritually *dead* in his or her sins. The spiritual condition of every lost sinner is to be spiritually dead (that is – spiritually separated from the Lord our God and from the life of godliness). Thus by character and nature every lost sinner walks after the *disobedient* ways of this spiritually dark world and of that wicked one, the devil, who governs the spiritual darkness of this world. Furthermore, every lost sinner conducts himself or herself in the *lusts* of his or her sinful flesh, giving himself or herself to the *selfish desires* of the flesh and of the mind. Even so, every lost sinner is under the *power* of spiritual darkness, having his or her heart and life *dominated* and *governed* by that darkness and having *no* spiritual power for victory over temptation and sin.

Yet in the riches of His mercy and grace and in the greatness of His love and kindness, the Lord our God has provided a way of spiritual deliverance in His Son, the Lord Jesus Christ, for us sinners. Through faith in the shed blood and sacrificial death of the Lord Jesus Christ upon the cross for eternal salvation from sin, a lost sinner is spiritually delivered from the power of darkness. (Colossians 1:13) Furthermore, through faith in the Lord Jesus Christ as eternal Savior from sin, a lost sinner is spiritually made alive through new spiritual birth. Through faith in Christ as Savior, we who were spiritually dead unto God in sin are now spiritually alive unto God in Christ. Romans 6:11 declares, ***"Likewise reckon ye also yourselves to be dead indeed unto sin, but alive unto God through Jesus Christ our Lord."***

Yea, through eternal salvation and new spiritual birth, we who were the children of darkness and of disobedience are now *the children of God and of light*. Now we are *no longer bound* under the power of spiritual darkness, having our heart and life dominated and governed thereby and having no spiritual power for victory over sinful lust. Now we have *newness of spiritual life*, and now we are *able to walk in the light* as children of light, even as God our heavenly

Father walks in the light. Yes, the spiritual *power for victory* over temptation and sinful lust is the heritage of every individual who is eternally saved and born again through faith in Jesus Christ as Savior. Thus Romans 6:12-13 gives the instructions, "*Let not sin therefore reign in your mortal body, that ye should obey it in the lusts thereof. Neither yield ye your members as instruments of unrighteousness unto sin: but yield yourselves unto God, as those that are alive from the dead, and your members as instruments of righteousness unto God.*"

Repent of Any Involvement in Sexual Sin

In the second place, *we must repent with a contrite heart of any involvement in the sin of sexual lust, adultery, and fornication.* God's Holy Word presents a three-fold instruction in Romans 13:12-13, saying, "*The night is far spent, the day is at hand: let us therefore cast off the works of darkness, and let us put on the armour of light. Let us walk honestly, as in the day; not in rioting and drunkenness, not in chambering and wantonness, not in strife and envying.*" Through the order of this instruction, we learn that in order to walk in the way of spiritual light and victory, we must *first put on* the spiritual armor of light. Furthermore, we learn that before we may put on the spiritual armor of light, we must *first cast off* the works of spiritual darkness.

What then is included among these works of darkness that we must cast off? The closing portion of verse 13 provides an answer, indicating through a three-fold couplet how we are not to walk – "*not in rioting and drunkenness, not in chambering and wantonness, not in strife and envying.*" Now, the second of these couplets mentions the sin of "chambering and wantonness." As we noted in the previous chapter, in this context the word "chambering" refers to sinful activities of the bedchamber; and the word "wantonness" refers to unbridled sexual lust. Before we may put on the armor of spiritual light and walk in the way of spiritual light, finding spiritual victory over the temptation and sin of sexual lust, adultery, and fornication, we must *first cast off* any prior involvement that we have had in the sin of sexual lust, adultery, and fornication.

351

How then can we cast off such prior involvement in this sin? The answer is found in one word – "Repent!" In Revelation 2:20-22 the Lord our God confronted the church in Thyatira, saying, *"Notwithstanding I have a few things against thee, because thou sufferest that woman Jezebel, which calleth herself a prophetess, to teach and to seduce my servants to commit fornication, and to eat things sacrificed unto idols. And I gave her space to repent of her fornication; and she repented not. Behold, I will cast her into a bed, and them that commit adultery with her into great tribulation, except they repent of their deeds."* To every believer who involves himself or herself in the sin of sexual lust, adultery, and fornication, the Lord our God grants a space of time to repent. Until one comes to repentance, our Lord's hand of chastening will be heavy upon that individual. Even so, David reported in Psalm 32:3-4 concerning his own sin of adultery with Bath-sheba, saying, *"When I kept silence, my bones waxed old through my roaring all the day long. For day and night thy hand was heavy upon me: my moisture is turned into the drought of summer. Selah."* Yet when one does come to repentance through broken-hearted confession, our Lord's hand of mercy will be open toward that individual. Proverbs 28:13 declares, *"He that covereth his sins shall not prosper: but whoso confesseth and forsaketh them shall have mercy."*

Our Lord will grant forgiveness of sin, even as David revealed in Psalm 32:5, *"I acknowledged my sin unto thee, and mine iniquity have I not hid. I said, I will confess my transgressions unto the LORD; and thou forgavest the iniquity of my sin."* Furthermore, He will renew a clean heart and a right spirit within and will restore unto the joy of His fellowship, even as David requested in Psalm 51:10-12, *"Create in me a clean heart, O God; and renew a right spirit within me. Cast me not away from thy presence; and take not thy Holy Spirit from me. Restore unto me the joy of thy salvation; and uphold me with thy free Spirit."* Finally, He will deliver from the dark pit of sin and will establish one's going in the way of spiritual light and victory, even as David reported in Psalm 40:2, *"He brought me up also out of an horrible pit, out of the miry clay, and set my feet upon a rock, and established my goings."* Through repentance with a contrite heart, an individual enters into the place of spiritual victory;

but without such repentance an individual remains in the pit of spiritual defeat.

Put On and Abide in Our Lord Jesus Christ

In the third place, *we must put on and abide in our Lord Jesus Christ each and every day as our armor of spiritual light.* As we learned in the previous point from Romans 13:12-13, we must cast off the works of spiritual darkness and put on the armor of spiritual light in order to walk in the way of spiritual light and victory. In the opening line of Romans 13:14, we find a repetition of the instruction to put on – *"But put ye on the Lord Jesus Christ."* God the Son, the Lord Jesus Christ our Savior, *is Himself* our spiritual armor of light. We must abide in Him and allow Him to abide in us throughout each day of our daily walk. He instructed us in John 15:4-5, *"Abide in me, and I in you. As the branch cannot bear fruit of itself, except it abide in the vine; no more can ye, except ye abide in me. I am the vine, ye are the branches. He that abideth in me, and I in him, the same bringeth forth much fruit: for without me ye can do nothing."* Without Him we *cannot* be spiritually victorious; but through Him we can be *all* victorious over any and all sin, including the sins of "chambering and wantonness." Even so, the apostle Paul gave testimony in Philippians 4:13, saying, *"I can do all things through Christ which strengtheneth me."*

We must set our trust in our Lord with all of our heart at all times. We must never rely upon our own understanding or upon our own strength to find victory over the sin of sexual lust, adultery, and fornication. Rather, we must *"be strong in the Lord, and in the power of his might."* (Ephesians 6:10) We must *"be strong in the grace that is in Christ Jesus."* (2 Timothy 2:1) We must be weak in ourselves and must trust in the Lord, *"that the power of Christ may rest upon [us]."* (2 Corinthians 12:9) We must trust *"in the LORD for ever: for in the LORD JEHOVAH is everlasting strength."* (Isaiah 26:4)

353

Walk after the Direction of the Holy Spirit

In the fourth place, *we must walk in and after the righteous direction of the indwelling Holy Spirit of God.* In Galatians 5:16 God's Holy Word declares, *"This I say then, Walk in the Spirit, and ye shall not fulfil the lust of the flesh."* The promise of victory is clearly revealed. We will find victory over the sinful desires of our flesh when we walk in and after the righteous direction of the Holy Spirit. The direction of the indwelling Holy Spirit is *always* contrary to the desires of our sinful flesh, even as verse 17 states, *"For the flesh lusteth against the Spirit, and the Spirit against the flesh: and these are contrary the one to the other: so that ye cannot do the things that ye would."* Now, the works of the flesh are revealed in verses 19-21; and adultery, fornication, and lasciviousness (unbridled sexual lust) are included among them. Thus when we walk in and after the righteous direction of the Holy Spirit, we shall not engage in the sins of adultery, fornication, and sexual lust, but shall have victory over them. The Holy Spirit's righteous direction is *always away* from such sin, and His almighty power is *always greater* than our sinful flesh. We must submit ourselves to His direction in order that He might empower us for victory.

Seek after the Wisdom of God's Word

In the fifth place, *we must seek enthusiastically after and apply our heart unto the wisdom of God's Holy Word.* In Proverbs 2:1-4 the instruction is given in the form of a prerequisite to a promise, *"My son, if thou wilt receive my words, and hide my commandments with thee; so that thou incline thine ear unto wisdom, and apply thine heart to understanding; yea, if thou criest after knowledge, and liftest up thy voice for understanding; if thou seekest her as silver, and searchest for her as for hid treasures."* This passage presents the instruction of a father to his son, and the greatest application of this passage centers upon the relationship of God our heavenly Father to His dear children. We who are the children of God should receive the words and hide the commandments of our heavenly Father within our hearts. We should incline our ears and apply our hearts to the wisdom of His Holy Word. We should cry after and seek for that wisdom with all enthusiasm of heart.

What then will be the result? Verses 5-9 give answer, *"Then shalt thou understand the fear of the LORD, and find the knowledge of God. For the LORD giveth wisdom: out of his mouth cometh knowledge and understanding. He layeth up sound wisdom for the righteous: he is a buckler to them that walk uprightly. He keepeth the paths of judgment, and preserveth the way of his saints. Then shalt thou understand righteousness, and judgment, and equity; yea, every good path."* The result of seeking enthusiastically after and applying our hearts unto the wisdom of God's Word is that we shall enter into a right relationship with the Lord our God (v. 5) and shall walk daily upon every good and righteous path (v. 9).

Yet there is one additional result. Verses 10-11 declare, *"When wisdom entereth into thine heart, and knowledge is pleasant unto thy soul; discretion shall preserve thee, understanding shall keep thee."* The discretion that the wisdom of God's Holy Word produces within one's heart will preserve and protect that individual from spiritual destruction. Yea, the sound wisdom of God's Word will serve as a buckler and shield to protect those who walk uprightly. Finally, in verses 12-22 we find that the discretion of God's wisdom from God's Word will preserve in a three-fold manner. The first is revealed in verse 12 – *"To deliver thee from the way of the evil man, from the man that speaketh froward things."* The second is revealed in verse 16 – *"To deliver thee from the strange woman, even from the stranger which flattereth with her words."* The third is revealed in verse 20 – *"That thou mayest walk in the way of good men, and keep the paths of the righteous."* Thus we understand that victory over the sin of adultery and fornication requires a faithful seeking after and applying of our hearts unto the wisdom of God's Holy Word. Yet we must also understand that this is not simply a gathering of Biblical knowledge. Rather, this must be a gleaning of Biblical wisdom, applied to the heart within and followed in the walk without.

Obey the Commandments of God's Word

In the sixth place, *we must obey the commandments of God's Holy Word in both its regulations and reproofs.* This truth flows directly out of the previous point. In Proverbs 6:23-24 God's Holy Word proclaims, *"For the commandment is a lamp; and the law is light; and reproofs of instruction are the way of life: to keep thee from the evil woman, from the flattery of the tongue of a strange woman."* We must not simply apply ourselves to learn the wisdom of God's Holy Word. We must also submit ourselves to obey the commands of God's Holy Word, and these commands will come to us in two forms. First, the commands of God's Word will come to us in the form of law, that is – in the form of rules and regulations to guide and govern the attitudes and actions of our hearts and lives. Second, the commands of God's Word will come to us in the form of reproofs of instruction, that is – in the form of reproof and rebuke to convict and correct us of the wrong attitudes and actions in our hearts and lives.

Now, as we submit ourselves to obey the rules and regulations of God's Holy Word and to turn at the reproof and rebuke of God's Holy Word, we shall be guided in the way of spiritual light and life and shall be guarded from the sin of adultery and fornication. The spiritual darkness of temptation and sin employs deception to ensnare us, even as the evil woman employs the deception of flattery to ensnare her victims. Yet those who faithfully obey the commandments of God's Holy Word in both its regulations and reproofs find that these very commandments are a lamp unto their feet and a light unto their path. This spiritual light will guide them to walk in the way of spiritual life and will guard them from falling into the pit of spiritual destruction.

Set Your Affection on Things Above

In the seventh place, *we must seek after and set our affection upon things above, not upon things on the earth.* In Colossians 3:1-2 God's Holy Word gives instruction, saying, *"If ye then be risen with Christ, seek those things which are above, where Christ sitteth on the right hand of God. Set your affection on things above, not on things on the earth.*" We must purposefully set the affection of our hearts (that is – the thoughts of our mind and the desires of our emotion) on the things of our Lord above. We must set our minds and hearts on the purpose and pleasure of our Lord in heaven above, not on the purpose and pleasure of our flesh on the earth beneath. In order that we may please our Lord in all things, we must not entangle our affection with the purposes and pleasures of this life. This must be our mind-set – to walk worthy of our Lord unto all pleasing.

Now, the two-fold motivation for setting our affection on the things of our Lord above is given in verses 3-4 – "*For ye are dead, and your life is hid with Christ in God. When Christ, who is our life, shall appear, then shall ye also appear with him in glory.*" First, we are to be motivated by the reality of our newness of spiritual life in Christ; and second, we are to be motivated by our reward at the return of Christ in glory. Then the spiritual victory of setting our affection on the things of our Lord above is given in verse 5 – "*Mortify therefore your members which are upon the earth; fornication, uncleanness, inordinate affection, evil concupiscence and covetousness, which is idolatry.*" When we set our affection on the purpose and pleasure of our Lord above, then we shall find the spiritual victory to mortify (put to death) the sinful desires of our flesh upon the earth, which include the sin of fornication and adultery.

Make a Covenant Not to Look or Think with Lust

In the eighth place, *we must make a covenant with our eyes and heart not to look or think upon another with lustful desire.* In Matthew 5:27-28 our Lord Jesus Christ gave the warning, "*Ye have heard that it was said by them of old time, Thou shalt not commit adultery; but I say unto you, That whosoever looketh on a woman to lust after her hath committed adultery with her already in his heart.*" The philosophy of the world, "You may look as long as you do not touch," is unacceptable with the Lord our God. Yea, in the sight of the Lord our God, a look with lustful desire is *already* the sin of adultery and fornication in one's heart. Even so, the tenth of the Ten Commandments that the Lord our God delivered unto the nation of Israel in Exodus 20, that they were not to covet, included the instruction, *"Thou shalt not covet thy neighbour's wife."* (Exodus 20:17) Furthermore, the opening portion of Proverbs 6:25 instructs concerning the adulterous woman, *"Lust not after her beauty in thine heart."*

Victory over the sin of physical adultery and fornication is rooted in victory over the sin of sexual lust in our hearts. Thus the man of God Job expressed his commitment on the matter in Job 31:1, saying, *"I made a covenant with mine eyes; why then should I think upon a maid?"* This upright servant of the Lord, who feared God and avoided evil, had made a covenant with his eyes and heart not to look or think upon a woman with lustful desire. In like manner, we each should also make such a binding covenant with our eyes and heart that we will not look or think upon another with lustful desire.

Make No Provision for the Desires of the Flesh

In the ninth place, *we must make no provision for the sinful desires of our flesh, but must put them to death.* In Romans 13:14 we find a two-fold instruction – *"But put ye on the Lord Jesus Christ, and make not provision for the flesh, to fulfil the lusts thereof."* Already in this study we have considered the first of these instructions – that we must put on and abide in our Lord Jesus Christ each and every day as our armor of spiritual light. As we have learned, by this means we shall be able to walk in the way of spiritual light and victory. Yet as we so walk in the way of spiritual light, we must also avoid making any provision for the desires and works of our sinful flesh. Such would include the sin of "chambering and wantonness" (that is – the sin of adultery, fornication, and sexual lust). This sin must not be fed and nurtured in any manner, whether by thoughts, fantasies, visual stimulations, verbal communications, emotional connections, physical contacts, plans, preparations, etc. We must not support it, savor it, or supply it in our hearts and lives. Rather, we must subdue it, starve it, and strangle it to death in our hearts and lives.

Even so, after pronouncing a warning against the sin of sexual lust in Matthew 5:27-28, our Lord Jesus Christ delivered a severe instruction in verses 29-30, saying, *"And if thy right eye offend thee, pluck it out, and cast it from thee: for it is profitable for thee that one of thy members should perish, and not that thy whole body should be cast into hell. And if thy right hand offend thee, cut it off, and cast it from thee: for it is profitable for thee that one of thy members should perish, and not that thy whole body should be cast into hell.*" Our Lord employed this severe instruction in this context in order to communicate that we must cut off and cast away from our lives anything that might cause us to fall into the sin of sexual lust, adultery, and fornication. Whatever it might be, no matter how dear it might be to us, if it makes provision for the sin of sexual lust, adultery, and fornication, it must be severely cut off and cast away without mercy.

Maintain a Healthy Physical Relationship within the Marriage

In the tenth and final place, *we must maintain a Biblically healthy physical relationship within the marriage.* As we have learned in a previous chapter, in 1 Corinthians 7:1-5 the Lord our God gives commandment and counsel to the husband and wife that they should maintain a healthy physical, sexual relationship with one another. In verse 2 God's Holy Word provides a reason for this, saying, *"Nevertheless, to avoid fornication, let every man have his own wife, and let every woman have her own husband."* Furthermore, in verse 5 the warning is given, *"Defraud ye not one the other, except it be with consent for a time, that ye may give yourselves to fasting and prayer; and come together again, that Satan tempt you not for your incontinency."* A healthy physical relationship within the marriage will help to provide for victory over the temptation and sin of fornication, adultery, and sexual lust. By itself it will not be enough, for spiritual victory over temptation and sin requires spiritual power. However, joined with a daily walk in the ways of the Lord, a healthy physical relationship within the marriage will provide a strong protection against sexual temptation and sin.

Truth for Meditation

The Biblical means by which we may flee away and find victory over the temptation and sin of adultery and fornication is that –

1. We must be eternally saved from the power of darkness through faith in the Lord Jesus Christ as our eternal Savior. (Eph. 2:1-3; Col. 1:13; Rom. 6:11-13)

2. We must repent with a contrite heart of any involvement in the sin of sexual lust, adultery, and fornication. (Rom. 13:12-13; Rev. 2:20-22; Psa. 32:3-5; 40:2; 51:10-12; Prov. 28:13)

3. We must put on and abide in our Lord Jesus Christ each and every day as our armor of spiritual light. (Rom. 13:14; John 15:4; Isa. 26:4; 2 Cor. 12:9; Eph. 6:10; Phil. 4:13; 2 Tim. 2:1)

4. We must walk in and after the righteous direction of the indwelling Holy Spirit of God. (Gal. 5:16-17)

5. We must seek enthusiastically after and apply our heart unto the wisdom of God's Holy Word. (Prov. 2:1-22)

6. We must obey the commandments of God's Holy Word in both its regulations and reproofs. (Prov. 6:23-24)

7. We must seek after and set our affection upon things above, not upon things on the earth. (Col. 3:1-5)

8. We must make a covenant with our eyes and heart not to look or think upon another with lustful desire. (Job 31:1; Exo. 20:17; Prov. 6:25; Matt. 5:27-28)

9. We must make no provision for the sinful desires of our flesh, but must put them to death. (Rom. 13:14; Matt. 5:27-30)

10. We must maintain a Biblically healthy physical relationship within the marriage. (1 Cor. 7:2-5)

Verses for Memorization

Romans 6:12-13: Let not sin therefore reign in your mortal body, that ye should obey it in the lusts thereof. Neither yield ye your members as instruments of unrighteousness unto sin: but yield yourselves unto God, as those that are alive from the dead, and your members as instruments of righteousness unto God.

Romans 13:14: But put ye on the Lord Jesus Christ, and make not provision for the flesh, to fulfil the lusts thereof.

Proverbs 6:23-24: For the commandment is a lamp; and the law is light; and reproofs of instruction are the way of life: to keep thee from the evil woman, from the flattery of the tongue of a strange woman

Matthew 5:28: But I say unto you, That whosoever looketh on a woman to lust after her hath committed adultery with her already in his heart.

Job 31:1: I made a covenant with mine eyes; why then should I think upon a maid?

28

Spiritual Leadership for the Home

In an earlier chapter of this book, we learned from God's Holy Word that the Lord our God has ordained for the man of the home to serve in the role of leadership for the home. In addition, we learned that this role of leadership is not primarily a matter of privilege, but of responsibility. Included in this responsibility is that of spiritual leadership for the home. This responsibility of spiritual leadership is revealed through the godly example of the man of God Joshua. In Joshua 24:14-15 Joshua challenged the children of Israel, saying, *"Now therefore fear the LORD, and serve him in sincerity and in truth: and put away the gods which your fathers served on the other side of the flood, and in Egypt; and serve ye the LORD. And if it seem evil unto you to serve the LORD, choose you this day whom ye will serve; whether the gods which your fathers served that were on the other side of the flood, or the gods of the Amorites, in whose land ye dwell: but as for me and my house, we will serve the LORD."*

The man of God Joshua made the spiritual decision and set the spiritual direction for his home. He did not take a vote from the members of his household on the matter. He simply took the responsibility to lead his household in the matter. He clearly declared for *both* himself *and* his household that they would serve the Lord. Even so, every man of God today is responsible to set the spiritual direction for his household, firmly and faithfully leading his wife and children in the right way. So then, what is involved in this responsibility of spiritual leadership for the home?

Choose for His Home to Reject the World's Ways

In the first place, the man of the home must lead his home spiritually by *choosing for his home to reject the direction and ways of the world.* In Joshua's challenge to the children of Israel, he set a choice before them. He challenged them to choose either to fear and serve the Lord "in sincerity and in truth" or to serve the false gods and ways of the lost world around them. He challenged them to choose which way they would follow and what god they would serve. If they did not desire to serve the Lord, he challenged them to choose whether they would serve the gods of Egypt whom their forefathers served or the gods of the people around them in the land of Canaan. *But*, as for himself and his household, in contrast to all other options, the man of God Joshua declared that they would serve the Lord.

With the contrasting conjunction "but," Joshua clearly revealed his rejection of the ways of the world. Others might choose to follow and serve the false ways of the world, *but* he would reject those false ways and would serve the Lord. Furthermore, the man of God Joshua established this rejection of the world's ways, not only for himself, but also for his household. Other households might follow and serve the false ways of the world, *but* he would *lead and direct* his household to serve the Lord. This is just where spiritual leadership for the home must begin. The man of the home is responsible to lead and direct his household to reject the ways of the world and to serve the Lord their God.

Choose for His Home to Serve the Lord

In the second place then, the man of the home must lead his home spiritually by *choosing for his home to serve the Lord in sincerity and truth.* In the opening portion of Joshua's challenge to the children of Israel, he gave a three-fold charge to them. This we find in Joshua 24:14 – "*Now therefore fear the LORD, and serve him in sincerity and in truth: and put away the gods which your fathers served on the other side of the flood, and in Egypt; and serve ye the LORD.*" Herein the man of God Joshua charged the people of God to walk in the fear of the Lord, to put away the false ways of the world, and to serve the Lord with their lives. In fact, he instructed them twice to serve the Lord, first as the evidence that they truly were walking in the fear of the Lord and second as the evidence that they truly had rejected the false ways of the world. Then at the end of verse 15, in concluding his challenge to the people of God, Joshua publicly proclaimed his own choice in the matter, both for himself and for his household – "*But as for me and my house, we will serve the LORD.*"

He charged the people to serve the Lord "in sincerity and in truth;" then he chose to lead and direct his own household in that very way. Joshua chose to lead and direct his household to serve the Lord, not simply with the outward show of hypocrisy, but *sincerely* with *the inward commitment* of the heart. Furthermore, he chose to lead and direct his household to serve the Lord, not simply according to the thoughts and ideas of their own mind, but *submissively* according to *the precepts and principles* of God's own truth. This is the nature of spiritual leadership for the home.

Love the Lord with All His Heart

In the third place, the man of the home must lead his home spiritually by *loving the Lord his God with all his heart, soul, and might.* In Deuteronomy 6:1-2 the man of God Moses set his focus upon the male leadership of the homes of Israel, saying, "*Now these are the commandments, the statutes, and the judgments, which the LORD your God commanded to teach you, that ye might do them in the land whither ye go to possess it: that thou mightest fear the LORD thy God, to keep all his statutes and his commandments, which I command thee, thou, and thy son, and thy son's son, all the days of thy life; and that thy days may be prolonged.*" Herein Moses set his focus upon the men of the homes, upon their sons who would rise up to be the men of the homes for the next generation, and upon their grandsons who would rise up to be the men of the homes for the generation thereafter.

365

With this focus Moses gave instruction under the inspiration of God the Holy Spirit concerning spiritual leadership for the home. In verses 4-9 he declared, *"Hear, O Israel: The LORD our God is one LORD: and thou shalt love the LORD thy God with all thine heart, and with all thy soul, and with all thy might. And these words, which I command thee this day, shall be in thine heart: and thou shalt teach them diligently unto thy children, and shalt talk of them when thou sittest in thine house, and when thou walkest by the way, and when thou liest down, and when thou risest up. And thou shalt bind them for a sign upon thine hand, and they shall be as frontlets between thine eyes. And thou shalt write them upon the posts of thy house, and on thy gates."* Having chosen for his home to reject the false ways of the world and to serve the Lord in sincerity and truth, the man of the home must now *live out* this choice in his *own* daily walk. He must walk each day in love for the Lord his God with all the *desire* of his heart, with all the *delight* of his soul, and with all the *diligence* of his might. Thereby he must serve for his household as an example of love for his Lord that through his example they might learn to love the Lord with all *their* heart, soul, and might also.

Root the Truth of God's Word in His Heart

In the fourth place, the man of the home must lead his home spiritually by *receiving and rooting the truth of God's Word in his heart*. The second instruction that Moses delivered in this context to the man of the home is found in verse 6 – *"And these words, which I command thee this day, shall be in thine heart."* Not only must the man of the home walk each day in love for the Lord with all his heart, soul, and might; but also he must open and direct his heart each day to learn the truth of God's Word. He must search the truth of God's Word daily (Acts 17:11) and must study therein to show himself *"approved unto God."* (2 Timothy 2:15) He must desire the pure and faithful truth of God's Word that he might grow thereby. (1 Peter 2:2) He must delight himself in the law and commandments of God's Word and must meditate therein day and night. (Psalm 1:2; 119:47-48) He must set his heart unto the truth of God's Word in order that he might fill his heart with that truth. He must let the truth of God's Word dwell in him *"richly in all wisdom."* (Colossians 3:16)

366

He must receive the truth of God's Word with meekness and not resistance, with submission and not stubbornness. (James 1:21) He must allow the truth of God's Word to convert the character of his soul and make him spiritually wise. (Psalm 19:7) He must root the truth of God's Word into his heart as the governing principle of his heart and life in order that he might seek *"to do according to all that is written therein."* (Joshua 1:8). As a sign upon his hand, he must receive God's truth as the governing principle for his actions; and as a frontlet before his eyes, he must receive God's truth as the governing principle for his decisions. Even so, in Deuteronomy 6:8 Moses gave the instruction, *"And thou shalt bind them for a sign upon thine hand, and they shall be as frontlets between thine eyes."* Yea, in Deuteronomy 11:18 Moses brought the two truths together, saying, *"Therefore shall ye lay up these my words in your heart and in your soul, and bind them for a sign upon your hand, that they may be as frontlets between your eyes."*

Diligently Teach the Truth of God's Word to His Household

In the fifth place, the man of the home must lead his home spiritually by *diligently teaching the truths of God's Word to his household.* In Deuteronomy 6:7 Moses gave the instruction, *"And thou shalt teach them diligently unto thy children, and shalt talk of them when thou sittest in thine house, and when thou walkest by the way, and when thou liest down, and when thou risest up."* When he sits in the house or walks by the way, when he lies down or rises up, yea at all times the man of the home must diligently teach his children the truths of God's Word and direct them in the way of God's Word. Day by day throughout the years of their upbringing, he is responsible to *"bring them up in the nurture and admonition of the Lord."* (Ephesians 6:4) He is to *nurture* his children with the *doctrinal truths* of God's Word and to *admonish* them with the *corrective reproofs* of God's Word. He is to enter into the ministry of discipling his children in the ways of the Lord, ever sharpening their heart's commitment, their mind's understanding, and their life's obedience. This is not to be a matter of passing neglect, but of pressing *diligence*, not of low importance, but of high *priority*. Each day that is lost is an opportunity that cannot be regained.

Furthermore, the man of the home is responsible to communicate God's truth unto his wife and to answer the spiritual questions of his wife. Speaking concerning wives, the opening portion of 1 Corinthians 14:35 declares, *"And if they will learn any thing, let them ask their husbands at home."* This indicates that the husband should be prepared to present the truth of God's Word in answer to his wife's questions and in response to her needs. He must ever have the truth of God's Word planted, rooted, and growing within his own heart in order that he might ever be sowing it into the hearts of his household.

Make the Truth of God's Word the Governing Principle

In the sixth place, the man of the home must lead his home spiritually by *setting forth the truth of God's Word as the governing principle for his household.* In Deuteronomy 6:9 Moses gave the instruction concerning the truths of God's Word, *"And thou shalt write them upon the posts of thine house, and on thy gate."* Certainly it is a worthy practice to post the words of Scripture at various places around one's house. Yet the full intent of this instruction runs deeper. Through the picture of this instruction, it illustrates that the truth of God's Word should be the governing principle for our private behavior within the home and our public behavior outside the home. For the children of Israel, God's truth was to be posted on the doorpost to convey the message that it was to govern the private behavior of the household as they entered into the home through the door. In addition, God's truth was to be posted on the gate to convey the message that it was to govern the public behavior of the household as they exited into the public through the gate. Even so, the man of the home is responsible through his example, leadership, and instruction to hold up and set forth God's truth as the governing principle for his household's behavior at all times in all things. Yea, the man of the home is responsible to lead his household to submit themselves at all times in all things under the governing authority of God's truth.

Commanding His Household to Walk in the Lord's Ways

In the seventh place, the man of the home must lead his home spiritually by *commanding his household to walk after him in the ways of the Lord.* In Genesis 18:19 the Lord our God spoke of the man of God Abraham, saying, *"For I know him, that he will command his children and his household after him, and they shall keep the way of the LORD, to do justice and judgment; that the LORD may bring upon Abraham that which he hath spoken of him."* In the previous point we encountered the principle of *submission* to the truth of God's Word. In this point we come to the corresponding principle of *obedience* to the truth of God's Word. The man of the home is responsible to lead and direct his household in obeying the Word of the Lord and in keeping the way of the Lord.

This is not simply to be a matter of suggestion and encouragement, but to be a matter of direction and commandment. The Lord our God honored Abraham because He knew that Abraham would *command* his household to "keep the way of the LORD." Abraham was not hopefully passive, but *authoritatively active* in his spiritual leadership over his household. Too many men are willing only to communicate God's truth unto their household, but not willing to command God's truth over their household. What a shameful lack of spiritual leadership! What a shameful failure of God-given responsibility! Day after day, year after year the man of the home must command his household, saying, "This is the way of the Lord; walk ye in it." Yet he must not simply command *them* to keep and walk in the way of the Lord. Rather, he *himself* must *first* keep and walk in the way of the Lord *and then* command his household to *follow after* him in keeping the way of the Lord. He must take the lead and set the example.

Walk before His Household in Full Assurance of Faith in the Lord

In the eighth place, the man of the home must lead his home spiritually by *walking before his household in full assurance of faith in the Lord.* Hebrews 11:7 commends the faith of the man of God Noah, saying, *"By faith Noah, being warned of God of things not seen as yet, moved with fear, prepared an ark to the saving of his house; by the which he condemned the world, and became heir of the righteousness which is by faith."* What a great deliverance Noah's faith in the Lord provided for his household! When every other individual on the face of the earth was killed under the fierce

369

judgment of the Lord, Noah's household, himself, his wife, his three sons, and their wives, were delivered from that judgment because *Noah* set *his* faith upon the Lord. Now, this was no momentary, short-lived faith. For one hundred twenty years, as he was preparing the ark, Noah maintained his faith in the Lord in contrast to all that had ever been seen or known. Up to that point in time, rain had never been seen, and a flood due to rain had never been known. Yet Noah walked by faith in the Lord, not by physical sight or human understanding. Also by his example Noah's household learned to walk by faith in the Lord after him. For one hundred twenty years, his household *joined him* by faith in preparing the ark.

❖ First then, Noah's faith was *a faith that was rooted in the Word of the Lord.* Hebrews 11:7 indicates that Noah prepared the ark because he had been warned of God concerning the coming flood. Rain had never been seen before. A flood had never been seen before. Yet the Lord had proclaimed by His absolutely true and faithful Word that He would *"bring a flood of waters upon the earth, to destroy all flesh, wherein is the breath of life, from under heaven."* (Genesis 6:17) In addition, the Lord God had commanded Noah by His Word to build an ark of gopher wood for the deliverance of his household. Noah rooted his faith in the Word of the Lord. Because *God* said it, Noah *believed* it. Thus he continued in preparing the ark for one hundred twenty years without any visual evidence for the flood. Thereby also he led and directed his household, as they joined him in preparing the ark, to root their faith in the absolute truth and faithfulness of God's Word.

❖ Furthermore, Noah's faith was *a faith that was founded upon the character of the Lord.* Hebrews 11:7 indicates that Noah prepared the ark because he was "moved with fear." Yet this was not the fear of man or the fear of circumstances. Rather, this was the fear of the Lord. Now, the fear of the Lord is not a spirit of terror that causes one to flee away from Him. Rather, it is a spirit of *reverence* that causes one to flee *unto Him in fullness of faith.* It is an understanding of our Lord's character that causes one to respond aright unto Him. Noah understood the Lord's righteous authority; thus he did not question the Lord's decision to destroy the inhabitants of the earth. Noah understood the Lord's almighty power; thus he did not doubt the Lord's ability to destroy the earth with a flood. And Noah understood the Lord's fierce judgment against evil and wickedness; thus he reverently trembled at the Lord's pronouncement that He would judge the earth. Yet Noah also understood the Lord's perfect wisdom; thus he did not question the Lord's command to build the ark. Noah understood the Lord's abundant grace; thus he did not doubt the Lord's promise to deliver his household within the ark. And Noah understood the Lord's faithful mercies; thus he unwaveringly trusted in the Lord's purpose and plan. Thereby also he led and directed his household to walk in the fear of the Lord and to found their faith upon the character of the Lord.

❖ Finally, Noah's faith was *a faith that motivated him to faithful obedience before the Lord.* Hebrews 11:7 indicates that Noah prepared the ark by faith. He believed the Word of the Lord concerning both the judgment of the flood over all the earth and the deliverance of the ark for his household. This full assurance of faith moved him to obey the commandment of the Lord in preparing the ark. "*According to all that God commanded him, so did he.*" (Genesis 6:22) This was not a short-lived, sporadic obedience. This was a long-term, faithful obedience for the entire one hundred twenty years that it took to build the ark. Noah's faith was *full,* and his obedience was *faithful.* Thereby also he led and directed his household to the faithful obedience of a full faith in the Lord.

Direct His Household to Confess and Put Away Sin

In the ninth place, the man of the home must lead his home spiritually by *directing his household to confess and put away the sinful things in their lives.* In Genesis 35:1-3 we read, "*And God said unto Jacob, Arise, go up to Bethel, and dwell there: and make there an altar unto God, that appeared unto thee when thou fleddest from the face of Esau thy brother. Then Jacob said unto his household, and to all that were with him, Put away the strange gods that are among you, and be clean, and change your garments: and let us arise, and go up to Bethel; and I will make there an altar unto God, who answered me in the day of my distress, and was with me in the way which I went."* When the Lord our God instructed Jacob to build an altar for worship at Bethel, the first step that Jacob took was to direct his household to put away the false gods that were among them and to be clean. In this case Jacob took the responsibility of spiritual leadership to direct his household to put away that which was contrary to God.

Even so, the man of the home today must take up this responsibility also. He must first be quick to confess and put away his *own* sin against the Lord that he might be spiritually clean in the Lord's sight. Then he must direct the members of his household to confess and put away sin from their lives that they also might be clean in the Lord's sight. Both for himself and for his household, the man of the home must ever hold forth the truths of Proverbs 28:13 and 1 John 1:9. *"He that covereth his sins shall not prosper: but whoso confesseth and forsaketh them shall have mercy." "If we confess our sins, he is faithful and just to forgive us our sins, and to cleanse us from all unrighteousness."*

Establish Standards to Guard against Worldliness

In the tenth place, the man of the home must lead his home spiritually by *establishing standards for his household to guard them against worldliness.* In Deuteronomy 7:25-26 the Lord our God instructed the men of Israel through His servant Moses, saying, *"The graven images of their gods shall ye burn with fire: thou shalt not desire the silver or gold that is on them, nor take it unto thee, lest thou be snared therein: for it is an abomination to the LORD thy God. Neither shalt thou bring an abomination into thine house, lest thou be a cursed thing like it: but thou shalt utterly detest it, and thou shalt utterly abhor it; for it is a cursed thing."*

The greatest temptation of worldliness that the children of Israel faced in that time concerned the idolatrous worship of false gods by the various heathen nations around them. Thus the graven images of these false gods were to be viewed as a hateful abomination before the Lord and to be burned completely with fire. Not even the silver or gold that adorned these graven images was to be desired and taken as wealth. It was *all* to be burned, lest the children of Israel be spiritually ensnared therein. The men of Israel were not to bring such worldly abominations into their homes and not to allow anyone else to bring such things into their homes. They were to establish a standard for their homes and households to guard them against the snare and curse of the world's false ways. They were utterly to detest and abhor these false ways and to lead and direct their household to do the same.

Even so, the man of the home today must also establish standards for his home and household to guard them against the snare and curse of worldliness. In the opening portion of Romans 12:2 we are commanded, *"And be not conformed to this world."* In 1 John 2:15-16 we are instructed and warned, *"Love not the world, neither the things that are in the world. If any man love the world, the love of the Father is not in him. For all that is in the world, the lust of the flesh, and the lust of the eyes, and the pride of life, is not of the Father, but is of the world."* Finally, in James 4:4 we are warned, *"Ye adulterers and adulteresses, know ye not that the friendship of the world is enmity with God? Whosoever therefore will be a friend of the world is the enemy of God."* Worldliness is still enmity with the Lord our God. It is still a hateful abomination in His sight, and the temptation to worldliness still abounds on every side at every turn, ever seeking to ensnare us and the members of our households. Thus we who are the men of our homes must ever stand guard and must establish a wall of standards for the protection of our households. In addition, we must lead and direct our households utterly to detest and abhor all worldliness.

Fight Valiantly for His Home against the Devil's Attacks

In the eleventh place, the man of the home must lead his home spiritually by *fighting valiantly to defend his household against the attacks of the devil.* In the time of Nehemiah, as the children of Israel at Jerusalem were in the process of rebuilding the walls of the city, they were under threat of attack from an outside force. Therefore, the man of God Nehemiah instructed the men of Israel to take up their weapons and to fight courageously in the strength of the Lord for the defense of their households. In Nehemiah 4:14

Nehemiah gave report, saying, *"And I looked, and rose up, and said unto the nobles, and to the rulers, and to the rest of the people, Be not ye afraid of them: remember the Lord, which is great and terrible, and fight for your brethren, your sons, and your daughters, your wives, and your houses."*

Now, in this time of the New Testament, our primary adversary is not a physical enemy of flesh and blood. Ephesians 6:12 declares, *"For we wrestle not against flesh and blood, but against principalities, against powers, against the rulers of the darkness of this world, against spiritual wickedness in high places."* Our primary adversary is a spiritual adversary. Our primary adversary is the devil and his forces of spiritual darkness and wickedness. Thus God's Word instructs us and warns us in 1 Peter 5:8-9, *"Be sober, be vigilant; because your adversary the devil, as a roaring lion, walketh about, seeking whom he may devour: whom resist stedfast in the faith, knowing that the same afflictions are accomplished in your brethren that are in the world."* To this James 4:7 adds the instruction, *"Submit yourselves therefore to God. Resist the devil, and he will flee from you."*

Through faith in and submission to the Lord our God, we must resist the devil. We must *"be strong in the Lord, and in the power of his might"* and must *"put on the whole armour of God, that* [we] *may be able to stand against the wiles of the devil."* (Ephesians 6:10-11) Yet we must recognize that our adversary the devil is not only walking about, seeking to devour us spiritually. He is walking about, seeking to devour the members of our households also. Thus we who are the men of our homes must stand against the attacks and wiles of the devil, not only for our own sakes, but also for the sakes of our households. We must not be afraid of our adversary the devil and his forces, but must trust in our great and almighty Lord, must be strong in His almighty strength, and must fight courageously and valiantly to defend our households against the devil's wiles and attacks.

374

Pray and Intercede Faithfully for His Household

In the twelfth and final place, the man of the home must lead his home spiritually by *praying and interceding faithfully for his household.* In Job 1:4-5 we read concerning the man of God Job, *"And his sons went and feasted in their houses, every one his day; and sent and called for their three sisters to eat and to drink with them. And it was so, when the days of their feasting were gone about, that Job sent and sanctified them, and rose up early in the morning, and offered burnt offerings according to the number of them all: for Job said, It may be that my sons have sinned, and cursed God in their hearts. Thus did Job continually."*

Continually the man of God Job was concerned for the spiritual condition of his household. Continually he was concerned that the members of his household might have sinned against the Lord, and continually he was concerned that they might have turned their hearts away from the Lord. Thus continually the man of God Job rose up early in the morning to sanctify and intercede for the members of his household. In that time of the Old Testament, such intercession required a burnt offering. Yet in this time of the New Testament, due to the eternal sacrifice of the eternal Lamb of God, the Lord Jesus Christ, upon the cross, we who are God's children may approach boldly unto God's throne of grace in prayer. Let us who are the men of our homes follow Job's example. Let us pray and intercede early and earnestly each day for the spiritual sanctification of the members of our households. Yea, God forbid that we should cease to pray for them.

Truth for Meditation

The man of the home must take up the responsibility to lead his home spiritually by –

1. Choosing for his home to reject the direction and ways of the world. (Josh. 24:14-15)

2. Choosing for his home to serve the Lord in sincerity and truth. (Josh. 24:14-15)

3. Loving the Lord his God with all his heart, soul, and might. (Deut. 6:4-5)

4. Receiving and rooting the truth of God's Word in his heart. (Deut. 6:6, 8; 11:18; Josh. 1:8; Psa. 1:2; 19:7; 119:47-48; Acts 17:11; Col. 3:16; 2 Tim. 2:15; Jam. 1:21; 1 Pet. 2:2)

5. Diligently teaching the truths of God's Word to his household. (Deut. 6:7; Eph. 6:4; 1 Cor. 14:35)

6. Setting forth the truth of God's Word as the governing principle for his household. (Deut. 6:9)

7. Commanding his household to walk after him in the ways of the Lord. (Gen. 18:19)

8. Walking before his household in full assurance of faith in the Lord. (Heb. 11:7; Gen. 6:22)

9. Directing his household to confess and put away the sinful things in their lives. (Gen. 35:2; Prov. 28:13; 1 John 1:9)

10. Establishing standards for his household to guard them against worldliness. (Deut. 7:25-26; Rom. 12:2; Jam. 4:4; 1 John 2:15-16)

11. Fighting valiantly to defend his household against the attacks of the devil. (Neh. 4:14; Eph. 6:10-12; Jam. 4:7; 1 Pet. 5:8-9)

12. Praying and interceding faithfully for his household. (Job 1:4-5)

Noah's faith, by which he led and directed his household, was –

1. A faith that was rooted in the Word of the Lord.

2. A faith that was founded upon the character of the Lord.

3. A faith that motivated him to faithful obedience before the Lord.

Verses for Memorization

Deuteronomy 6:5-6: And thou shalt love the LORD thy God with all thine heart, and with all thy soul, and with all thy might. And these words, which I command thee this day, shall be in thine heart.

Deuteronomy 11:18: Therefore shall ye lay up these my words in your heart and in your soul, and bind them for a sign upon your hand, that they may be as frontlets between your eyes.

Deuteronomy 7:26: Neither shalt thou bring an abomination into thine house, lest thou be a cursed thing like it: but thou shalt utterly detest it, and thou shalt utterly abhor it; for it is a cursed thing.

29

One-Flesh Unity

As has been presented and emphasized often throughout this book, in the beginning the Lord our God delivered the three foundational principles for a good marriage relationship in Genesis 2:24. There He proclaimed, "*Therefore shall a man leave his father and his mother, and shall cleave unto his wife; and they shall be one flesh.*" The third of these foundational principles indicates that the husband and the wife are both required to pursue, develop, and maintain one-flesh unity in their marriage relationship together.

As has also been presented and emphasized throughout this book, the husband has the God-given responsibility to take the lead in pursuing, developing, and maintaining this one-flesh unity within the marriage relationship. This we conclude from the fact that the first two of the three foundational principles are directed *only* toward the husband, whereas the third is directed toward *both* the husband and the wife. The husband has the *first responsibility* to leave the priority of his relationship with his parents and to replace it with the priority of his relationship with his wife. Furthermore, in giving his relationship with his wife the place of priority over all other human relationships, the husband is to "cleave unto his wife," ever considering and loving her as the very bone of his bone and the very flesh of his flesh. (Ephesians 5:28-31) He is to hold her dear to his heart in love; he is to hold her tight to himself in commitment; and he is to hold her near to his side in one-flesh unity and communion. In like manner, the wife is to *cooperate* with her husband in pursuing, developing, and maintaining the one-flesh unity of their marriage relationship together. The husband is to take the lead in this pursuit of one-flesh unity, and the wife is to cooperate with him in pursuing one-flesh unity.

Now, God's Holy Word presents a number of principles concerning the pursuit of unity between individuals. In their immediate context, these principles deal with unity and communion among God's people. Yet certainly they may also be applied to the pursuit of unity and communion between a husband and wife. If these principles should be employed and applied for *Christian* unity and communion between fellow believers, then how much more should they be employed and applied for the *one-flesh* unity and communion between a husband and wife. Yea, Psalm 133:1-3 exclaims, ***"Behold, how good and how pleasant it is for brethren to dwell together in unity! It is like the precious ointment upon the head, that ran down upon the beard, even Aaron's beard: that went down to the skirts of his garments; as the dew of Hermon, and as the dew that descended upon the mountains of Zion: for there the LORD commanded the blessing, even life for evermore."*** Even so, would it not also be appropriate to exclaim, "Behold, how good and how pleasant it is for a husband and wife to dwell together in unity!" Certainly such unity is also as beautifully pleasant as the precious ointment upon the head of Aaron the high priest and as refreshingly good as the dew upon the mountains of Zion.

Walk after the Will and Way of Christ

In the first place, the pursuit of unity and communion between a husband and wife requires *a walk after the will and way of Christ*. The only way that a husband and wife can have one-flesh unity of heart, soul, and mind together is if they both are conformed to and governed by one standard will and mindset. Whose will and mindset should then be that standard, governing will and mindset? In the prayer of the apostle Paul for the believers at Rome in Romans 15:5-6, the answer may be found – ***"Now the God of patience and***

380

consolation grant you to be likeminded one toward another according to Christ Jesus: that ye may with one mind and one mouth glorify God, even the Father of our Lord Jesus Christ." This is to be the standard for like-mindedness and unity – *according to Christ Jesus.*

The will and way of Christ Jesus our Lord is to be the standard unto which the husband and the wife are each to submit themselves, by which each are to be governed in their daily living, and through which they may develop and maintain one-flesh unity together. Such may be illustrated by a triangle in which the top point represents our Lord Jesus Christ and the two side points of the base represent the husband and the wife respectively. As the husband and the wife each move upward on their respective side toward the central point of Christ, they will also be drawing closer to one another.

In like manner, the apostle Paul instructed the believers at Philippi under the inspiration of God the Holy Spirit in Philippians 3:15-16, saying, *"Let us therefore, as many as be perfect, be thus minded: and if in any thing ye be otherwise minded, God shall reveal even this unto you. Nevertheless, whereto we have already attained, let us walk by the same rule, let us mind the same thing."* One-flesh unity requires that the husband and wife "walk by the same rule" and "mind the same thing."

What then is to be the standard (rule) and mindset by which they are to walk and to be thus minded? The apostle's testimony in verse 8 reveals the answer – *"Yea doubtless, and I count all things but loss for the excellency of the knowledge of Christ Jesus my Lord: for whom I have suffered the loss of all things, and do count them but dung, that I may win Christ."* Again his testimony in verse 10 reveals the answer – *"That I may know him, and the power of his resurrection, and the fellowship of his sufferings, being made conformable unto his death."* Yet again his testimony in verses 13-14 reveals the answer – *"Brethren, I count not myself to have apprehended: but this one thing I do, forgetting those things which are behind, and reaching forth unto those things which are before, I press toward the mark for the prize of the high calling of God in*

Christ Jesus." Then the opening portion of verse 15 presents the instruction, *"Let us therefore, as many as be perfect, be thus minded."* The standard mindset by which a husband and wife may find one-flesh unity together is that they each pursue after the excellency of the knowledge of Christ Jesus our Lord. The knowledge and fellowship of Christ Jesus our Lord *is* the standard for unity and communion within the marriage relationship.

Even so, in John 17:20-23 our Lord Jesus Christ prayed for all believers, saying, *"Neither pray I for these alone, but for them also which shall believe on me through their word; that they all may be one; as thou, Father, art in me, and I in thee, that they also may be one in us: that the world may believe that thou hast sent me. And the glory which thou gavest me I have given them; that they may be one, even as we are one: I in them, and thou in me, that they may be made perfect in one; and that the world may know that thou hast sent me, and hast loved them, as thou hast loved me."* Herein our Lord Jesus Christ revealed the standard for unity among God's people – "that they also may be one *in Us.*" Just as a husband and wife walk in fellowship with God their heavenly Father and Jesus Christ His Son, even so they will find the one-flesh unity of their marriage relationship to be perfected.

Finally, Philippians 2:1-4 delivers the instruction for unity, *"If there be therefore any consolation in Christ, if any comfort of love, if any fellowship of the Spirit, if any bowels and mercies, fulfil ye my joy, that ye be likeminded, having the same love, being of one accord, of one mind. Let nothing be done through strife or vainglory; but in lowliness of mind let each esteem other better than themselves. Look not every man on his own things, but every man also on the things of others."* Then the standard mindset by which such unity may be found is revealed in verse 5-8, *"Let this mind be in you, which was also in Christ Jesus: who, being in the form of God, thought it not robbery to be equal with God: but made himself of no reputation, and took upon him the form of a servant, and was made in the likeness of men: and being found in fashion as a man, he humbled himself, and became obedient unto death, even the death of the cross."* Only as the husband and wife walk each day in the humble, servant-mindedness of Christ shall they find one-flesh unity in their marriage relationship together. Indeed, the pursuit of unity and communion between a husband and wife requires *above all else* a walk after the will and way of Christ.

Walk after the Direction of the Holy Spirit

In the second place, the pursuit of unity and communion between a husband and wife requires *a walk in and after the direction of the Holy Spirit*. Philippians 2:1 speaks of the *"fellowship of the Spirit;"* and Ephesians 4:3 gives the instruction, saying, *"Endeavoring to keep the unity of the Spirit in the bond of peace."* Christian unity among God's people is produced and perfected by the Holy Spirit of God. In like manner, the one-flesh unity between a husband and wife is also produced and perfected by the Holy Spirit of God. Thus the husband and wife must daily heed the instruction of Galatians 5:16 – *"This I say then, Walk in the Spirit, and ye shall not fulfil the lust of the flesh."*

According to the truth of Galatians 5:16-26; 6:7-8; and Romans 8:4-6, 12-13, there are two opposing motivations by which we who are God's children might walk. On the one hand, we might walk (as the Lord our God intends) according to the godly direction of the Holy Spirit. On the other hand, we might walk according to the selfish desires of our sinful flesh. If the husband and the wife walk according to the selfish desires of their sinful flesh, that selfishness will produce strife and division between them. However, if the husband and the wife walk according to the godly direction of the Holy Spirit, the fruit of the Spirit will be born out in their behavior (Galatians 5:22-23); and their one-flesh unity will be perfected thereby.

Walk in Spirit-filled Love

In the third place, the pursuit of unity and communion between a husband and wife requires *a walk in Spirit-filled love toward one another*. Philippians 2:1 speaks of the "comfort of love;" and verse 2 declares, *"Fulfil ye my joy, that ye be likeminded, having the same love, being of one accord, of one mind."* In addition, Colossians 2:2 speaks of believers' hearts *"being knit together in love."* Spirit-filled love is at the center of Christian unity among God's people. In like manner, Spirit-filled love is also at the center of one-flesh unity between a husband and wife. Without such love a husband and wife will never find the one-flesh unity that the Lord our God intends for their marriage relationship. Therefore, they must follow all that God's Holy Word reveals concerning love.

As we have previously learned, their love must be motivated by our Lord's first love toward them. Furthermore, their love must be characterized by the sacrifice of self for the benefit of the other, by a longsuffering and forbearing spirit toward the other, by kindness in attitude, word, and action toward the other, by humility and selflessness rather than pride and selfishness, by joy and rejoicing in righteousness and not in unrighteousness, by a spirit of trust and hope toward the other, by a forgiving spirit toward the other, by an affectionate spirit toward the other, and by a pure heart and fervent spirit toward the other. As the husband and the wife pursue such Spirit-filled love with one another, their one-flesh unity will be perfected thereby.

Walk in Affectionate Care

In the fourth place, the pursuit of unity and communion between a husband and wife requires *a walk in affectionate care for one another.* Philippians 2:1 speaks of *"bowels and mercies;"* and 1 Peter 3:8 gives the instruction, saying, *"Finally, be ye all of one mind, having compassion one of another, love as brethren, be pitiful, be courteous."* In addition, Romans 12:15-16 gives the instruction, *"Rejoice with them that do rejoice, and weep with them that weep. Be of the same mind one toward another. Mind not high things, but condescend to men of low estate. Be not wise in your own conceits."* Christian unity among God's people requires "bowels and mercies" toward one another (that is – affections and compassions). It requires that believers have compassion and sympathy toward one another, that they be tenderhearted ("pitiful") toward one another, and that they be courteous toward one another.

In like manner, the one-flesh unity between a husband and wife also requires affectionate care, compassion, and courtesy toward one another. They each must be touched in heart with the feeling of the other's situation, rejoicing with the other when the other rejoices and weeping with the other when the other weeps. As they maintain such affection for one another, their one-flesh unity will be strengthened thereby.

Walk in a Peaceable Spirit

In the fifth place, the pursuit of unity and communion between a husband and wife requires *a walk in a peaceable spirit toward one another*. After Philippians 2:2 gives instruction for Christian unity, the opening portion of verse 3 adds, *"Let nothing be done through strife or vainglory."* In addition, 1 Corinthians 1:10 gives the counsel, *"Now I beseech you, brethren, by the name of our Lord Jesus Christ, that ye all speak the same thing, and that there be no divisions among you; but that ye be perfectly joined together in the same mind and in the same judgment."* Christian unity among God's people requires that believers never be moved to pursue strife and contention with one another, but that they ever be motivated to pursue peace with one another. Thus the counsel is given in 2 Corinthians 13:11, *"Finally, brethren, farewell. Be perfect, be of good comfort, be of one mind, live in peace; and the God of love and peace shall be with you."* In addition, Ephesians 4:3 counsels believers to be *"endeavoring to keep the unity of the Spirit in the bond of peace."*

In like manner, one-flesh unity within the marriage relationship requires that the husband and wife never be moved to pursue strife with one another, but that they ever be motivated to pursue peace with one another. With as much earnestness as they each are spiritually able, they each must live peaceably with the other. They each must speak with gentle, gracious words toward the other. They each must be slow to annoyance and anger at the other. They each must not retaliate against the other, but must return good for evil in word and action. Then their one-flesh unity will be protected against divisions, damage, and destruction by "the bond of peace."

Walk in Humbleness of Mind

In the sixth place, the pursuit of unity and communion between a husband and wife requires *a walk in humbleness of mind before one another*. After Philippians 2:2 gives instruction for Christian unity, verse 3 continues, saying, *"Let nothing be done through strife or vainglory; but in lowliness of mind let each esteem other better than themselves."* Christian unity among God's people requires a spirit of humility in their relationship to one another. It requires a rejection of the fleshly desire for vainglory (that is – self-glory). It requires a true heart-esteem of others as better than self. It requires the choice to be nothing more than a servant unto others. It requires a humble submission of self in faithful obedience unto the Lord and in self-sacrifice for others. Even so, the instruction is given in verses 5-8 for us to follow our Lord Jesus Christ's example of humility and servanthood – *"Let this mind be in you, which was also in Christ Jesus: who, being in the form of God, thought it not robbery to be equal with God: but made himself of no reputation, and took upon him the form of a servant, and was made in the likeness of men: and being found in fashion as a man, he humbled himself, and became obedient unto death, even the death of the cross."*

In like manner, one-flesh unity between a husband and wife requires a spirit of humility in their marriage relationship together. They each must reject all fleshly desire for self-glory and must esteem the other as more important than self. They each must choose to be the servant of the other and to sacrifice self for the other. Then as they humbly serve one another and sacrifice for one another, it will ever draw them closer to one another. Yet if they walk in pride and self-advancement, it will only breed strife and contention between them. Even so, the opening half of Proverbs 13:10 warns, *"Only by pride cometh contention;"* and the opening half of Proverbs 28:25 adds, *"He that is of a proud heart stirreth up strife."* Only as the husband and wife pursue the place of humble service and sacrifice for one another will they find the place of one-flesh unity with one another.

Walk in Unselfishness

In the seventh and final place, the pursuit of unity and communion between a husband and wife requires *a walk in unselfishness toward one another*. After Philippians 2:2 gives instruction for Christian unity, verse 4 adds, *"Look not every man on his own things, but every man also on the things of others."* Yea, this was the mindset of our Lord Jesus Christ when He *"made himself of no reputation, and took upon him the form of a servant, and was made in the likeness of men."* (Philippians 2:7) When He came into the world as God in the flesh, He came not for His own sake, but for our sakes. He *"came not to be ministered unto, but to minister, and to give his life a ransom for many."* (Matthew 20:28) Even so, we are instructed in Philippians 2:5, *"Let this mind be in you, which was also in Christ Jesus."* Thus we read about the unity of the believers at Jerusalem in Acts 4:32 – *"And the multitude of them that believed were of one heart and of one soul: neither said any of them that ought of the things which he possessed was his own; but they had all things common."*

In like manner, one-flesh unity between a husband and wife requires a spirit of unselfishness in their marriage relationship together. They each must not look after and consider only his or her own things, but must also look after and consider the things of the other. They each must not simply seek to please self, but must seek to please the other and to bear the burdens of the other. They each must not consider the things of the home (especially the monetary assets and material possessions) to be one's own as opposed to the other's, but must consider all such things to be the common possession of both. Then their one-flesh unity will be supported by a *selflessly giving* spirit, rather than strained by a *selfishly taking* spirit.

Truth for Meditation

The pursuit of one-flesh unity and communion between a husband and wife requires –

1. A walk after the will and way of Christ. (Rom. 15:5-6; Phil. 2:1-8; 3:8, 10, 13-16; John 17:20-23)

2. A walk in and after the direction of the Holy Spirit. (Phil. 2:1-2; Gal. 5:16, 22-23)

3. A walk in Spirit-filled love toward one another. (Phil. 2:1-2; Col. 2:2)

4. A walk in affectionate care for one another. (Phil. 2:1-2; 1 Pet. 3:8; Rom. 12:15-16)

5. A walk in a peaceable spirit toward one another. (Phil. 2:2-3; 1 Cor. 1:10; 2 Cor. 13:11; Eph. 4:3)

6. A walk in humbleness of mind before one another. (Phil. 2:2-3, 5-8; Prov. 13:10; 28:25)

7. A walk in unselfishness toward one another. (Phil. 2:2, 4-5, 7; Acts 4:32)

Verses for Memorization

Ephesians 4:3: Endeavoring to keep the unity of the Spirit in the bond of peace.

Philippians 2:2-4: Fulfil ye my joy, that ye be likeminded, having the same love, being of one accord, of one mind. Let nothing be done through strife or vainglory; but in lowliness of mind let each esteem other better than themselves. Look not every man on his own things, but every man also on the things of others.

30

Serving the Lord Together

One reason for a husband and wife to walk in one-flesh unity together is that they might serve the Lord in cooperation together. Now, as the members of a church are "fitly joined together and compacted," that Christian unity among them stimulates, supports, strengthens, and significantly enhances the ministry effectiveness of that church body. Ephesians 4:16 reveals the truth, saying, *"From whom the whole body fitly joined together and compacted by that which every joint supplieth, according to the effectual working in the measure of every part, maketh increase of the body unto the edifying of itself in love."* Through the Spirit-filled contribution of each member to the ministry of the church and through the Spirit-filled cooperation of each member with each other member of the church, the entire church body is increased, edified, and unified in love. In like manner, the one-flesh unity between a husband and wife will stimulate, support, strengthen, and significantly enhance their service for the Lord together as a unit. In what ways then ought a husband and wife to serve the Lord together in unity?

Walk in Righteousness before God Together

In the first place, the husband and wife ought *to walk in righteousness before God together*. In Genesis 6:5-13 we find that the generation of mankind in Noah's day was a wicked generation, that it was corrupt before God, and that it was filled with violence. Thus we find that the Lord God determined to destroy that generation of mankind with a worldwide flood. Yet in Genesis 6:8-9 we find that Noah "found grace in the eyes of the LORD" because he was a just man, and was perfect in his generation, and walked with God. Thus in Genesis 6:14-21 we find that the Lord God commanded Noah to build an ark for the deliverance of his household and of the animals. Finally, in Genesis 6:22 we find that Noah obeyed God's commandment according to all that he had been commanded; and in Genesis 7:1 we find that Noah was seen to be righteous before God in his generation.

Yet Noah did not walk alone in righteousness and obedience before God. For the one hundred twenty years that it took to build the ark, Noah's wife faithfully walked in righteousness and obedience before God together with Noah. Although that entire generation opposed Noah's walk and proclamation of righteousness and obedience, yet his wife faithfully stood in unity with him throughout that one hundred twenty years. In addition, Noah's three sons followed after him and walked in righteousness and obedience before God together with their father. Yet they also did not stand alone, for each of their wives faithfully stood in unity with them throughout that one hundred twenty years. Thus we understand that four separate couples faithfully served the Lord *together* by walking in righteousness before God *together*; and this they did in the midst of that wicked, corrupt, and violent generation.

In like manner, in Luke 1:6 we read concerning the priest Zacharias and his wife Elisabeth, "*And they were both righteous before God, walking in all the commandments and ordinances of the Lord blameless.*" They both walked in righteousness before God *together*. They both walked in obedience to all the commandments of the Lord *together*. They both served the Lord faithfully *together*. Thus the Lord our God chose them to be the parents of the Messiah's forerunner, John the Baptist. In like manner, the Lord our God is searching today in the midst of our wicked, corrupt generation for married couples who will walk in righteousness before Him together. Just as the husband and wife are to pursue one-flesh unity together, even so they ought to pursue a unified walk in righteousness and obedience before God together.

Obey the Call of God Together

In the second place, the husband and wife ought *to obey the call of God together*. In Hebrews 11:8 we read concerning Abraham's call from God and concerning Abraham's obedience to that call – *"By faith Abraham, when he was called to go out into a place which he should after receive for an inheritance, obeyed; and he went out, not knowing whither he went."* The account of this call is recorded in Genesis 12:1-3 where we read, *"Now the LORD had said unto Abram, Get thee out of thy country, and from thy kindred, and from thy father's house, unto a land that I will shew thee: and I will make of thee a great nation, and I will bless thee, and make thy name great; and thou shalt be a blessing: and I will bless them that bless thee, and curse him that curseth thee: and in thee shall all families of the earth be blessed."* Then Abraham's obedience to the call of God is recorded in the opening portion of verse 4 – *"So Abraham departed, as the LORD had spoken unto him."*

The Lord our God called Abraham to serve Him by leaving his country, his kindred, and his father's house in order to travel unto an unknown land; and Abraham obeyed the call of God. Yet Abraham did not obey this call alone. As his helper who was meet for him, Abraham's wife obeyed the call of God with him. Even so, the opening portion of Genesis 12:5 reports, *"And Abram took Sarai his wife, and Lot his brother's son."* Abraham and his wife obeyed the call of God together. For this reason, the Lord later opened Sarah's barren womb and granted them a son in their old age. For this reason also, the Lord began the process of creating from them a great nation out of which the Lord's Messiah and the world's Savior might come forth.

In like manner, the Lord our God is still calling men to serve Him today. In fact, every man who is a child of God is called by God to some aspect of service for God. The Lord our God does not call every man to leave his country or to leave his kindred in order to serve in the ministry and work of the Lord. The Lord our God may simply call a man to serve Him in some ministry capacity within his local church. Yet the Lord our God does indeed call every man who is a child of God to some form of service for Him; and when our Lord calls a man to serve Him, He does not call that man alone. He also calls that man's wife to serve in unity with her husband as an helper meet for Him. The Lord our God is searching today for married couples who will obey His call for service together. Just as the husband and wife are to pursue one-flesh unity together, even so they ought to pursue a unified obedience to the call of God together.

Walk by Faith in God Together

In the third place, the husband and wife ought *to walk by faith in God together*. In Hebrews 11:23 we read concerning Moses' parents, ***"By faith Moses, when he was born, was hid three months of his parents, because they saw he was a proper child; and they were not afraid of the king's commandment."*** Every step of the way Moses' father and mother walked by faith in God. They saw that Moses was a goodly and proper child and *believed* that God had a great purpose for his life. Although the king of Egypt had made a decree to drown every boy that was born to the Israelites, Moses' father and mother hid him away and nourished him up for three months in their house because they *believed* that God would protect him and them. Throughout those three months they were not filled with fear over the king's commandment because they *believed* with full assurance of faith in God's grace and power to overcome. Then at the end of three months, when they could no longer hide Moses in their house, they placed him in an ark of bulrushes and set it among the reeds and rushes by the river's brink, *believing* that God would take care of him. In fact, they positioned his older sister some distance away to watch him, not in order to guard him from trouble, but in order to know *"what would be done to him."* (Exodus 2:4) Although they did not know what God would do, they *believed* with full assurance of faith that God would indeed do something on the behalf of their son. Thus God brought forth the king's own daughter to adopt Moses as her own and thereby to protect him from death. (Exodus 2:1-10)

In like manner, the Lord our God is searching today for married couples who will walk by faith in Him together. He is searching for married couples who will entrust their marriage, their children, and their homes unto His wisdom, His grace, and His care. He is searching for married couples who will believe and trust in His good purpose in all things, whether in their individual lives, in their marriage relationship, or in their children's lives. He is searching for married couples who will believe and trust in His perfect will so as to follow Him no matter what the cost. He is searching for married couples who will believe and trust in His abundant grace so as not to fear the troubles of life or the opposition of mankind. He is searching for married couples who will believe and trust in His unfailing faithfulness so as not to fear the unknown future, but to expect Him to bring forth great and mighty things which they know not. (Jeremiah 33:3)

Glorify the Lord Our God Together

In the fourth place, the husband and wife ought *to glorify the Lord our God together.* In Romans 15:5-6 the apostle Paul expressed his burden for the believers at Rome that the Lord our God might develop Christian unity among them. There he declared, *"Now the God of patience and consolation grant you to be likeminded one toward another according to Christ Jesus: that ye may with one mind and one mouth glorify God, even the Father of our Lord Jesus Christ."* Now, from verse 6 we learn one of the reasons for such Christian unity among God's people – that they might "with one mind and one mouth glorify God" together. Even so, one of the reasons for the one-flesh unity of the marriage relationship between the husband and wife is that they also might glorify the Lord our God together. The one-flesh unity of the marriage relationship is not simply that the husband and wife might focus their love upon one another, but also that they might focus their love together upon the Lord. Their hearts are to be knit together in one-flesh unity in order that the spirit of their minds together and the words of their mouths together might be lifted up in spiritual harmony unto the praise, and honor, and glory of our Lord God's holy name.

Continue in Prayer unto God Together

In the fifth place, the husband and wife ought *to continue in prayer unto God together*. In Acts 1:14 we read concerning the Christian unity among that first assembly of believers who waited at Jerusalem for the promised gift of the Holy Spirit. Yet they were not simply assembled in unity. Their Christian unity moved them to continue in unified prayer and supplication together. Thus we read, *"These all continued with one accord in prayer and supplication, with the women, and Mary the mother of Jesus, and with his brethren."* Even so, one of the reasons for the one-flesh unity of the marriage relationship between the husband and wife is that they also might continue in prayer unto God together. Certainly they each ought to maintain a personal, private prayer life before the Lord that is faithful and fervent, unceasing and unfainting. Yet they also ought to continue in prayer and supplication together. As decisions need to be made for the marriage and home, they ought to seek God's wisdom through prayer together. As troubles strike against the marriage and home, they ought to seek God's help through prayer together. As conflicts must be mended within the marriage and home, they ought to seek God's grace through prayer together. Such prayer together should flow out of their one-flesh unity and will further strengthen their one-flesh unity.

Worship the Lord Our God Together

In the sixth place, the husband and wife ought *to worship the Lord our God together*. In Psalm 55:14 the man of God David speaks of the spiritual unity that he had with another, saying, *"We took sweet counsel together, and walked unto the house of God in company."* Now, in the full context of this psalm, David was expressing his complaint that this friend had turned against him. However, in verse 14 David spoke of that time before when they were yet in unified friendship and fellowship together. During that time of unified friendship and fellowship, they had walked unto the house of God and worshipped the Lord their God together. In like manner, the husband and wife, in the one-flesh unity of their marriage relationship, ought to go and worship God together at the assembling of their local church. They ought to go unto the house of God as a married unit and ought to find sweet, spiritual fellowship together in their worship of God.

Minister in the Work of God Together

In the seventh place, the husband and wife ought *to minister in the work of God together*. In Acts 18:24-25 we read about the man of God Apollos, *"And a certain Jew named Apollos, born at Alexandria, an eloquent man, and mighty in the Scriptures, came to Ephesus. This man was instructed in the way of the Lord; and being fervent in the spirit, he spake and taught diligently the things of the Lord, knowing only the baptism of John."* Yet Apollos was in need of some further training in the truth of God; and the Lord our God employed a husband and wife team, Aquila and Prascilla, for the task. Thus we read in verse 26, *"And he began to speak boldly in the synagogue: whom when Aquila and Priscilla had heard, they took him unto them, and expounded unto him the way of God more perfectly."* Here we find that this husband and wife ministered together in expounding the truth of God more perfectly unto Apollos. Together they were used of the Lord to *edify* a fellow believer.

Furthermore, from Romans 16:3-4 we learn that this husband and wife team were faithful helpers of the apostle Paul in his work for the Lord. There the apostle declared, *"Greet Priscilla and Aquila, my helpers in Christ Jesus: who have for my life laid down their own necks: unto whom not only I give thanks, but also all the churches of the Gentiles."* This ministry of help actually began when this couple first met the apostle in Corinth. In Acts 18:1-3 we read, *"After these things Paul departed from Athens, and came to Corinth; and found a certain Jew named Aquila, born in Pontus, lately come from Italy, with his wife Priscilla; (because that Claudius had commanded all Jews to depart from Rome:) and came unto them. And because he was of the same craft, he abode with them, and wrought: for by their occupation they were tentmakers."* From that time forward this husband and wife continued their ministry of help toward the apostle. Together they were used of the Lord to *encourage* a fellow believer.

395

Finally, from 1 Corinthians 16:19 we learn that this husband and wife team extended their efforts of ministry toward the work of the Lord as a whole. There the apostle Paul gave report, "*The churches of Asia salute you. Aquila and Priscilla salute you much in the Lord, with the church that is in their house.*" Here we find two ways in which this husband and wife had extended their efforts of ministry toward the work of the Lord as a whole. First, they sent a message of salute to the believers at Corinth and thereby extended their heart-felt encouragement and support toward those fellow believers and their church ministry. Second, they opened their own house as a place for their local church to assemble and thereby sacrificed of themselves for the sake of the Lord's work. Together they *gave support* and *made sacrifice* for the work of the Lord. In like manner, our Lord is searching today for married couples who will minister in His work together. He is searching for married couples who will minister together in edifying and encouraging fellow believers and in giving support and making sacrifice for His work.

Strive for the Faith of the Gospel Together

In the eighth place, the husband and wife ought *to strive for the faith of the gospel together*. In Philippians 1:27 the apostle Paul exhorted the believers at Philippi under the inspiration of God the Holy Spirit, saying, "*Only let your conversation be as it becometh the gospel of Christ: that whether I come and see you, or else be absent, I may hear of your affairs, that ye stand fast in one spirit, with one mind striving together for the faith of the gospel.*" The apostle was greatly concerned for the progress of the gospel within this spiritually dark world. For this reason, he instructed the believers at Philippi to maintain a character and conduct that was worthy of the gospel of Christ. For this reason also, he encouraged them to maintain Christian unity in order that they might strive together for the faith of the gospel.

As our Lord Jesus Christ indicated in his prayer in John 17:21-23, Christian unity among God's people is a great tool whereby God our heavenly Father draws the spiritually lost of this world to believe on Jesus Christ as God the Son and Savior from sin. Furthermore,

Christian unity among God's people is a Biblical means whereby the shining forth of God's people as the light of this spiritually dark world is intensified. (Matthew 5:14-16 & Philippians 2:1-4, 14-16) Finally, Christian unity among God's people provides a strong motivation by which fellow believers are encouraged in their relationship with one another to stand fast and strive faithfully for the spread of the gospel of Christ.

In like manner, the one-flesh unity between a husband and wife serves in a similar manner for them as a ministering team. The one-flesh unity in their marriage relationship will be a tool whereby God our heavenly Father may draw the lost to believe on the Lord Jesus Christ as their eternal Savior. Furthermore, the one-flesh unity in their marriage relationship will be a means whereby their light will shine more brightly. Finally, the one-flesh unity in their marriage relationship will provide mutual support and encouragement for them to stand fast and strive faithfully together for the spread of Christ's gospel. Just as our Lord Jesus Christ sent forth his disciples in couples, two-by-two, even so the one-flesh unity of the husband and wife allow them to strive together in such a couple also.

Stand Fast against Opposition Together

In the ninth place, the husband and wife ought *to stand fast against opposition together.* Again in Philippians 1:27 we consider the apostle's exhortation concerning Christian unity – *"Only let your conversation be as it becometh the gospel of Christ: that whether I come and see you, or else be absent, I may hear of your affairs, that ye stand fast in one spirit, with one mind striving together for the faith of the gospel."* Here we take notice that Christian unity "in one spirit" was presented as a foundation for these believers to "stand fast" in the faith. Even so, the exhortation continues in verse 28, saying, *"And in nothing terrified by your adversaries: which is to them an evident token of perdition, but to you of salvation, and that of God."*

The ability of God's people to stand fast without fear against the opposition and persecution of their adversaries is greatly strengthened by their Christian unity together. If one stumbles in the way, then others are available to help him up. If one becomes weak under the pressure, then others are available to give him support. If one is under more severe attack, then others are available to stand at his side. Thus the truth is given in Ecclesiastes 4:9-12, "*Two are better than one; because they have a good reward for their labour. For if they fall, the one will lift up his fellow: but woe to him that is alone when he falleth; for he hath not another to help him up. Again, if two lie together, then they have heat: but how can one be warm alone? And if one prevail against him, two shall withstand him; and a threefold cord is not quickly broken.*" Even so, the one-flesh unity between a husband and wife will greatly strengthen their ability to stand fast in the faith while in the face of temptation, tribulation, opposition, and persecution. In one-flesh unity they will be available to help one another, support one another, and encourage one another.

Raise Up Godly Children Together

In the tenth and final place, the husband and wife ought *to raise up godly children together.* In the opening half of Malachi 2:15 the Lord our God presented one of His reasons for the one-flesh unity of the marriage relationship. There we read, "*And did not he make one? Yet had he the residue of the spirit. And wherefore one? That he might seek a godly seed.*" The Lord our God is seeking for married couples who will raise up a godly generation to love Him, obey His voice, walk in His ways, cleave unto Him, and serve Him with all their hearts and lives. Furthermore, the Lord our God has determined that the one-flesh unity of the marriage relationship between a husband and wife will serve as a significant foundation for this purpose. Thus the Lord our God is searching for married couples who will pursue one-flesh unity together in order that they might raise up a godly generation together.

Truth for Meditation

A husband and wife ought to serve the Lord together by –

1. Walking in righteousness before God together. (Gen. 6:22; 7:1; Luke 1:6)

2. Obeying the call of God together. (Gen. 12:1-5; Heb. 11:8)

3. Walking by faith in God together. (Heb. 11:23; Ex. 2:1-4)

4. Glorifying the Lord our God together. (Rom. 15:5-6)

5. Continuing in prayer unto God together. (Acts 1:14)

6. Worshiping the Lord our God together. (Psa. 55:14)

7. Ministering in the work of God together. (Acts 18:1-3, 26; Rom. 16:3-4; 1 Cor. 16:19)

8. Striving for the faith of the gospel together. (Phil. 1:27)

9. Standing fast against opposition together. (Phil. 1:27-28; Eccl. 4:9-12)

10. Raising up godly children together. (Mal. 2:15)

Verses for Memorization

Romans 15:5-6: Now the God of patience and consolation grant you to be likeminded one toward another according to Christ Jesus; that ye may with one mind and one mouth glorify God, even the Father of our Lord Jesus Christ.

Ecclesiastes 4:9-10: Two are better than one; because they have a good reward for their labour. For if they fall, the one will lift up his fellow: but woe to him that is alone when he falleth; for he hath not another to help him up.

31

For the Troubled Marriage
(Part 1)

For the sake of this chapter, the phrase "troubled marriage" shall refer, not to those times when a marriage is troubled by pressures or attacks from without, but to those times when a marriage is troubled by conflict and strife from within. It refers to those times when the one-flesh unity of the marriage relationship is strained and separated by conflict and contention, strife and division, anger and bitterness, etc. between a husband and wife.

Now, every married couple experiences some times of such trouble. When two individuals who possess a sinful, selfish flesh must live in close, constant contact with one another, as is the case in the one-flesh relationship of marriage, their selfish flesh will at times stir up conflict and strife between them. The solution for such times of conflict and strife is to be found in the Biblical principles of love, communication, confession, forgiveness, and a peaceable spirit that have been presented in earlier chapters of this book. If the husband and the wife will faithfully follow these principles of God's Holy Word, then the times of conflict and strife in their marriage relationship will be *resolved* and *mended*. Thereby also the one-flesh unity of their marriage relationship will be *protected* and *strengthened*.

Yet some husbands and wives selfishly and stubbornly refuse to follow these principles of God's Holy Word. If *both* the husband

and the wife walk in such selfishness and stubbornness, there is *no hope whatsoever* for the conflict and strife between them to be resolved and mended. Their selfishness and stubbornness will only *feed* the conflict and strife between them, causing their marriage relationship to become more and more troubled until it is finally broken. The principle of James 1:15 is clear – *"Then when lust* [that is – selfish desire] *hath conceived, it bringeth forth sin: and sin, when it is finished, bringeth forth death."* This principle applies equally as well to the marriage relationship as it does to an individual's life. Within the marriage relationship selfishness and sinfulness will only bring forth the death of the marriage.

On the other hand, there are many cases in which *one* spouse does indeed desire to follow the principles of God's Holy Word, while the other spouse refuses to do so. In such a case what is that spouse to do? God's Holy Word provides specific instruction concerning this matter, and to this instruction we must turn. In 1 Peter 3:1-2 God's Word speaks to the wife of a husband who is living in disobedience to God's Word, saying, *"Likewise, ye wives, be in subjection to your own husbands; that, if any obey not the word, they also may without the word be won by the conversation of the wives; while they behold your chaste conversation coupled with fear."* Then after some further instruction to the wives in verses 3-6, God's Word speaks in verse 7 to the husband of a wife who is living in disobedience to God's Word, saying, *"Likewise, ye husbands, dwell with them according to knowledge, giving honour unto the wife, as unto the weaker vessel, and as being heirs together of the grace of life; that your prayers be not hindered."* Although this verse does not specifically mention the disobedience of the wife as verse 1 specifically mentioned the disobedience of the husband, yet the word "likewise" with which this verse begins looks back to the case of the wife with a disobedient husband and reveals that it speaks similarly to the case of a husband with a disobedient wife.

Yet verse 1 also begins with the word "likewise." Thus not only does this word "likewise" at the beginning of verse 7 look back to the case of verses 1-6, but also this word "likewise" both at the beginning of verse 1 and verse 7 looks back to the previous case of 1 Peter

402

2:21-25. Therein our Lord and Savior Jesus Christ is presented as an example of patient suffering though He had done no wrong. In verses 21-23 we read, *"For even hereunto were ye called: because Christ also suffered for us, leaving us an example, that ye should follow his steps: who did no sin, neither was guile found in his mouth: who, when he was reviled, reviled not again; when he suffered, he threatened not; but committed himself to him that judgeth righteously."*

Yet even this case of Christ's example for us to follow is not the beginning of the context, for Christ's example of patient suffering is presented in support of the principle that is revealed in verses 19-20. There we are informed, *"For this is thankworthy, if a man for conscience toward God endure grief, suffering wrongfully. For what glory is it, if, when ye be buffeted for your faults, ye shall take it patiently? But if, when ye do well, and suffer for it, ye take it patiently, this is acceptable with God."* The full context begins with the principle of 1 Peter 2:19-20 and extends to Christ's example of patient suffering, then to the wife's case with a disobedient husband, and then to the husband's case with a disobedient wife. For the rest of this chapter, let us then consider the principles and precepts of this passage in their application to a spouse who desires to follow the principles of God's Word while his or her spouse refuses to do so.

Humbly Acknowledge Your Own Selfishness and Sin

In the first place, the spouse who desires to follow the principles of God's Word must *humbly acknowledge and patiently accept the consequences to his or her own selfishness and sin.* In the opening half of 1 Peter 2:20 this principle is revealed through a question – *"For what glory is it, if, when ye be buffeted for your faults, ye shall take it patiently?"* Often when a marriage is troubled, the spouse who claims the "high ground" of God's principles will lay *all* of the blame for the conflict and strife upon the other spouse. Yet it is very rarely true in such conflict and strife that one spouse is responsible for *all* of the fault. Yea, it is very rarely true that only one spouse has contributed *all* of the selfishness and sin that created the conflict and strife.

403

Thus the spouse who desires to follow the principles of God's Word *must* humbly acknowledge *every* element of selfishness and sin that he or she has contributed to the conflict. Even if these elements of selfishness and sin were in response to the selfishness and sin of the other, still they contributed to the conflict and must be humbly confessed as sin both to the Lord and to the other. The one who truly desires to follow God's principles will specifically acknowledge each fault of selfish, sinful attitude, word, or action with a broken and contrite spirit of *humility*. This will not be a casual confession of general, human faultiness. Rather, this will be a humble confession of specific, sinful faults.

In addition, the spouse who desires to follow the principles of God's Word *must* patiently accept the consequences to his or her own contribution of fault in the matter. Our own faults will bring forth some form of "buffeting" (that is – some form of chastening and consequence). This is the certain principle of Galatians 6:7 – "***Be not deceived; God is not mocked: for whatsoever a man soweth, that shall he also reap.***" The one who truly desires to follow God's principles will accept this "buffeting" with a spirit of *patience*, not of blame-shifting or complaining. Such is the spirit of one who is truly contrite and humble over his or her own fault of selfishness and sin. Yea, such is the spirit of one who *truly* desires to follow the principles of God's Word – *humbly acknowledging* one's *own* fault of selfishness and sin and *patiently accepting* the consequences to one's *own* fault of selfishness and sin. A spirit of blame-shifting or complaining, however, reveals that the claim to the "high ground" of God's principles is only lying hypocrisy.

Take Suffering with Joyful Patience and Faithful Continuance

In the second place, the spouse who desires to follow the principles of God's Word must *take suffering in and for well doing with joyful patience and with faithful continuance*. 1 Peter 2:19 declares, "***For this is thankworthy, if a man for conscience toward God endure grief, suffering wrongfully.***" The closing portion of verse 20 adds, "***But if, when ye do well, and suffer for it, ye take it patiently, this is acceptable with God.***" Just such a spirit of joyful patience in wrongful suffering and of faithful continuance in well doing is acceptable and well pleasing unto the Lord our God, whereas a spirit of complaining or quitting is unacceptable and displeasing in His sight.

Even so, the opening portion of 1 Peter 3:14 presents suffering in and for well doing as a happy condition, saying, *"But and if ye suffer for righteousness' sake, happy are ye;"* and 1 Peter 4:14 adds, *"If ye be reproached for the name of Christ, happy are ye; for the spirit of glory and of God resteth upon you: on their part he is evil spoken of, but on your part he is glorified."* Certainly this is not because such suffering is so enjoyable. Rather, this is because patient suffering in and for well doing glorifies the Lord our God. It indicates that He is so worthy of our reverence and our love that no price of suffering or sacrifice is too great to pay in serving Him. Thus the one who truly desires to follow God's principles will endure grief, suffering wrongfully, not simply with grudging patience, but with *joyful* patience. Yea, this is the very command of the Lord our God in 1 Peter 4:12-13 – *"Beloved, think it not strange concerning the fiery trial which is to try you, as though some strange thing happened unto you: but rejoice, inasmuch as ye are partakers of Christ's sufferings; that, when his glory shall be revealed, ye may be glad also with exceeding joy."* A complaining spirit against the wrongful suffering or a weary spirit in the well doing is the way of disobedience.

Furthermore, the one who truly desires to follow God's principles must not be troubled in heart over wrongful suffering, but must continue to sanctify the Lord God in his or her heart. 1 Peter 3:14-16 gives the instruction, *"But and if ye suffer for righteousness' sake, happy are ye: and be not afraid of their terror, neither be troubled; but sanctify the Lord God in your hearts: and be ready always to give an answer to every man that asketh you a reason of the hope that is in you with meekness and fear: having a good conscience; that, whereas they speak evil of you, as of evildoers, they may be ashamed that falsely accuse your good conversation in Christ."* The focus of the heart must remain upon the Lord. If the focus of the heart is set upon the wrongful suffering, it will become troubled by a spirit of complaint or discouragement. Rather, in the face of wrongful suffering, the spouse who desires to follow the principles of God's Word must be even more driven to focus his or her heart upon the Lord to love, honor, serve, and trust Him.

Return Back Blessing for Verbal Attack and Mistreatment

In the third place, the spouse who desires to follow the principles of God's Word must *not return verbal attack for verbal attack or mistreatment for mistreatment, but instead blessing.* In 1 Peter 2:21-23 our Lord Jesus Christ is presented as an example for us to follow of wrongful suffering. There we read, *"For even hereunto were ye called: because Christ also suffered for us, leaving us an example, that ye should follow his steps: who did no sin, neither was guile found in his mouth: who, when he was reviled, reviled not again; when he suffered, he threatened not; but committed himself to him that judgeth righteously."* When our Lord Jesus Christ was reviled (that is – verbally attacked and abused), He did not revile back in return. He refrained from any manner of corrupt communication, evil speaking, and deceitful manipulation, even when others mistreated Him. Furthermore, when He suffered under such mistreatment, He did not develop or demonstrate a threatening attitude back in return.

Even so, the one who truly desires to follow God's principles will walk in our Lord's steps after His example. Yea, the instruction is given in 1 Peter 3:9, *"Not rendering evil for evil, or railing for railing: but contrariwise blessing; knowing that ye are thereunto called, that ye should inherit a blessing."* This is the behavior unto which the Lord our God has called us and upon which He has promised His blessing. Thus if the spouse who rejects God's principles disrespects, verbally attacks, or mistreats the spouse who desires to follow God's principles, the spouse who truly desires to follow God's principles will not return back disrespect, verbal attack, or mistreatment. Rather, he or she will return back blessing in loving spirit, respectful attitude, gracious words, and kind actions.

Yea, in Matthew 5:44 our Lord Jesus Christ revealed this principle of returning back good unto those who do us evil, saying, *"But I say unto you, Love your enemies, bless them that curse you, do good to them that hate you, and pray for them which despitefully use you, and persecute you."* Again God's Word reveals this principle in 1 Thessalonians 5:15, saying, *"See that none render evil for evil unto any man; but ever follow that which is good, both among yourselves, and to all men."* Yet again God's Word reveals the principle in Proverbs 25:21-22, saying, *"If thine enemy be hungry, give him bread to eat; and if he be thirsty, give him water to drink: for thou shalt heap coals of fire upon his head, and the LORD shall reward thee."* Finally, God's Word reveals the warning and principle in Romans 12:21, saying, *"Be not overcome of evil, but overcome evil with good."*

In times of mistreatment the spouse who truly desires to follow God's principles will not be defensive, abrasive, argumentative, deceptive, or manipulative. Rather, he or she will refrain from speaking any evil or deception, will avoid any attitude or action of evil response, will focus on doing good for and toward the other, and will seek and pursue after peace as much as he or she is able. Even so, the instruction is given in 1 Peter 3:10-11, *"For he that will love life, and see good days, let him refrain his tongue from evil, and his lips that they speak no guile. Let him eschew evil, and do good; let him seek peace, and ensue it."* To the one who will follow this path of behavior, the promise of God's Word is delivered in the opening portion of verse 12, *"For the eyes of the Lord are over the righteous, and his ears are open unto their prayers."* Over such our Lord's favor will be poured out, and for such He will hear and answer their prayers. Yet to the one who will not follow this path of behavior, the warning of God's Word is delivered in the closing portion of the verse, *"But the face of the Lord is against them that do evil."* To return back evil for evil is to do evil, and against such our Lord's anger will be kindled.

Commit Your Case by Faith unto the Lord Your God

In the fourth place, the spouse who desires to follow the principles of God's Word must *commit his or her case by faith unto the faithful deliverance and just judgment of almighty God.* Again from 1 Peter 2:23 we consider the example of our Lord Jesus Christ for us to follow in wrongful suffering – *"Who, when he was reviled, reviled not again; when he suffered, he threatened not; but committed himself to him that judgeth righteously.*" When our Lord was mistreated, He did not fight back in His own defense. Rather, He committed Himself and His case into the hand of God the Father, trusting that the Father would indeed judge righteously in His way in His time. During His ministry upon this earth, our Lord did not take vengeance into His own hand. Rather, He gave place unto the Father's wrath, trusting that the Father would be faithful to care for Him, deliver Him, and reward Him in the goodness of His will.

Even so, the one who truly desires to follow God's principles will walk after our Lord's example. Yea, the instruction is given 1 Peter 4:19, "*Wherefore let them that suffer according to the will of God commit the keeping of their souls to him in well doing, as unto a faithful Creator.*" Indeed the Lord our God is faithful unto those who trust in Him and walk after Him. He has established His faithfulness unto the very heavens in greatness, and He will not allow His faithfulness to fail. (Psalm 89:1-2, 33) With unfailing faithfulness He will ever strengthen and care for His own and will never forsake them in their time of need. In Isaiah 41:10 our Lord proclaims His promise, "*Fear thou not; for I am with thee: be not dismayed; for I am thy God: I will strengthen thee; yea, I will help thee; yea, I will uphold thee with the right hand of my righteousness.*"

Thus in the midst of any wrongful suffering and grief, the spouse who truly desires to follow the principles of God's Word will ever maintain his or her trust in the Lord God of heaven and earth. He or she will entrust his or her defense and deliverance into the keeping of God's hand. He or she will not take any form of vengeance (pay-back), whether in attitude, word, or action, into his or her own hand. Rather, he or she will depend upon the Lord's almighty strength to continue in well doing and will thereby continue in that well doing while patiently waiting on and faithfully trusting in the Lord's hand of deliverance. Even so, the instruction is given in Proverbs 20:22, "*Say not thou, I will recompense evil; but wait on the LORD, and he shall save thee.*" He or she will join with David from Psalm 62:1-2, saying, "*Truly my soul waiteth upon God: from him cometh my salvation. He only is my rock and my salvation; he is my defence; I shall not be greatly moved;"* and again from verses 5-7, saying, *"My soul, wait thou only upon God; for my expectation is from him. He only is my rock and my salvation: he is my defence; I shall not be moved. In God is my salvation and my glory: the rock of my strength, and my refuge, is in God."*

Furthermore, the spouse who truly desires to follow the principles of God's Word will ever give place unto God's wrath, trusting Him to judge in righteousness as He wills to do. The instruction is given in Romans 12:19, *"Dearly beloved, avenge not yourselves, but rather give place unto wrath: for it is written, Vengeance is mine; I will repay, saith the Lord."* The one who truly desires to follow God's principles will join with the psalmist from Psalm 94:21-23, saying, *"They gather themselves together against the soul of the righteous, and condemn the innocent blood. But the LORD is my defence; and my God is the rock of my refuge. And he shall bring upon them their own iniquity, and shall cut them off in their own wickedness; yea, the LORD our God shall cut them off."*

Truth for Meditation

When one spouse refuses to follow the principles of God's Word, the other spouse must –

1. Humbly acknowledge and patiently accept the consequences to his or her own selfishness and sin. (1 Peter 2:20)

2. Take suffering in and for well doing with joyful patience and with faithful continuance. (1 Peter 2:19-20; 3:14-16; 4:12-14)

3. Not return verbal attack for verbal attack or mistreatment for mistreatment, but instead blessing. (1 Peter 2:21-23; 3:9-12; Prov. 25:21-22; Matt. 5:44; Rom. 12:21; 1 Thess. 5:15)

4. Commit his or her case by faith unto the faithful deliverance and just judgment of almighty God. (1 Peter 2:21-23; 4:19; Psa. 62:1-2, 5-7; 94:21-23; Prov. 20:22; Isa. 41:10; Rom. 12:19)

Verses for Memorization

1 Peter 2:20: For what glory is it, if, when ye be buffeted for your faults, ye shall take it patiently? But if, when ye do well, and suffer for it, ye take it patiently, this is acceptable with God.

1 Peter 3:9: Not rendering evil for evil, or railing for railing: but contrariwise blessing; knowing that ye are thereunto called, that ye should inherit a blessing.

Romans 12:21: Be not overcome of evil, but overcome evil with good.

1 Peter 4:19: Wherefore let them that suffer according to the will of God commit the keeping of their souls to him in well doing, as unto a faithful Creator.

Proverbs 20:22: Say not thou, I will recompense evil; but wait on the LORD, and he shall save thee.

Psalm 62:1-2: Truly my soul waiteth upon God: from him cometh my salvation. He only is my rock and my salvation; he is my defence; I shall not be greatly moved.

32

For the Troubled Marriage
(Part 2)

Now, having considered the two principles from the counsel of God's Word in 1 Peter 2:19-20 and the two principles from Christ's example of wrongful suffering in 1 Peter 2:21-23, we come to the specific case of the wife with a disobedient husband in 1 Peter 3:1-6. Herein we also find two principles specifically for the wife to follow.

As the Wife, Subject Yourself to Your Husband's Headship

In the first place, the wife who truly desires to follow the principles of God's Word *must subject herself under her husband's headship authority while living daily in pure behavior.* In 1 Peter 3:1-2 God's Word gives instruction, saying, *"Likewise, ye wives, be in subjection to your own husbands; that, if any obey not the word, they also may without the word be won by the conversation of the wives; while they behold your chaste conversation coupled with fear."*

Yes, the wife is to be subject unto her own husband *even when* he is living in disobedience to the principles of God's Word. Her husband's unsubmissive and disobedient spirit toward his Head, the Lord Jesus Christ, does not grant her the right to have an unsubmissive and disobedient spirit toward him. Rather, the Lord God Himself requires that she walk daily in pure behavior (chaste conversation) coupled with a respectful and submissive spirit toward her husband. In fact, God's Word reveals that this is the means by which the wife should seek to win her husband unto the way of godliness. She is specifically *not* to attempt to change her husband through the word of preaching, or rebuke, or instruction. Rather, she is to seek to win her husband through her *pure behavior and submissive spirit.*

Now, certainly the wife is not to obey her husband if he directs her to do something that the Lord our God has specifically forbidden in His Word, such as deceit, theft, fornication, drunkenness, etc. In such cases the wife ought to obey the commandment of God rather than the direction of her husband. Furthermore, if her husband forbids her to do something that the Lord our God has specifically commanded of her and for which He has given personal responsibility to her, such as to meditate on God's Word daily and to pray without ceasing, the wife should also obey God rather than her husband. Yet even in such cases of disobedience, the wife must maintain all due respect in spirit unto her husband as the Lord God Himself has also commanded her. On the other hand, in any case where there is no direct violation of God's Word, the wife is required to subject herself under her husband's authority and to obey his direction, no matter how annoying, unpleasant, overbearing, unreasonable, displeasing, objectionable, or contrary to her own desires she may find that authority and direction.

As the Wife, Focus on the Inward Beauty of a Meek and Quiet Spirit

In the second place, the wife who truly desires to follow the principles of God's Word *must not be focused on the vanity of outward beauty, but on the inward beauty of a meek and quiet spirit.* In 1 Peter 3:3-6 God's Holy Word gives instruction, saying, "*Whose adorning let it not be that outward adorning of plaiting the hair, and of wearing of gold, or of putting on of apparel; but let it be the hidden man of the heart, in that which is not corruptible, even the ornament of a meek and quiet spirit, which is in the sight of God of great price. For after this manner in the old time the holy women also, who trusted in God, adorned themselves, being in subjection unto their own husbands: even as Sara obeyed Abraham, calling him lord: whose daughters ye are, as long as ye do well, and are not afraid with any amazement.*"

412

According to God's Word in Proverbs 31:30, outward beauty is vain; and social favor is deceitful. However, a woman who walks in the godliness of the fear of the Lord shall be well pleasing unto the Lord and shall find the favor of the Lord. Now, such a walk in godliness begins with "the hidden man of the heart." In particular, it involves the heart attitude of a meek and quiet spirit. This is a form of adorning that is not corruptible. Yea, this is an ornament of beauty that is in the sight of the Lord our God an ornament of great price and great attraction. Yea, this is the spirit with which the holy and godly women of the past adorned themselves. If she truly desires to follow God's principles, the wife must maintain this heart attitude of a meek and quiet spirit. If she will not do so, she only reveals that any claim to the "high ground" of God's principles is only lying hypocrisy.

So then, what is the nature of a meek and quiet spirit? First, it is a true attitude of the heart, not simply an external show of behavior. Regardless of her words or actions, if the wife's spirit is not right toward her husband, then her heart is not right before God. The Lord our God looks on the heart, and He knows the spirit of attitude that the wife actually has toward her husband. He is the One who requires a meek and quiet spirit of her and who views such a spirit with great favor. Second, it is an attitude of the heart that governs and pervades the words and actions of the behavior. The tone of the wife's words and the spirit of the wife's actions will ever portray meekness and peacefulness, rather than selfishness and stubbornness. Third and finally, a meek and quiet spirit is one of humble selflessness, patient gentleness, and peaceable kindness. It is not selfish, manipulative, self-assertive, contentious, loud, stubborn, or abrasive. With such a spirit the wife will not push to get her own way, but will give up her own way for the sake of peace. She will not push herself forward to take the lead, but will submit herself to the lead of her husband. She will not manipulate or nag her husband until he gives in to her wishes, but will patiently serve her husband for his good and benefit. She will not speak with *"grievous words"* (Proverbs 15:1), but with *"the law of kindness"* (Proverbs 31:26).

Indeed this was the manner of the godly and holy women of the past – to set their trust in God, to be adorned with a meek and quiet

413

spirit, and to be in subjection unto their own husbands. 1 Peter 3:7 specifically mentions the example of Sarah in her meek and quiet spirit of submission and obedience to her husband Abraham. Yet one other example from the Old Testament would be profitable for our consideration – the example of Abigail, the wife of Nabal. In 1 Samuel 25:3 God the Holy Spirit revealed that she was "*a woman of good understanding, and of a beautiful countenance.*" Now, a beautiful countenance in the view of God the Holy Spirit would be that of a woman who was adorned with the beautiful ornament of a meek and quiet spirit.

Yet Abigail was married to an ungodly man who rebelled against God's principles. In 1 Samuel 25:3 God the Holy Spirit revealed that her husband Nabal was a "churlish" man and "evil in his doings." He was hard-hearted, mean-spirited, and stiff-necked in his character and disagreeable, malignant, and wicked in his behavior. Again in verse 17 Nabal's servants reported that he was "such a son of Belial" that no one could speak to him. He was good for nothing, ungodly, and evil in his demeanor. Yet again in verse 25 his wife reported that he was a man of folly (that is – of senselessness, disgracefulness, and vileness). To this man Abigail had been married for many years, yet she maintained a right spirit throughout those years. Yea, she was even willing to take the responsibility and consequences of his faults upon herself. (1 Samuel 25:18-28) He was her husband; and regardless of his ungodly character, as a virtuous woman who trusted in the Lord, she would do him good and not evil all the days of her life. (Proverbs 31:12) The Lord honored her trust, and in His time He did indeed judge Nabal for his wicked ways. (1 Samuel 25:36-38)

In conclusion, the principle must again be emphasized that the wife must seek to win her husband to the ways of the Lord through her pure behavior coupled with a meek and quiet spirit of submission and respect. This is the method of influence that the Lord our God will approve and bless – that the husband might be won through the behavior of his wife, as he beholds from day to day her pure behavior coupled with a right spirit. On the other hand, the wife is *not* to employ the preaching of truth or the reproofs of instruction to win her husband to the ways of the Lord. 1 Peter 3:1 directly states that the husband is to be won "without the word." Furthermore, the wife must not employ the deceit of manipulation, the persistence of nagging, or the force of contention to change her husband's ways. Such methods of influence are not approved of our Lord and will not be blessed by Him. In fact, although such methods may appear to be profitable in the short term, they will certainly create more trouble in the marriage and do more damage to the marriage in the long term.

Now, having considered the case of the wife with a disobedient husband in 1 Peter 3:1-6, we come to the case of the husband with a disobedient wife in 1 Peter 3:7. Herein we also find two principles specifically for the husband to follow, just as we had found two principles for the wife.

As the Husband, Seek to Dwell at Harmony with Your Wife

In the first place, the husband who truly desires to follow the principles of God's Word *must seek to know his wife as an individual and must dwell at harmony with her in that knowledge.* In the opening portion of 1 Peter 3:7, God's Word gives instruction, saying, *"**Likewise, ye husbands, dwell with them according to knowledge.**"* In this context the instruction for the husband to "dwell with" his wife means that he is to live at harmony with her. In addition, this harmonious living is to be in accord with his knowledge of his wife. The husband who truly desires to follow God's principles must ever seek to know his wife better as an individual person and must ever live at harmony with her in that knowledge.

Yes, the husband is to live at harmony with his wife *even when* she is living in disobedience to the principles of God's Word. His wife's disregard and disrespect of the Lord does not grant him the right to disregard and disrespect her in their marriage relationship. Rather, the Lord our God requires that he daily pursue a harmonious relationship with his wife. Certainly he is not to be in harmony with her rejection of and rebellion against any of the principles of God's Word. Yet in any aspect of their relationship where his wife is not in direct contradiction to God's Word, the husband is required to live at harmony with her, no matter how contrary her desires may be to his own interests and preferences.

Even so, the husband who truly desires to follow God's principles will put forth the effort and energy to know his wife's personal joys and burdens, likes and dislikes, delights and annoyances, pleasures and pains, strengths and weaknesses, hopes and fears. He will lovingly, attentively, considerately, and faithfully listen to her each day. He will not pull away from his wife or allow his heart to grow cold and hard toward her. Rather, he will draw nigh unto her in every area that is Biblically acceptable and will ever maintain a loving and tender heart toward her. In addition, if he truly desires to follow God's principles, the husband will put forth the effort and energy to behave in a manner that will produce harmony in his relationship with his wife. When he comes to know that something bothers his wife, he will put forth every Biblically acceptable effort to avoid that thing; and when he comes to know that something pleases his wife, he will put forth every Biblically acceptable effort to pursue that thing.

As the Husband, Specifically Give Honor unto Your Wife

In the second place, the husband who truly desires to follow the principles of God's Word *must specifically give honor unto his wife by preferring her above himself in their relationship.* In the opening portion of 1 Peter 3:7, God's Word continues the instruction, saying, **"Likewise, ye husbands, dwell with them according to knowledge, giving honour unto the wife."** Regardless of his wife's attitude, words, and actions, the husband must honor his wife as a precious treasure. Each day throughout each step of the day, he must pour out honor unto her from the fullness of his heart in specific, tangible ways of his own attitude, words, and actions. He will not seek to beat his wife into repentance and righteousness through some manner of force. Rather, He will seek to honor his wife unto repentance and righteousness. This is the spirit that the husband is required to maintain toward his wife; and if he will not do so, he only reveals that any claim to the "high ground" of God's principles is only lying hypocrisy.

Even so, if the husband truly desires to follow God's principles, he will not take his wife and her efforts of labor for granted; and he will not treat her as an unimportant inferior or a worthless possession.

Rather, as Romans 12:10 teaches, in honor he will to prefer her above himself in the matters of their relationship. Furthermore, he will not tear down or tear into his wife verbally. Rather, he will bless her and praise her for the fruit of her hands. Finally, he will not mistreat, misuse, marginalize, manipulate, malign, mock, menace, or manhandle his wife. Rather, he will behave toward his wife in such a manner as to magnify her and to minister unto her. In all, if the husband truly desires to follow the principles of God's Word, he will express and demonstrate respect and appreciation for his wife's thoughts, feelings, opinions, suggestions, time, efforts, and labor wherever they are not contrary to God's Word.

Now, these principles for both the husband and the wife ought to be followed with commitment and faithfulness at all times within the marriage relationship. However, at those times when the marriage is troubled by conflict and strife, these principles need to be followed with a greater intensity of commitment and faithfulness.

Truth for Meditation

When the husband refuses to follow the principles of God's Word, the wife must –

1. Subject herself under her husband's headship authority while living daily in pure behavior. (1 Peter 3:1-2)

2. Not be focused on the vanity of outward beauty, but on the inward beauty of a meek and quiet spirit. (1 Peter 3:3-6)

When the wife refuses to follow the principles of God's Word, the husband must –

1. Seek to know his wife as an individual and must dwell at harmony with her in that knowledge. (1 Peter 3:7)

2. Specifically give honor unto his wife by preferring her above himself in their relationship. (1 Peter 3:7)

Verses for Memorization

1 Peter 3:1-2: Likewise, ye wives, be in subjection to your own husbands; that, if any obey not the word, they also may without the word be won by the conversation of the wives; while they behold your chaste conversation coupled with fear.

Romans 12:10: Be kindly affectioned one to another with brotherly love; in honour preferring one another.

33

An Heritage of the Lord

In Psalm 127:3-5 God's Word speaks concerning children in the home, saying, *"Lo, children are an heritage of the LORD: and the fruit of the womb is his reward. As arrows are in the hand of a mighty man; so are children of the youth. Happy is the man that hath his quiver full of them: they shall not be ashamed, but they shall speak with the enemies in the gate."* Here we find two general truths concerning children in the home. First, we learn that children are a good reward from the Lord; and second, we learn that children are a great responsibility before the Lord.

A Good Reward from the Lord

Concerning the truth that children are *a good reward* from the Lord, the closing half of Psalm 127:3 specifically refers to them as "His reward." Furthermore, the opening half of the verse refers to children as "an heritage of the Lord." Both of these phrases reveal that the Lord our God intends for us to view children as a precious gift and valuable privilege from His hand.

❖ First, this means that each and every child must be received as *a gift given directly by the Lord Himself.* They are *His* heritage and *His* reward to the parents. Thus it is not right for any parent either personally or emotionally to reject a child because that child does not meet expectations, even if the child is a girl and not the boy desired, or a boy and not the girl desired, or a "mistake" and not in the plan, or a child with some form of handicap. Each and every physical, mental, and emotional attribute and ability of the child was predetermined by the Lord even before that child was formed in the mother's womb. (Psalm 139:16) What, therefore, God hath sent forth in His will, let not man reject.

❖ Second, this means that each and every child must be viewed as *a precious treasure of the Lord's loving-kindness.* They are His *heritage* to the parents. Each and every child is of great value in our Lord's sight. Thus each and every child is to be of great value in the parents' sight, and each and every child is to be treated with godly love and responsible care by the parents.

❖ Third, this means that having children must be pursued as *a positive prospect of the Lord's will.* They are His *reward* to the parents. Certainly it is not our Lord's will that every married couple should bring forth children into the world. In such cases our Lord may call this couple to the ministry of adoption or to concentrate themselves in some other form of ministry. Yet every married couple should have a desire to bring forth and raise up children for our Lord's glory. The prospect of having children should not be viewed *negatively* as a great restriction to the couple's freedom, or as a great expense to the financial status, or as a great hindrance to the chosen career, or as a great burden on the desired life-style, or as a great detriment to the wife's figure, etc. This viewpoint is contrary to the view of our Lord. Rather, the prospect of having children should be viewed *positively* as a great reward and blessing from the Lord. It is good in our Lord's sight; thus it should be good in the married couple's sight.

The Second Evidence

The second evidence that children are a good reward from the Lord is that married couples are commanded with a command of *blessing* to bring forth children into this world. In Genesis 1:27 God's Word speaks of the creation of the man and the woman as a married couple, saying, "***So God created man*** [that is – mankind] ***in His own image,*** *in the image of God created he him; male and female created he them.*" Then in the opening portion of verse 28, God's principles for each married couple is given, "*And God blessed them, and God said unto them, Be fruitful, and multiply, and replenish the earth, and subdue it.*" In like manner, this principle was delivered to Noah and his three sons in Genesis 9:1 where we read, "*And God blessed Noah and his sons, and said unto them, Be fruitful, and multiply, and replenish the earth.*"

This means that each married couple should attempt to bring forth children in obedience to our Lord's command. Certainly if our Lord does not allow a couple to bring forth children, they are not in sinful disobedience to the Lord's command. They were prevented according to God's own will. Yet if a couple refuses even to seek the privilege of bringing forth children, they are indeed in disobedience to our Lord's command. In addition, this means that each married couple should regard the prospect of having children as a blessing of the Lord. The command of Genesis 1:28 is *a command of blessing.* The Lord our God *blessed* us in giving this command and thereby in granting us this privilege. What, therefore, God hath called a blessing, let not man call a curse.

The Third Evidence

The third evidence that children are a good reward from the Lord is that God's Word considers children to be the fruitfulness of a married couple. In both Genesis 1:28 and Genesis 9:1, the instruction to bring forth children is presented in the two words – "*Be fruitful.*" In fact, the word "fruitful" is used ten times in the book of Genesis as a reference to bringing forth children into the world. Certainly this word indicates a positive viewpoint on the matter of having children. A barren tree, vine, or field of crop is a condition of grief and sorrow for a farmer. Yet a fruitful tree, vine, or field of crop is certainly a condition for joy and happiness. In like manner, the fruitfulness of having children ought to be a pursuit of joy and happiness for a married couple. This means that each married couple should ask the Lord to grant this blessing of fruitfulness and should thank the Lord for every child that He grants.

The Fourth Evidence

The fourth and final evidence that children are a good reward from the Lord is that having and raising up children for the Lord is one of our Lord's purposes for marriage. In Malachi 2:15 the question is asked – Why did the Lord our God make the one-flesh marriage relationship? In the midst of the verse the answer is given, *"That he might seek a godly seed."* This is the desire of the Lord our God – that children might be brought forth and raised up to walk in godliness for His glory. Yea, raising up children for the Lord's glory should be the third highest priority for a married couple. The first priority should be their personal walk with the Lord each day. The second priority should be the growth of a good, godly marriage relationship together. The third priority should be to raise up a godly generation for the Lord. This means that each married couple should attempt to bring forth children in honor of our Lord's purpose. In addition, this means that each married couple should be pleased to bring forth and raise up children according to our Lord's pleasure.

A Great Responsibility before the Lord

The Lord our God does not simply desire that a married couple should bring forth children into this world. He also desires that they should take up the responsibility to raise up those children in this world. Yet He does not simply desire that those children should be raised to be healthy, good, and successful children. Rather, the Lord our God desires that those children should be raised to be godly in their character and to serve Him in their conduct. Thus we come to the second general truth of Psalm 127:3-5 – that children are *a great responsibility* before the Lord.

Concerning this truth that children are a great responsibility before the Lord, the opening portion of Psalm 127:3 declares, *"Lo, children are an heritage of the LORD."* Now, the word "heritage" reveals not only that children are a valuable privilege granted from our Lord's hand, but also that children are an important *stewardship* entrusted by our Lord's hand. They are *His heritage* that He has *entrusted* unto the parents' care in order that the parents might bring them up according to *His purpose.*

What then is the purpose of our Lord concerning the up bringing of the children for which He has entrusted them unto the parents' care? In Malachi 2:15 we find the answer – *"That he might seek a godly seed."* This is our Lord's stewardship unto the parents in granting them children – that they should raise up their children to be a *godly* generation for the Lord. This means that the parents must bring up their children unto the knowledge of eternal salvation from sin through faith alone in God the Son, the Lord Jesus Christ, as their personal Redeemer and Savior. This means that the parents must bring up their children to love and worship the Lord their God with all their heart, soul, mind, and strength as the foundational priority of their lives. This means that the parents must bring up their children to walk by full assurance of faith in the all-sufficiency of the Lord, trusting Him with all their hearts and not leaning at all upon their own understanding or ability. This means that the parents must bring up their children to walk in complete surrender to the perfect will of the Lord, humbling themselves before Him and obeying His direction in all things. Finally, this means that the parents must bring up their children to deny the desires of their sinful flesh, to separate themselves from this sinful world, and to resist the temptations of the devil.

This is the standard by which the stewardship of parenting is to be examined. On the one hand, if the children grow up to be a godly generation for the Lord, then the work of parenting has been successful. On the other hand, if the children do not grow up to be a godly generation for the Lord, then the work of parenting has not been successful. Children that are brought up to be a godly generation – This is the stewardship to which the Lord our God has called the parents, and this is the standard by which the Lord our God examines the work of parenting.

The Second Evidence

The second evidence that children are a great responsibility before the Lord is that God's Word commands parents to teach God's truth unto their children *diligently*. In Deuteronomy 6:5-7 the instruction is given, *"And thou shalt love the LORD thy God with all thine heart, and with all thy soul, and with all thy might. And these words, which I command thee this day, shall be in thine heart: and thou shalt teach them diligently unto thy children, and shalt talk of them when thou sittest in thine house, and when thou walkest by the way, and when thou liest down, and when thou risest up."* In like manner, in the New Testament passage of Ephesians 6:4, the instruction is given, *"And, ye fathers, provoke not your children to wrath: but bring them up in the nurture and admonition of the Lord."*

This means that the parents must commit their own hearts and lives in love to the Lord their God. Children will reject the teaching of God's truth from their parents if they see that their parents themselves have no heart of love for the Lord. On the other hand, if the parents themselves walk in love for the Lord and cleave only unto Him, it will serve as a great foundation of example on which to build the teaching of their children in the truth of God's Word. This also means that the parents themselves must delight in and meditate upon the truth of God's Word throughout every day. The parents cannot teach truths unto their children that they have not yet made their own. Thus the parents must continually study the truths of God's Word in order to make it their own, and thereby in order to teach it diligently unto their children. Finally, this means that the parents must employ the Word of God as the standard of truth for every principle that they teach to their children, for every purpose in which they direct their children, for every warning that they set before their children, and for every discipline by which they correct their children.

The Third Evidence

The third evidence that children are a great responsibility before the Lord is that God's Word calls parents to correct and discipline their children faithfully. In Proverbs 13:24 the principle is given, *"He that spareth his rod hateth his son: but he that loveth him chasteneth him betimes."* Thus Proverbs 19:18 gives the instruction, *"Chasten thy son while there is hope, and let not thy soul spare for his crying."* Again Proverbs 22:15 gives the principle, *"Foolishness is bound in the heart of a child; but the rod of correction shall drive it far from him."* Thus again Proverbs 23:13-14 gives the instruction,

"Withhold not correction from the child: for if thou beatest him with the rod, he shall not die. Thou shalt beat him with the rod, and shalt deliver his soul from hell." Yet again Proverbs 29:15 gives the principle, *"The rod and reproof give wisdom: but a child left to himself bringeth his mother to shame."* Thus again Proverbs 29:17 gives the instruction, *"Correct thy son, and he shall give thee rest; yea, he shall give delight unto thy soul."*

By nature the foolishness of sin and immaturity is bound in the heart of every child. Indeed, it is rooted deeply and intertwined tightly therein. Only by the correction of faithful discipline will that foolishness of sin and immaturity be driven out of and far from that child's heart and life so that the wisdom of godliness and maturity might enter therein. This means that the parents must employ correction and discipline in love throughout each child's upbringing early, diligently, efficiently, consistently, and faithfully. They must not withhold correction. They must not spare for the child's crying. They must not leave the child to his own way. They must not neglect the child's correction and discipline. If they do, that child will bring them to shame. Yet if they are faithful in that child's correction and disciple, that child will give delight unto their souls.

The Fourth Evidence

The fourth and final evidence that children are a great responsibility before the Lord is that children who are brought up to walk in godliness and wisdom will bring joy to the parents' hearts, whereas children who walk in ungodliness and foolishness will bring grief to the parents' hearts. In Proverbs 10:1 the two principles are given, *"A wise son maketh a glad father: but a foolish son is the heaviness of his mother."* Thus in Proverbs 23:15-16 the father declares, *"My son, if thine heart be wise, my heart shall rejoice, even mine. Yea, my reins shall rejoice, when thy lips speak right things."* Even so, verses 24-25 proclaim, *"The father of the righteous shall greatly rejoice: and he that begetteth a wise child shall have joy of him. Thy father and thy mother shall be glad, and she that bare thee shall rejoice."* However, Proverbs 17:21 warns, *"He that begetteth a fool doeth it to his sorrow: and the father of a fool hath no joy."* To this verse 25 adds, *"A foolish son is a grief to his father, and bitterness to her that bare him."*

Even so, we return to Psalm 127:4-5 where the truth is revealed, *"As arrows are in the hand of a mighty man; so are children of the youth. Happy is the man that hath his quiver full of them: they shall not be ashamed, but they shall speak with the enemies in the gate."* Now, many have employed the "quiver full" phrase in verse 5 to indicate that a married couple should bring forth as great a number of children as is biologically possible. Yet the whole picture of verses 4-5 emphasizes a greater matter of responsibility.

That which ties together the picture of these two verses is the reference to arrows. In verse 4 "children of the youth" are compared to arrows, yet not just to any arrows. Specifically they are compared to arrows "in the hand of a mighty man." Now, a skilled mighty man would have been particular only to use arrows that were well made. Yet arrows of that time were not produced in a factory, but were produced by hand. Yea, a skilled mighty man of that time would likely have had a part in the production of his own arrows. In his hand the shaft, head, nock, and fletching of the arrow would have been well prepared for the most effective use of that arrow. Thus in these two verse the picture is not simply of a man who has his quiver full of as many arrows as he can hold, but of a skilled mighty man who has put forth careful effort to have his quiver full of *well prepared* arrows. This is the man who can go forth with the happy confidence that his arrows will effectively accomplish their purpose.

Even so, it is not simply the married couple who has as many children as they are biologically able who will experience joy and rejoicing in their children. In fact, according to the truth of God's own Word in Proverbs 10:1; 17:21 & 17:25, the more of their children who go astray unto foolishness and ungodliness, the more grief and sorrow the parents will experience. Rather, it is the parents who diligently raise up their children unto wisdom and godliness who shall be joyful, happy, and not ashamed. Not as they fill up their quiver with a great number of children, but as they fill up their quiver with children *of godly character* shall they find joy and rejoicing. These are the parents who shall be able to defend themselves against the reproaches of their enemies. Even so, in Proverbs 27:11 the father gave instruction to his son, saying, "*My son, be wise, and make my heart glad, that I may answer him that reproacheth me.*" Only as his son walked in godly wisdom would the father experience gladness of heart and defense against reproach. This then is the great responsibility of parents before the Lord – to fill up their quiver with *well raised* children *of godly character and godly wisdom.*

Truth for Meditation

The evidence that children are a good reward from the Lord is that –

1. God's Word calls children the heritage and the reward of the Lord. (Psa. 127:3)

2. God's Word commands married couples with a command of blessing to bring forth children. (Gen. 1:28; 9:1)

3. God's Word considers children to be the fruitfulness of a married couple. (Gen. 1:28; 9:1)

4. God's Word communicates that bringing forth children is a divine purpose for marriage. (Mal. 2:15)

The evidence that children are a great responsibility before the Lord is that –

1. God's Word communicates that raising up godly children is the Lord's stewardship unto the parents. (Psa. 127:3; Mal. 2:15)

2. God's Word commands parents to teach God's truth unto their children diligently. (Deut. 6:5-7; Eph. 6:4)

3. God's Word calls parents to correct and discipline their children faithfully. (Prov. 13:24; 19:18; 22:15; 23:13:14; 29:15, 17)

4. God's Word considers godly and mature children to be a joy to their parents' hearts. (Prov. 10:1; 17:21, 25; 23:15-16, 24-25; 27:11; Psa. 127:4-5)

Verses for Memorization

Psalm 127:3: Lo, children are an heritage of the LORD; and the fruit of the womb is His reward.

Ephesians 6:4: And, ye fathers, provoke not your children to wrath: but bring them up in the nurture and admonition of the Lord.

Proverbs 13:24: He that spareth his rod hateth his son: but he that loveth him chasteneth him betimes.

Proverbs 29:15: The rod and reproof give wisdom: but a child left to himself bringeth his mother to shame.

Proverbs 29:17: Correct thy son, and he shall give thee rest; yea, he shall give delight unto thy soul.

Proverbs 23:24: The father of the righteous shall greatly rejoice: and he that begetteth a wise child shall have joy of him.

Proverbs 17:25: A foolish son is a grief to his father, and bitterness to her that bare him.

34

For the Sake of the Home

In Proverbs 3:33 the warning and promise is proclaimed, *"The curse of the LORD is in the house of the wicked: but he blesseth the habitation of the just."* The Lord our God has given great and precious promises to the man and woman of God who will follow His precepts and principles in their personal walk, marriage relationship, and home life. Many of these promises are for the benefit and blessing of their household. Yet the Lord our God has given serious and sobering warnings concerning the household of that man or woman who will not follow His precepts and principles. In this concluding chapter of our study, let us consider these promises and warnings.

Concerning the relationships of the home, Psalm 128:1-4 gives the promise, *"Blessed is every one that feareth the LORD; that walketh in his ways. For thou shalt eat the labour of thine hands: happy shalt thou be, and it shall be well with thee. Thy wife shall be as a fruitful vine by the sides of thine house: thy children like olive plants round about thy table. Behold, that thus shall the man be blessed that feareth the LORD."*

Concerning the spiritual richness of the home, Psalm 112:1-3 gives the promise, *"Praise ye the LORD. Blessed is the man that feareth the LORD, that delighteth greatly in his commandments. His seed shall be mighty upon earth: the generation of the upright shall*

be blessed. Wealth and riches shall be in his house: and his righteousness endureth for ever." In addition, Proverbs 15:6 gives the promise and the warning, "**In the house of the righteous is much treasure: but in the revenues of the wicked is trouble.**"

Concerning the enduring strength of the home, Proverbs 12:7 gives the promise, "**The wicked are overthrown, and are not: but the house of the righteous shall stand.**" In like manner, Proverbs 14:11 gives the warning and the promise, "**The house of the wicked shall be overthrown: but the tabernacle of the upright shall flourish.**" Thus Proverbs 24:3-4 declares, "**Through wisdom is an house builded; and by understanding it is established: and by knowledge shall the chambers be filled with all precious and pleasant riches.**" In addition, Proverbs 14:1 declares, "**Every wise woman buildeth her house: but the foolish plucketh it down with her hands.**"

Concerning the financial stability of the home, Proverbs 21:20 gives the promise and the warning, "**There is treasure to be desired and oil in the dwelling of the wise; but a foolish man spendeth it up.**" Thus Proverbs 24:3-4 declares, "**Through wisdom is an house builded; and by understanding it is established: and by knowledge shall the chambers be filled with all precious and pleasant riches.**"

Concerning the upbringing of the children, Proverbs 22:6 gives the promise, "**Train up a child in the way he should go: and when he is old, he will not depart from it.**" In addition, Proverbs 23:13-14 gives the promise, "**Withhold not correction from the child: for if thou beatest him with the rod, he shall not die. Thou shalt beat him with the rod, and shalt deliver his soul from hell.**" Finally, Proverbs 29:17 gives the promise, "**Correct thy son, and he shall give thee rest; yea, he shall give delight unto thy soul.**"

Concerning God's hand upon the children, Psalm 102:28 gives the promise, "**The children of thy servants shall continue, and their seed shall be established before thee.**" Again Proverbs 20:7 gives the promise, "**The just man walketh in his integrity: his children are blessed after him.**" Yet again Psalm 112:1-2 gives the promise, "**Praise ye the LORD. Blessed is the man that feareth the LORD,** *that delighteth greatly in his commandments. His seed shall be mighty upon earth: the generation of the upright shall be blessed."* And yet again Psalm 25:12-13 gives the promise, *"What man is he that feareth the LORD? Him shall he teach in the way that he shall choose. His soul shall dwell at ease; and his seed shall inherit the earth."* Finally, Proverbs 11:21 gives the promise, *"Though hand join in hand, the wicked shall not be unpunished: but the seed of the righteous shall be delivered."*

On the other hand, concerning God's judgment upon a home, the opening portion of Proverbs 3:33 gives the warning, *"The curse of the LORD is in the house of the wicked."* In like manner, the opening portion of Proverbs 15:25 gives the warning, *"The LORD will destroy the house of the proud."* Thus the opening portion of Proverbs 14:11 declares, *"The house of the wicked shall be overthrown."* Even so, Jeremiah 22:13 gives the warning, *"Woe unto him that buildeth his house by unrighteousness, and his chambers by wrong; that useth his neighbour's service without wages, and giveth him not for his work."* Again the opening portion of Proverbs 15:27 gives the warning, *"He that is greedy of gain troubleth his own house."* Yet again the opening portion of Proverbs 11:29 gives the warning, *"He that troubleth his own house shall inherit the wind."* Finally, Proverbs 17:13 gives the warning, *"Whoso rewardeth evil for good, evil shall not depart from his house."*

The opening half of Psalm 127:1 makes the truth abundantly clear – *"Except the LORD build the house, they labour in vain that build it."* The Lord's help and blessing upon a home is absolutely necessary in order for that marriage and home to be built up and established with strength and stability. Without His gracious help and blessing, all of the effort and energy that is expended to build up and establish that marriage and home will be completely in vain. Thus the husband and the wife must ever follow after the will and way of the Lord for the success of their marriage and home.

SCRIPTURE INDEX

Also Available From
Shepherding the Flock Ministries
www.shepherdingtheflock.com

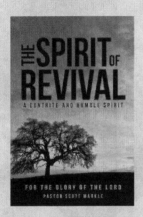

THE SPIRIT OF REVIVAL
A CONTRITE AND HUMBLE SPIRIT

A Biblical study of the inseparable relationship between Biblical humility and spiritual revival, including studies in:
Isaiah 57:15-21
James 4:1-10
2 Chronicles 7:12-14
Psalm 51:1-19
Isaiah 66:1-5
(200 pages)

THE TENDER MERCIES
OF THE LORD
COMFORT IN OUR LORD'S TENDER CARE

A biblical study concerning the Lord's tender mercies toward His own in order to provide spiritual confidence, courage, and comfort through the truth of our Lord's tender care. *(127 pages)*

GOD'S OWN WORD
On The Fear of the Lord

Chapter Contents
(82 pages)

The Fear of the Lord
The Terror of the Lord –
Because of His Glory
The Fear of God's People –
Because His Hand Is with Them
Learning to Fear the Lord
The Benefits of Fearing the Lord
If You Will Not Fear the Lord
The Terror of the Lord –
Because of Our Sin

GOD'S OWN WORD
On Our Fears

Chapter Contents
(80 pages)

Fear Thou Not
Fear in the Midst of Affliction
I Will Fear No Evil
Afraid of Man
Delivered from Fear
Fear as a Judgment from the Lord